Oh My Goddess! 1

ああっ女神さまっ

STORY AND ART BY
Kosuke Fujishima

ORIGINAL TRANSLATION BY
Dana Lewis, Alan Gleason,
AND Toren Smith

LETTERING AND TOUCH-UP BY
Susie Lee AND Betty Dong
WITH Tom2K

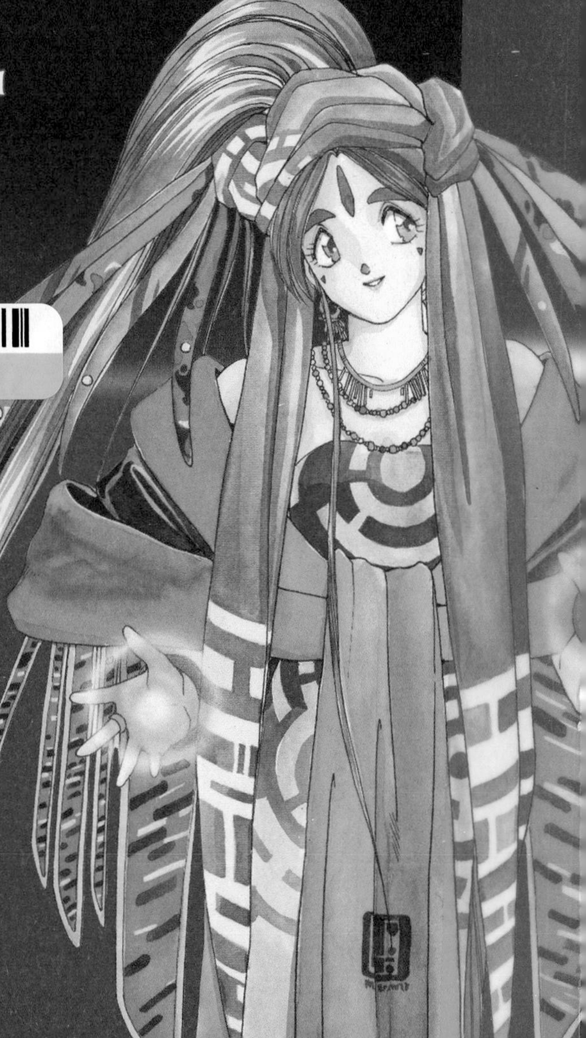

DARK HORSE MANGA™

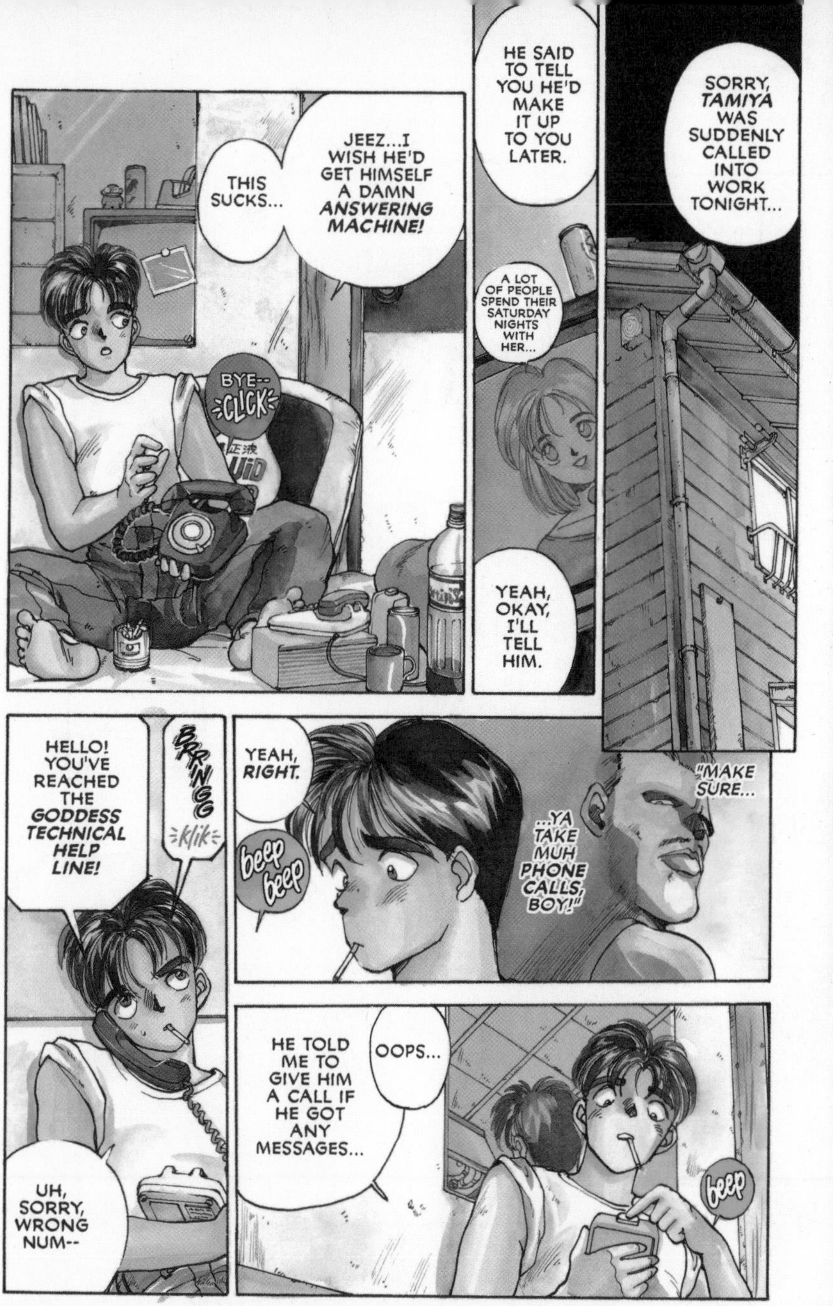
SORRY, *TAMIYA* WAS SUDDENLY CALLED INTO WORK TONIGHT...
HE SAID TO TELL YOU HE'D MAKE IT UP TO YOU LATER.
A LOT OF PEOPLE SPEND THEIR SATURDAY NIGHTS WITH HER...
YEAH, OKAY, I'LL TELL HIM.
JEEZ...I WISH HE'D GET HIMSELF A DAMN *ANSWERING MACHINE!*
THIS SUCKS...
BYE-- CLICK
"MAKE SURE...
...YA TAKE MUH *PHONE CALLS*, BOY!"
YEAH, *RIGHT.*
beep beep
OOPS...
HE TOLD ME TO GIVE HIM A CALL IF HE GOT ANY MESSAGES...
beep
BRRINGG
klik
HELLO! YOU'VE REACHED THE *GODDESS TECHNICAL HELP LINE!*
UH, SORRY, WRONG NUM--

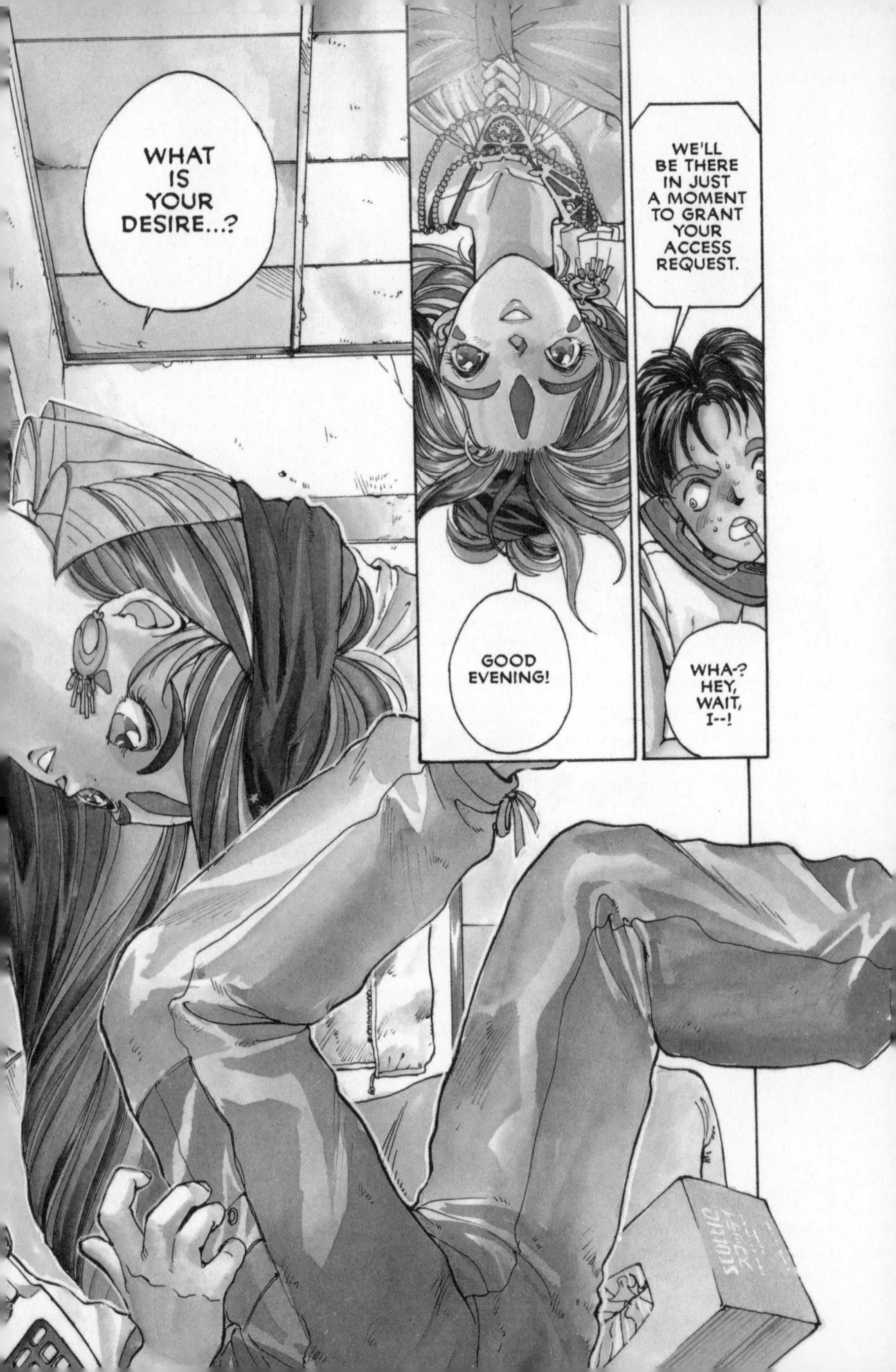
WE'LL BE THERE IN JUST A MOMENT TO GRANT YOUR ACCESS REQUEST.
WHA-? HEY, WAIT, I--!
GOOD EVENING!
WHAT IS YOUR DESIRE...?

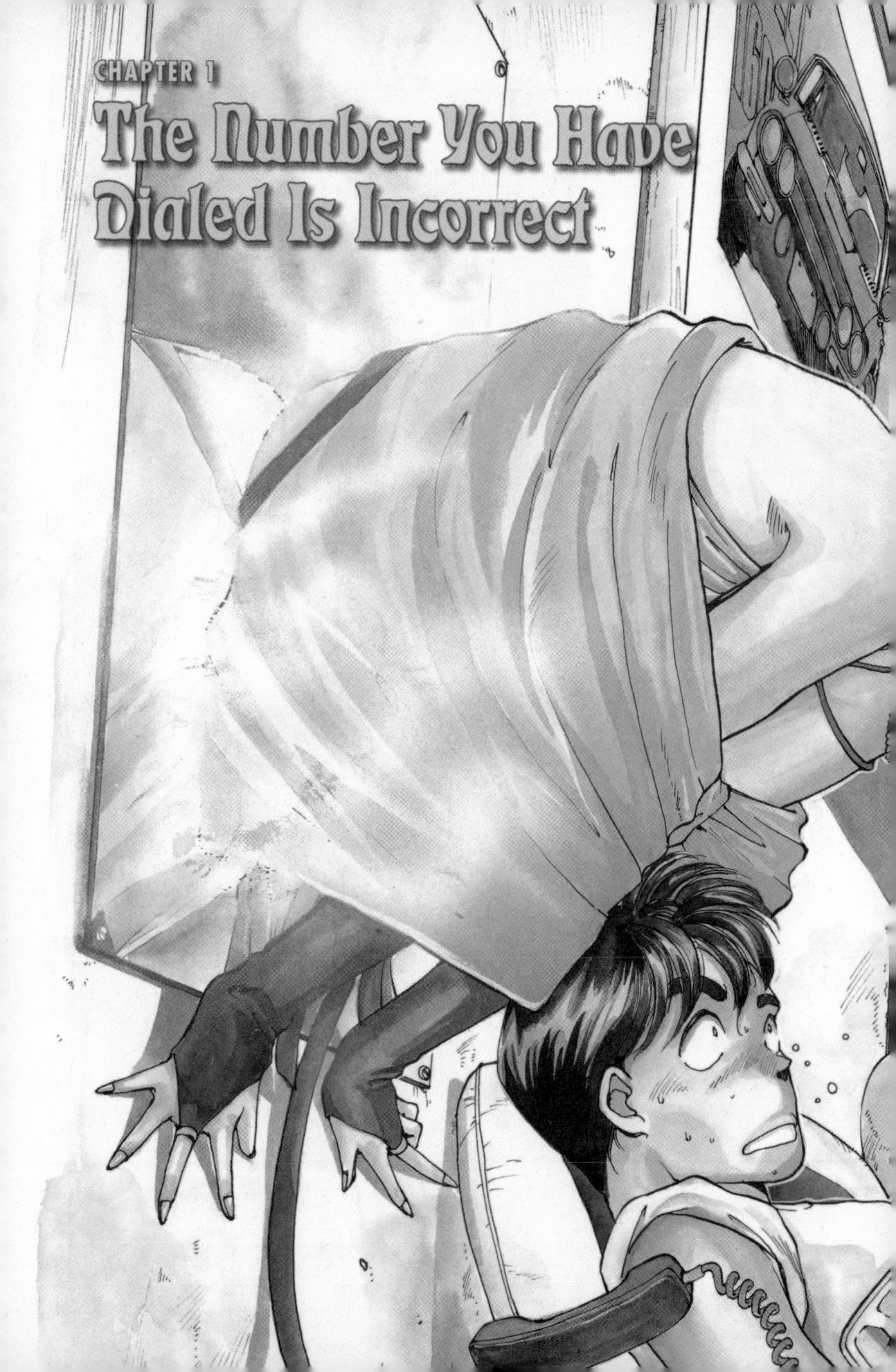
CHAPTER 1
The Number You Have
Dialed Is Incorrect

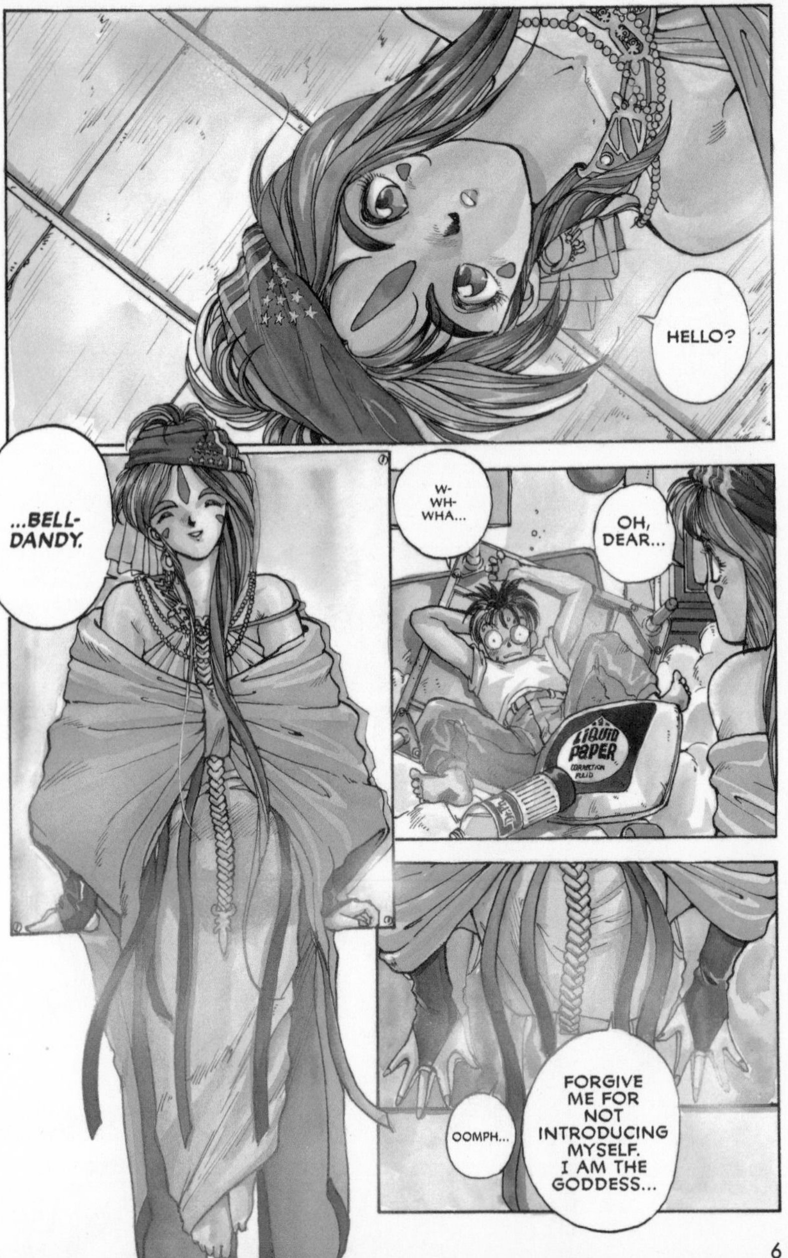
HELLO?
OH, DEAR...
W-WH-WHA...
FORGIVE ME FOR NOT INTRODUCING MYSELF. I AM THE GODDESS...
OOMPH...
...BELL-DANDY.
LIQUID PAPER
CORRECTION FLUID

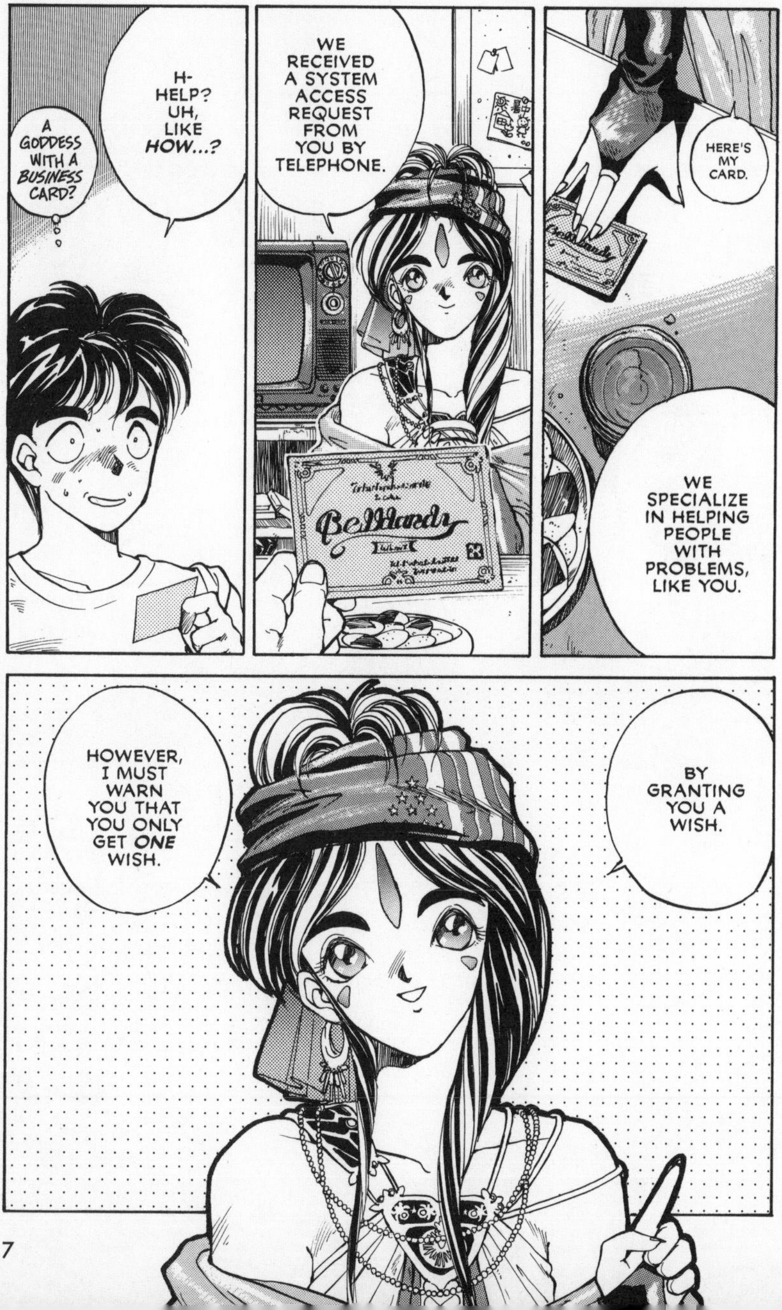
HERE'S MY CARD.
WE SPECIALIZE IN HELPING PEOPLE WITH PROBLEMS, LIKE YOU.
WE RECEIVED A SYSTEM ACCESS REQUEST FROM YOU BY TELEPHONE.
H- HELP? UH, LIKE *HOW...?*
A GODDESS WITH A *BUSINESS* CARD?
BY GRANTING YOU A WISH.
HOWEVER, I MUST WARN YOU THAT YOU ONLY GET *ONE* WISH.

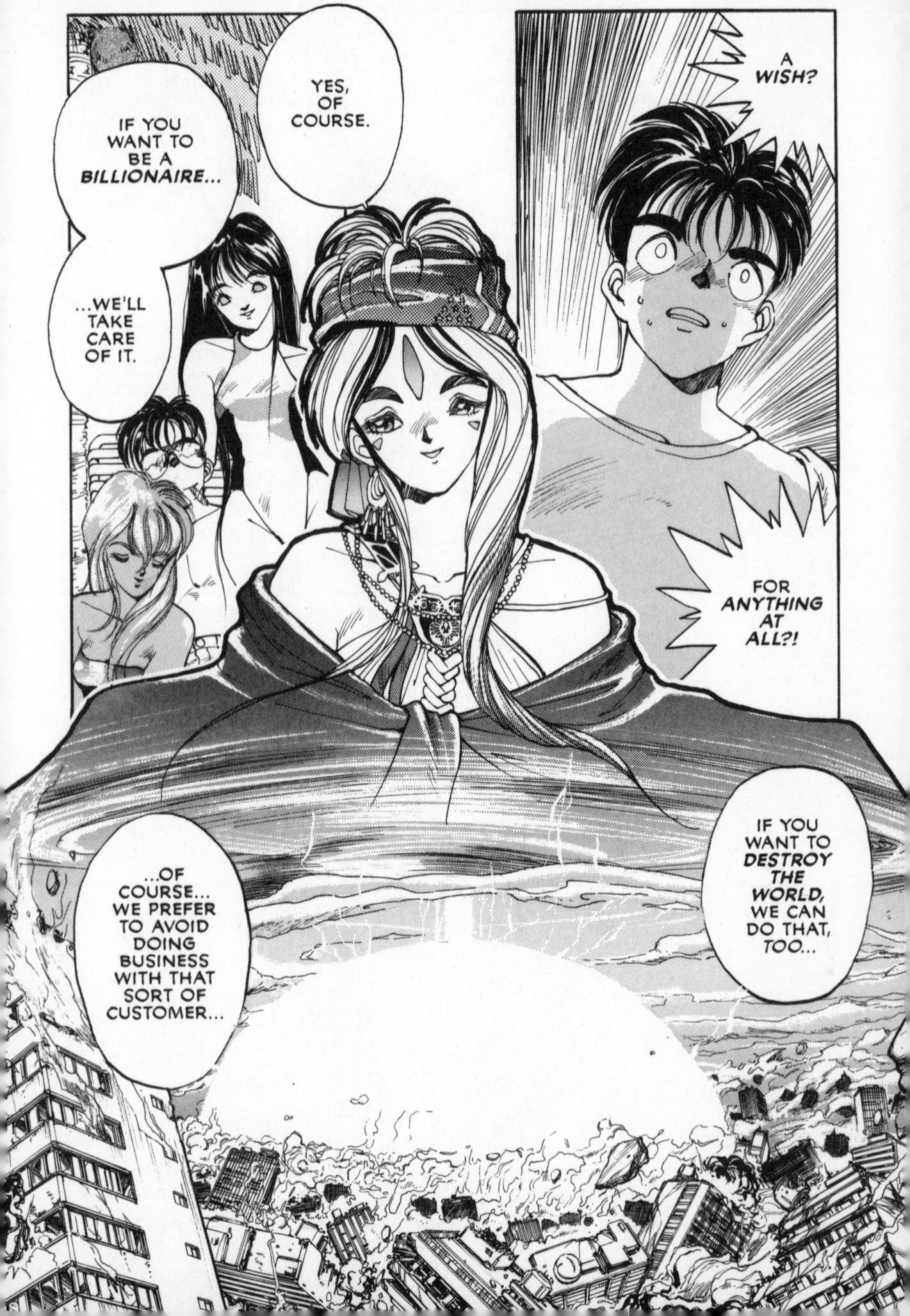
A *WISH?*
FOR *ANYTHING AT ALL?!*
YES, OF COURSE.
IF YOU WANT TO BE A *BILLIONAIRE...*
...WE'LL TAKE CARE OF IT.
IF YOU WANT TO *DESTROY THE WORLD,* WE CAN DO THAT, *TOO...*
...OF COURSE... WE PREFER TO AVOID DOING BUSINESS WITH THAT SORT OF CUSTOMER...

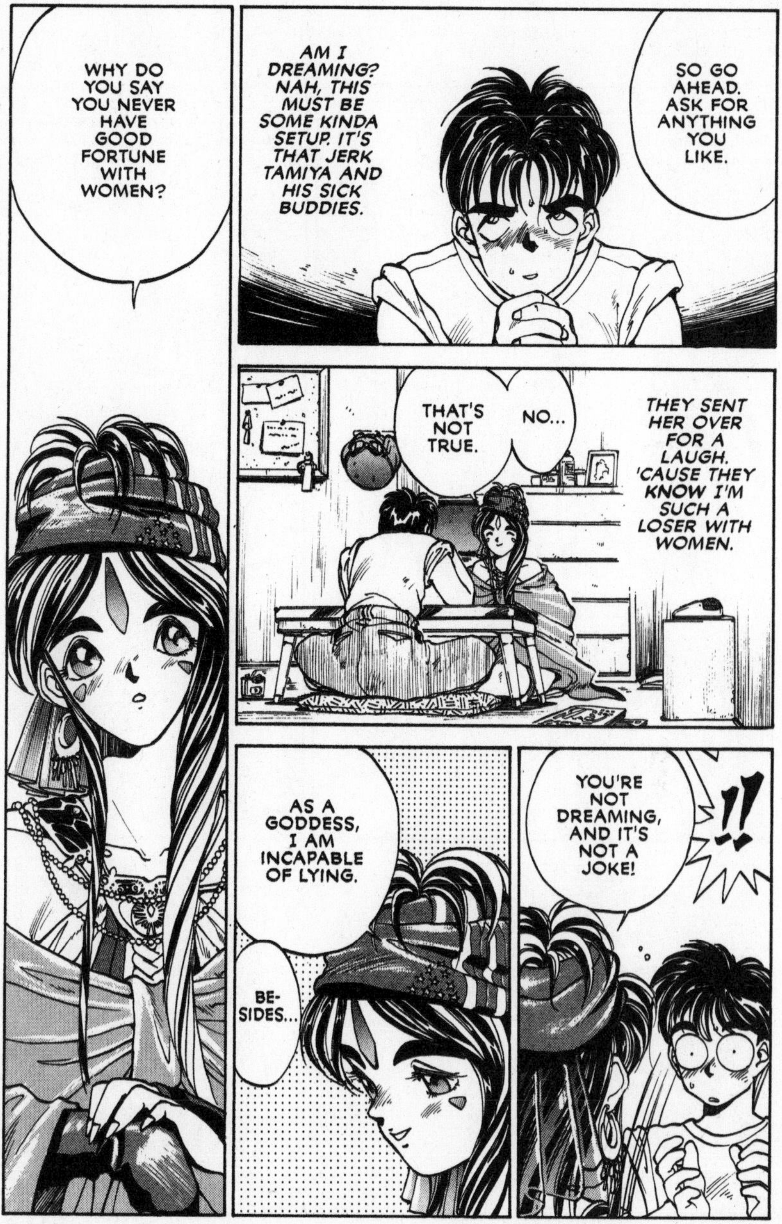
SO GO AHEAD. ASK FOR ANYTHING YOU LIKE.
AM I DREAMING? NAH, THIS MUST BE SOME KINDA SETUP. IT'S THAT JERK TAMIYA AND HIS SICK BUDDIES.
THEY SENT HER OVER FOR A LAUGH. 'CAUSE THEY KNOW I'M SUCH A LOSER WITH WOMEN.
NO...
THAT'S NOT TRUE.
!!
YOU'RE NOT DREAMING, AND IT'S NOT A JOKE!
AS A GODDESS, I AM INCAPABLE OF LYING.
BE-SIDES...
WHY DO YOU SAY YOU NEVER HAVE GOOD FORTUNE WITH WOMEN?

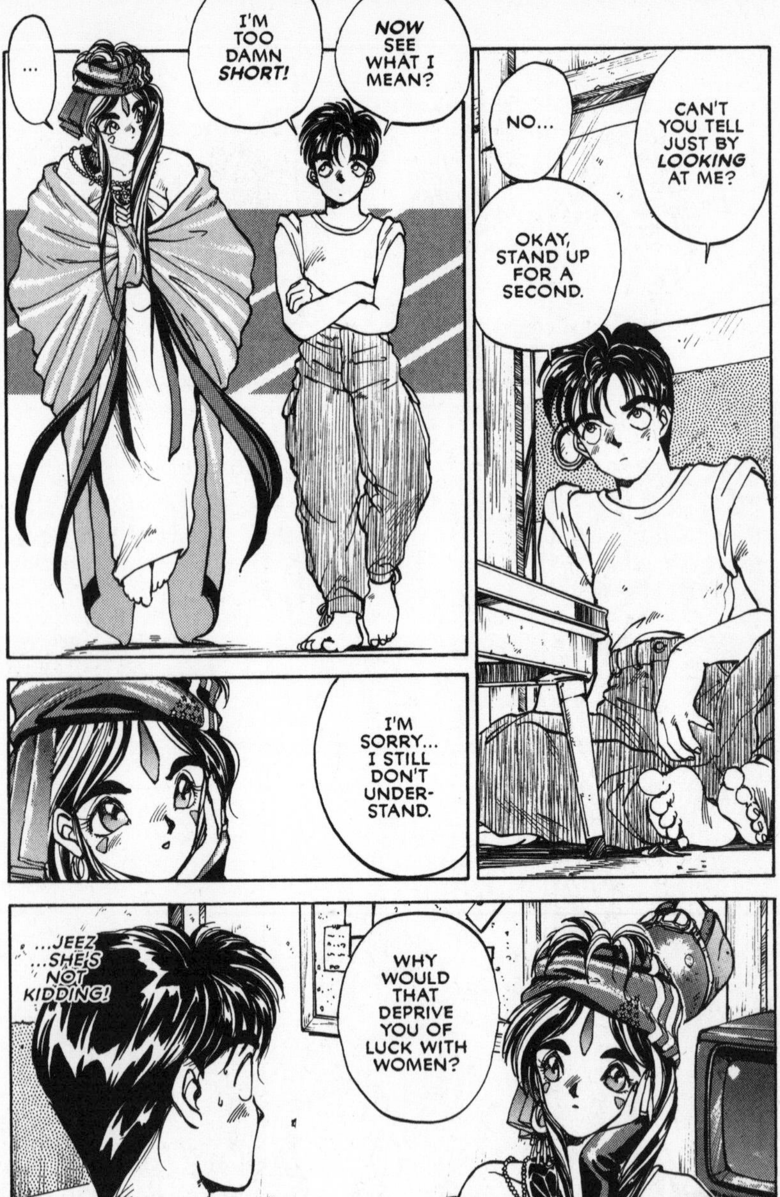
CAN'T YOU TELL JUST BY *LOOKING* AT ME?
NO...
OKAY, STAND UP FOR A SECOND.
NOW SEE WHAT I MEAN?
I'M TOO DAMN *SHORT!*
...
I'M SORRY... I STILL DON'T UNDER-STAND.
WHY WOULD THAT DEPRIVE YOU OF LUCK WITH WOMEN?
...JEEZ ...SHE'S NOT KIDDING!

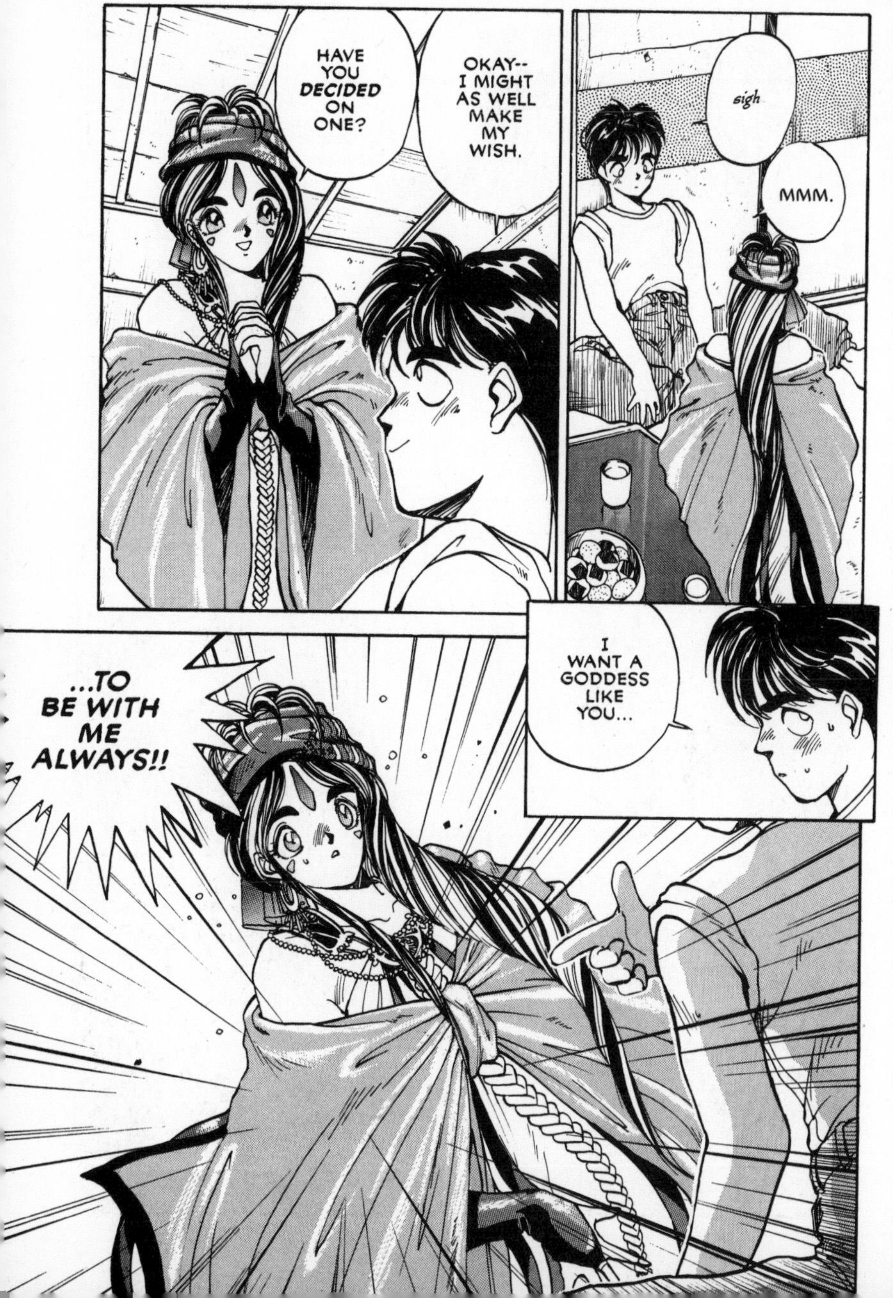
HAVE YOU DECIDED ON ONE?
OKAY-- I MIGHT AS WELL MAKE MY WISH.
sigh
MMM.
I WANT A GODDESS LIKE YOU...
...TO BE WITH ME ALWAYS!!

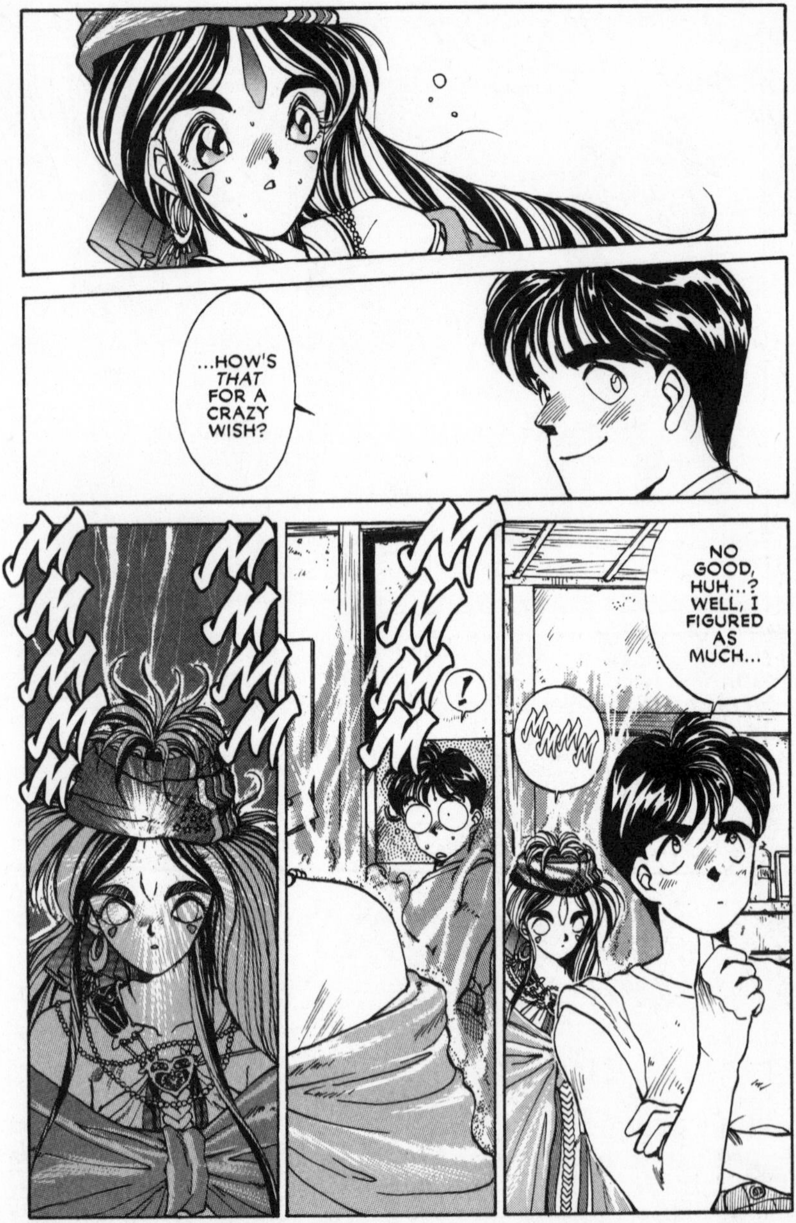
...HOW'S *THAT* FOR A CRAZY WISH?
NO GOOD, HUH...? WELL, I FIGURED AS MUCH...
MMMM
MMMMM
!
MMMMM
MMMMM

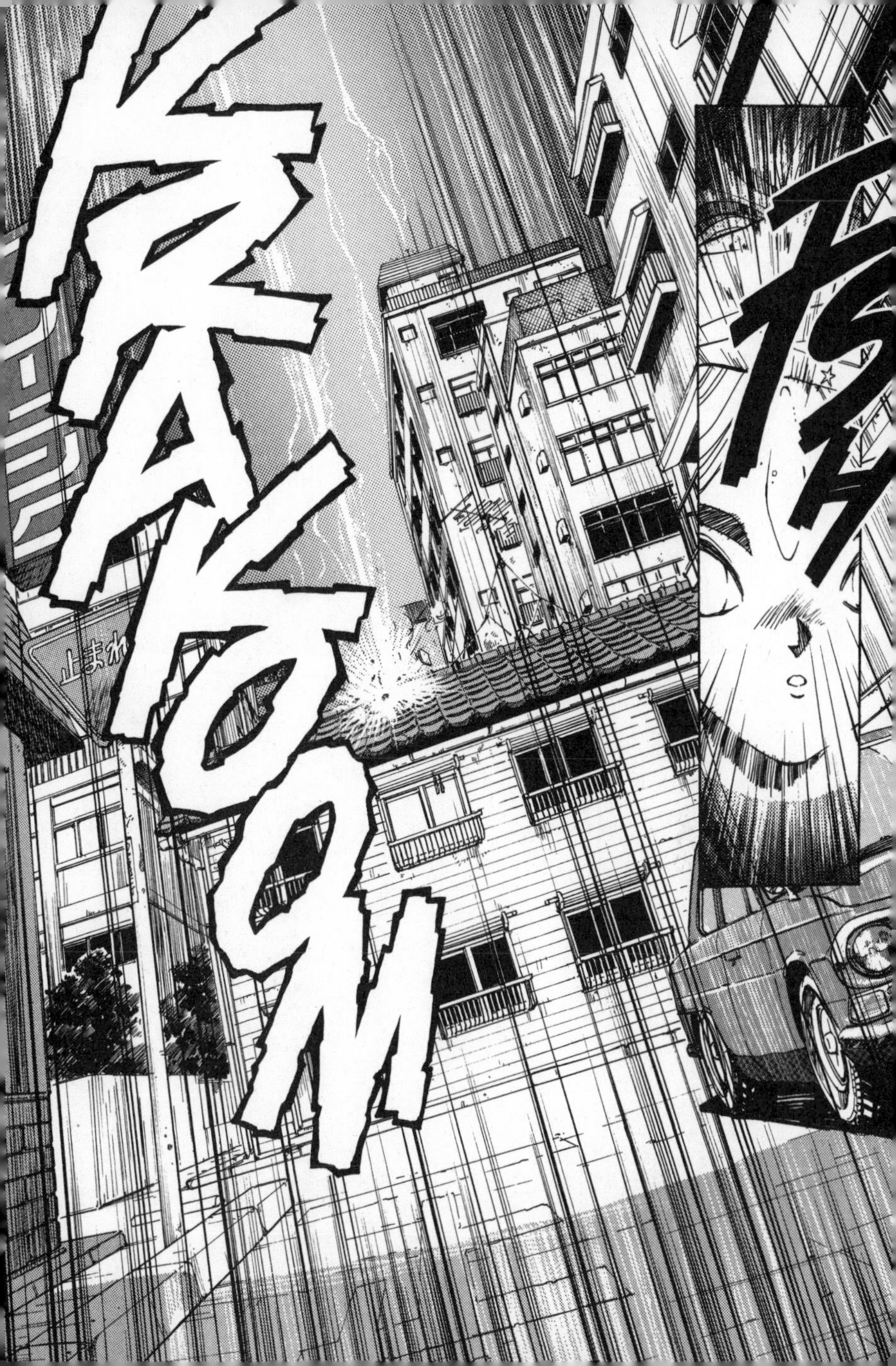
TSH
KABOOM
止まれ

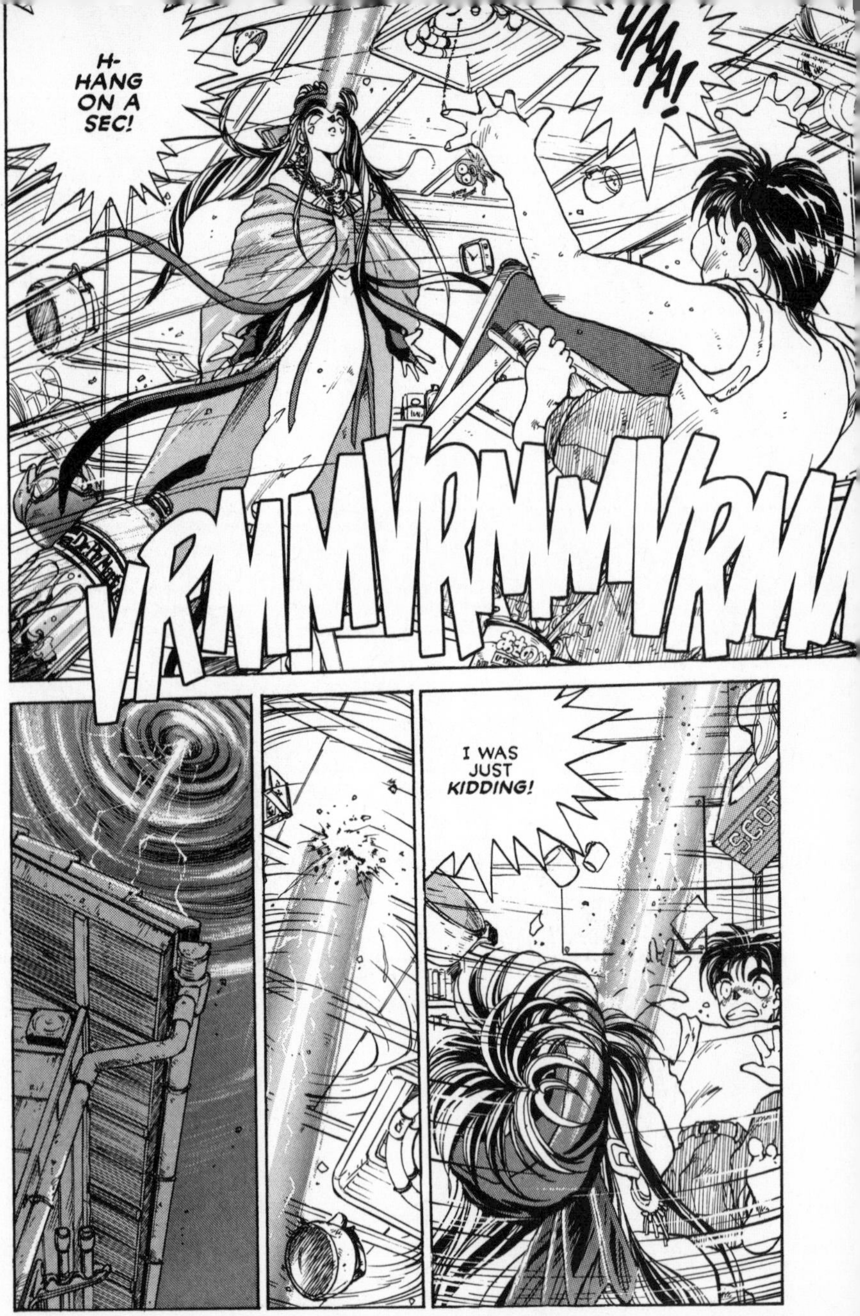
YAAAA!
H-HANG ON A SEC!
VRMMVRMMVRM
I WAS JUST KIDDING!

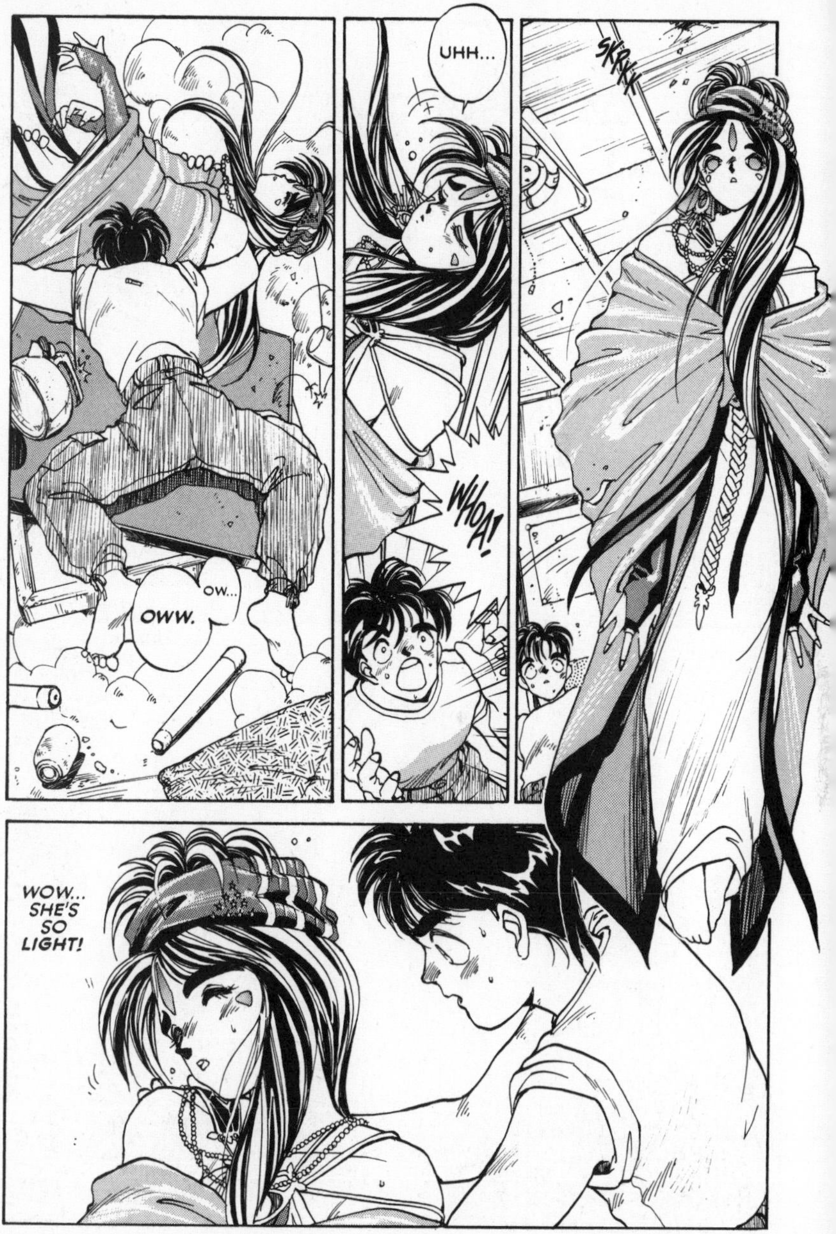
SKRKK
UHH...
WHOA!
OW...
OWW.
WOW... SHE'S SO LIGHT!

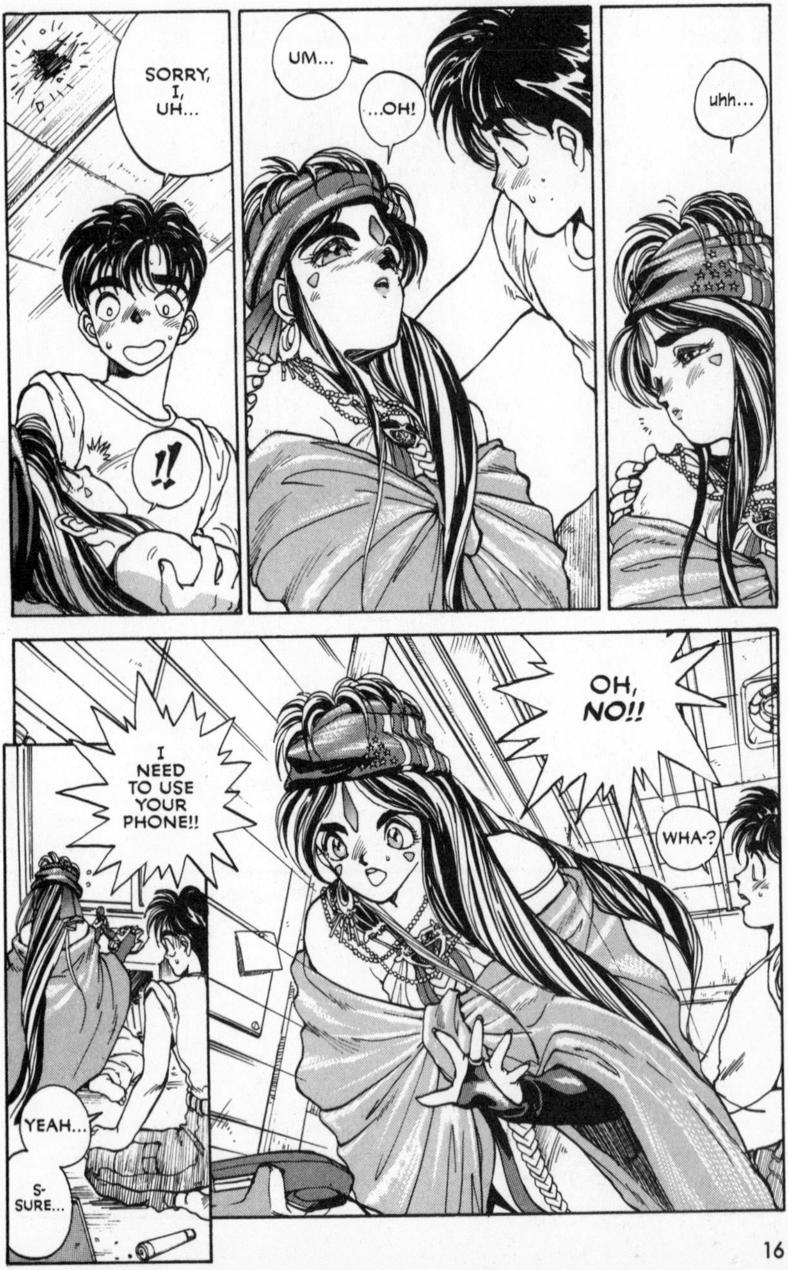
uhh...
UM...
...OH!
SORRY, I, UH...
!!
OH, NO!!
WHA-?
I NEED TO USE YOUR PHONE!!
YEAH...
S-SURE...

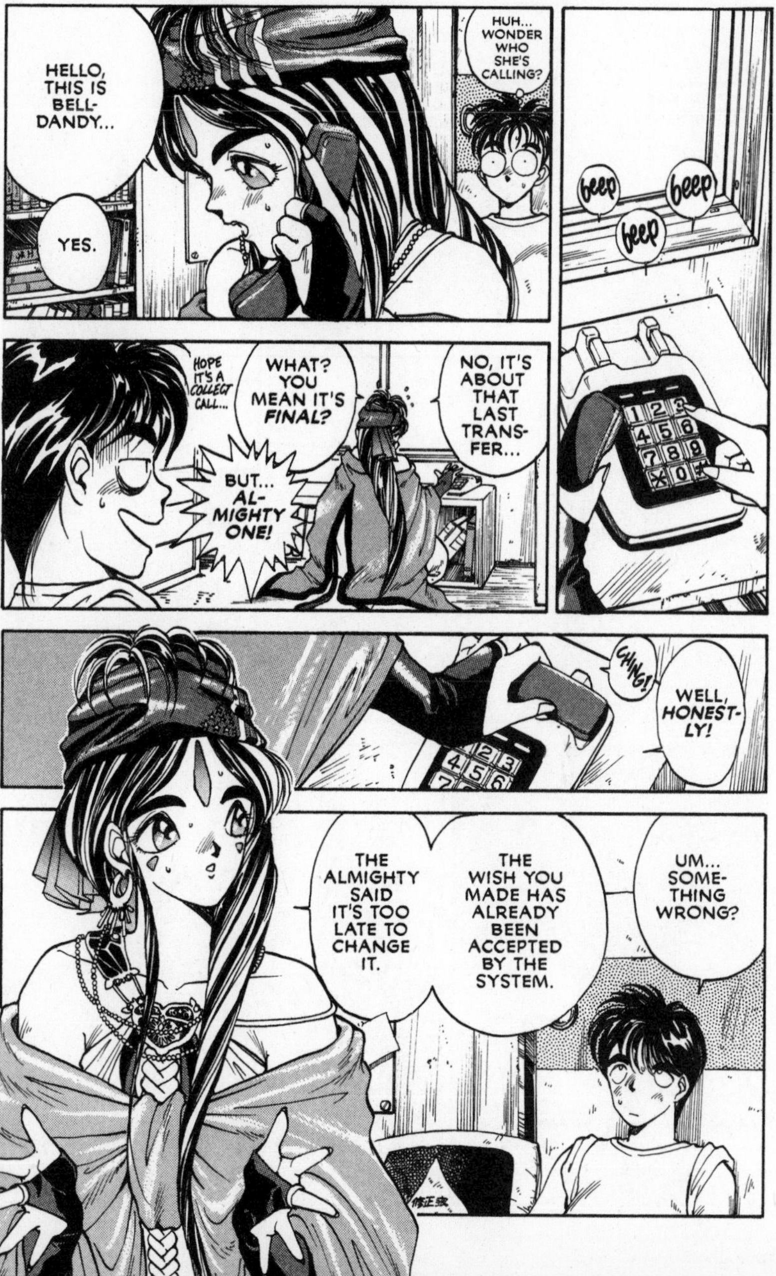
beep
beep
beep
HUH... WONDER WHO SHE'S CALLING?
HELLO, THIS IS BELL-DANDY...
YES.
NO, IT'S ABOUT THAT LAST TRANSFER...
WHAT? YOU MEAN IT'S *FINAL?*
HOPE IT'S A COLLECT CALL...
BUT... ALMIGHTY ONE!
WELL, HONESTLY!
CHING!
UM... SOMETHING WRONG?
THE WISH YOU MADE HAS ALREADY BEEN ACCEPTED BY THE SYSTEM.
THE ALMIGHTY SAID IT'S TOO LATE TO CHANGE IT.
修正液

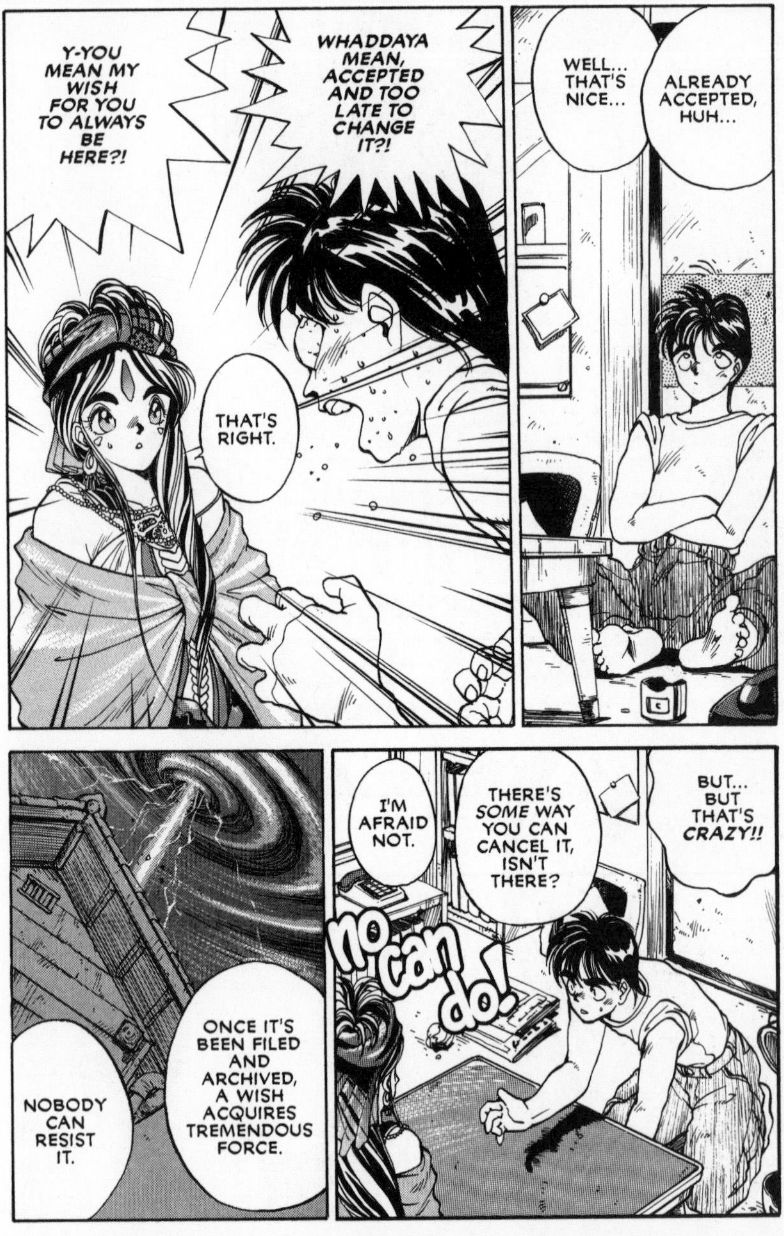
ALREADY ACCEPTED, HUH...
WELL... THAT'S NICE...
WHADDAYA MEAN, ACCEPTED AND TOO LATE TO CHANGE IT?!
Y-YOU MEAN MY WISH FOR YOU TO ALWAYS BE HERE?!
THAT'S RIGHT.
BUT... BUT THAT'S *CRAZY!!*
THERE'S *SOME* WAY YOU CAN CANCEL IT, ISN'T THERE?
I'M AFRAID NOT.
no can do!
ONCE IT'S BEEN FILED AND ARCHIVED, A WISH ACQUIRES TREMENDOUS FORCE.
NOBODY CAN RESIST IT.

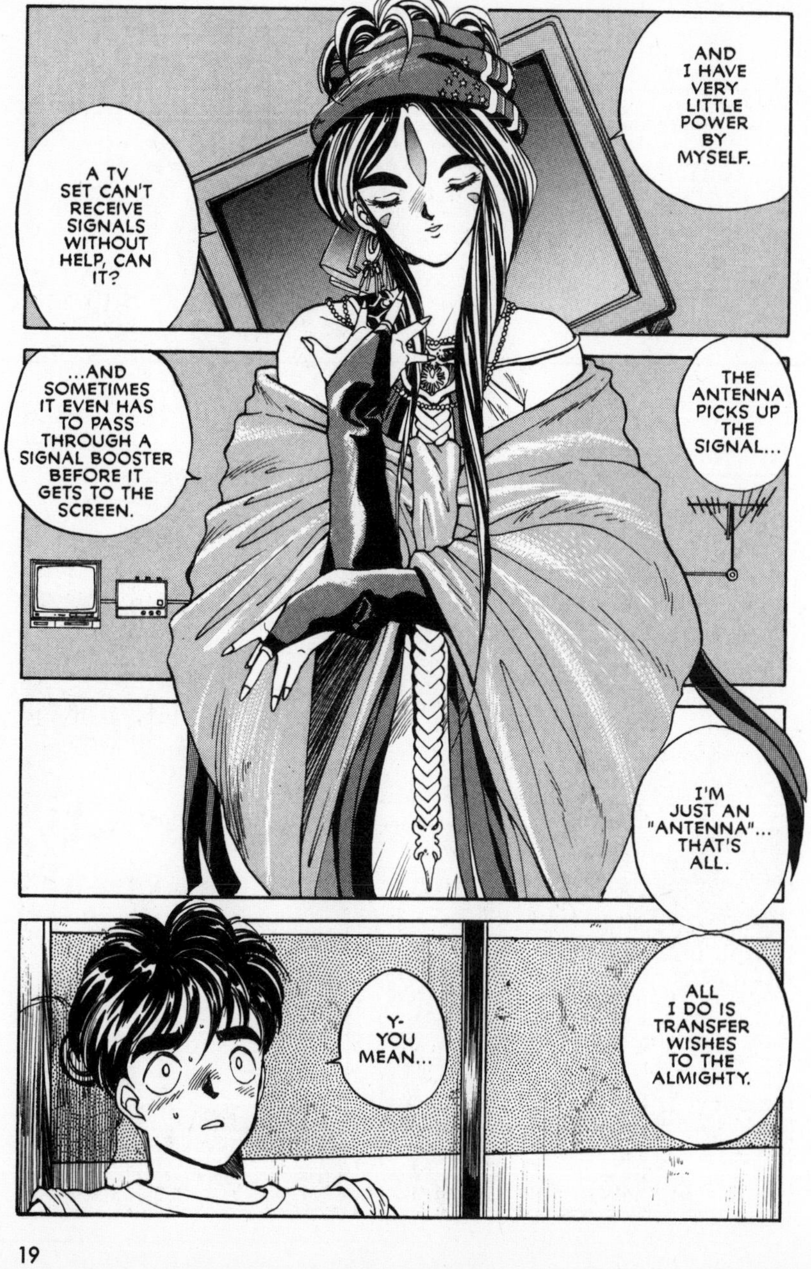
AND I HAVE VERY LITTLE POWER BY MYSELF.
A TV SET CAN'T RECEIVE SIGNALS WITHOUT HELP, CAN IT?
THE ANTENNA PICKS UP THE SIGNAL...
...AND SOMETIMES IT EVEN HAS TO PASS THROUGH A SIGNAL BOOSTER BEFORE IT GETS TO THE SCREEN.
I'M JUST AN "ANTENNA"... THAT'S ALL.
ALL I DO IS TRANSFER WISHES TO THE ALMIGHTY.
Y-YOU MEAN...

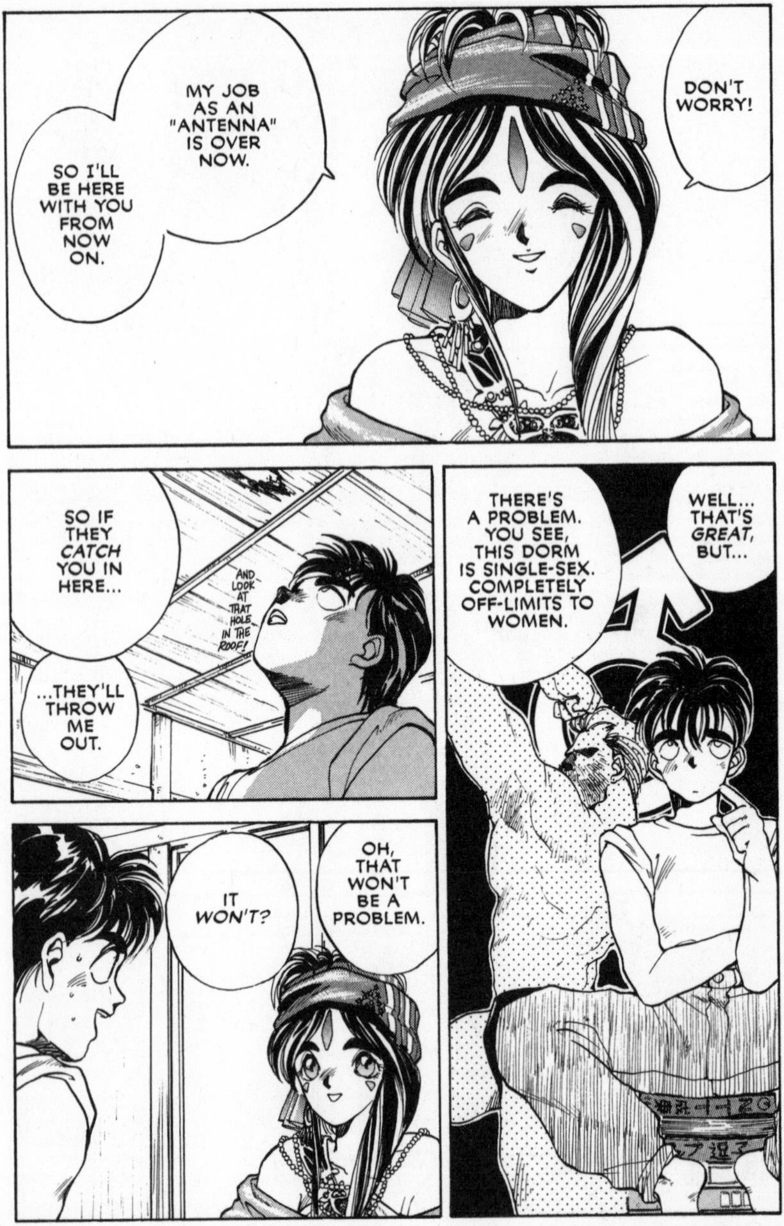
DON'T WORRY!
MY JOB AS AN "ANTENNA" IS OVER NOW.
SO I'LL BE HERE WITH YOU FROM NOW ON.
WELL... THAT'S *GREAT,* BUT...
THERE'S A PROBLEM. YOU SEE, THIS DORM IS SINGLE-SEX. COMPLETELY OFF-LIMITS TO WOMEN.
SO IF THEY *CATCH* YOU IN HERE...
AND LOOK AT THAT HOLE IN THE ROOF!
...THEY'LL THROW ME OUT.
OH, THAT WON'T BE A PROBLEM.
IT *WON'T?*

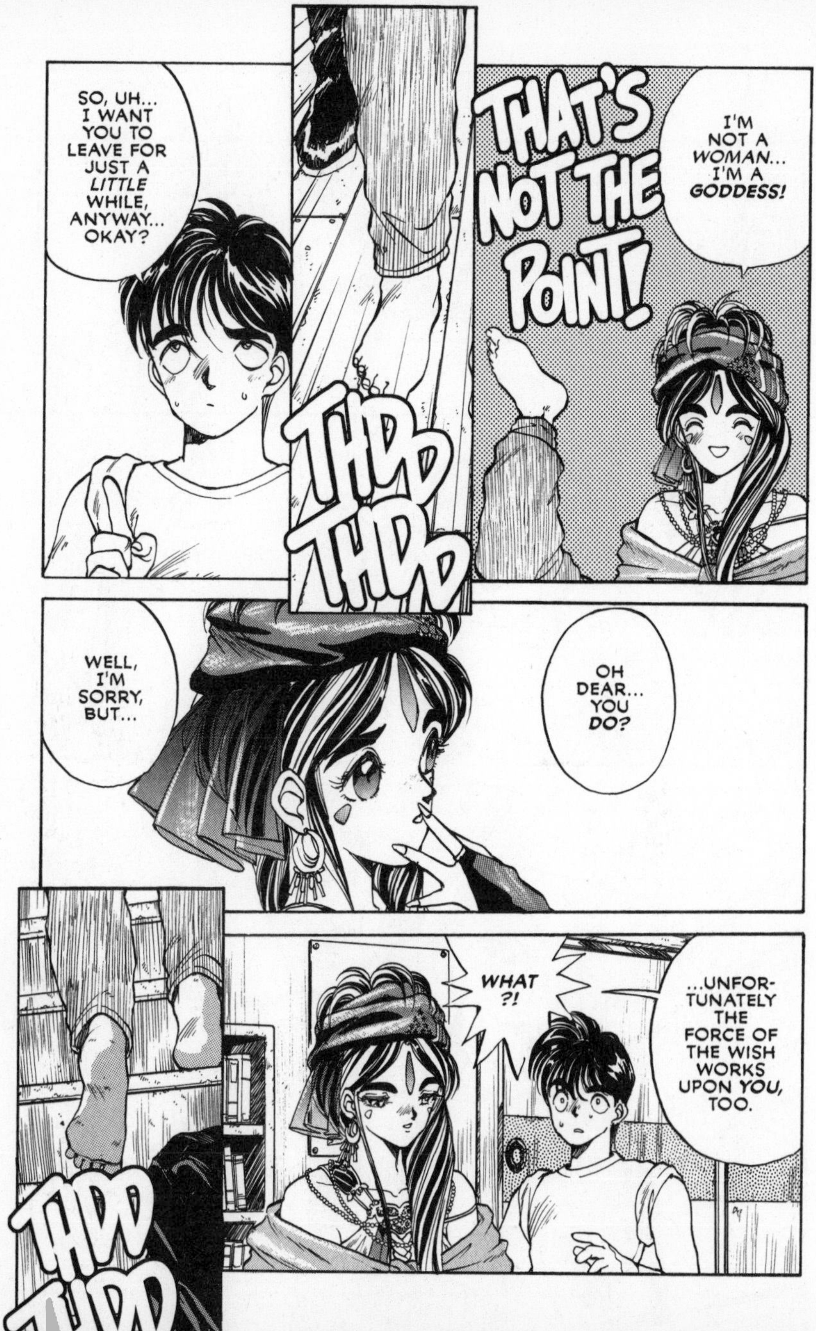
I'M NOT A WOMAN... I'M A GODDESS!
THAT'S NOT THE POINT!
THDD THDD
SO, UH... I WANT YOU TO LEAVE FOR JUST A LITTLE WHILE, ANYWAY... OKAY?
OH DEAR... YOU DO?
WELL, I'M SORRY, BUT...
...UNFORTUNATELY THE FORCE OF THE WISH WORKS UPON YOU, TOO.
WHAT?!
THDD THDD

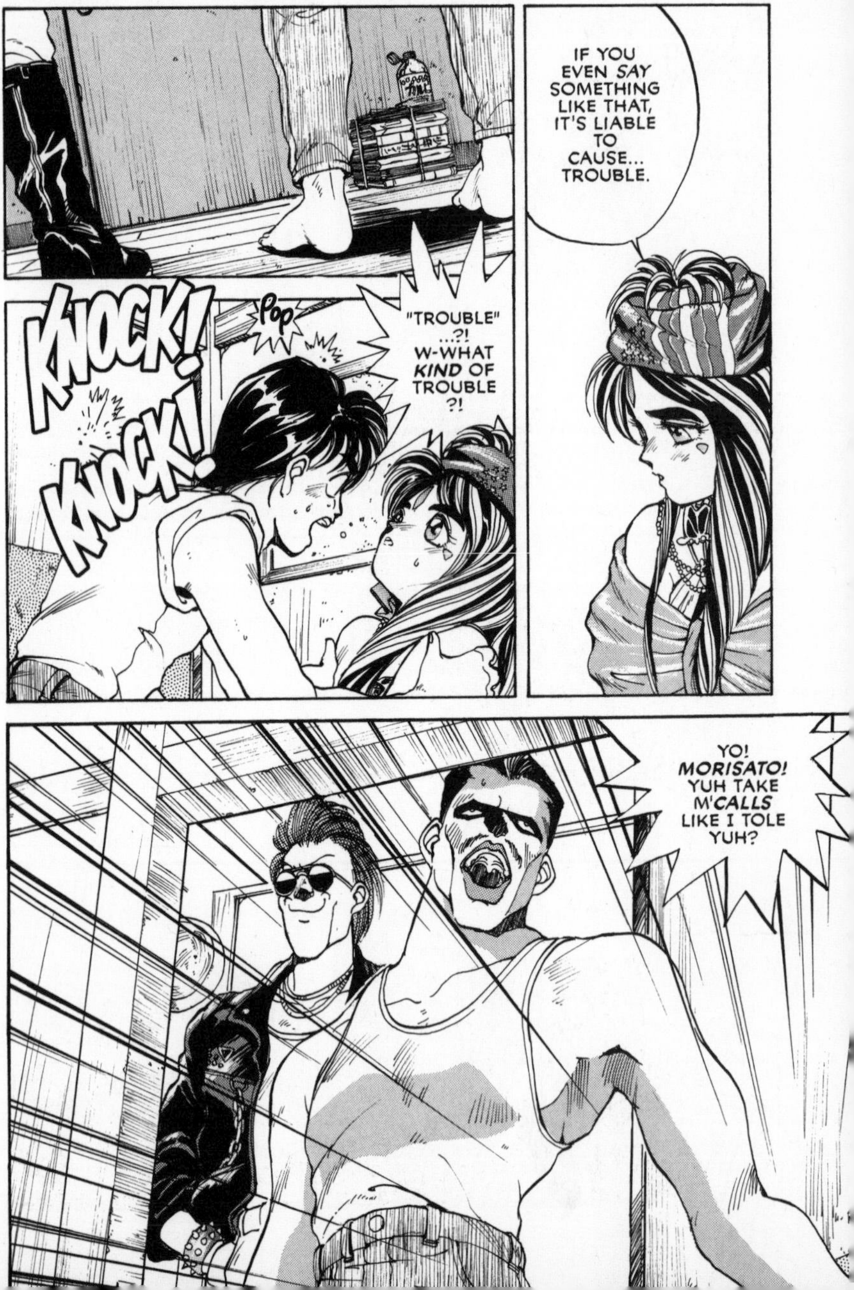
IF YOU EVEN SAY SOMETHING LIKE THAT, IT'S LIABLE TO CAUSE... TROUBLE.
"TROUBLE" ...?! W-WHAT KIND OF TROUBLE ?!
Pop
KNOCK!
KNOCK!
YO! MORISATO! YUH TAKE M'CALLS LIKE I TOLE YUH?

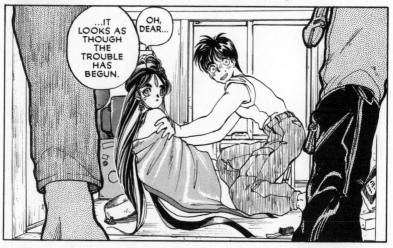

...IT LOOKS AS THOUGH THE TROUBLE HAS BEGUN.

OH, DEAR...

YUH KNOW DA *ROOLS*, MORISATO.

SNAP

why, you...

hmf!

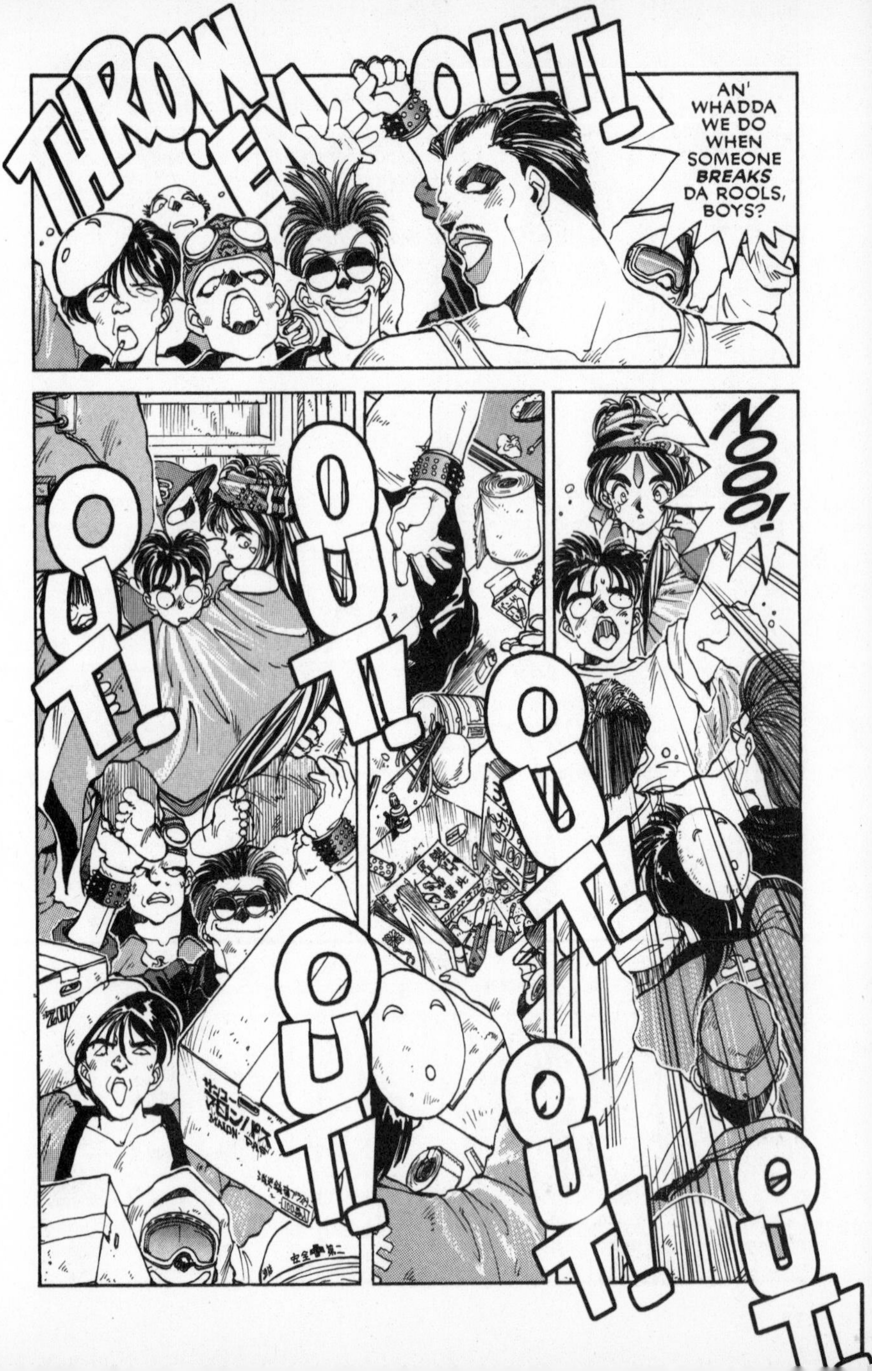
AN' WHADDA WE DO WHEN SOMEONE *BREAKS* DA ROOLS, BOYS?
THROW 'EM OUT!!
NOOOO!
OUT!!
OUT!!
OUT!!
OUT!!
OUT!
OUT!
OUT!

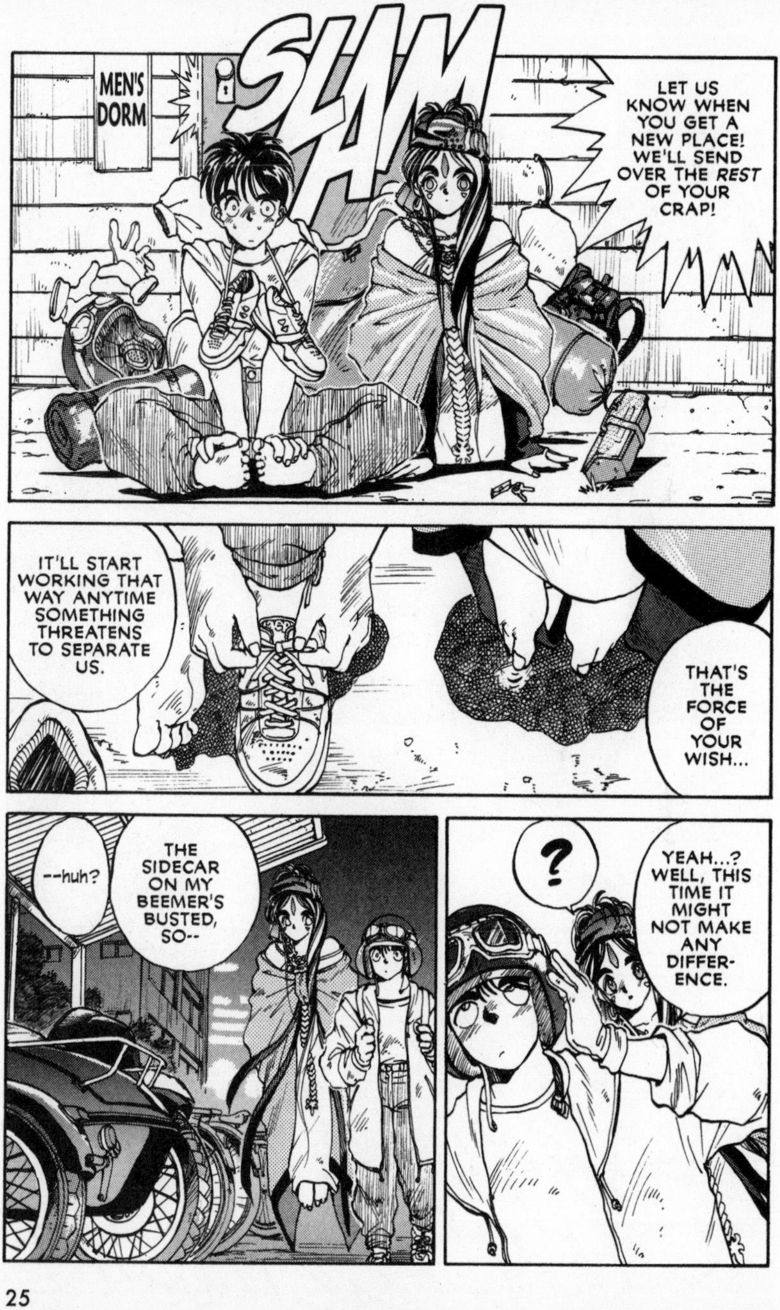
SLAM
LET US KNOW WHEN YOU GET A NEW PLACE! WE'LL SEND OVER THE *REST* OF YOUR CRAP!
MEN'S DORM
THAT'S THE FORCE OF YOUR WISH...
IT'LL START WORKING THAT WAY ANYTIME SOMETHING THREATENS TO SEPARATE US.
YEAH...? WELL, THIS TIME IT MIGHT NOT MAKE ANY DIFFERENCE.
?
THE SIDECAR ON MY BEEMER'S BUSTED, SO--
--huh?

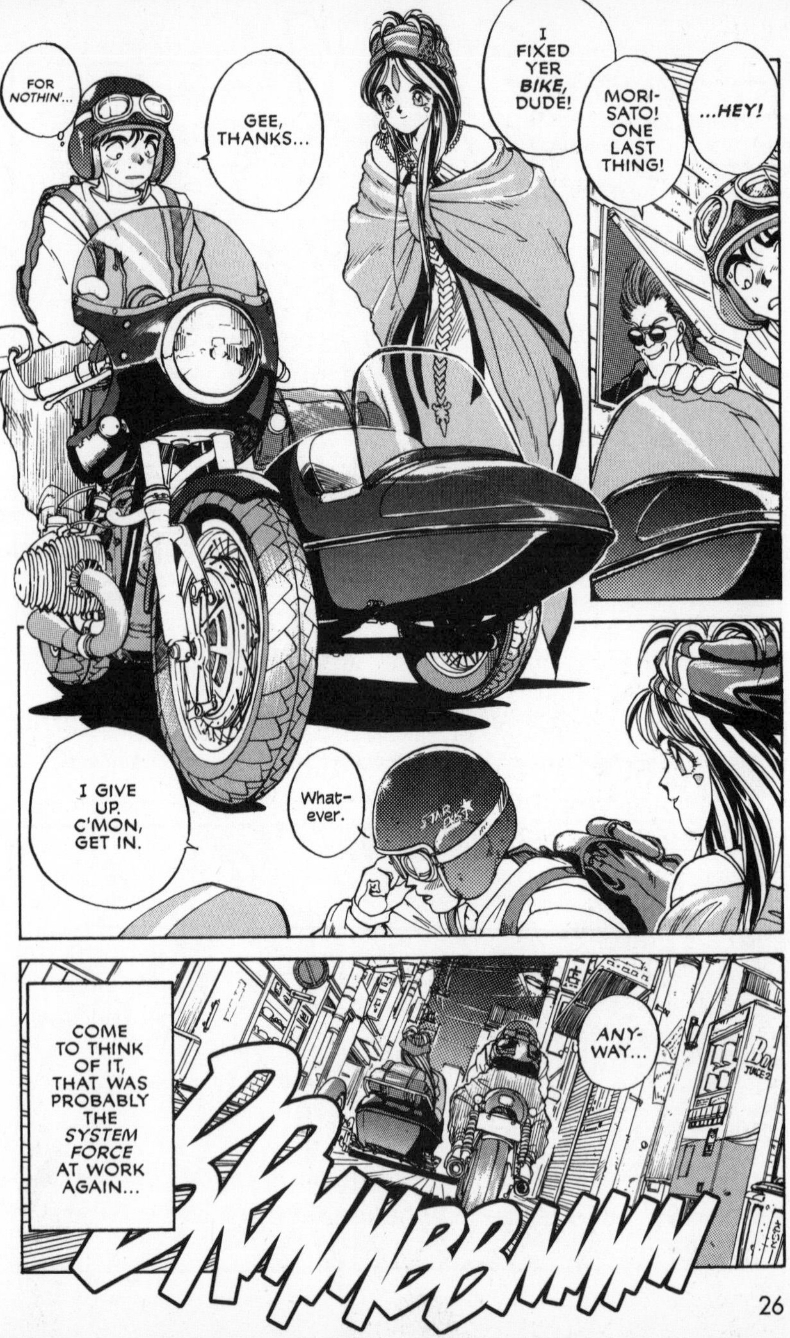
...HEY!
MORI-SATO! ONE LAST THING!
I FIXED YER *BIKE,* DUDE!
GEE, THANKS...
FOR *NOTHIN'...*
What-ever.
I GIVE UP. C'MON, GET IN.
ANY-WAY...
COME TO THINK OF IT, THAT WAS PROBABLY THE *SYSTEM FORCE* AT WORK AGAIN...

CHAPTER 2

Lair of the Anime Mania

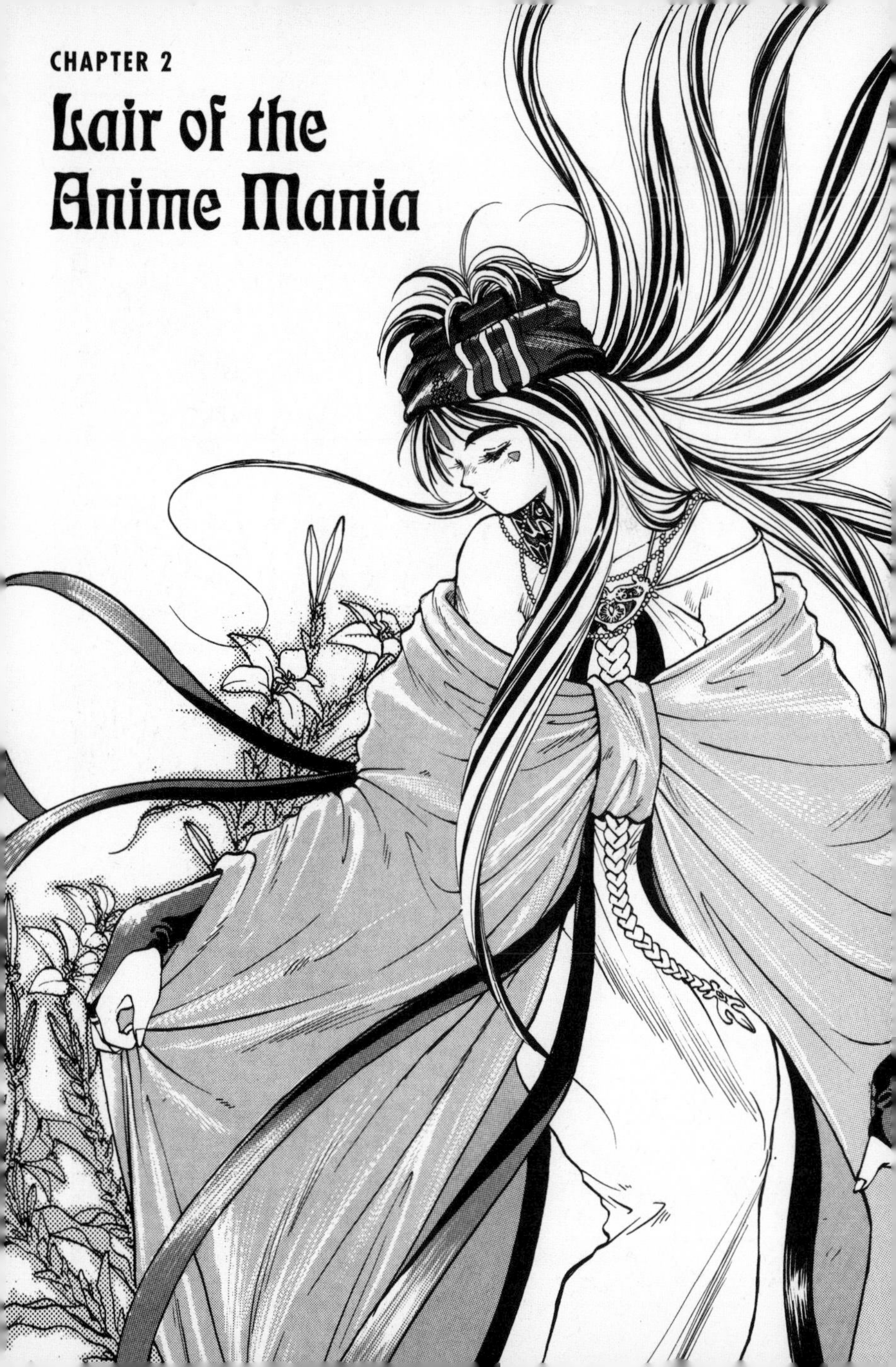

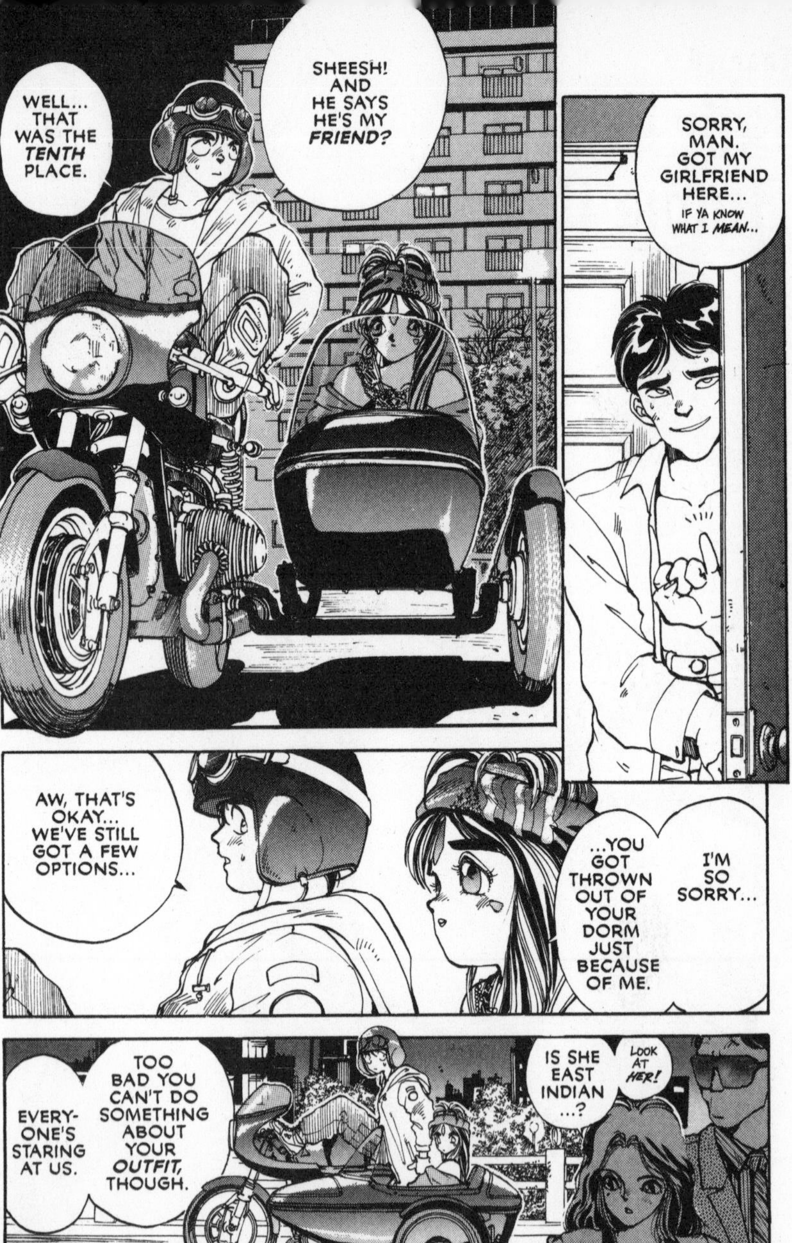
SORRY, MAN. GOT MY GIRLFRIEND HERE... IF YA KNOW WHAT I *MEAN*...
SHEESH! AND HE SAYS HE'S MY *FRIEND?*
WELL... THAT WAS THE *TENTH* PLACE.
I'M SO SORRY...
...YOU GOT THROWN OUT OF YOUR DORM JUST BECAUSE OF ME.
AW, THAT'S OKAY... WE'VE STILL GOT A FEW OPTIONS...
LOOK AT *HER!*
IS SHE EAST INDIAN ...?
TOO BAD YOU CAN'T DO SOMETHING ABOUT YOUR *OUTFIT,* THOUGH.
EVERY-ONE'S STARING AT US.

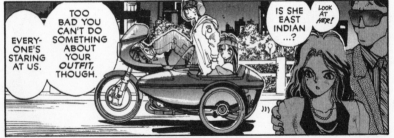

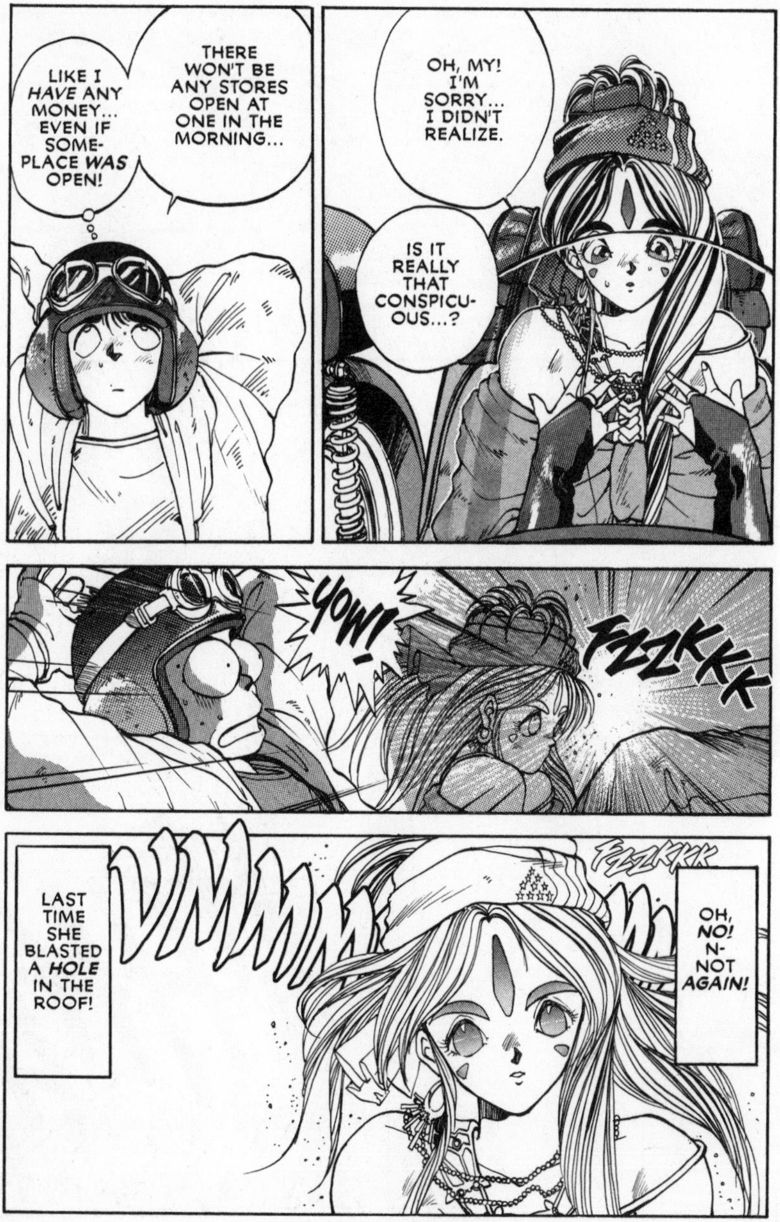
OH, MY! I'M SORRY... I DIDN'T REALIZE.
IS IT REALLY THAT CONSPICU-OUS...?
THERE WON'T BE ANY STORES OPEN AT ONE IN THE MORNING...
LIKE I *HAVE* ANY MONEY... EVEN IF SOME-PLACE *WAS* OPEN!
FZZKKKK
YOW!
OH, *NO!* N-NOT *AGAIN!*
FZZKKK
VMMMM
LAST TIME SHE BLASTED A *HOLE* IN THE ROOF!

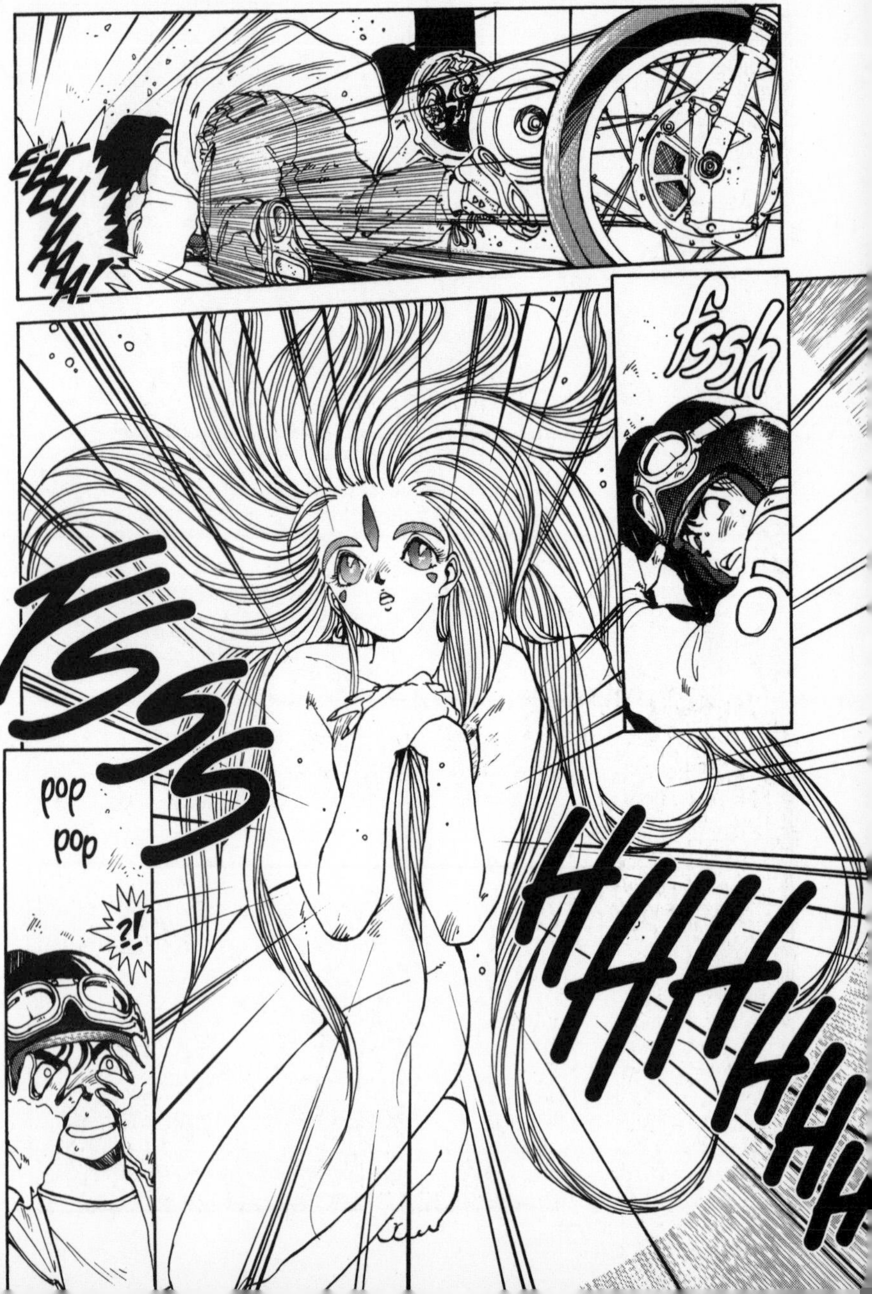
EEEEUWAAA!
fssh
FSSS
HHHHHH
pop
pop
?!

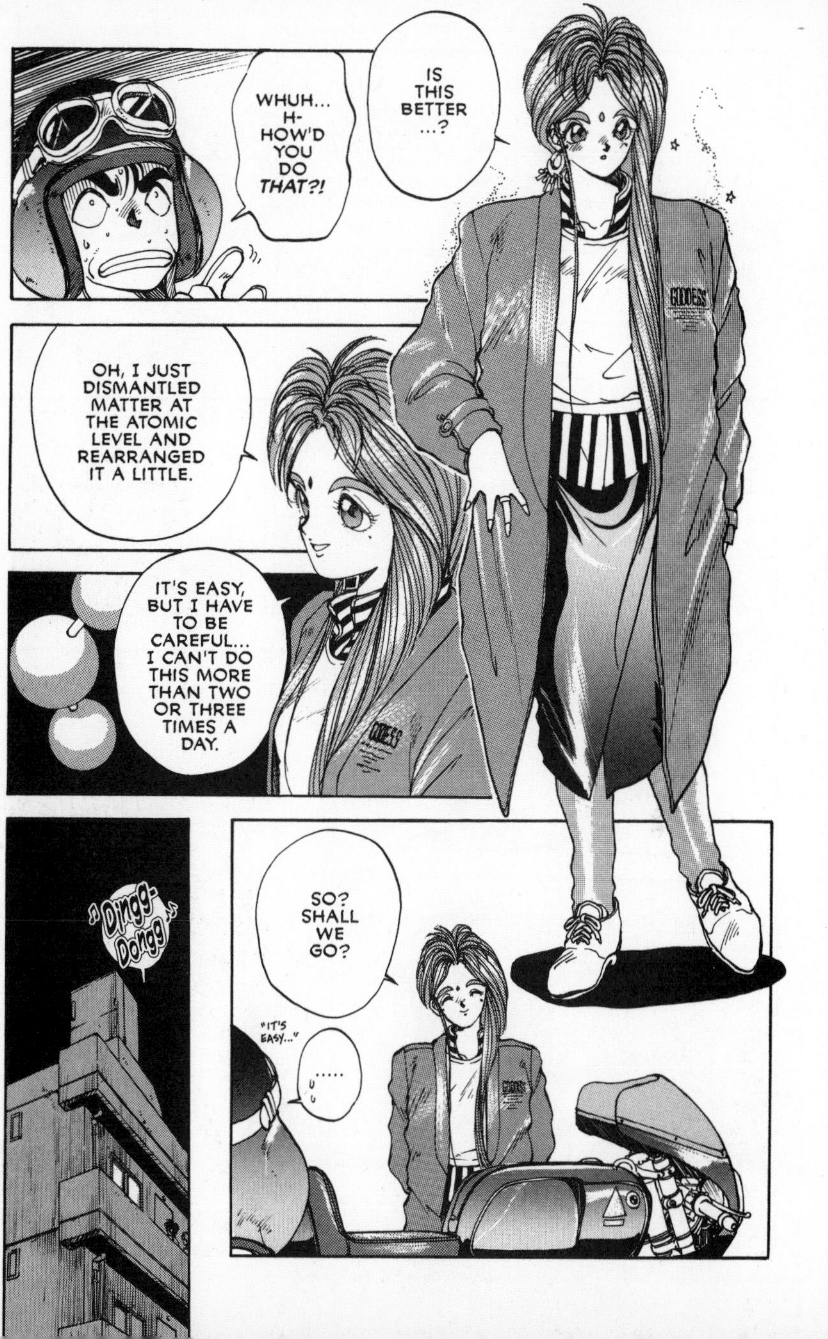
IS THIS BETTER ...?
WHUH... H-HOW'D YOU DO *THAT?!*
OH, I JUST DISMANTLED MATTER AT THE ATOMIC LEVEL AND REARRANGED IT A LITTLE.
IT'S EASY, BUT I HAVE TO BE CAREFUL... I CAN'T DO THIS MORE THAN TWO OR THREE TIMES A DAY.
SO? SHALL WE GO?
"IT'S EASY..."
.....
Dingg-Dongg

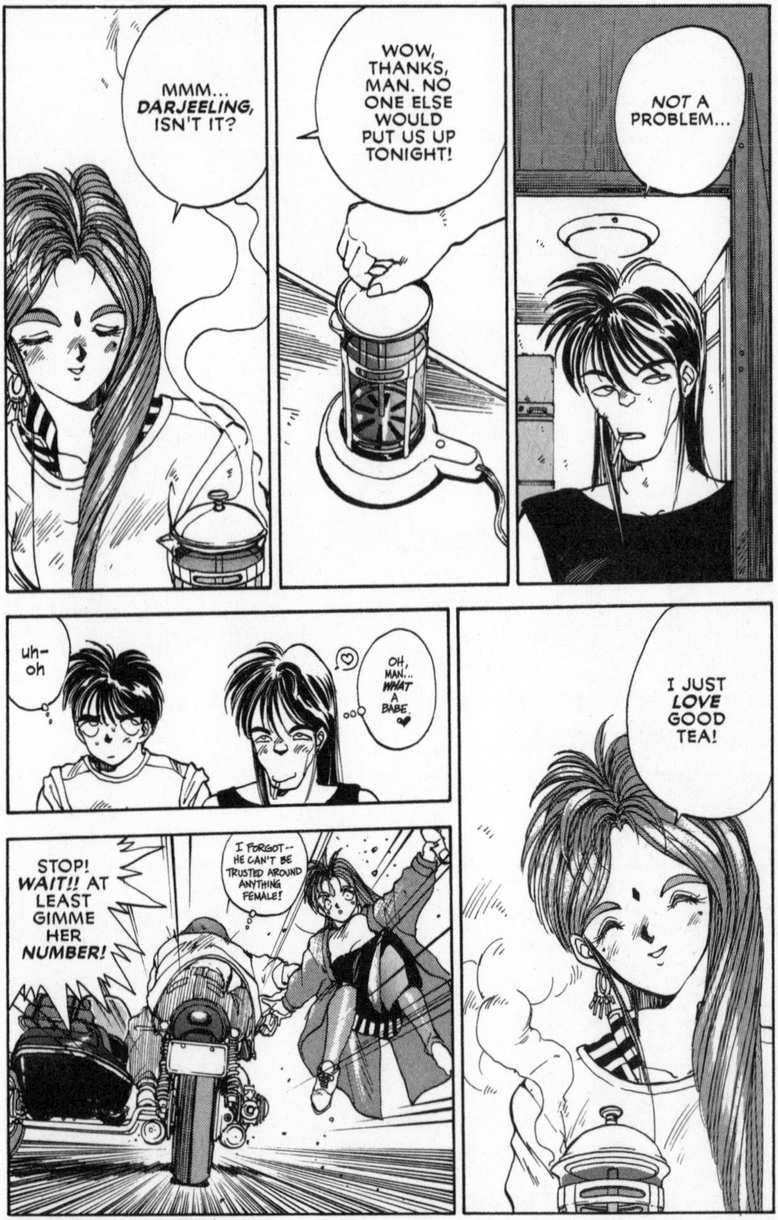
NOT A PROBLEM...
WOW, THANKS, MAN. NO ONE ELSE WOULD PUT US UP TONIGHT!
MMM... DARJEELING, ISN'T IT?
I JUST LOVE GOOD TEA!
OH, MAN... WHAT A BABE.
uh-oh
I FORGOT-- HE CAN'T BE TRUSTED AROUND ANYTHING FEMALE!
STOP! WAIT!! AT LEAST GIMME HER NUMBER!

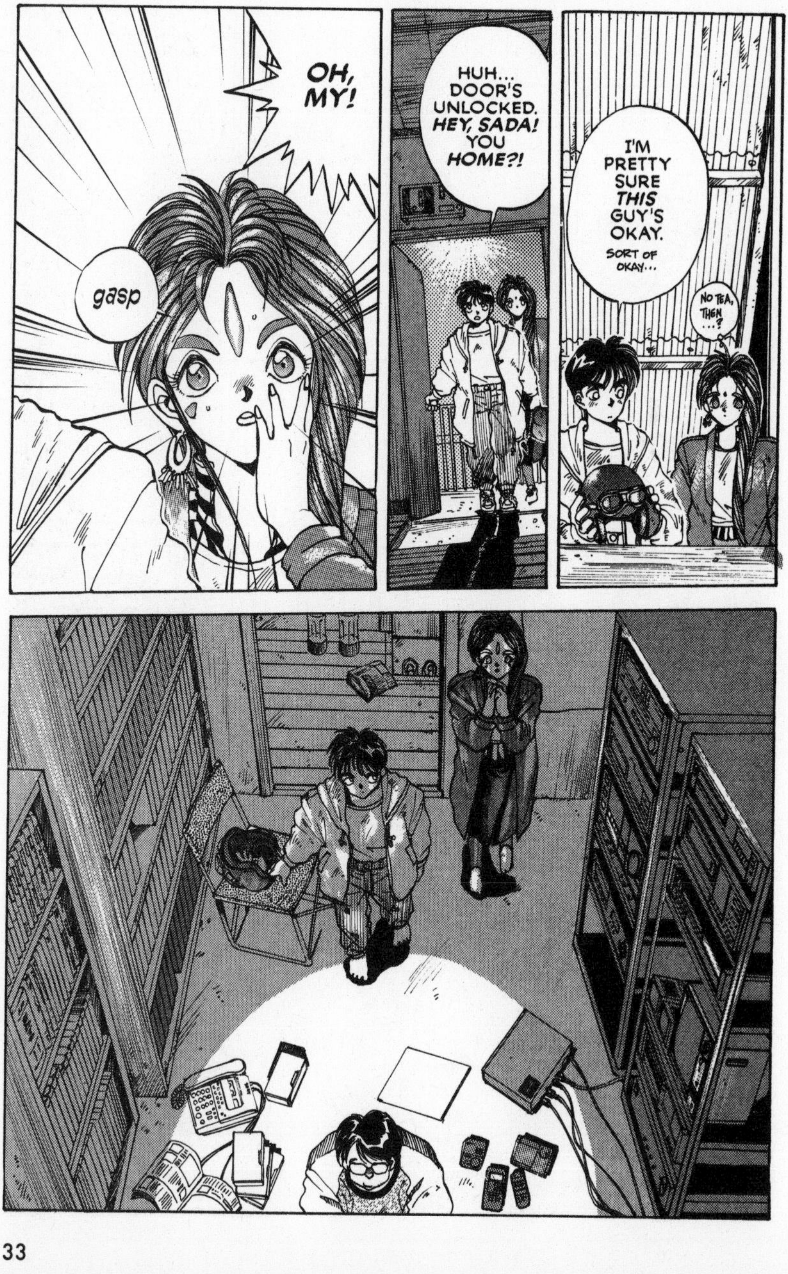
I'M PRETTY SURE THIS GUY'S OKAY.
SORT OF OKAY...
NO TEA, THEN...?
HUH... DOOR'S UNLOCKED. HEY, SADA! YOU HOME?!
OH, MY!
gasp

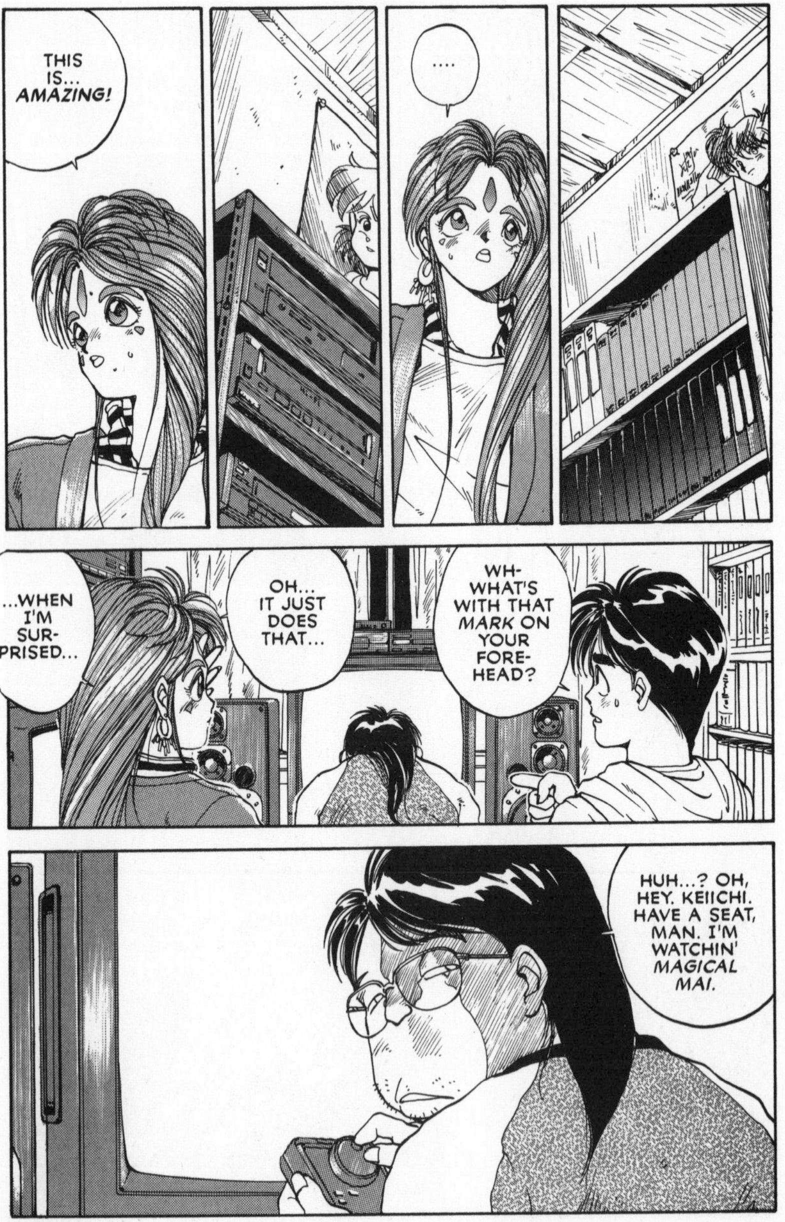
....
THIS IS... *AMAZING!*
WH- WHAT'S WITH THAT *MARK* ON YOUR FOREHEAD?
OH... IT JUST DOES THAT...
...WHEN I'M SURPRISED...
HUH...? OH, HEY. KEIICHI. HAVE A SEAT, MAN. I'M WATCHIN' *MAGICAL MAI.*

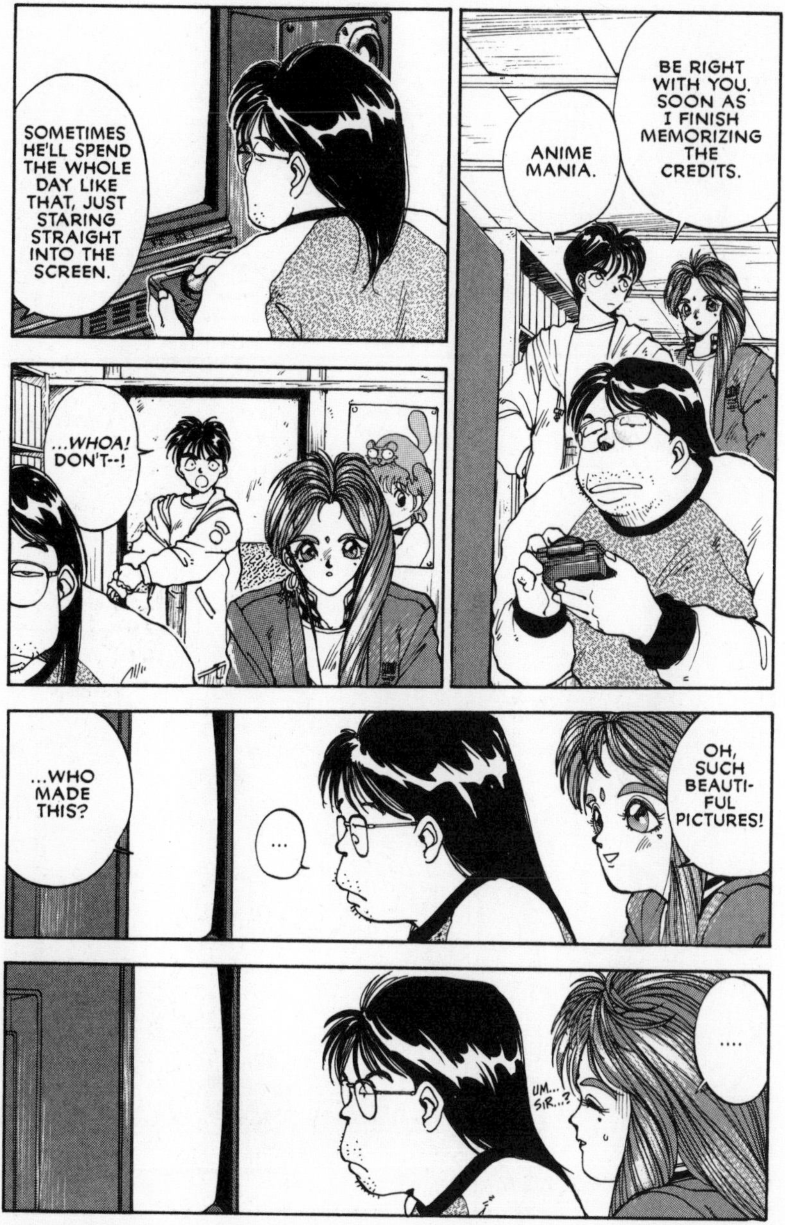
BE RIGHT WITH YOU. SOON AS I FINISH MEMORIZING THE CREDITS.
ANIME MANIA.
SOMETIMES HE'LL SPEND THE WHOLE DAY LIKE THAT, JUST STARING STRAIGHT INTO THE SCREEN.
...WHOA! DON'T--!
OH, SUCH BEAUTI-FUL PICTURES!
...
...WHO MADE THIS?
....
UM... SIR...?

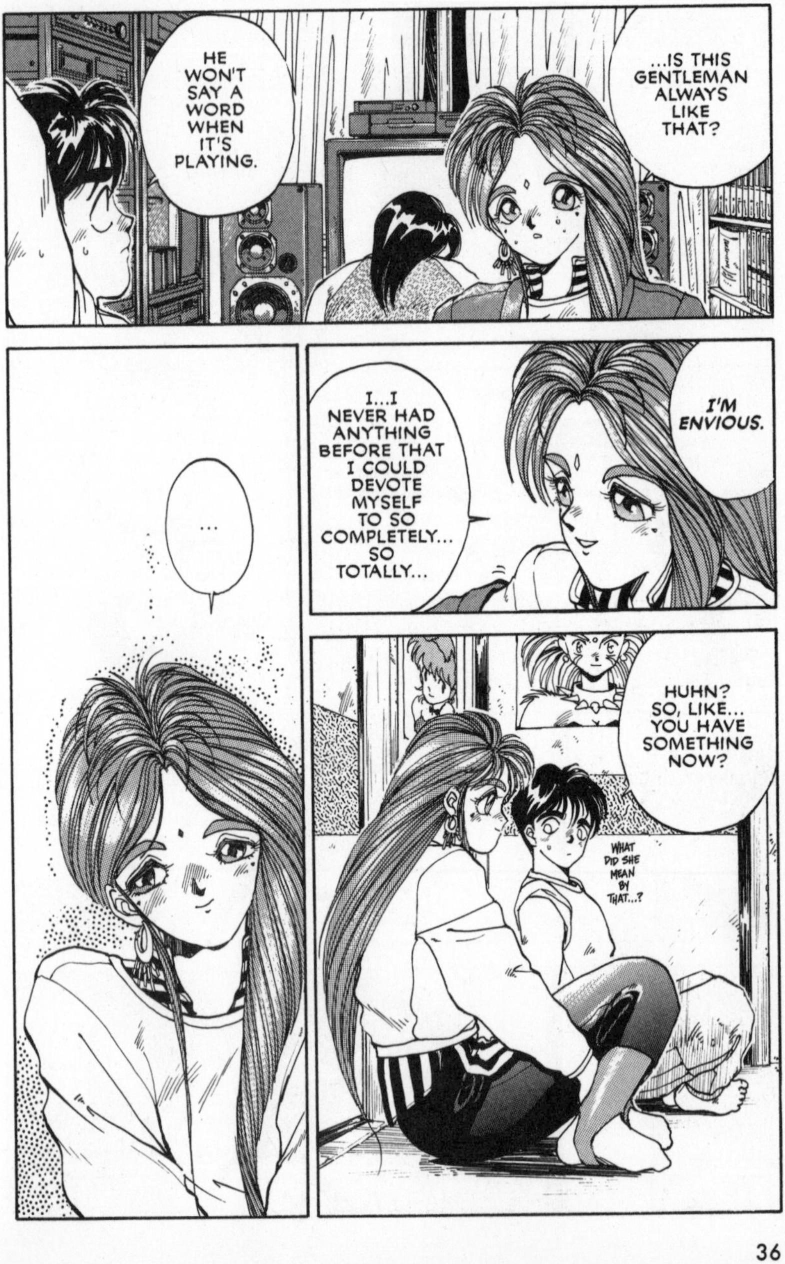
...IS THIS GENTLEMAN ALWAYS LIKE THAT?
HE WON'T SAY A WORD WHEN IT'S PLAYING.
I'M ENVIOUS.
I...I NEVER HAD ANYTHING BEFORE THAT I COULD DEVOTE MYSELF TO SO COMPLETELY... SO TOTALLY...
HUHN? SO, LIKE... YOU HAVE SOMETHING NOW?
WHAT DID SHE MEAN BY THAT...?
...

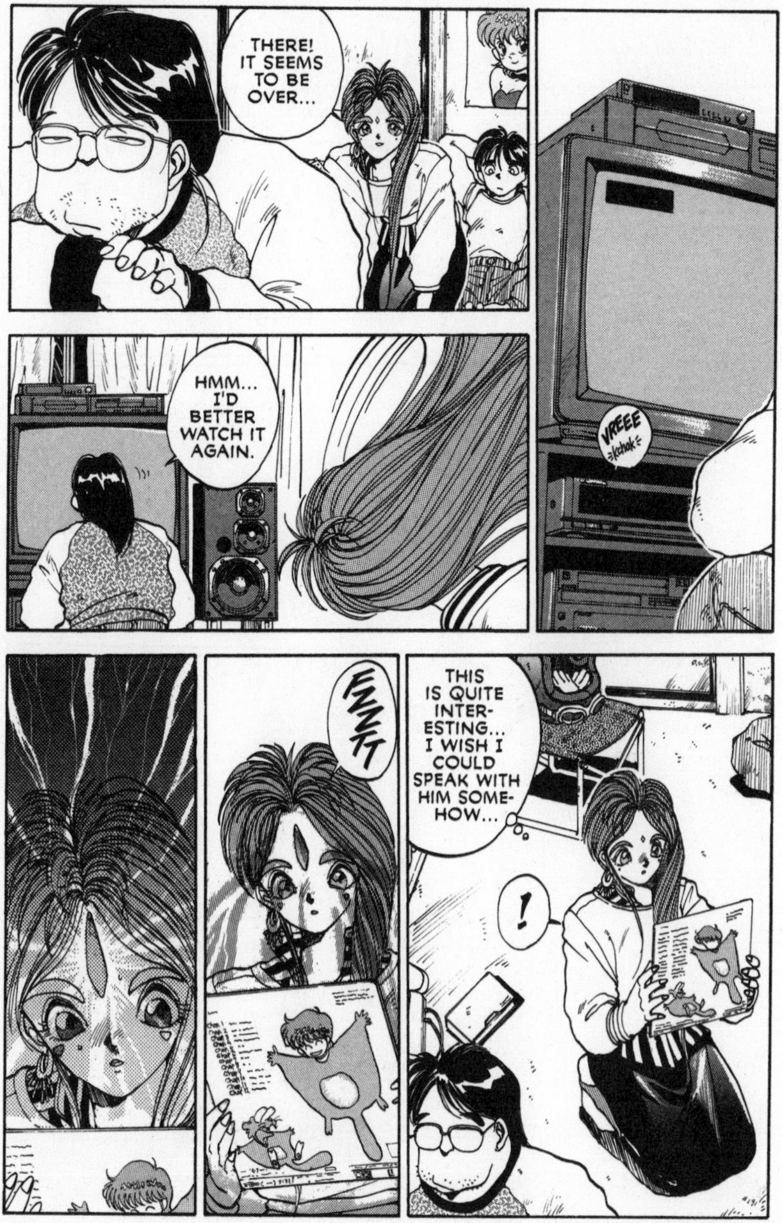
VREEE
kchak
THERE! IT SEEMS TO BE OVER...
HMM... I'D BETTER WATCH IT AGAIN.
THIS IS QUITE INTERESTING... I WISH I COULD SPEAK WITH HIM SOMEHOW...
!
FZZZT

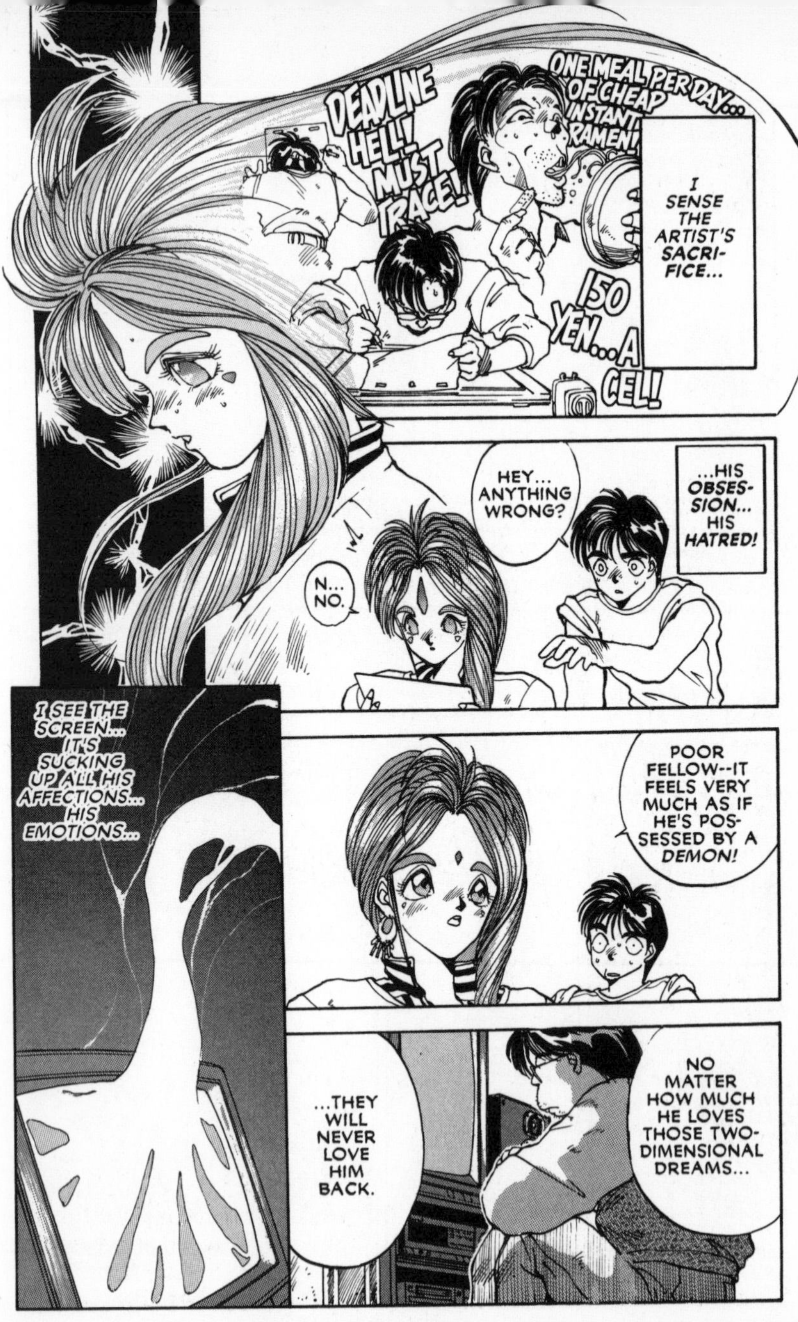
ONE MEAL PER DAY... OF CHEAP INSTANT RAMEN!
I SENSE THE ARTIST'S SACRI-FICE...
DEADLINE HELL! MUST TRACE!
150 YEN...A CEL!
...HIS OBSES-SION... HIS HATRED!
HEY... ANYTHING WRONG?
N... NO.
POOR FELLOW--IT FEELS VERY MUCH AS IF HE'S POS-SESSED BY A DEMON!
NO MATTER HOW MUCH HE LOVES THOSE TWO-DIMENSIONAL DREAMS...
...THEY WILL NEVER LOVE HIM BACK.
I SEE THE SCREEN... IT'S SUCKING UP ALL HIS AFFECTIONS... HIS EMOTIONS...

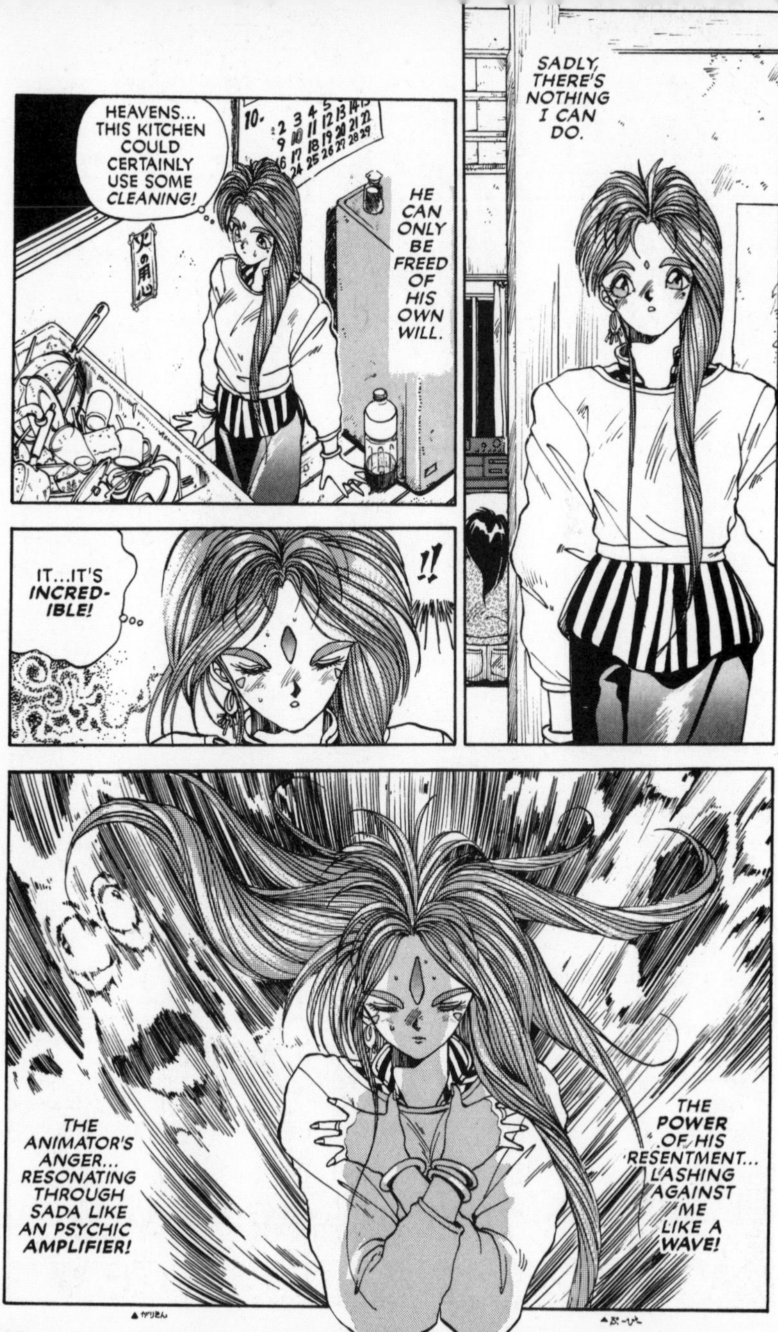
SADLY, THERE'S NOTHING I CAN DO.
HE CAN ONLY BE FREED OF HIS OWN WILL.
HEAVENS... THIS KITCHEN COULD CERTAINLY USE SOME *CLEANING!*
火の用心
!!
IT...IT'S *INCRED-IBLE!*
THE POWER OF HIS RESENTMENT... LASHING AGAINST ME LIKE A **WAVE!**
THE ANIMATOR'S ANGER... RESONATING THROUGH SADA LIKE AN PSYCHIC **AMPLIFIER!**

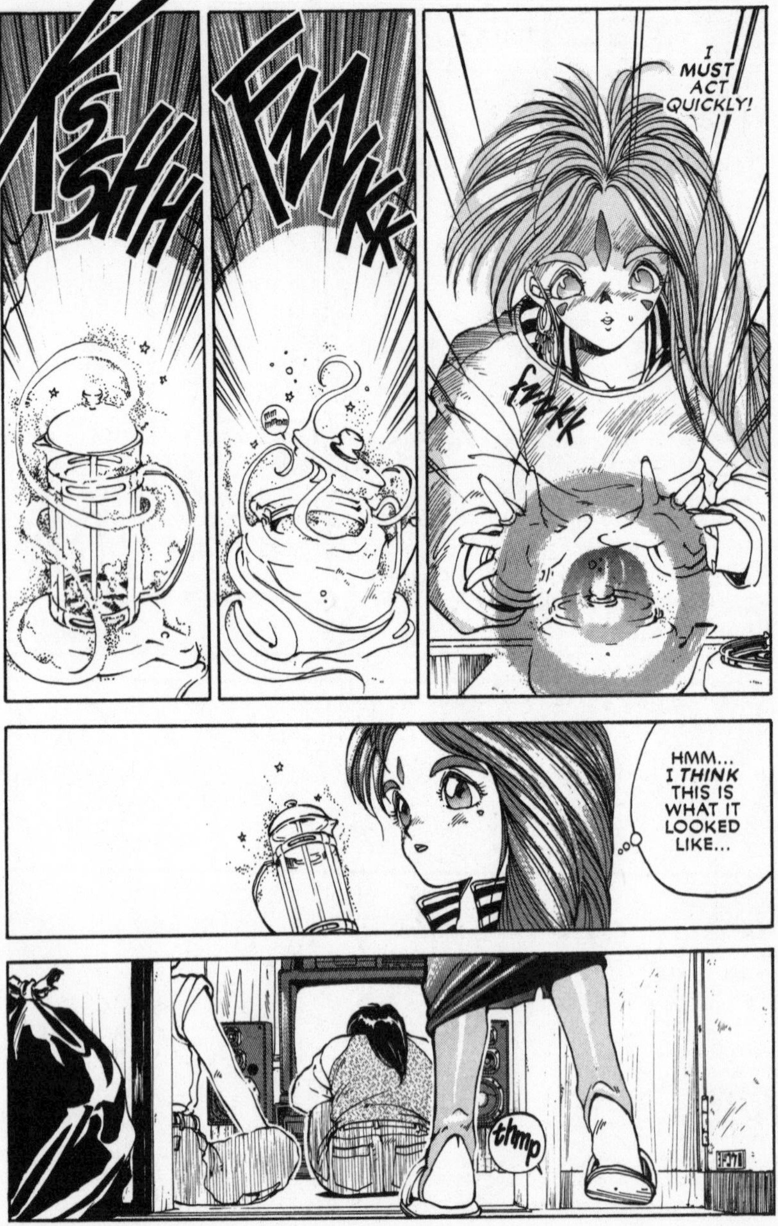
I MUST ACT QUICKLY!
fzzkk
FZZKK
KSHH
HMM... I *THINK* THIS IS WHAT IT LOOKED LIKE...
thmp

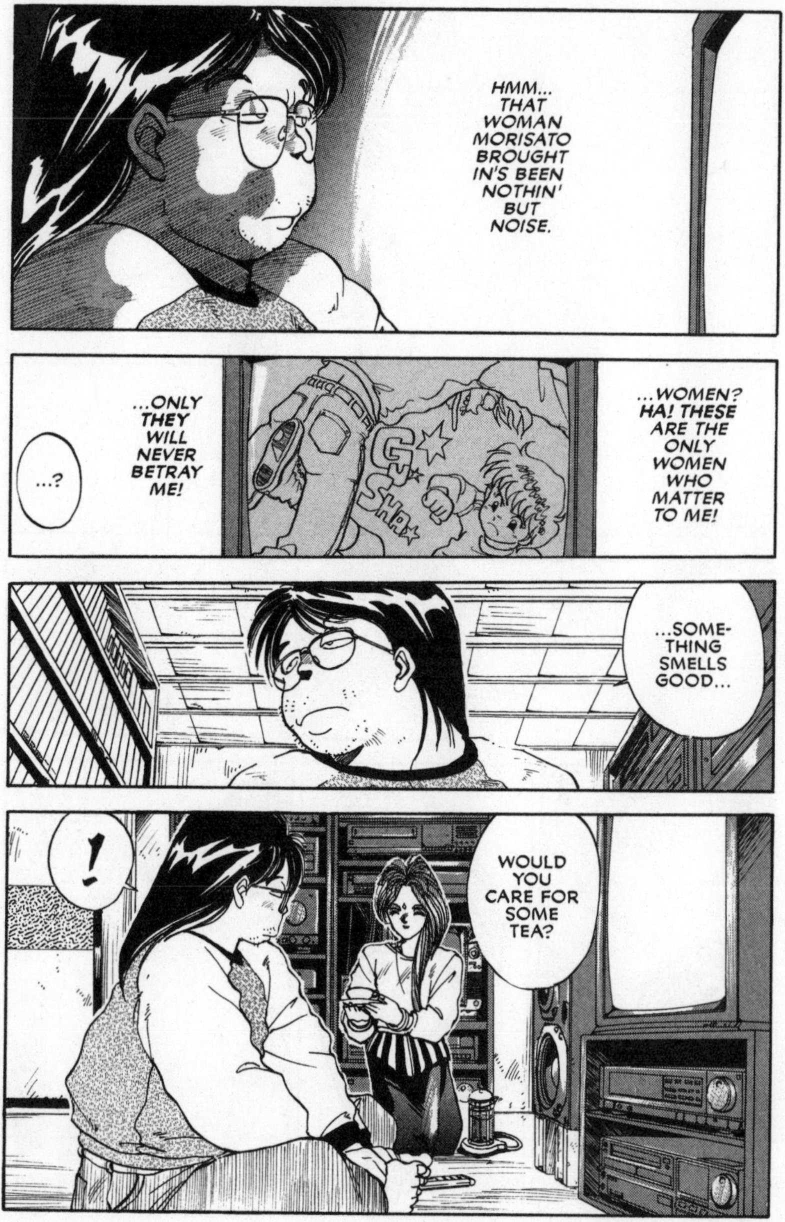
HMM... THAT WOMAN MORISATO BROUGHT IN'S BEEN NOTHIN' BUT NOISE.
...WOMEN? HA! THESE ARE THE ONLY WOMEN WHO MATTER TO ME!
...ONLY THEY WILL NEVER BETRAY ME!
...?
...SOME-THING SMELLS GOOD...
WOULD YOU CARE FOR SOME TEA?
!

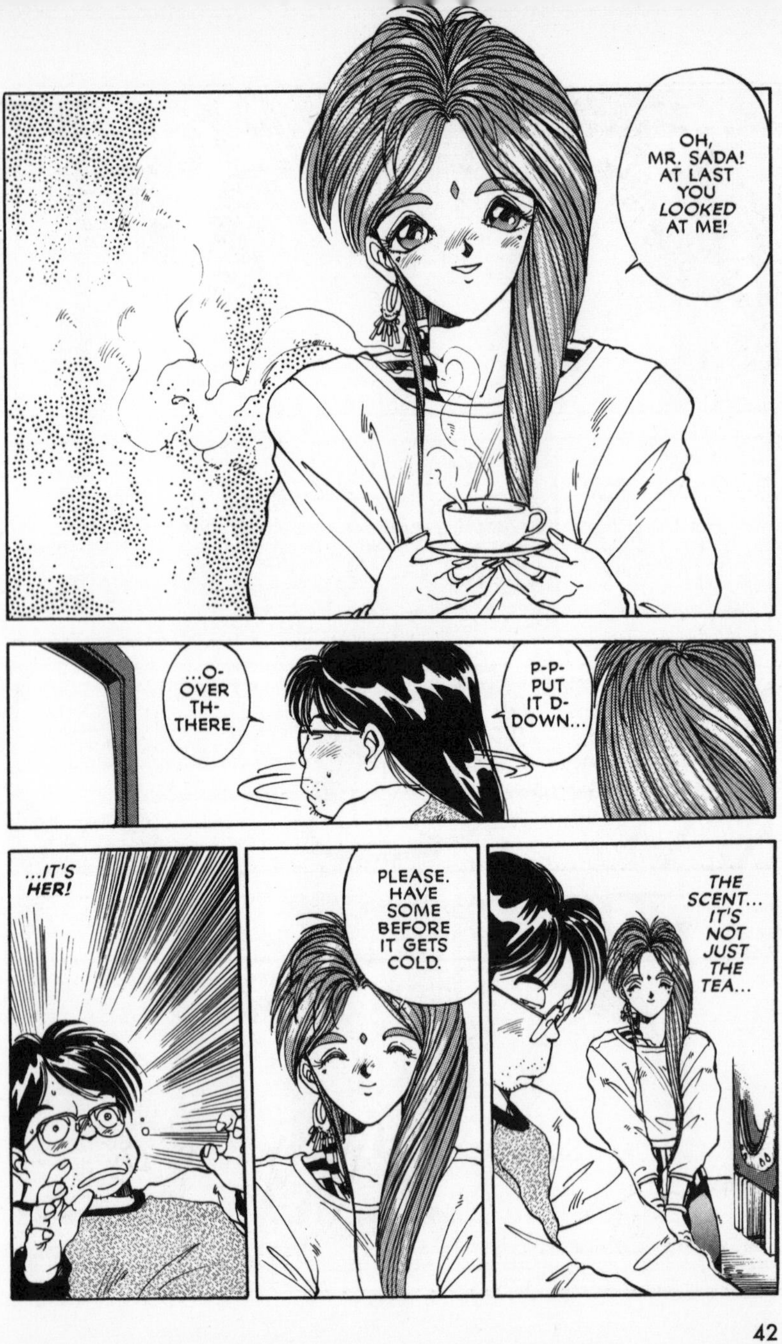
OH, MR. SADA! AT LAST YOU *LOOKED* AT ME!
P-P-PUT IT D-DOWN...
...O-OVER TH-THERE.
THE SCENT... IT'S NOT JUST THE TEA...
PLEASE. HAVE SOME BEFORE IT GETS COLD.
...IT'S ***HER!***

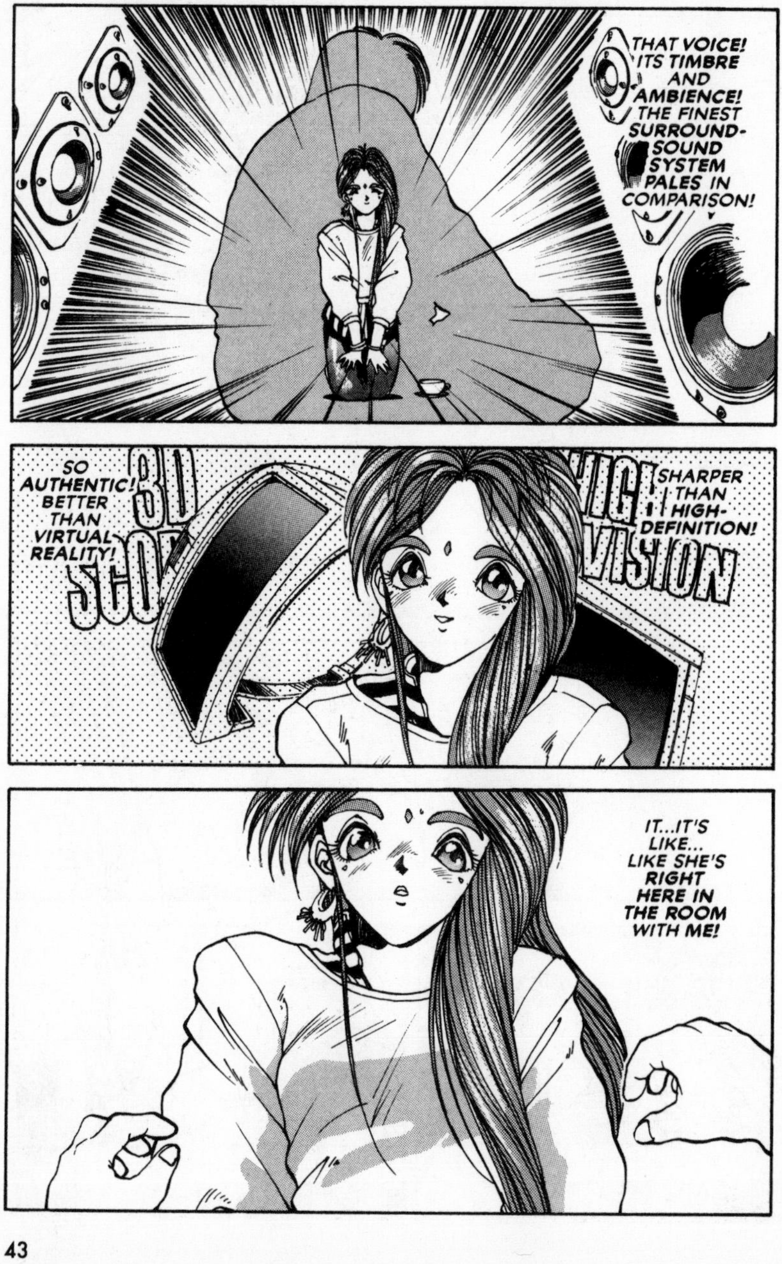
THAT VOICE! ITS TIMBRE AND AMBIENCE! THE FINEST SURROUND-SOUND SYSTEM PALES IN COMPARISON!
SHARPER THAN HIGH-DEFINITION!
VISION
3D
SO AUTHENTIC! BETTER THAN VIRTUAL REALITY!
IT...IT'S LIKE... LIKE SHE'S RIGHT HERE IN THE ROOM WITH ME!

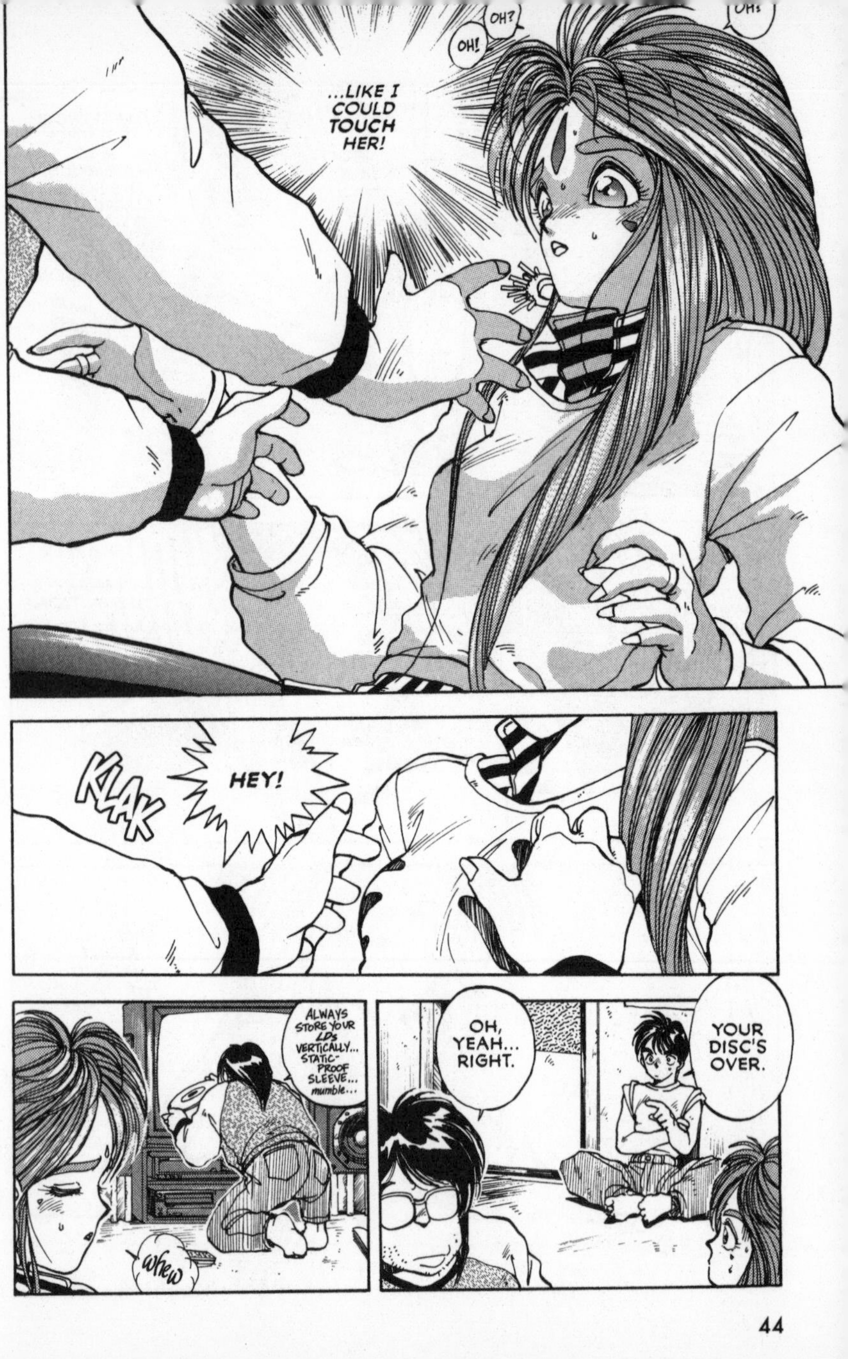
OH!
OH?
OH!
...LIKE I COULD TOUCH HER!
HEY!
KLAK
YOUR DISC'S OVER.
OH, YEAH... RIGHT.
ALWAYS STORE YOUR LDs VERTICALLY... STATIC-PROOF SLEEVE... mumble...
whew

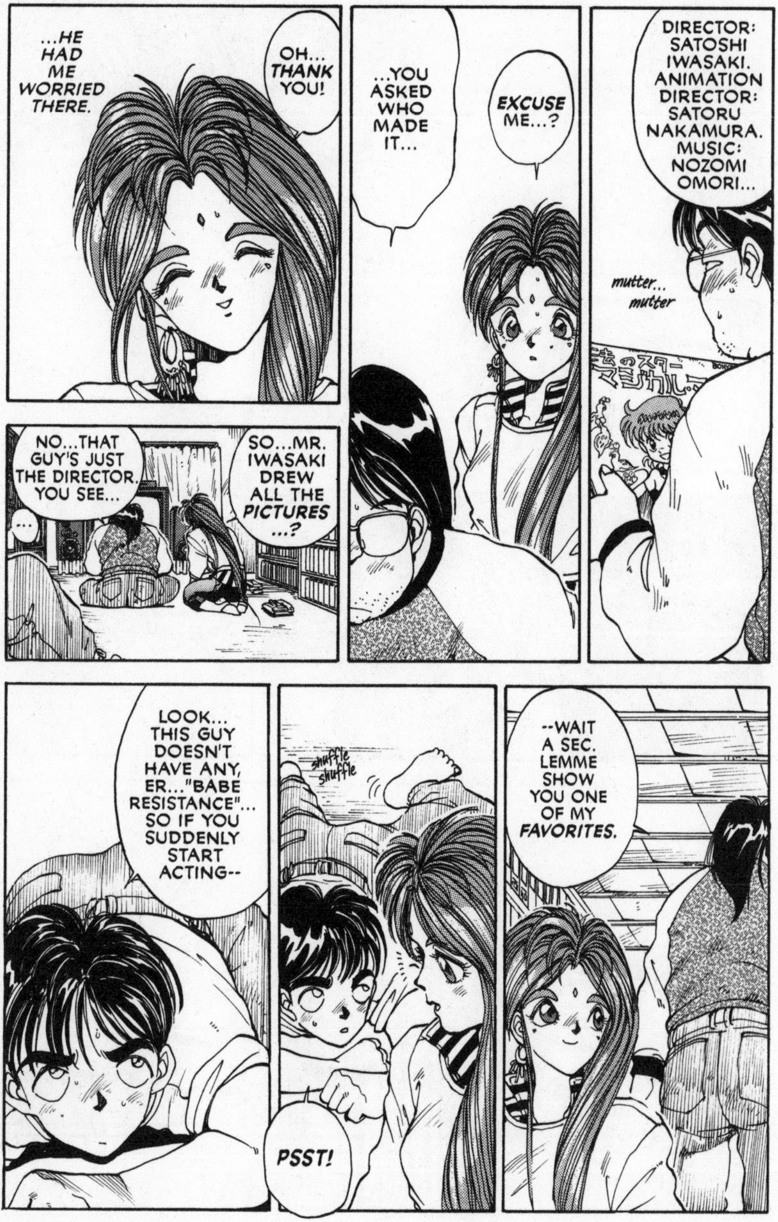
DIRECTOR: SATOSHI IWASAKI. ANIMATION DIRECTOR: SATORU NAKAMURA. MUSIC: NOZOMI OMORI...
mutter... mutter
EXCUSE ME...?
...YOU ASKED WHO MADE IT...
OH... THANK YOU!
...HE HAD ME WORRIED THERE.
SO...MR. IWASAKI DREW ALL THE PICTURES ...?
NO...THAT GUY'S JUST THE DIRECTOR. YOU SEE...
...
--WAIT A SEC. LEMME SHOW YOU ONE OF MY FAVORITES.
shuffle shuffle
PSST!
LOOK... THIS GUY DOESN'T HAVE ANY, ER..."BABE RESISTANCE"... SO IF YOU SUDDENLY START ACTING--

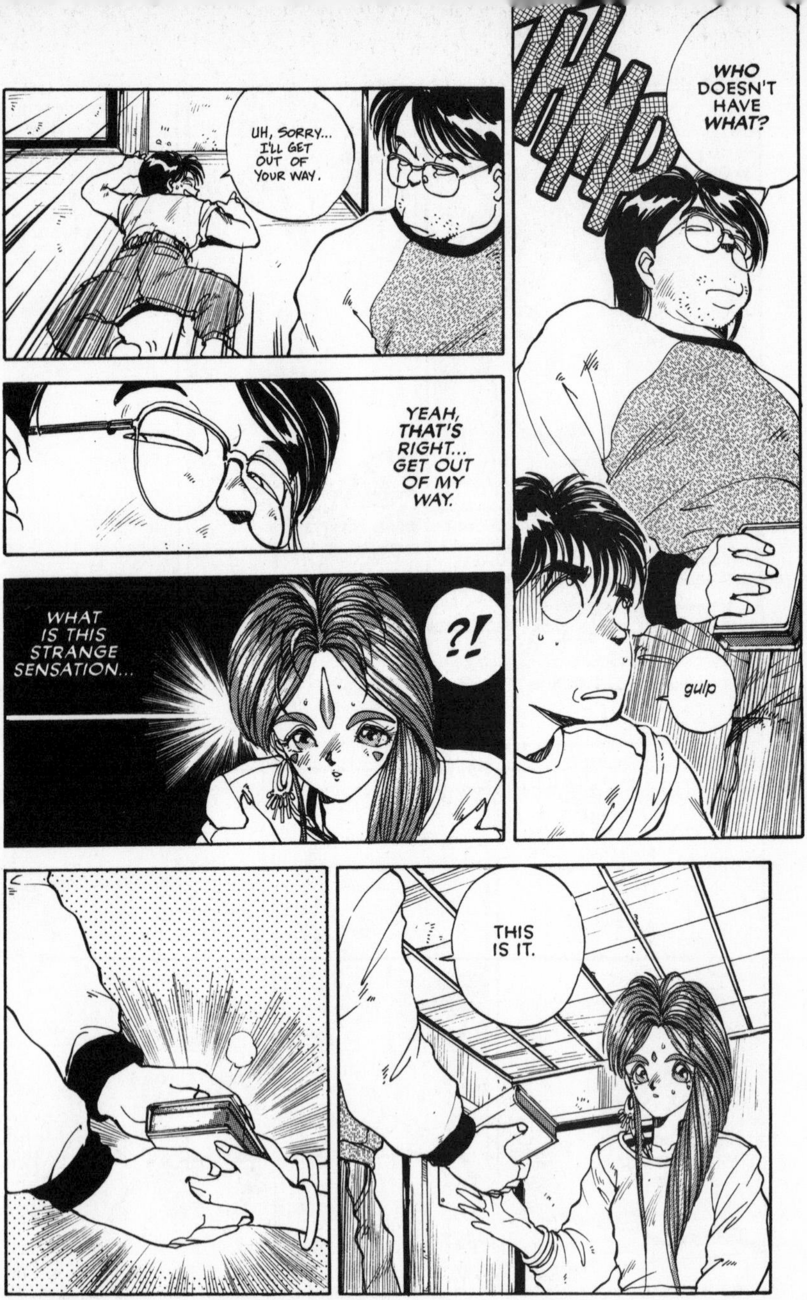
WHO DOESN'T HAVE WHAT?
THMP
gulp
UH, SORRY... I'LL GET OUT OF YOUR WAY.
YEAH, THAT'S RIGHT... GET OUT OF MY WAY.
?!
WHAT IS THIS STRANGE SENSATION...
THIS IS IT.

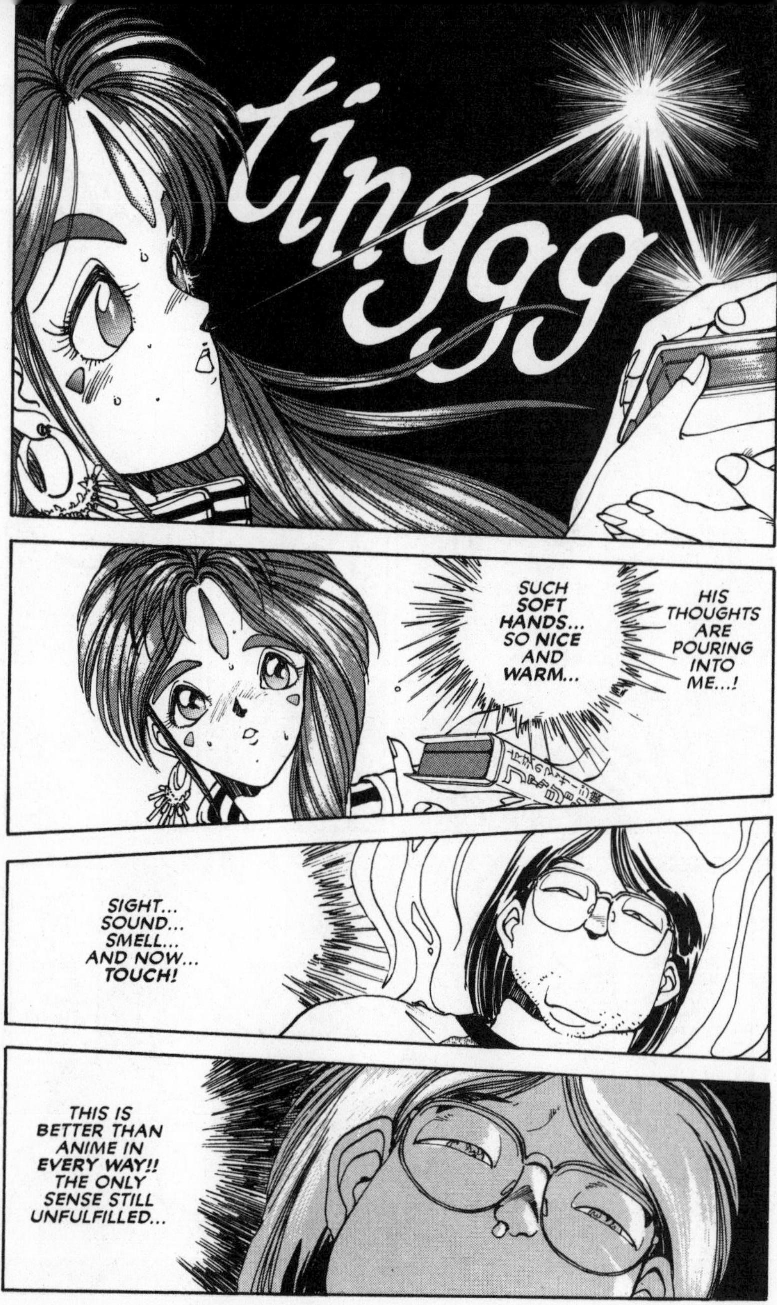
tinggg
HIS THOUGHTS ARE POURING INTO ME...!
SUCH SOFT HANDS... SO NICE AND WARM...
SIGHT... SOUND... SMELL... AND NOW... TOUCH!
THIS IS BETTER THAN ANIME IN EVERY WAY!! THE ONLY SENSE STILL UNFULFILLED...

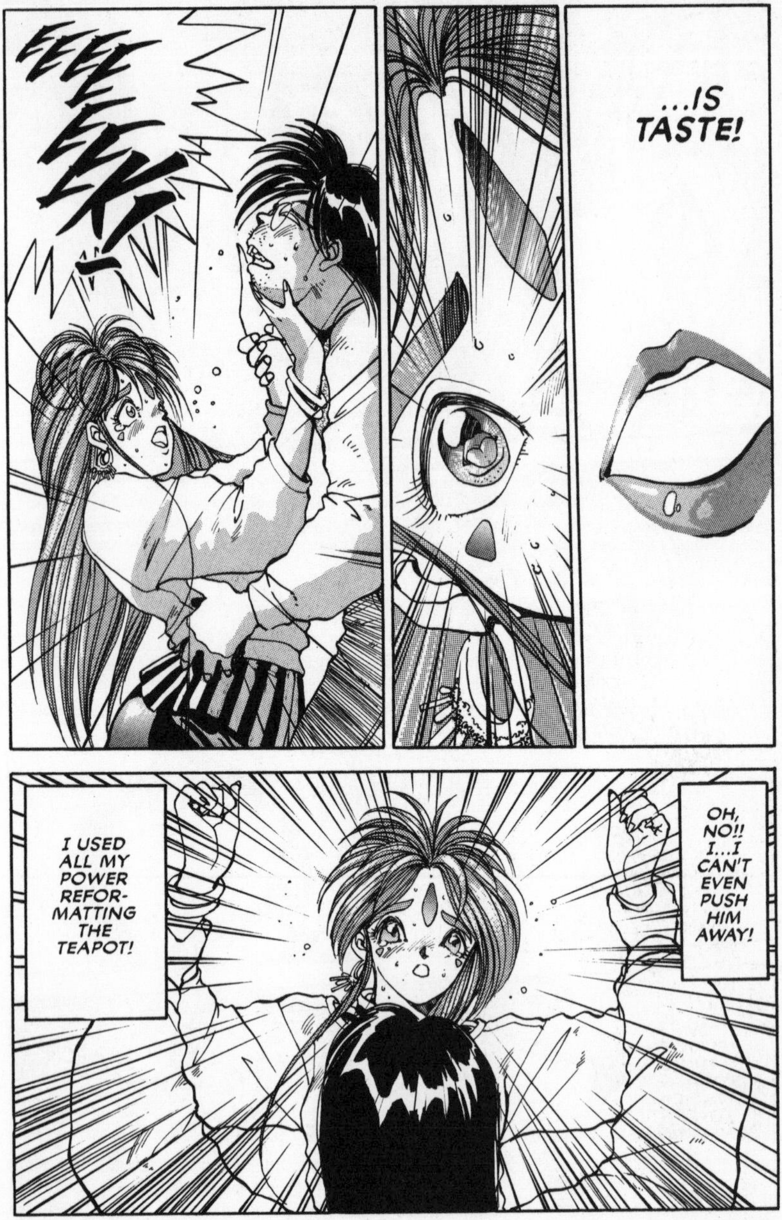
...IS TASTE!
EEEEEEEK!
OH, NO!! I...I CAN'T EVEN PUSH HIM AWAY!
I USED ALL MY POWER REFOR-MATTING THE TEAPOT!

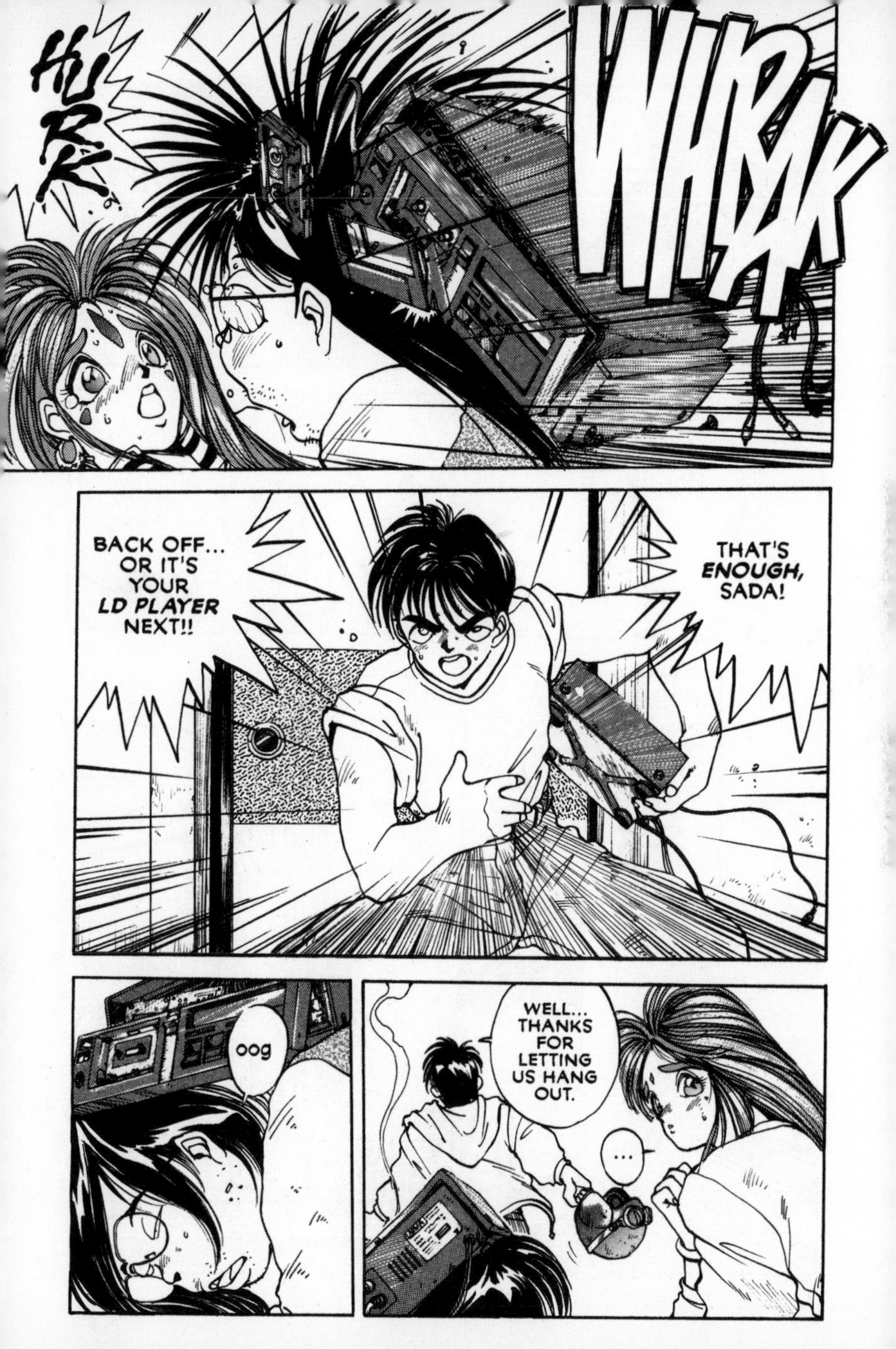
WHAK
HURK!
THAT'S *ENOUGH,* SADA!
BACK OFF... OR IT'S YOUR *LD PLAYER* NEXT!!
WELL... THANKS FOR LETTING US HANG OUT.
...
oog

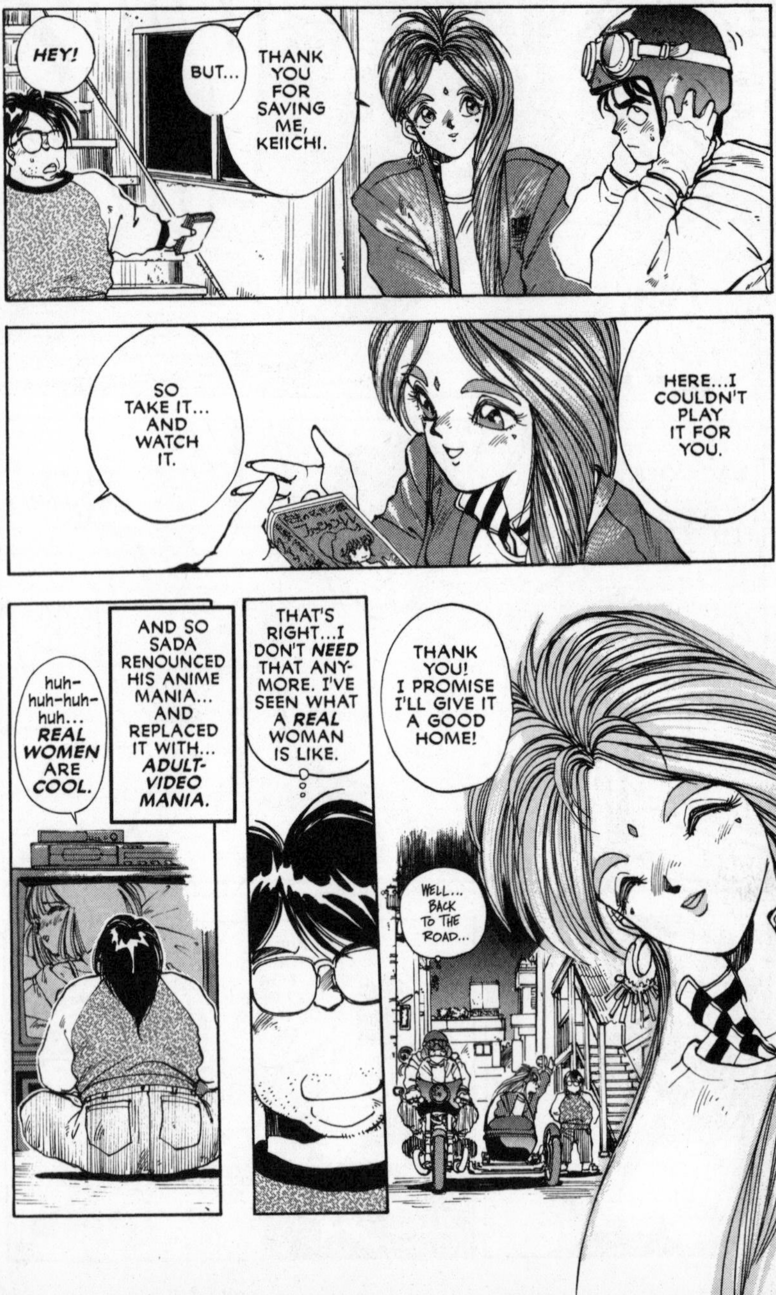
THANK YOU FOR SAVING ME, KEIICHI.
BUT...
HEY!
HERE...I COULDN'T PLAY IT FOR YOU.
SO TAKE IT... AND WATCH IT.
THANK YOU! I PROMISE I'LL GIVE IT A GOOD HOME!
WELL... BACK TO THE ROAD...
THAT'S RIGHT...I DON'T *NEED* THAT ANY-MORE. I'VE SEEN WHAT A *REAL* WOMAN IS LIKE.
AND SO SADA RENOUNCED HIS ANIME MANIA... AND REPLACED IT WITH... *ADULT-VIDEO MANIA.*
huh-huh-huh-huh... *REAL WOMEN* ARE *COOL.*

CHAPTER 3

A Man's Home Is His... Temple?

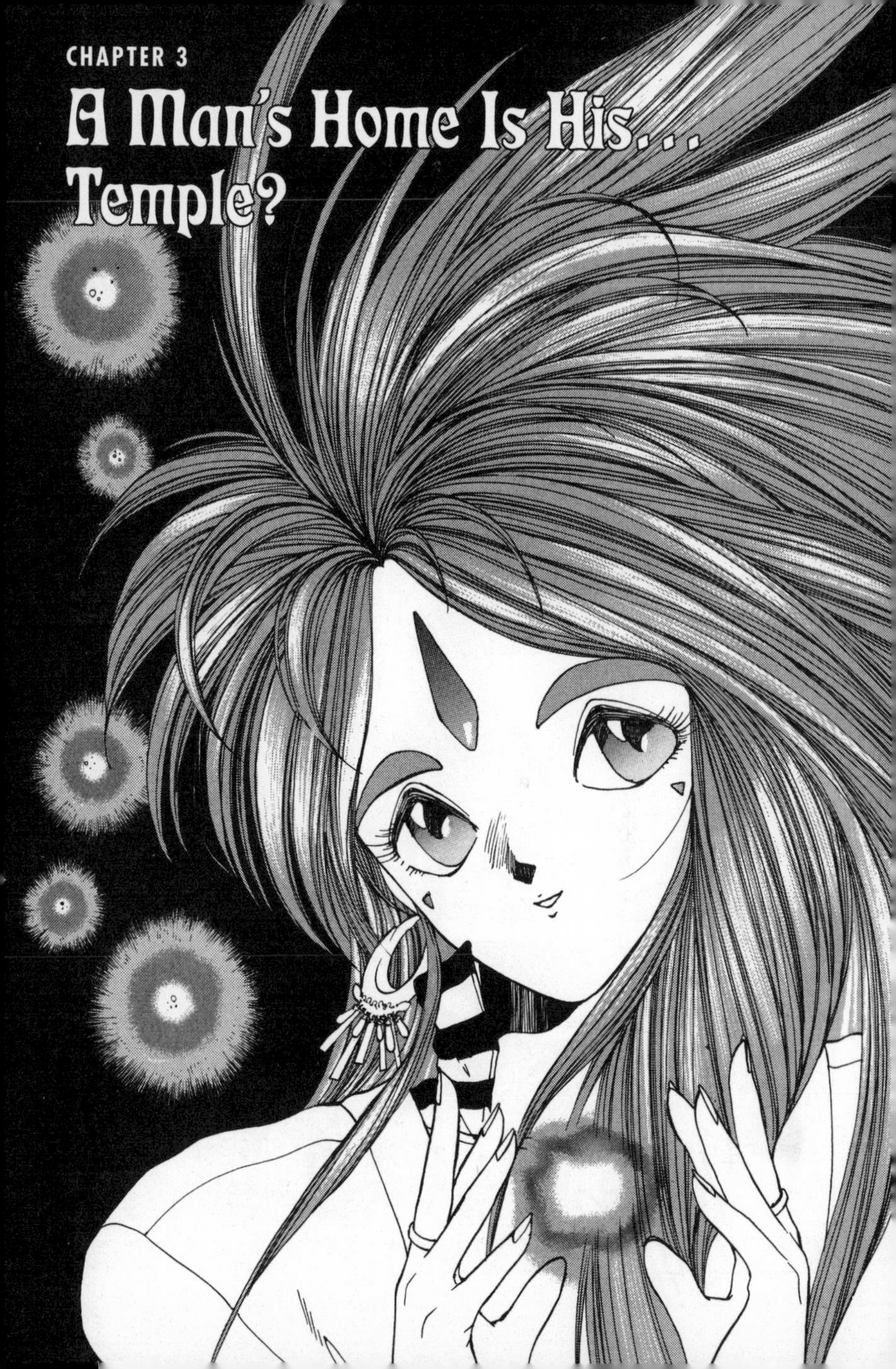

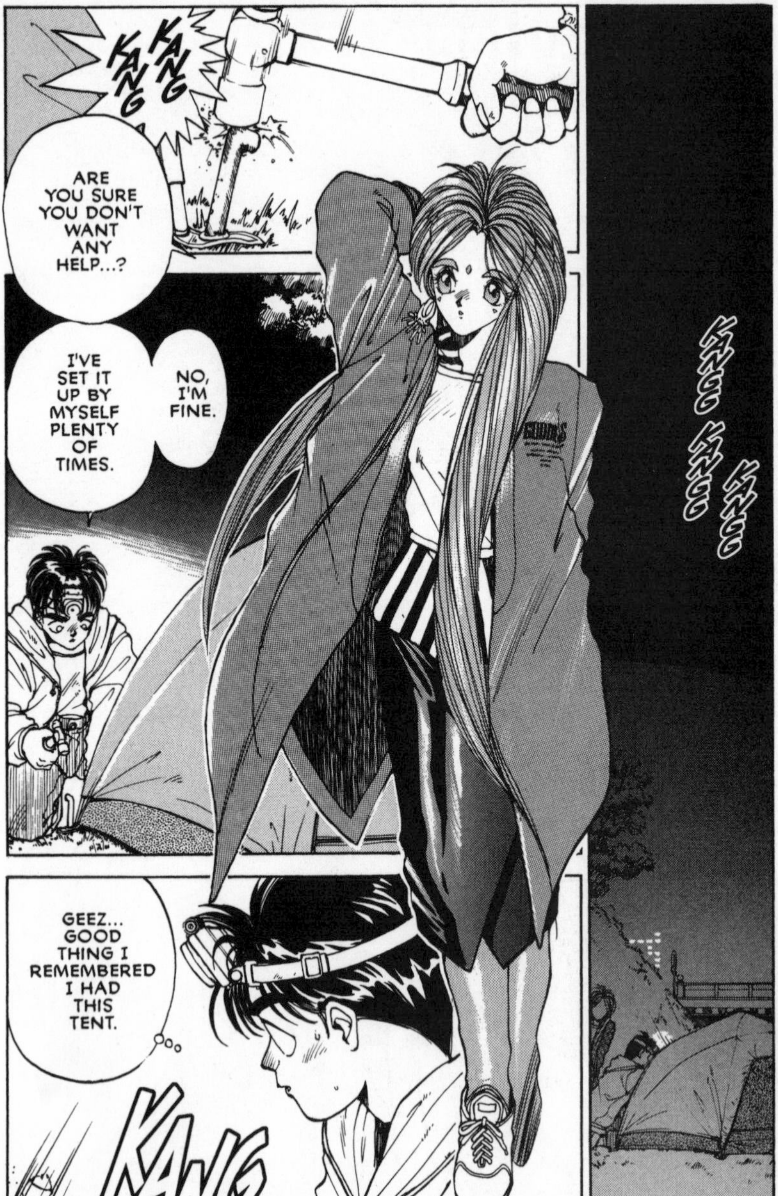
KANG KANG KANG
KANG KANG
ARE YOU SURE YOU DON'T WANT ANY HELP...?
NO, I'M FINE.
I'VE SET IT UP BY MYSELF PLENTY OF TIMES.
GEEZ... GOOD THING I REMEMBERED I HAD THIS TENT.
KANG

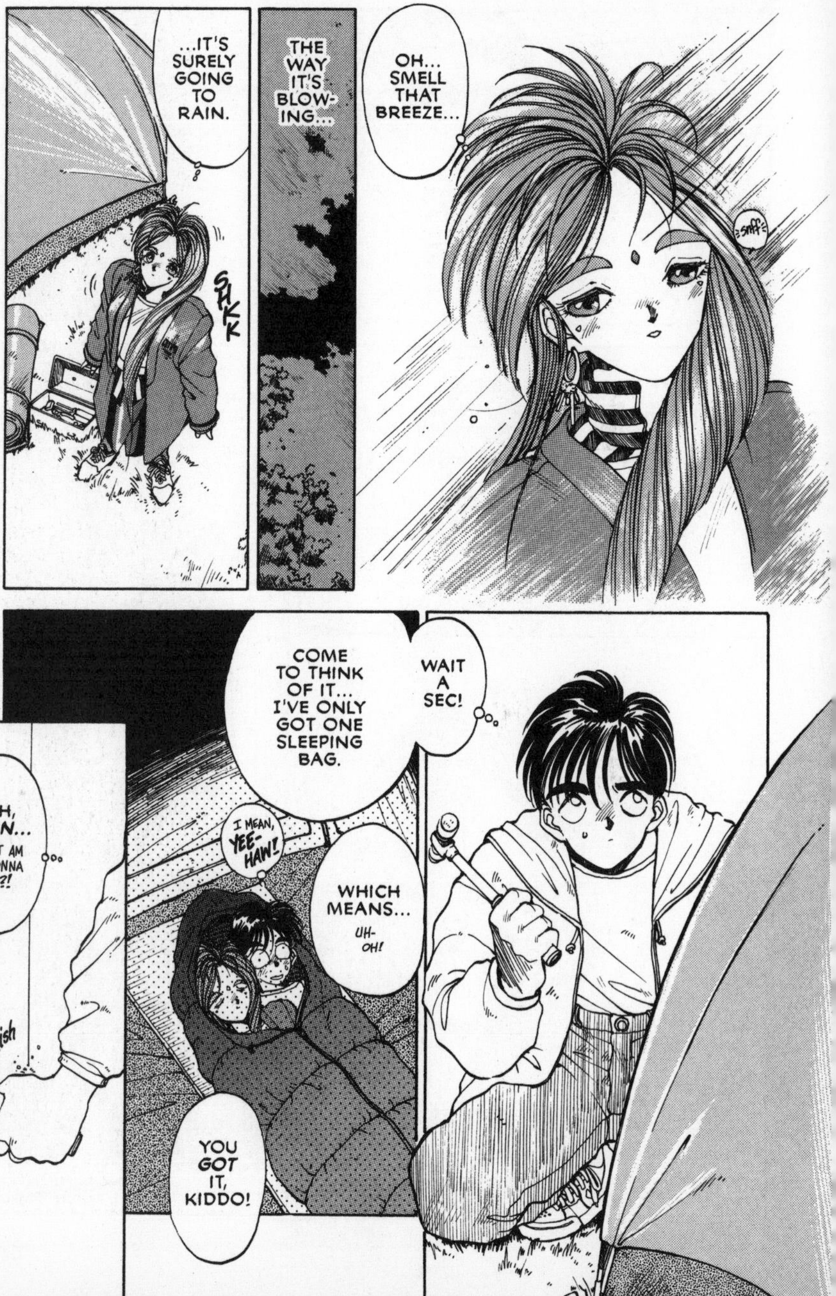
OH... SMELL THAT BREEZE...
snff
THE WAY IT'S BLOWING...
...IT'S SURELY GOING TO RAIN.
SHKK
WAIT A SEC!
COME TO THINK OF IT... I'VE ONLY GOT ONE SLEEPING BAG.
WHICH MEANS...
UH-OH!
I MEAN, YEE-HAW!
YOU GOT IT, KIDDO!
OH, MAN... WHAT AM I GONNA DO?!
plish

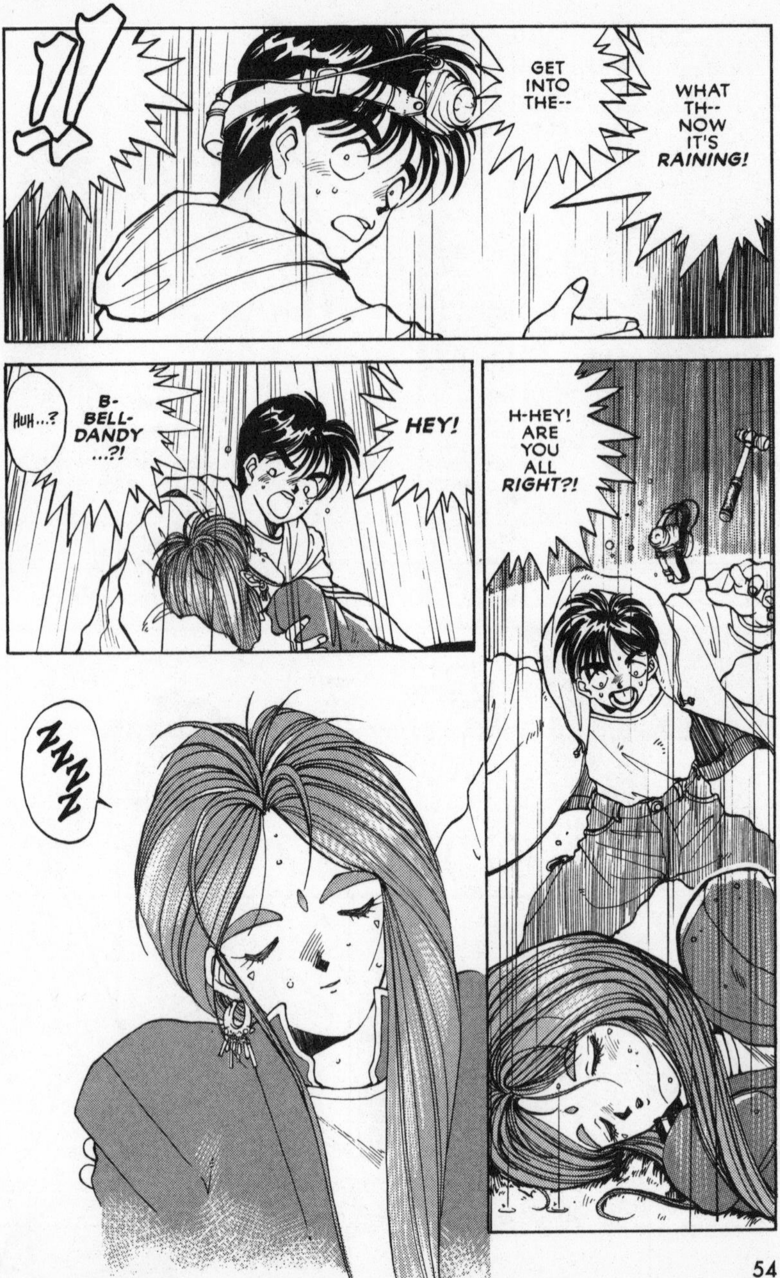

WHAT TH-- NOW IT'S RAINING!
GET INTO THE--
!!
H-HEY! ARE YOU ALL RIGHT?!
HEY!
B-BELL-DANDY ...?!
HUH...?
ZZZZ

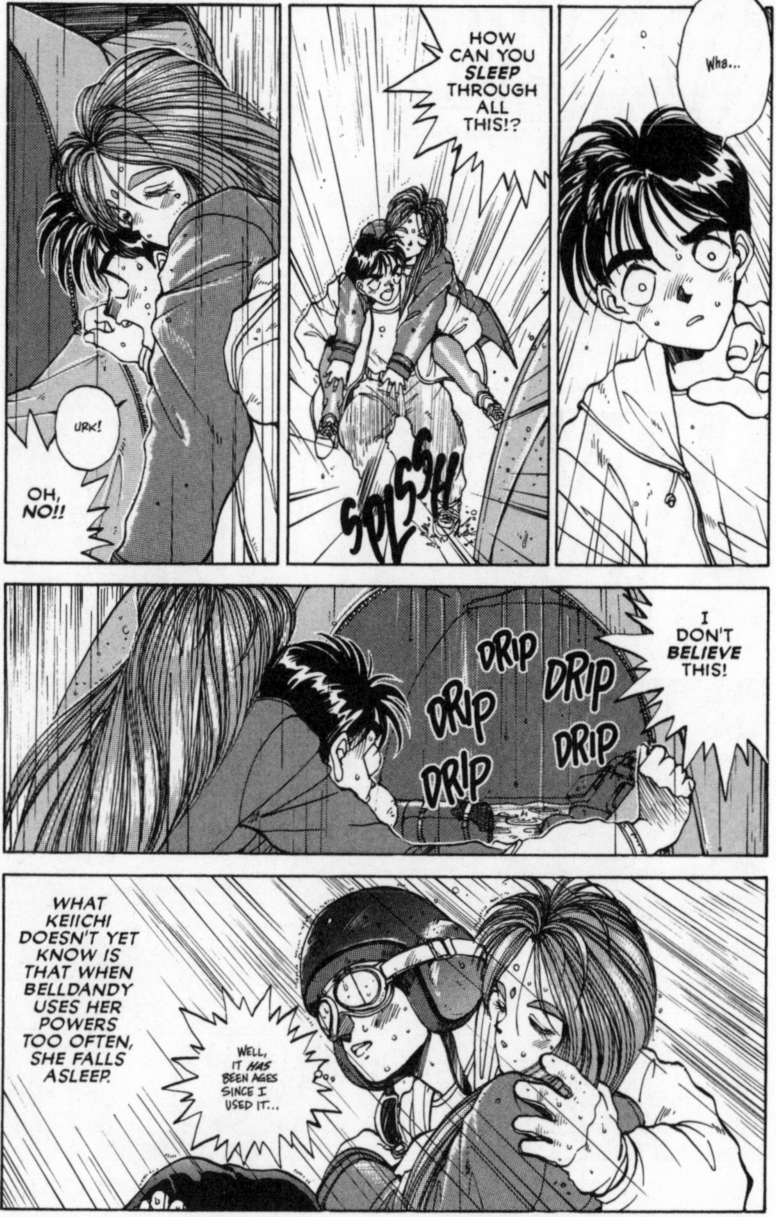
Wha...
HOW CAN YOU *SLEEP* THROUGH ALL THIS!?
SPLSSH
URK!
OH, *NO!!*
I DON'T *BELIEVE* THIS!
DRIP
DRIP
DRIP
DRIP
DRIP
WELL, IT *HAS* BEEN AGES SINCE I USED IT...
WHAT KEIICHI DOESN'T YET KNOW IS THAT WHEN BELLDANDY USES HER POWERS TOO OFTEN, SHE FALLS ASLEEP.

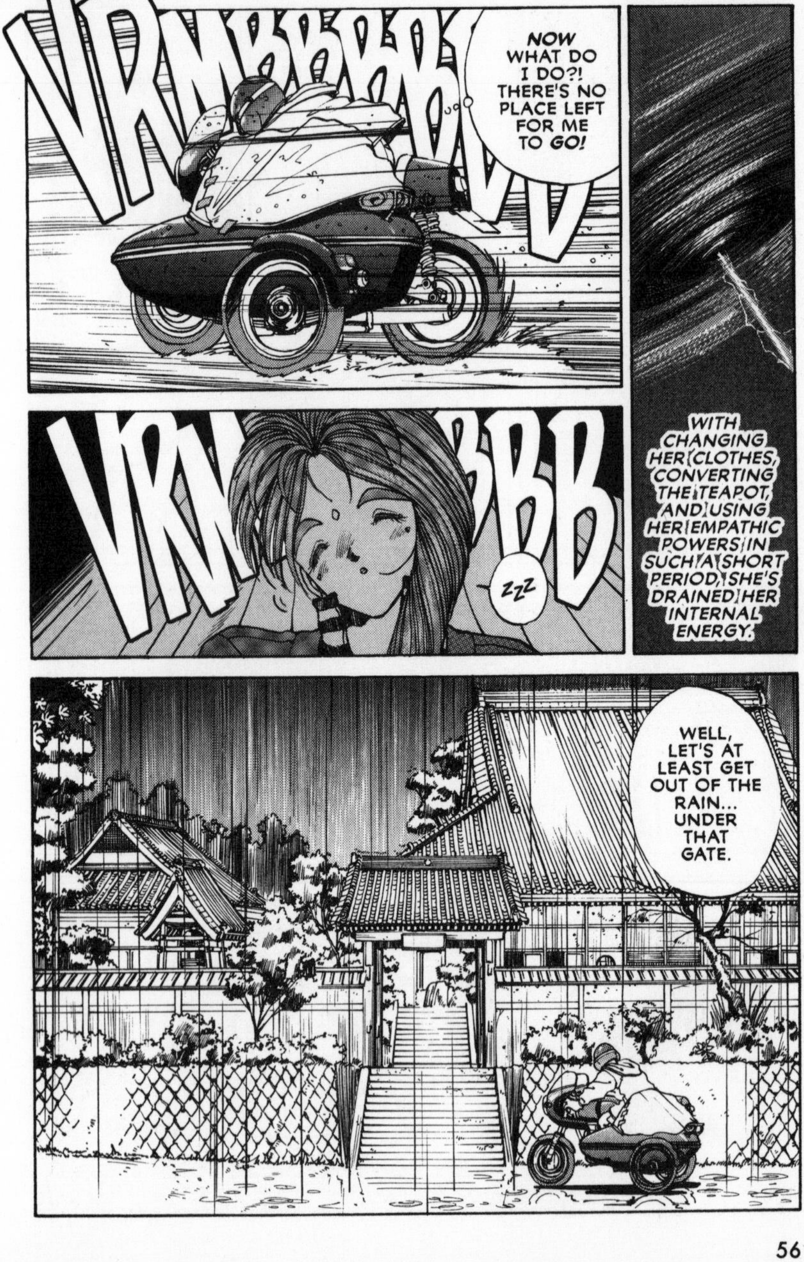
WITH CHANGING HER CLOTHES, CONVERTING THE TEAPOT, AND USING HER EMPATHIC POWERS IN SUCH A SHORT PERIOD, SHE'S DRAINED HER INTERNAL ENERGY.
NOW WHAT DO I DO?! THERE'S NO PLACE LEFT FOR ME TO GO!
ZZZ
WELL, LET'S AT LEAST GET OUT OF THE RAIN... UNDER THAT GATE.

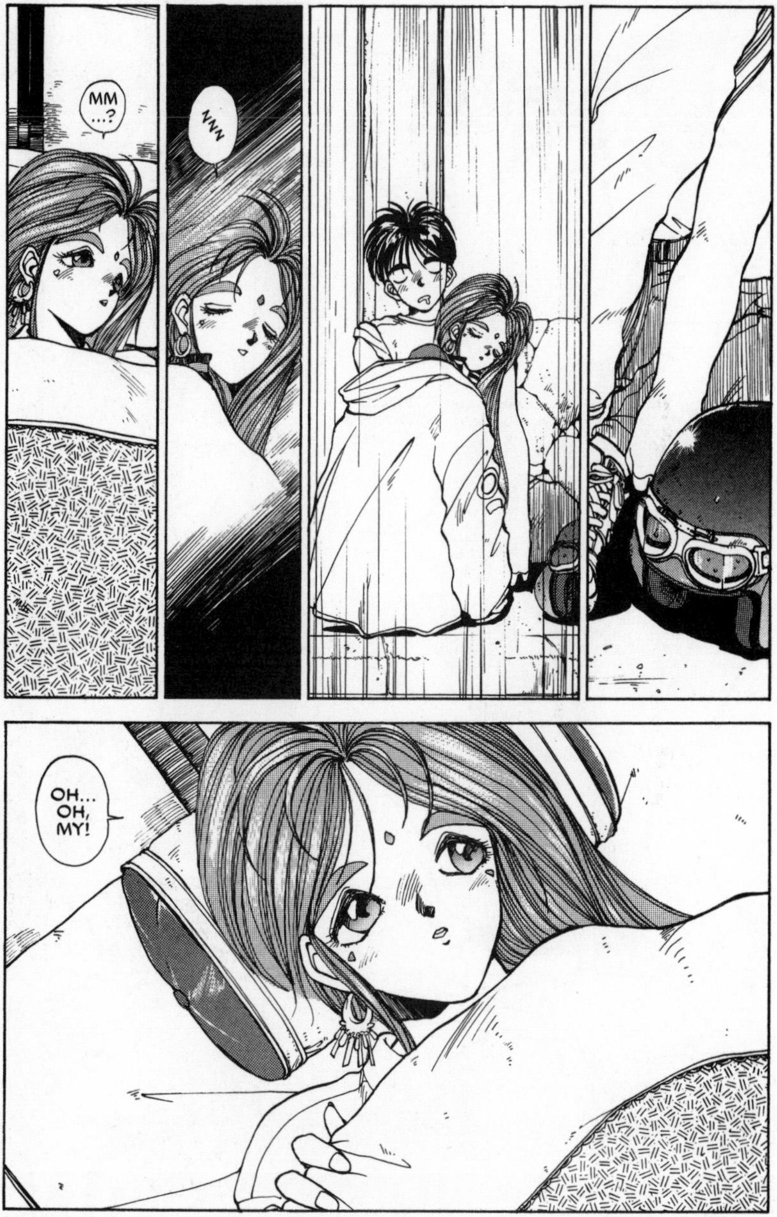
NNN
MM ...?
OH... OH, MY!

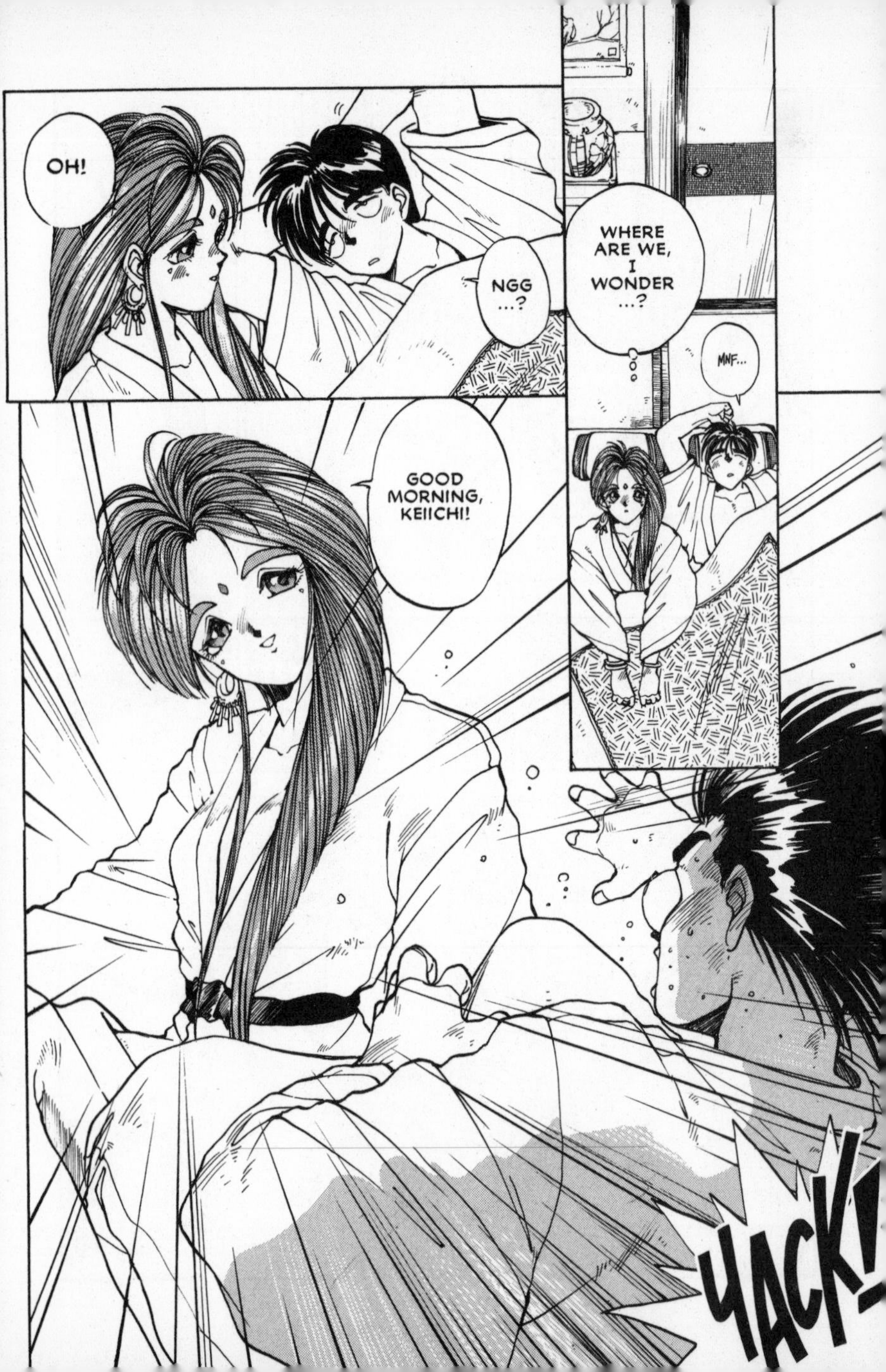
WHERE ARE WE, I WONDER ...?
MNF...
NGG ...?
OH!
GOOD MORNING, KEIICHI!
YACK!

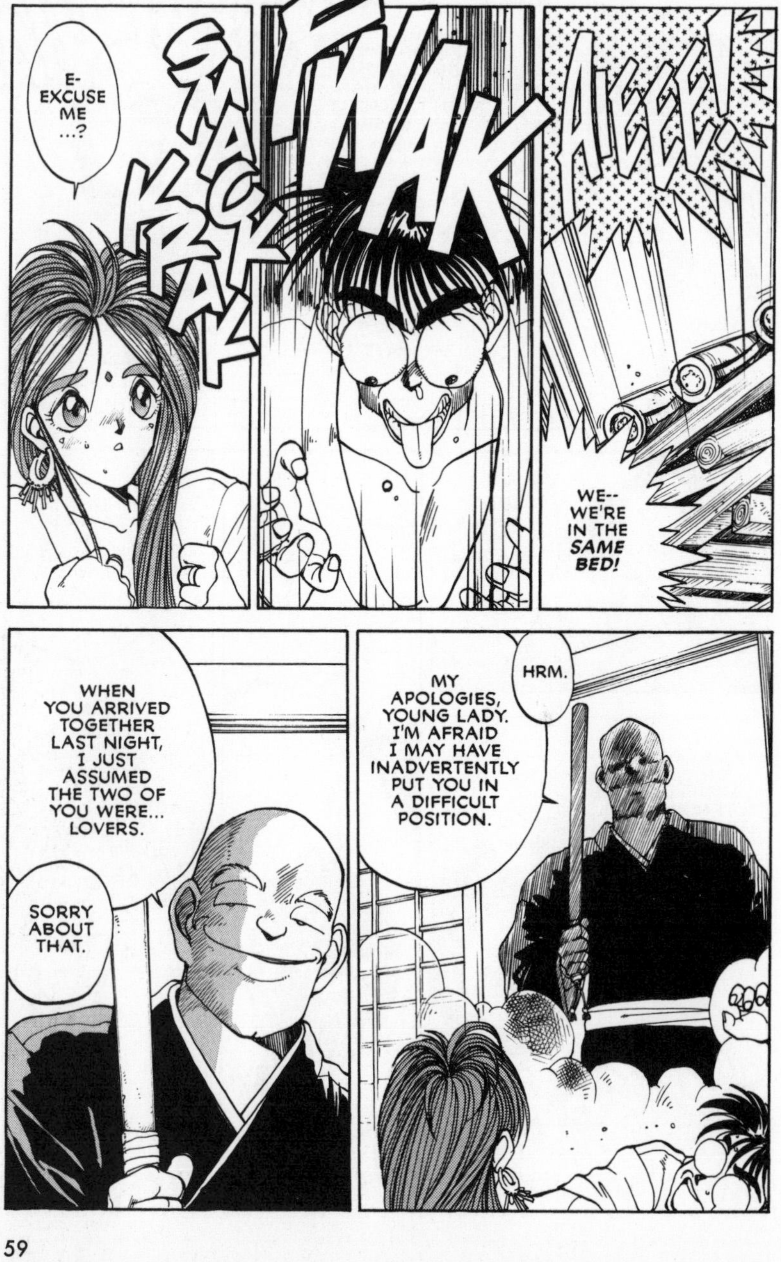
AEEE!
WE-- WE'RE IN THE *SAME BED!*
FWAK
SMACK KRAK KRAK
E-EXCUSE ME ...?
HRM.
MY APOLOGIES, YOUNG LADY. I'M AFRAID I MAY HAVE INADVERTENTLY PUT YOU IN A DIFFICULT POSITION.
WHEN YOU ARRIVED TOGETHER LAST NIGHT, I JUST ASSUMED THE TWO OF YOU WERE... LOVERS.
SORRY ABOUT THAT.

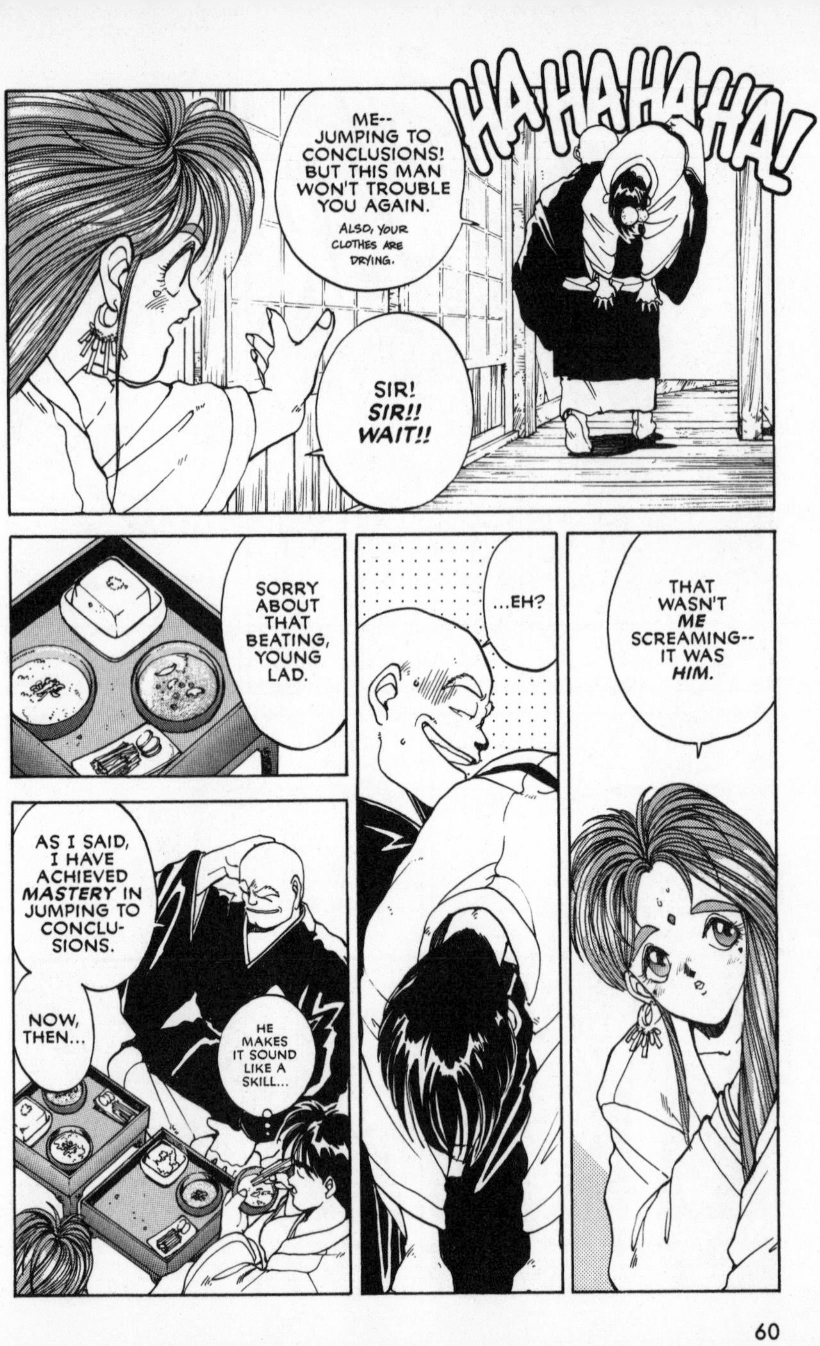
HAHAHAHA!
ME-- JUMPING TO CONCLUSIONS! BUT THIS MAN WON'T TROUBLE YOU AGAIN.
ALSO, YOUR CLOTHES ARE DRYING.
SIR! SIR!! WAIT!!
THAT WASN'T ME SCREAMING-- IT WAS HIM.
...EH?
SORRY ABOUT THAT BEATING, YOUNG LAD.
AS I SAID, I HAVE ACHIEVED MASTERY IN JUMPING TO CONCLUSIONS.
NOW, THEN...
HE MAKES IT SOUND LIKE A SKILL...

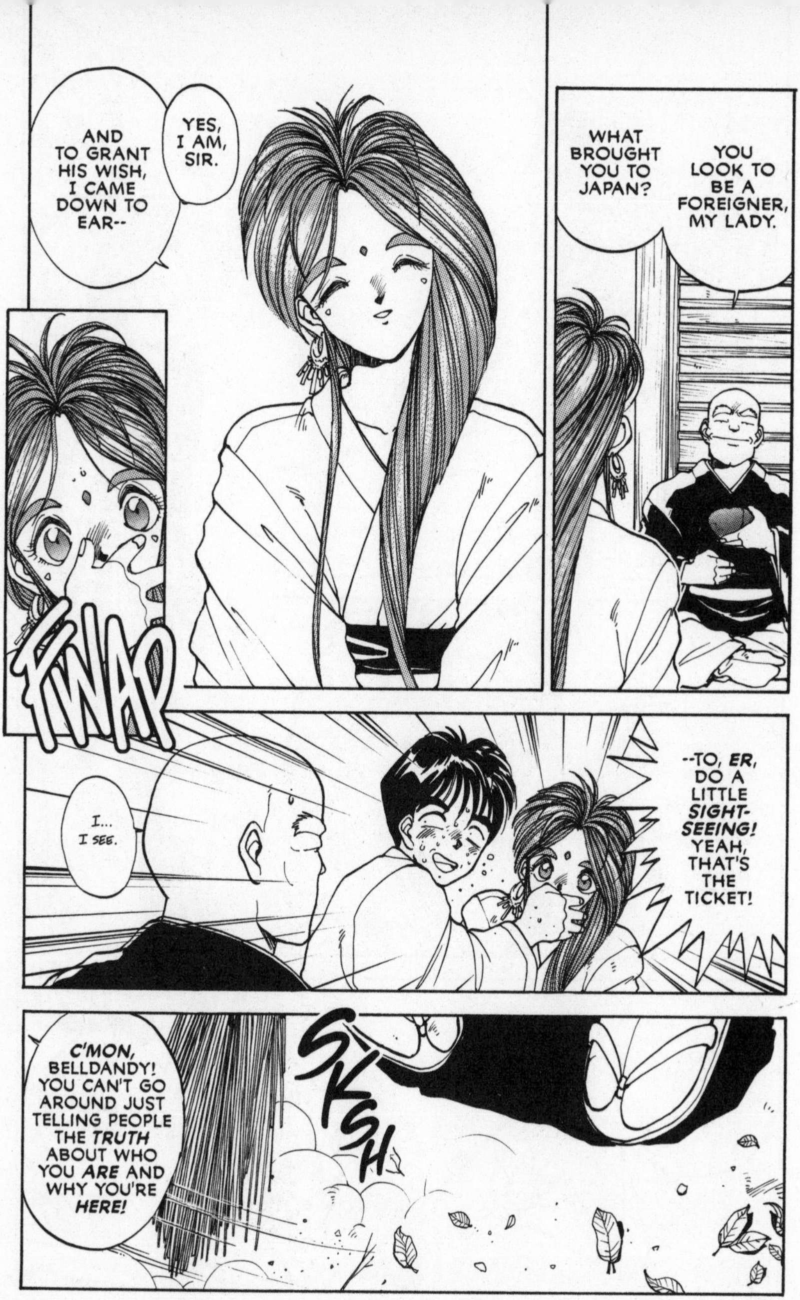

YOU LOOK TO BE A FOREIGNER, MY LADY.
WHAT BROUGHT YOU TO JAPAN?
YES, I AM, SIR.
AND TO GRANT HIS WISH, I CAME DOWN TO EAR--
FWAP
--TO, *ER*, DO A LITTLE *SIGHT-SEEING!* YEAH, THAT'S THE TICKET!
I... I SEE.
SKSH
C'MON, BELLDANDY! YOU CAN'T GO AROUND JUST TELLING PEOPLE THE *TRUTH* ABOUT WHO YOU *ARE* AND WHY YOU'RE *HERE!*

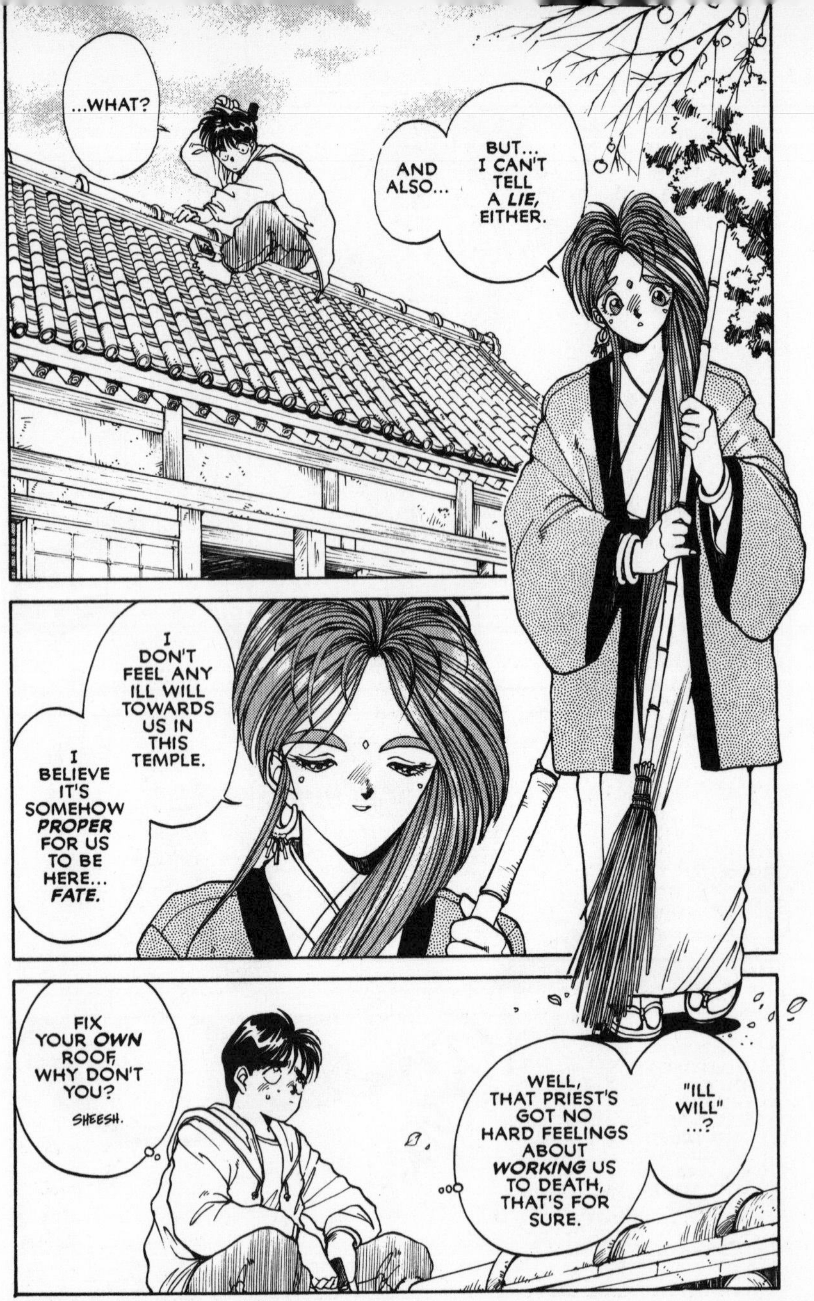
BUT... I CAN'T TELL A *LIE*, EITHER.
AND ALSO...
...WHAT?
I DON'T FEEL ANY ILL WILL TOWARDS US IN THIS TEMPLE.
I BELIEVE IT'S SOMEHOW *PROPER* FOR US TO BE HERE... *FATE*.
"ILL WILL" ...?
WELL, THAT PRIEST'S GOT NO HARD FEELINGS ABOUT *WORKING* US TO DEATH, THAT'S FOR SURE.
FIX YOUR *OWN* ROOF, WHY DON'T YOU?
SHEESH.

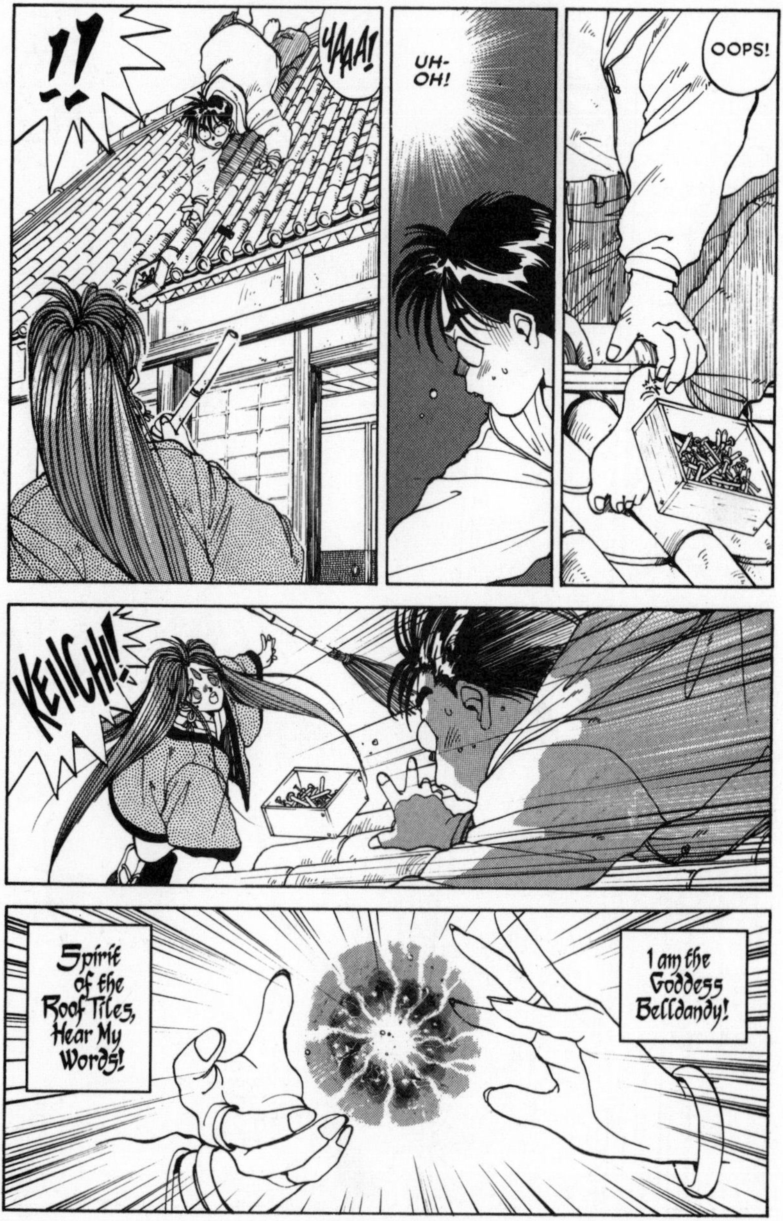
OOPS!
UH-OH!
YAAAA!
!!
KEIICHI!
I am the Goddess Belldandy!
Spirit of the Roof Tiles, Hear My Words!

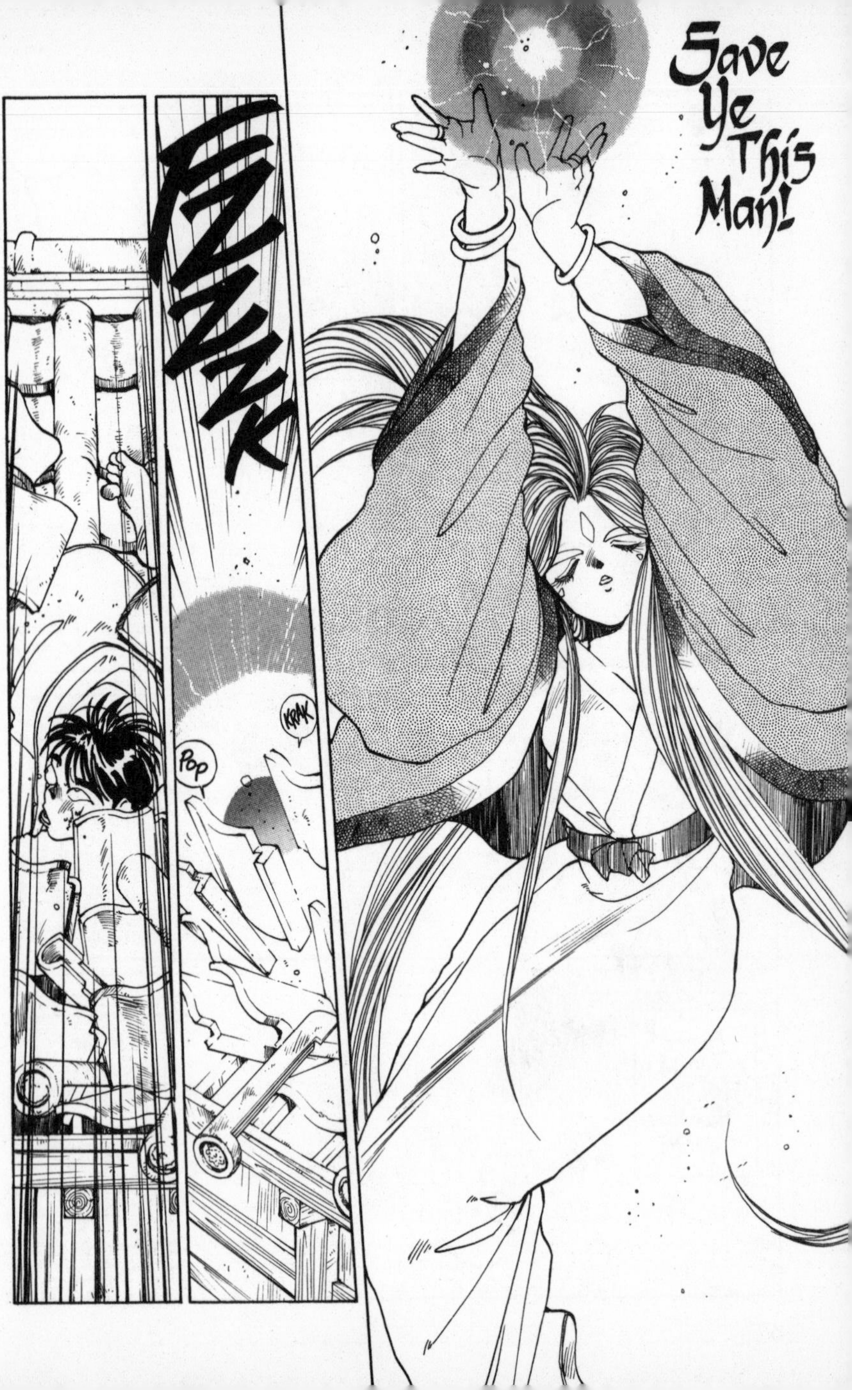
Save Ye This Man!
FZNNK
KRAK
POP

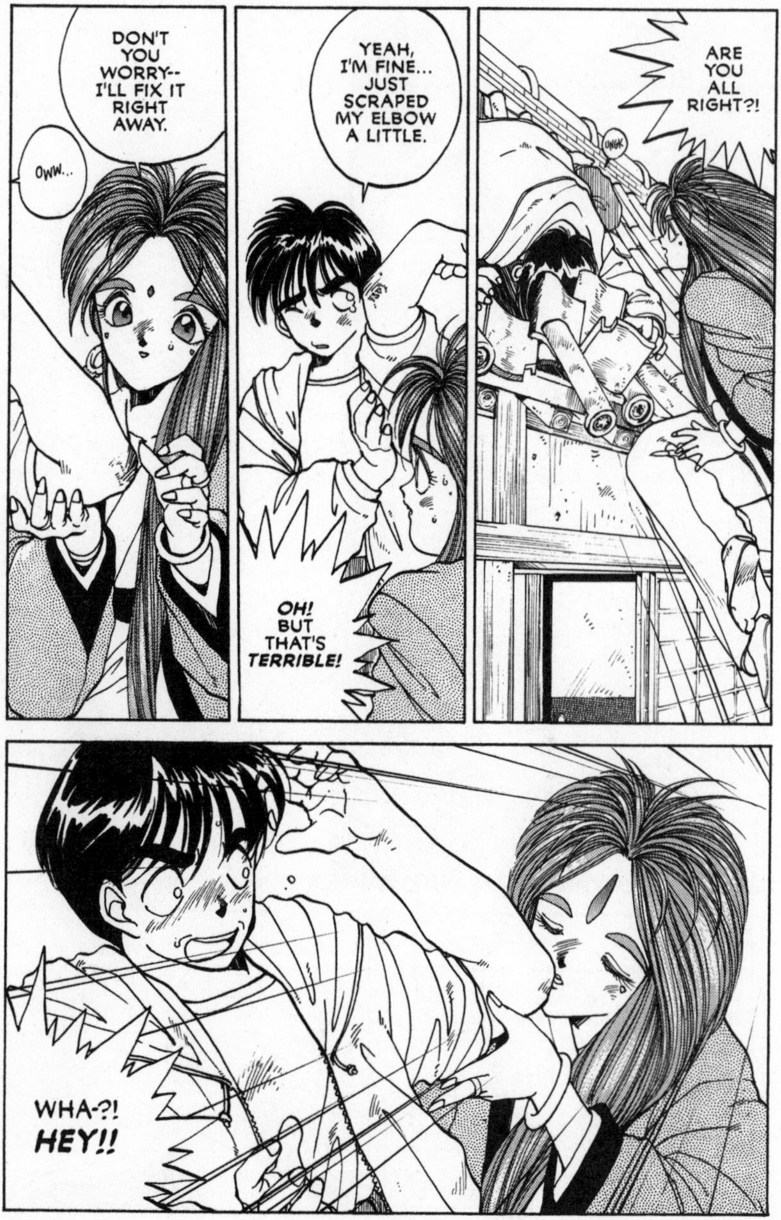
ARE YOU ALL RIGHT?!
UNGK
YEAH, I'M FINE... JUST SCRAPED MY ELBOW A LITTLE.
OH! BUT THAT'S *TERRIBLE!*
DON'T YOU WORRY-- I'LL FIX IT RIGHT AWAY.
OWW...
WHA-?! **HEY!!**

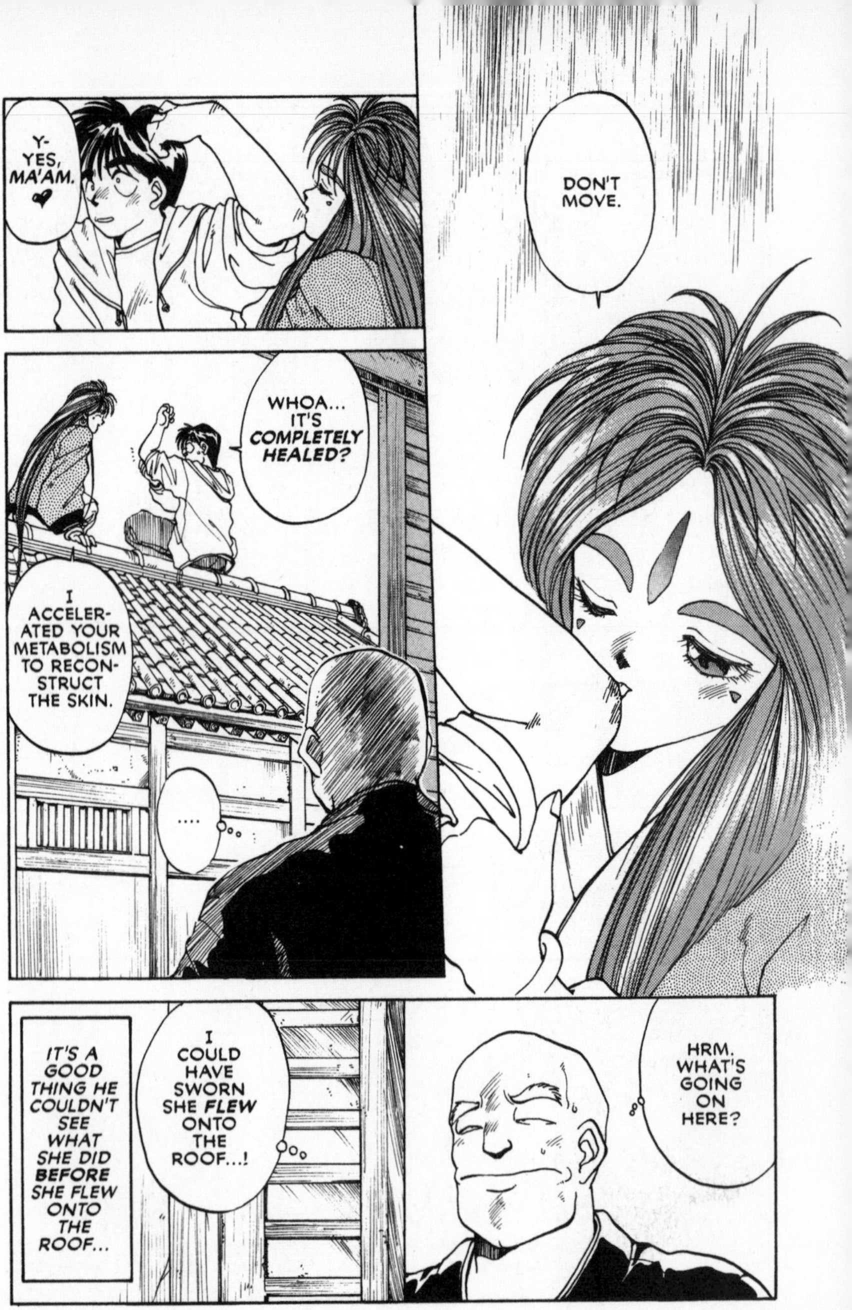
DON'T MOVE.
Y-YES, MA'AM. ♥
WHOA... IT'S *COMPLETELY HEALED?*
I ACCELERATED YOUR METABOLISM TO RECONSTRUCT THE SKIN.
....
HRM. WHAT'S GOING ON HERE?
I COULD HAVE SWORN SHE *FLEW* ONTO THE ROOF...!
IT'S A GOOD THING HE COULDN'T SEE WHAT SHE DID **BEFORE** *SHE FLEW ONTO THE ROOF...*

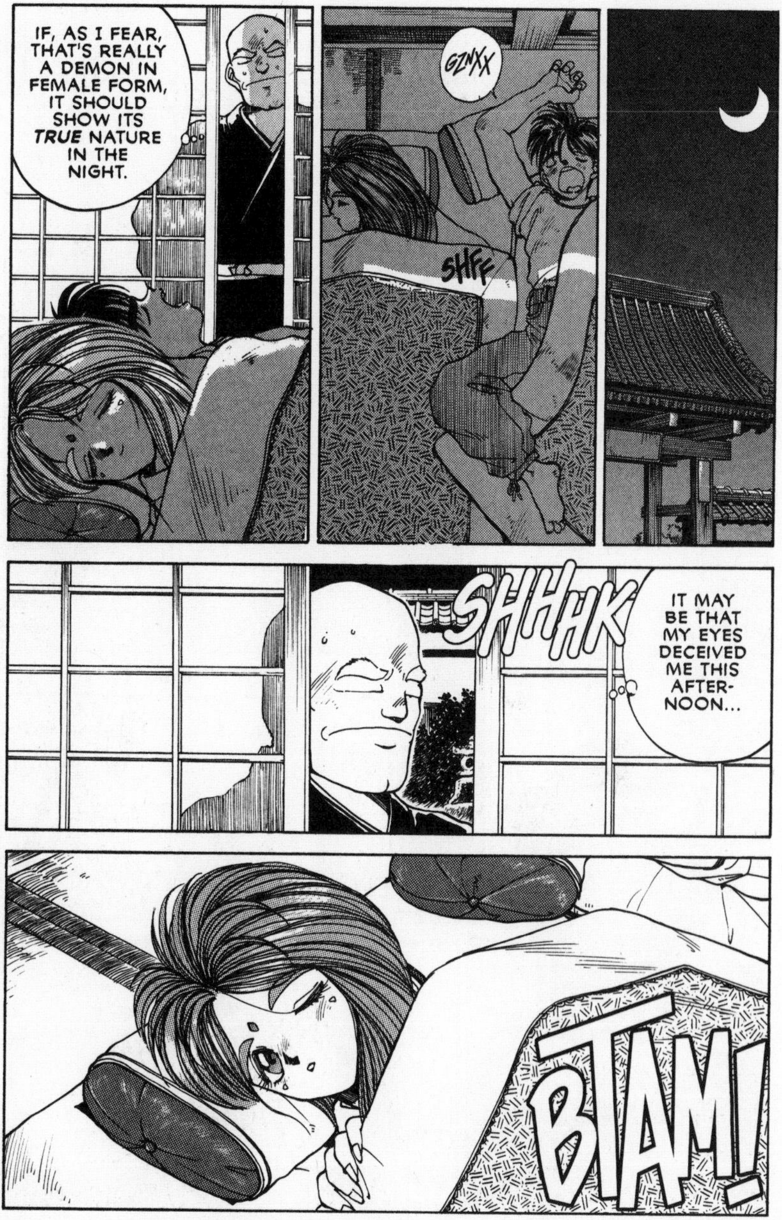
GZNXX
SHFF
IF, AS I FEAR, THAT'S REALLY A DEMON IN FEMALE FORM, IT SHOULD SHOW ITS *TRUE* NATURE IN THE NIGHT.
IT MAY BE THAT MY EYES DECEIVED ME THIS AFTER-NOON...
SHHHK
BTAM!

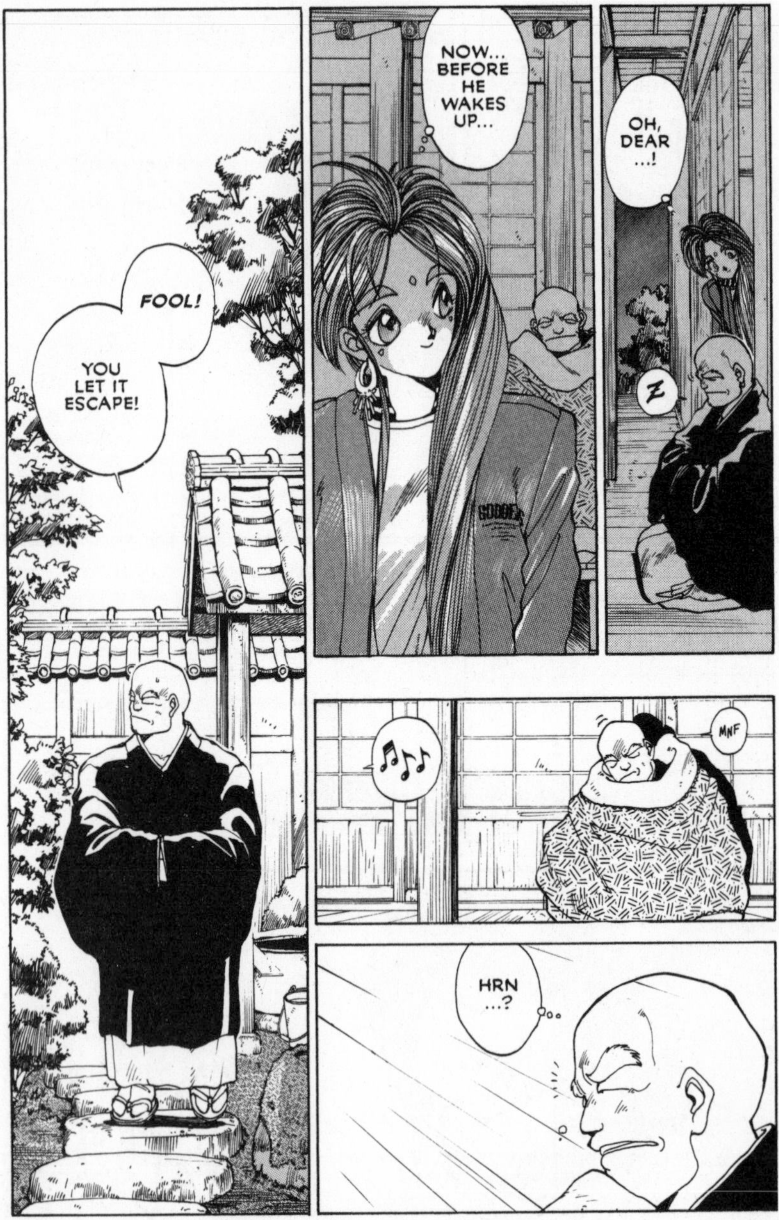
OH, DEAR ...!
Z
NOW... BEFORE HE WAKES UP...
MNF
HRN ...?
FOOL!
YOU LET IT ESCAPE!

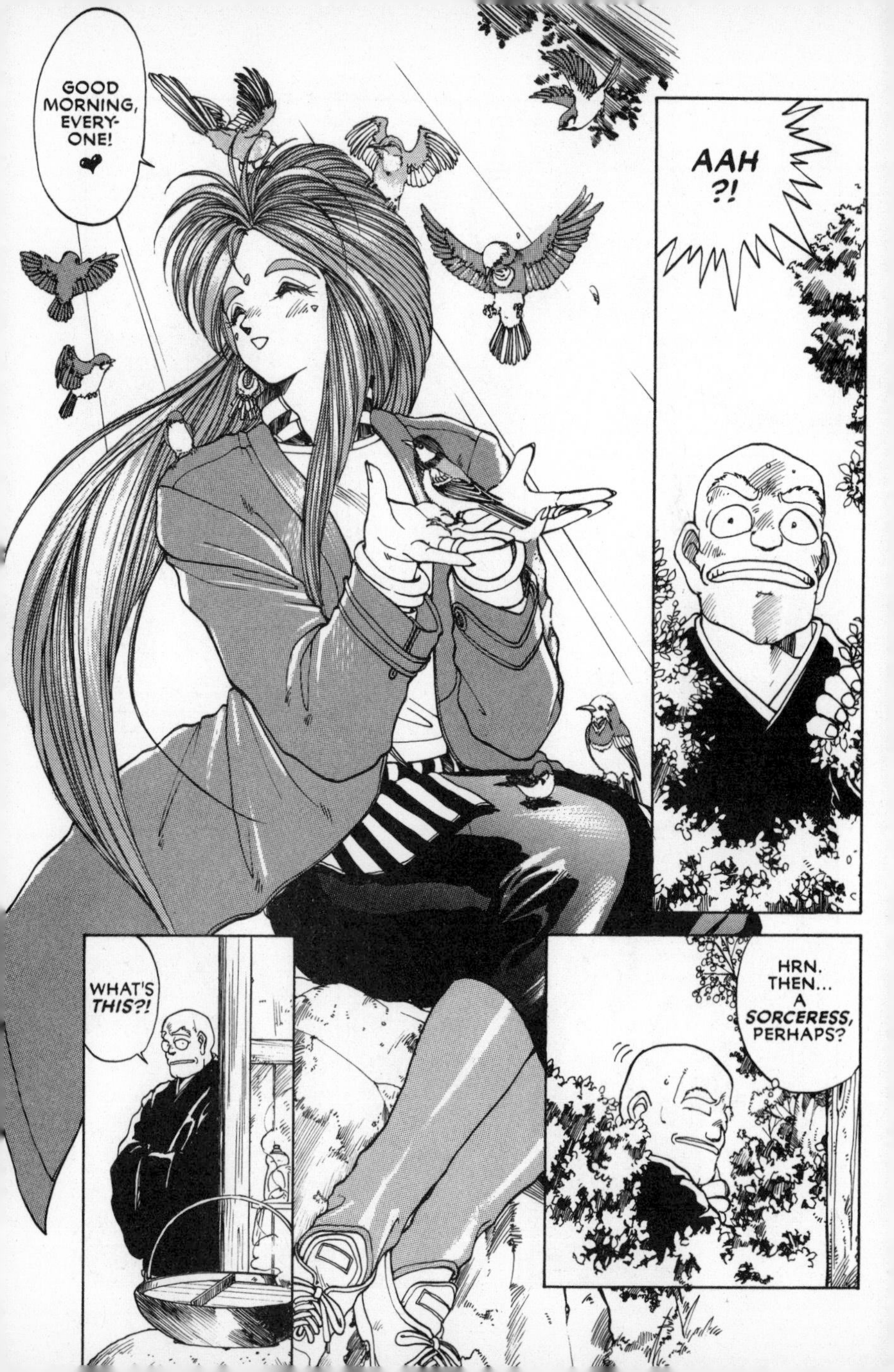
AAH ?!
GOOD MORNING, EVERY-ONE! ♥
HRN. THEN... A *SORCERESS*, PERHAPS?
WHAT'S *THIS?!*

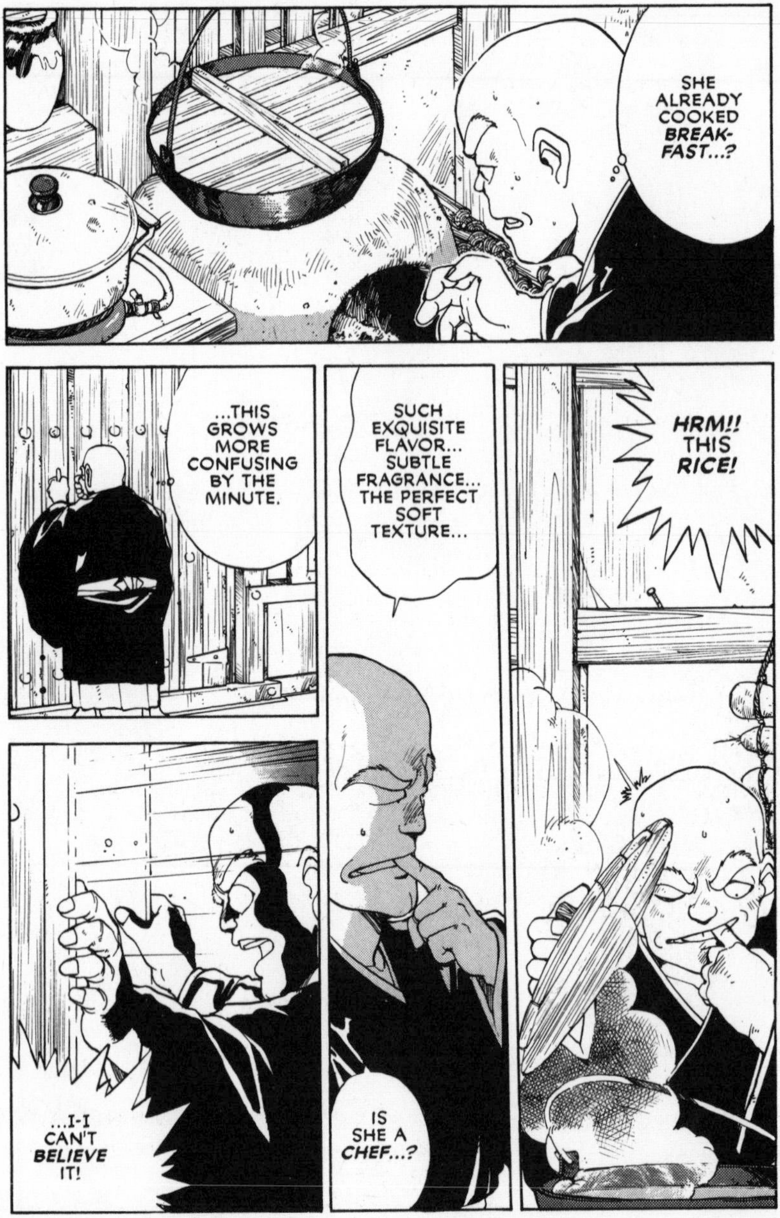
SHE ALREADY COOKED BREAK-FAST...?
HRM!! THIS RICE!
SUCH EXQUISITE FLAVOR... SUBTLE FRAGRANCE... THE PERFECT SOFT TEXTURE...
IS SHE A CHEF...?
...THIS GROWS MORE CONFUSING BY THE MINUTE.
...I-I CAN'T BELIEVE IT!

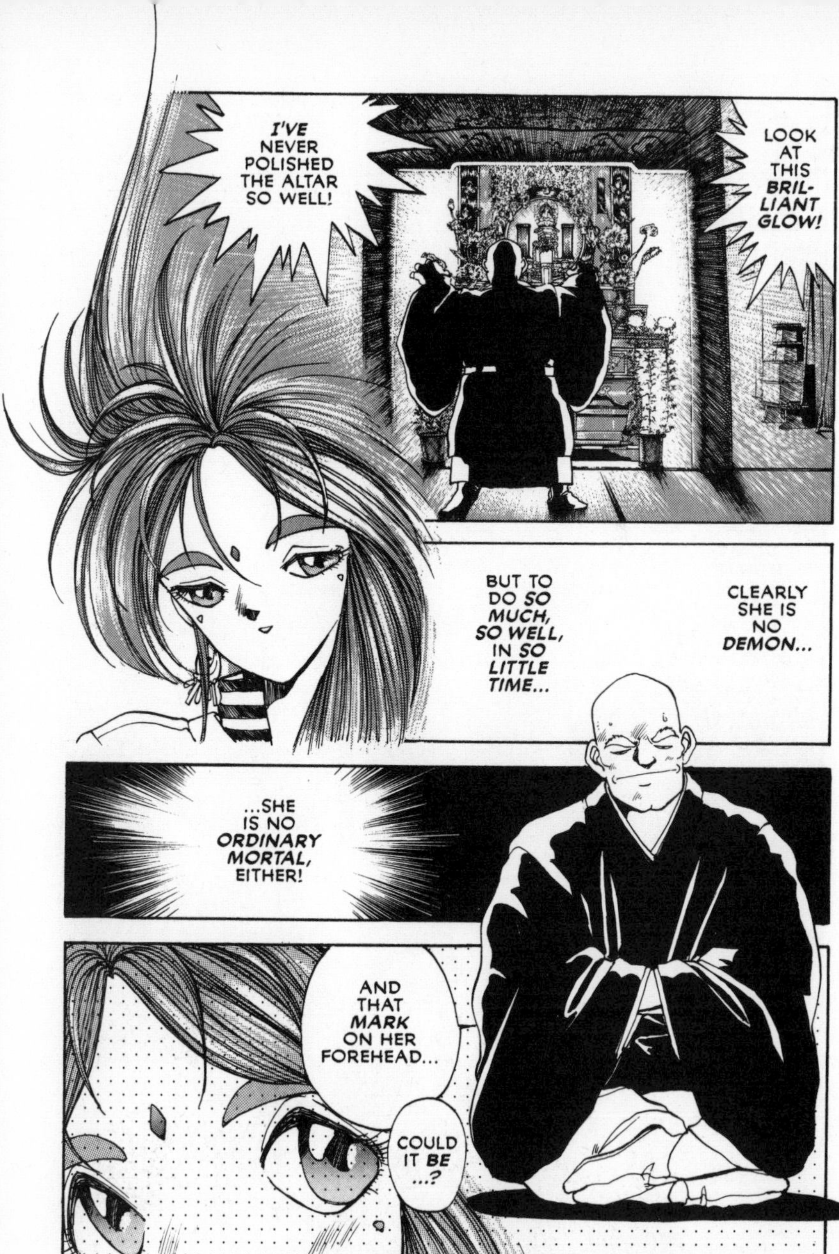
LOOK AT THIS BRILLIANT GLOW!
I'VE NEVER POLISHED THE ALTAR SO WELL!
CLEARLY SHE IS NO DEMON...
BUT TO DO SO MUCH, SO WELL, IN SO LITTLE TIME...
...SHE IS NO ORDINARY MORTAL, EITHER!
AND THAT MARK ON HER FOREHEAD...
COULD IT BE ...?

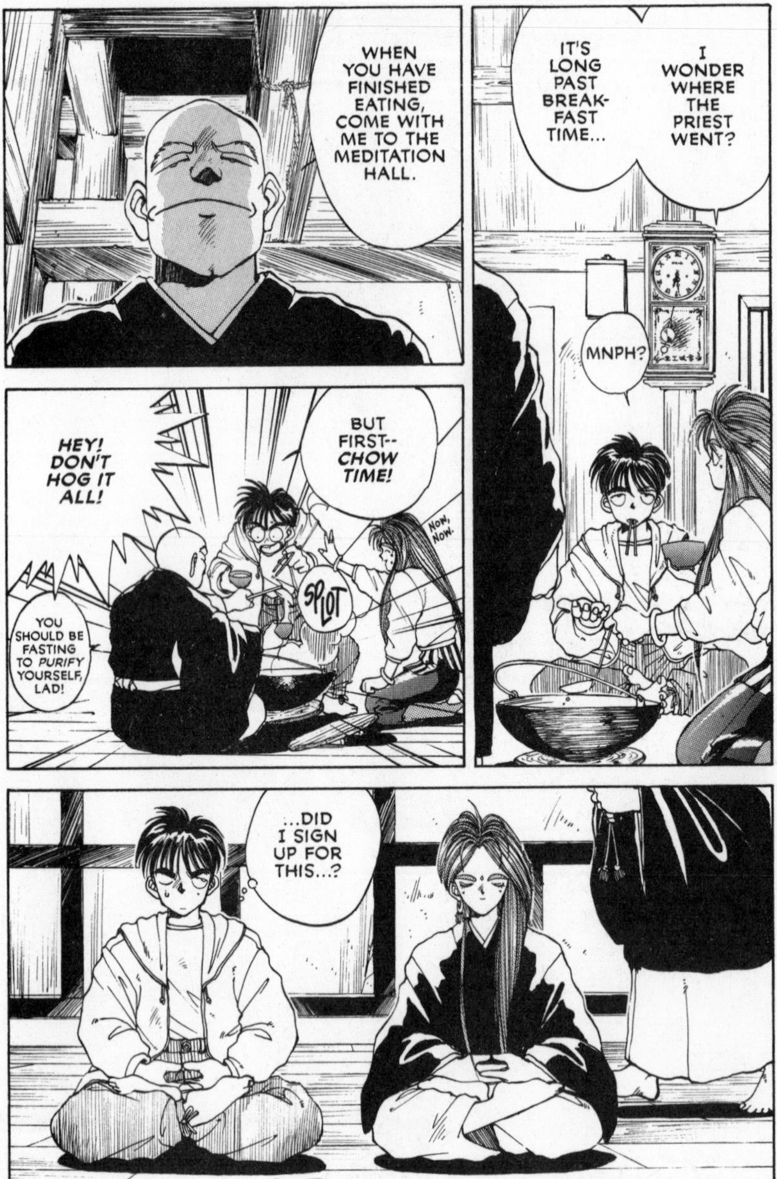

IT'S LONG PAST BREAKFAST TIME... I WONDER WHERE THE PRIEST WENT?
MNPH?
WHEN YOU HAVE FINISHED EATING, COME WITH ME TO THE MEDITATION HALL.
BUT FIRST-- *CHOW TIME!*
NOW, NOW.
HEY! DON'T HOG IT ALL!
SPLOT
YOU SHOULD BE FASTING TO *PURIFY* YOURSELF, LAD!
...DID I SIGN UP FOR THIS...?

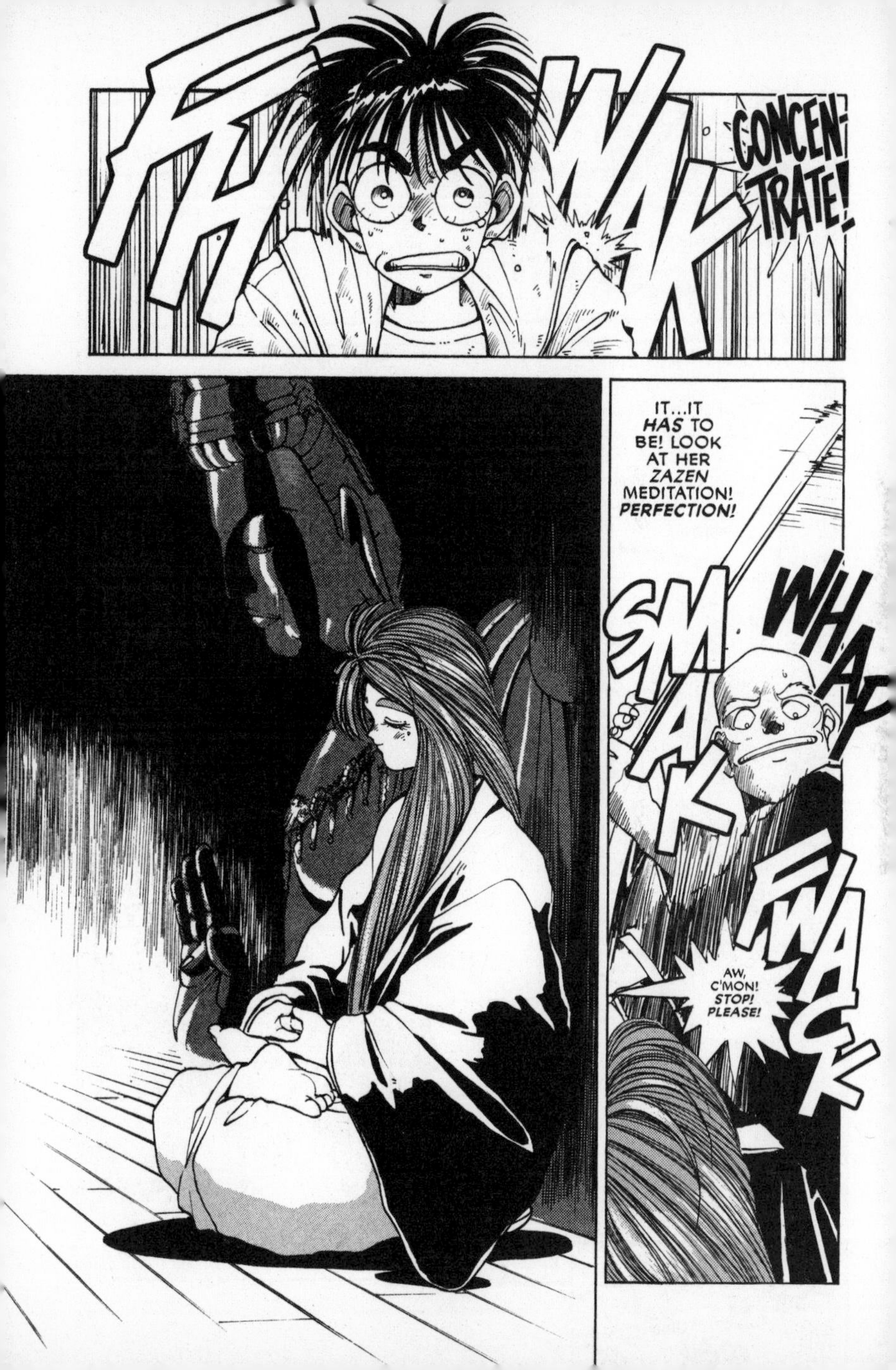
FWAK
CONCEN-TRATE!
IT...IT *HAS* TO BE! LOOK AT HER *ZAZEN* MEDITATION! ***PERFECTION!***
SMAK
WHAP
FWACK
AW, C'MON! ***STOP! PLEASE!***

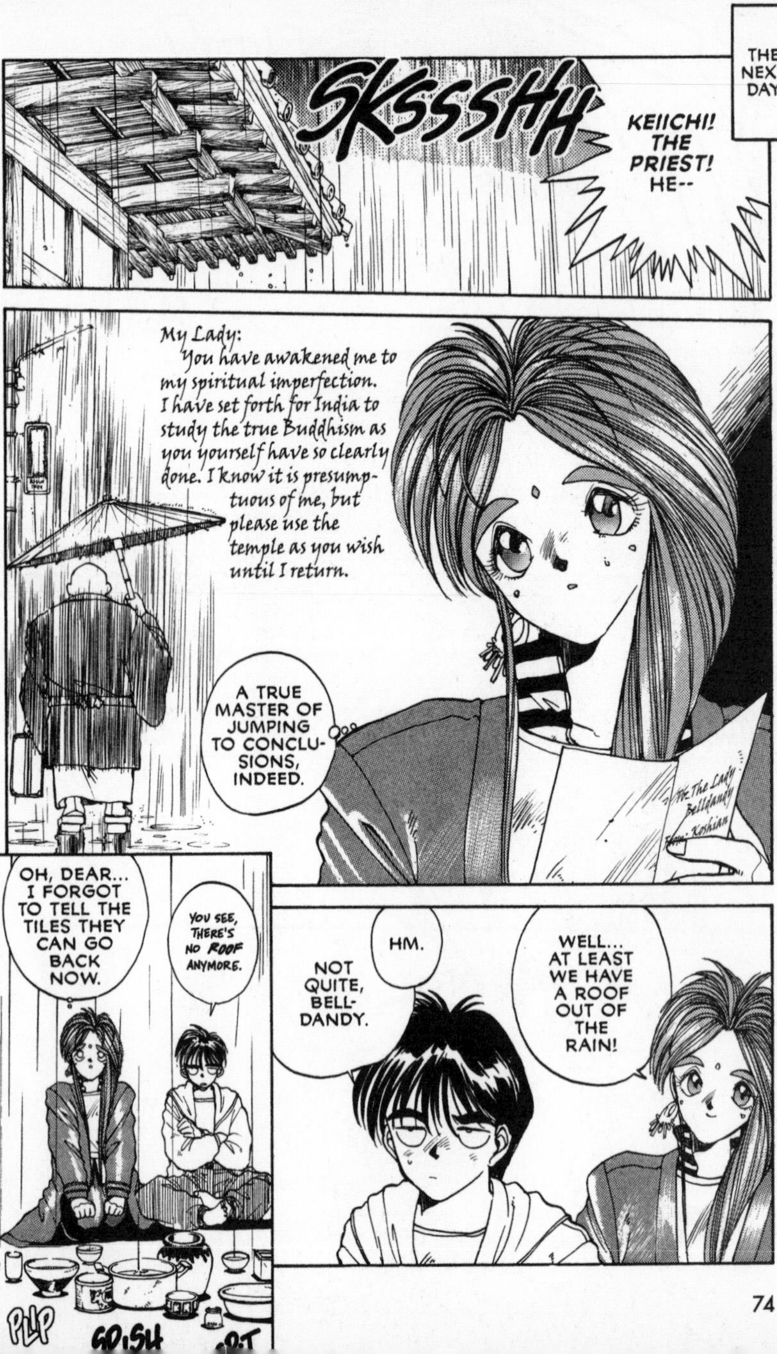
THE NEXT DAY
SKSSSHH
KEIICHI! THE PRIEST! HE--
My Lady:
You have awakened me to my spiritual imperfection. I have set forth for India to study the true Buddhism as you yourself have so clearly done. I know it is presumptuous of me, but please use the temple as you wish until I return.
A TRUE MASTER OF JUMPING TO CONCLUSIONS, INDEED.
To: The Lady Belldandy
From: Koshian
WELL... AT LEAST WE HAVE A ROOF OUT OF THE RAIN!
HM.
NOT QUITE, BELL-DANDY.
OH, DEAR... I FORGOT TO TELL THE TILES THEY CAN GO BACK NOW.
YOU SEE, THERE'S NO ROOF ANYMORE.
PLIP

CHAPTER 4

College Exchange Goddess

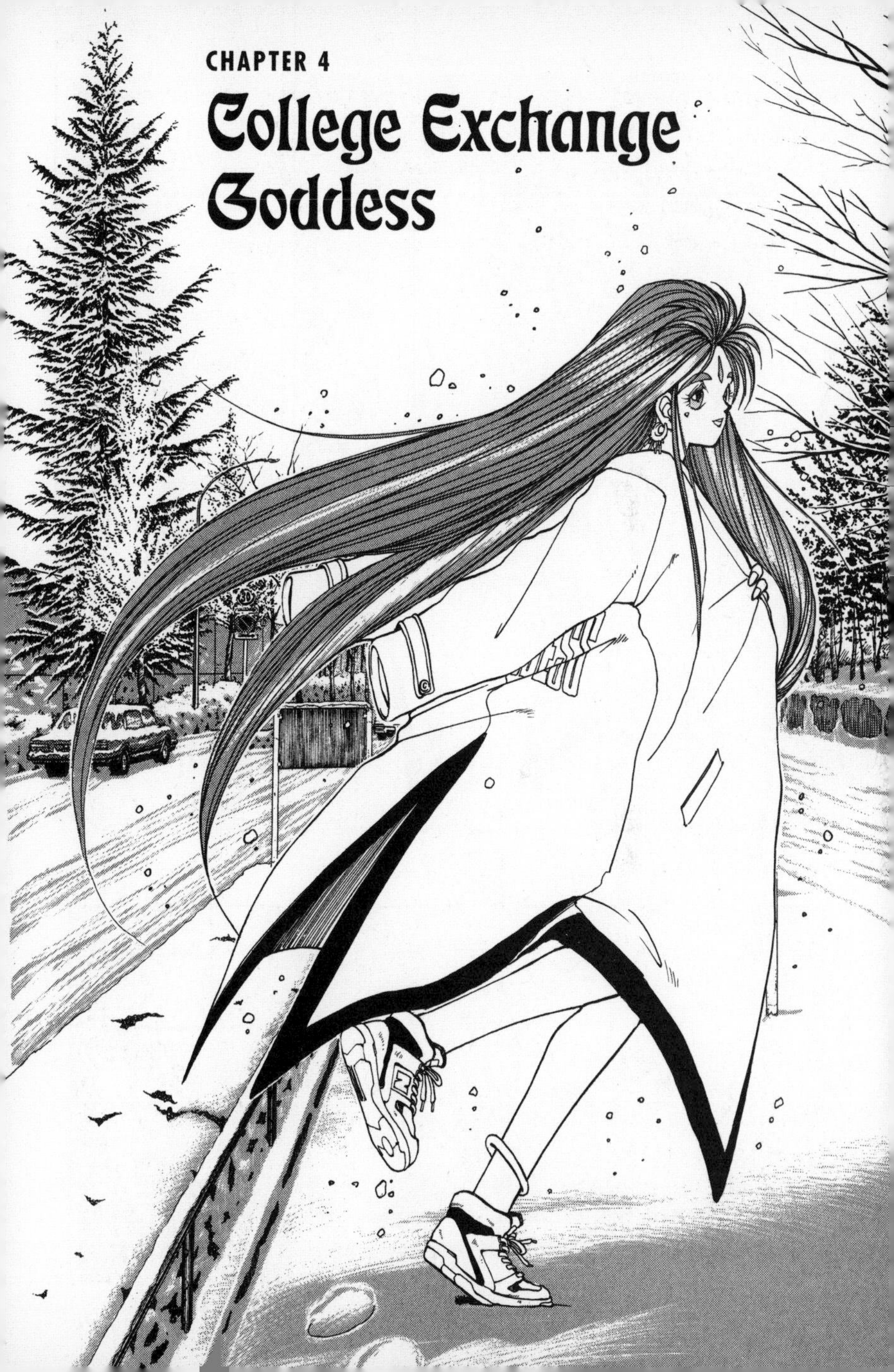

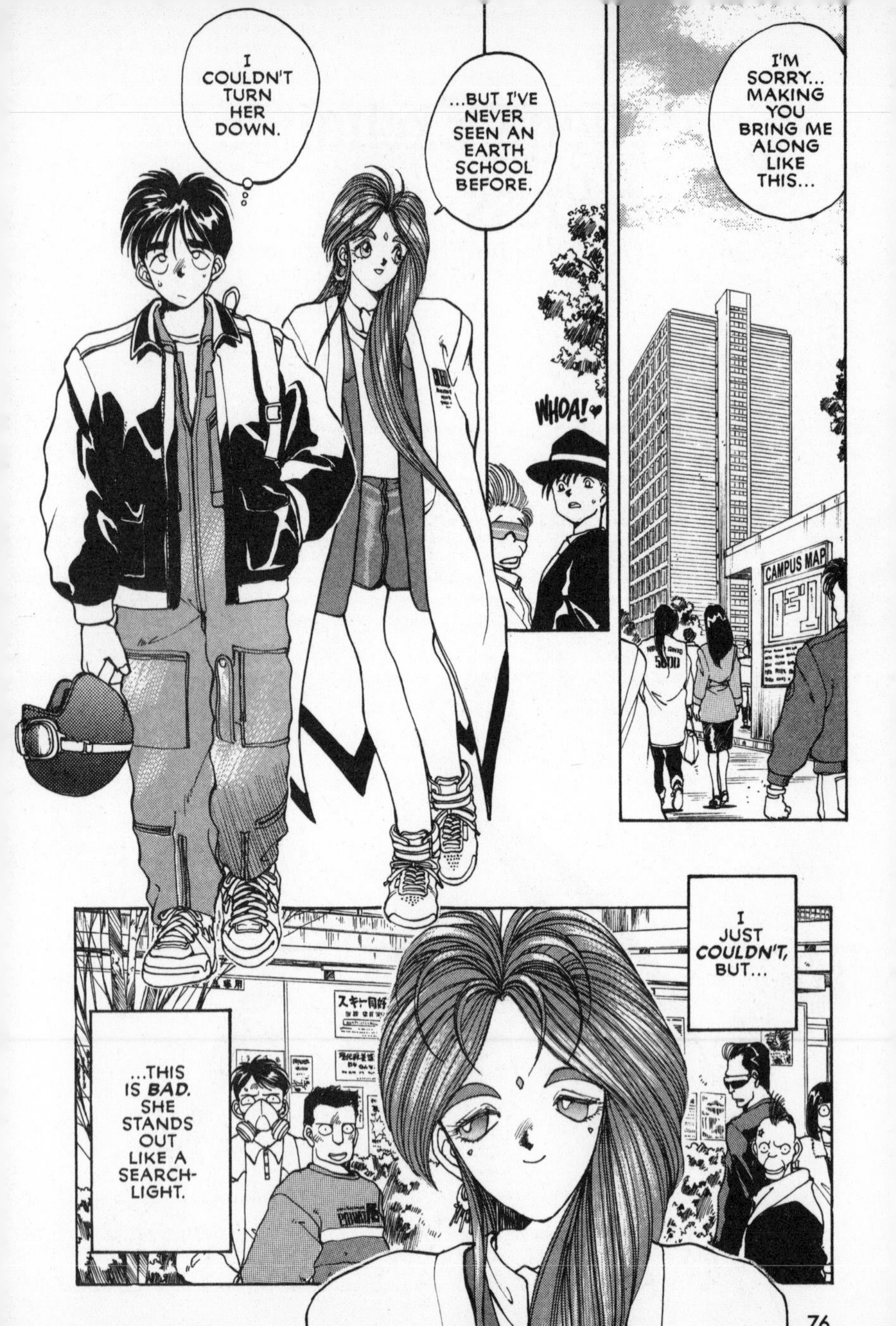
I'M SORRY... MAKING YOU BRING ME ALONG LIKE THIS...
CAMPUS MAP
WHOA!♥
...BUT I'VE NEVER SEEN AN EARTH SCHOOL BEFORE.
I COULDN'T TURN HER DOWN.
I JUST *COULDN'T,* BUT...
...THIS IS *BAD.* SHE STANDS OUT LIKE A SEARCH-LIGHT.

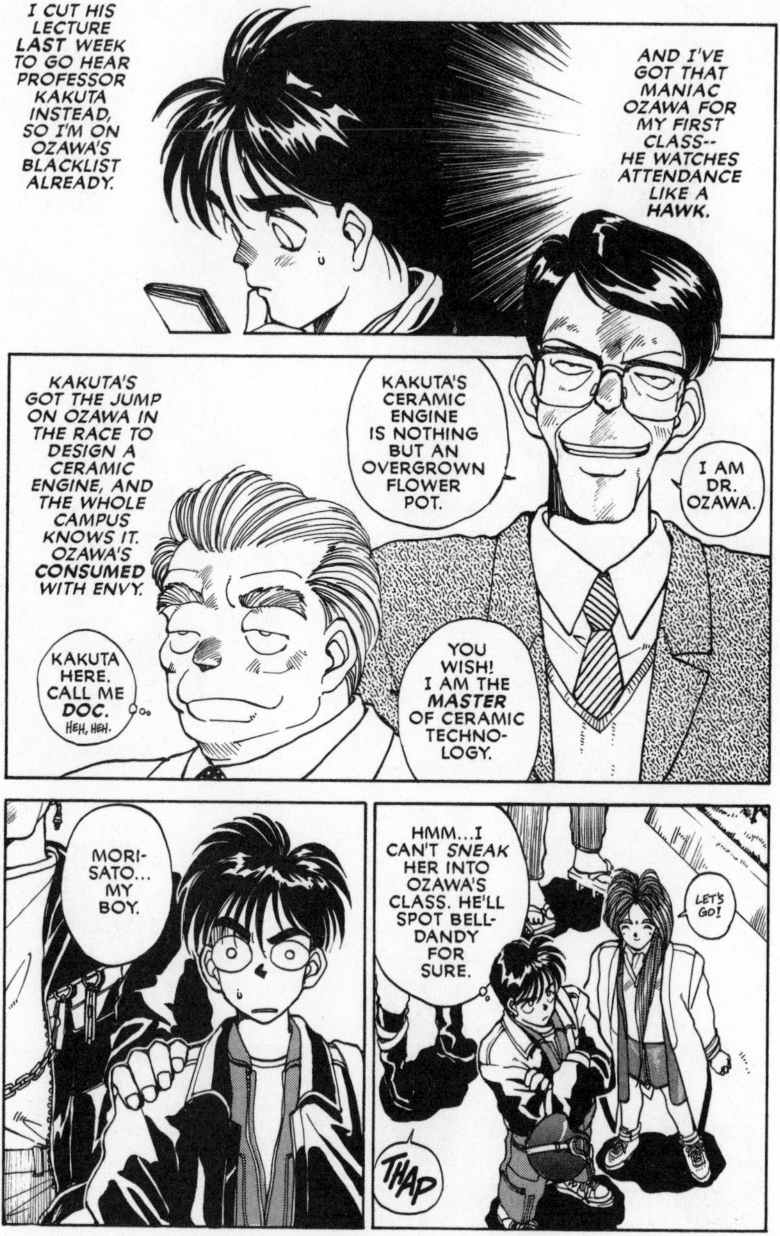
AND I'VE GOT THAT MANIAC OZAWA FOR MY FIRST CLASS-- HE WATCHES ATTENDANCE LIKE A **HAWK.**
I CUT HIS LECTURE **LAST** WEEK TO GO HEAR PROFESSOR KAKUTA INSTEAD, SO I'M ON OZAWA'S BLACKLIST ALREADY.
I AM DR. OZAWA.
KAKUTA'S CERAMIC ENGINE IS NOTHING BUT AN OVERGROWN FLOWER POT.
KAKUTA'S GOT THE JUMP ON OZAWA IN THE RACE TO DESIGN A CERAMIC ENGINE, AND THE WHOLE CAMPUS KNOWS IT. OZAWA'S **CONSUMED** WITH ENVY.
YOU WISH! I AM THE ***MASTER*** OF CERAMIC TECHNOLOGY.
KAKUTA HERE. CALL ME **DOC.**
HEH, HEH.
LET'S GO!
HMM...I CAN'T *SNEAK* HER INTO OZAWA'S CLASS. HE'LL SPOT BELLDANDY FOR SURE.
THAP
MORI-SATO... MY BOY.

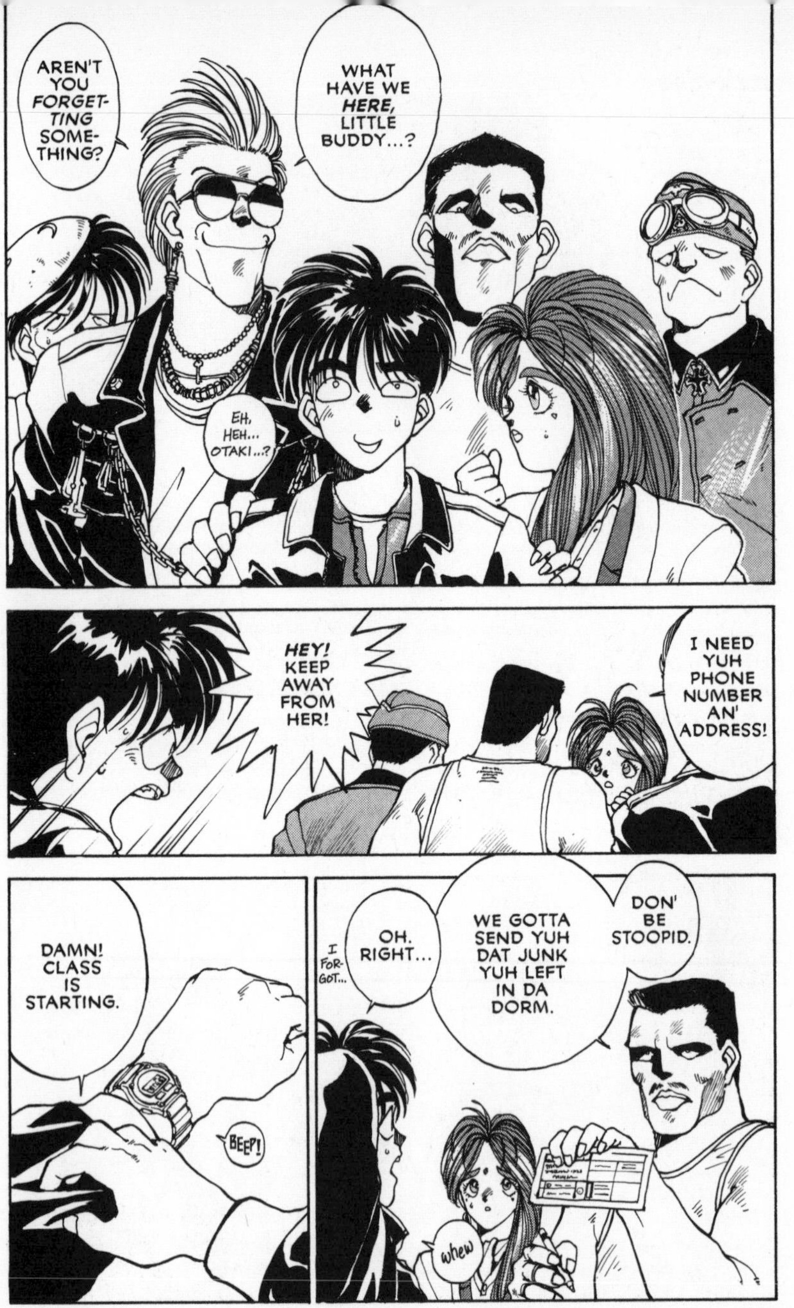
WHAT HAVE WE *HERE,* LITTLE BUDDY...?
AREN'T YOU *FORGETTING* SOMETHING?
EH, HEH... OTAKI...?
I NEED YUH PHONE NUMBER AN' ADDRESS!
HEY! KEEP AWAY FROM HER!
DON' BE STOOPID.
WE GOTTA SEND YUH DAT JUNK YUH LEFT IN DA DORM.
OH. RIGHT...
I FORGOT...
whew
DAMN! CLASS IS STARTING.
BEEP!

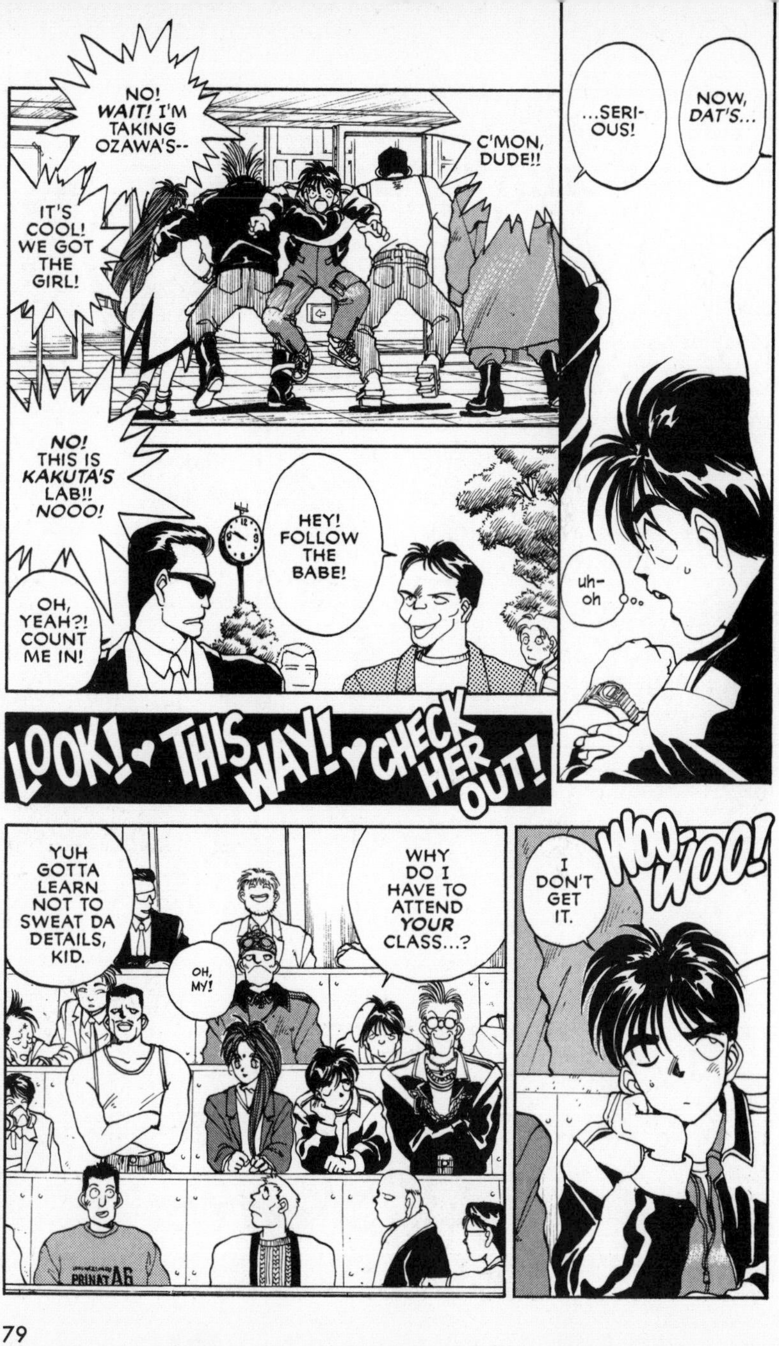
NOW, DAT'S...
...SERI-OUS!
uh-oh
C'MON, DUDE!!
NO! WAIT! I'M TAKING OZAWA'S--
IT'S COOL! WE GOT THE GIRL!
NO! THIS IS KAKUTA'S LAB!! NOOO!
HEY! FOLLOW THE BABE!
OH, YEAH?! COUNT ME IN!
LOOK! THIS WAY! CHECK HER OUT!
WOO-WOO!
I DON'T GET IT.
WHY DO I HAVE TO ATTEND YOUR CLASS...?
OH, MY!
YUH GOTTA LEARN NOT TO SWEAT DA DETAILS, KID.

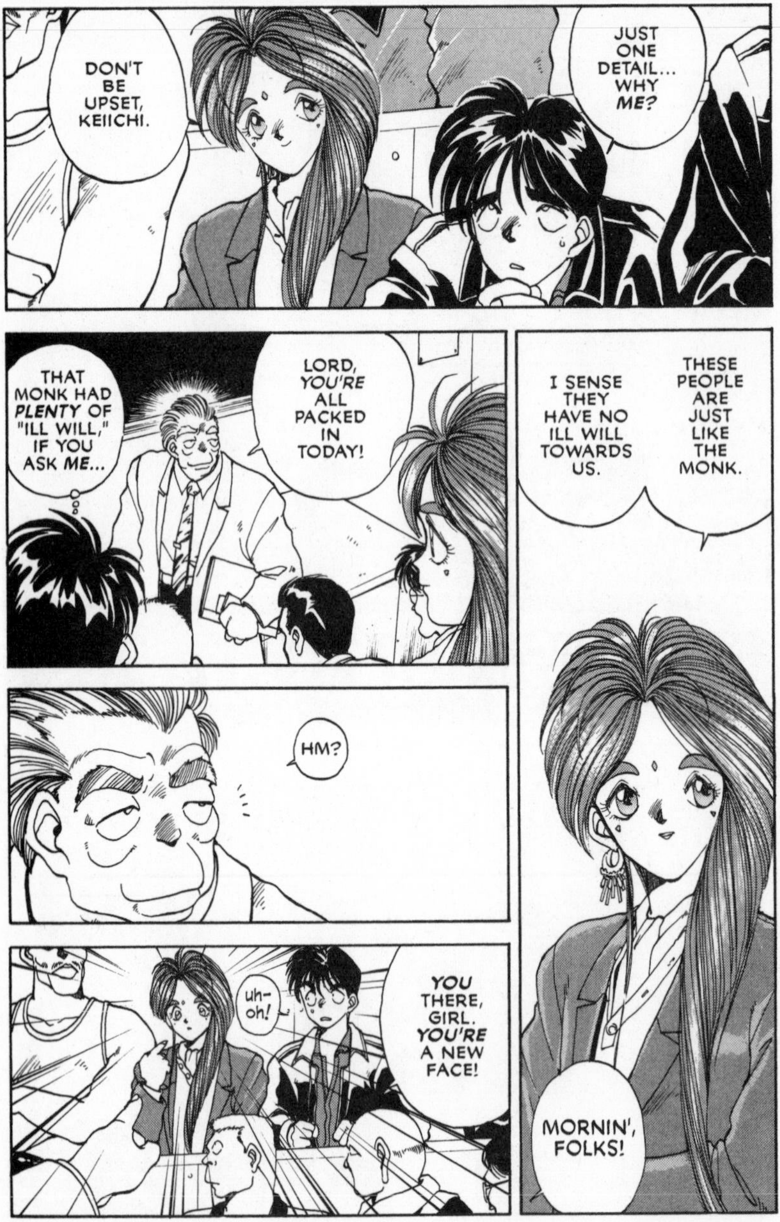
JUST ONE DETAIL... WHY *ME?*
DON'T BE UPSET, KEIICHI.
THESE PEOPLE ARE JUST LIKE THE MONK.
I SENSE THEY HAVE NO ILL WILL TOWARDS US.
MORNIN', FOLKS!
LORD, *YOU'RE* ALL PACKED IN TODAY!
THAT MONK HAD *PLENTY* OF "ILL WILL," IF YOU ASK *ME*...
HM?
YOU THERE, GIRL. *YOU'RE* A NEW FACE!
uh-oh!

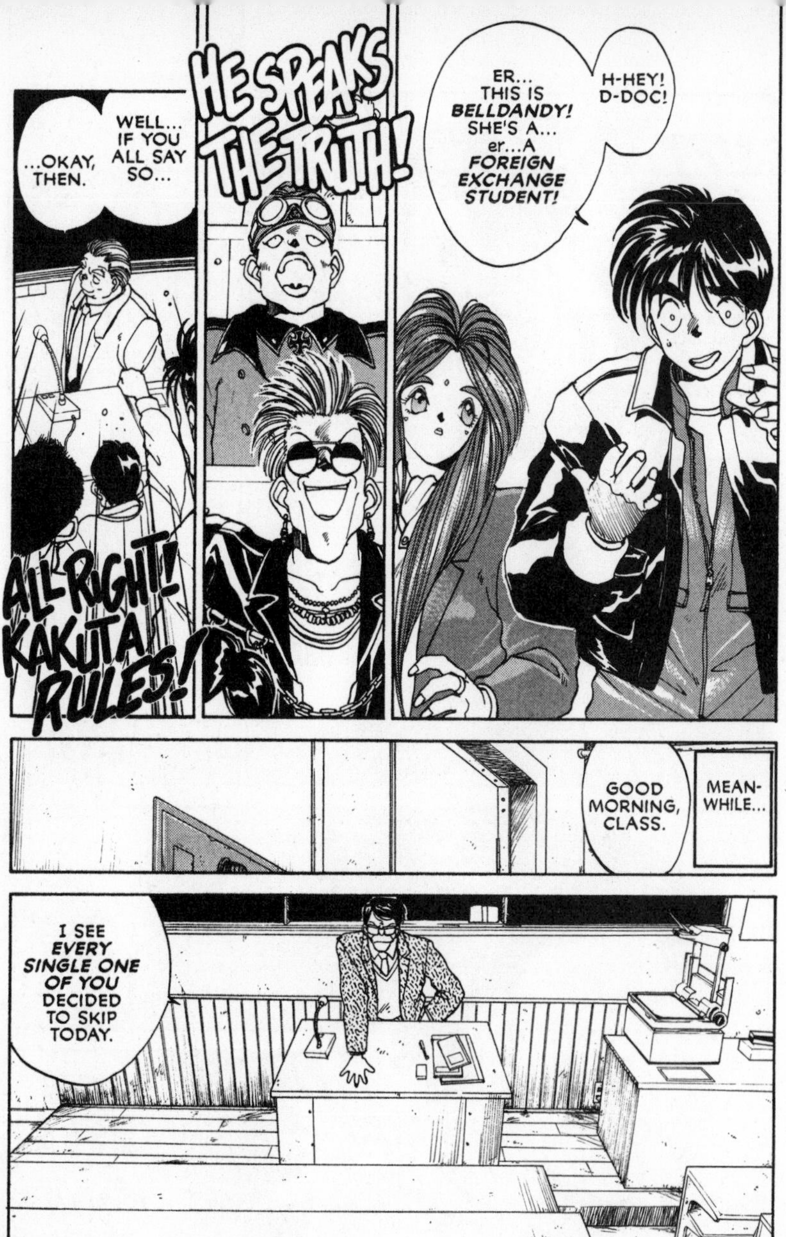
H-HEY! D-DOC!
ER... THIS IS BELLDANDY! SHE'S A... er...A FOREIGN EXCHANGE STUDENT!
HE SPEAKS THE TRUTH!
WELL... IF YOU ALL SAY SO...
...OKAY, THEN.
ALL RIGHT! KAKUTA RULES!
MEAN-WHILE...
GOOD MORNING, CLASS.
I SEE EVERY SINGLE ONE OF YOU DECIDED TO SKIP TODAY.

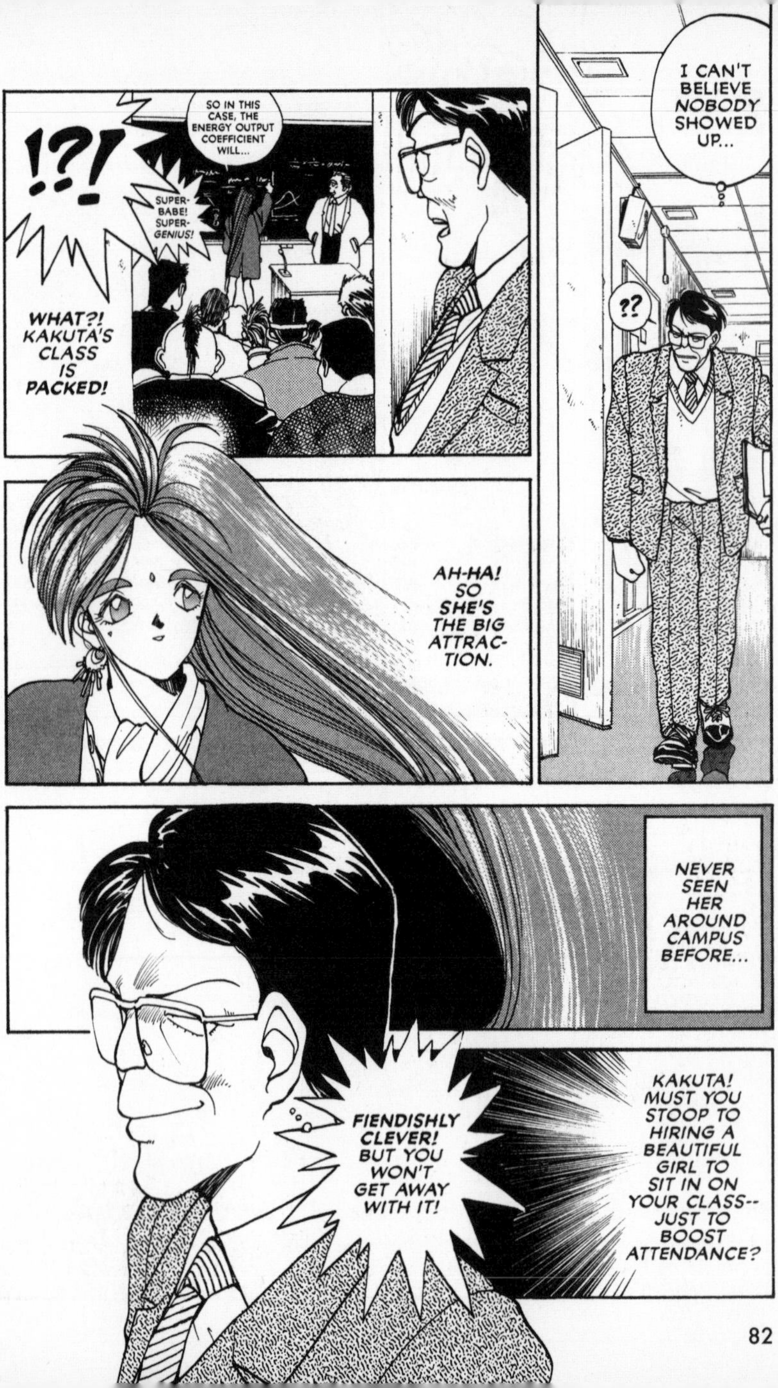
I CAN'T BELIEVE NOBODY SHOWED UP...
??
SO IN THIS CASE, THE ENERGY OUTPUT COEFFICIENT WILL...
!?!
SUPER-BABE! SUPER-GENIUS!
WHAT?! KAKUTA'S CLASS IS PACKED!
AH-HA! SO SHE'S THE BIG ATTRAC-TION.
NEVER SEEN HER AROUND CAMPUS BEFORE...
KAKUTA! MUST YOU STOOP TO HIRING A BEAUTIFUL GIRL TO SIT IN ON YOUR CLASS-- JUST TO BOOST ATTENDANCE?
FIENDISHLY CLEVER! BUT YOU WON'T GET AWAY WITH IT!

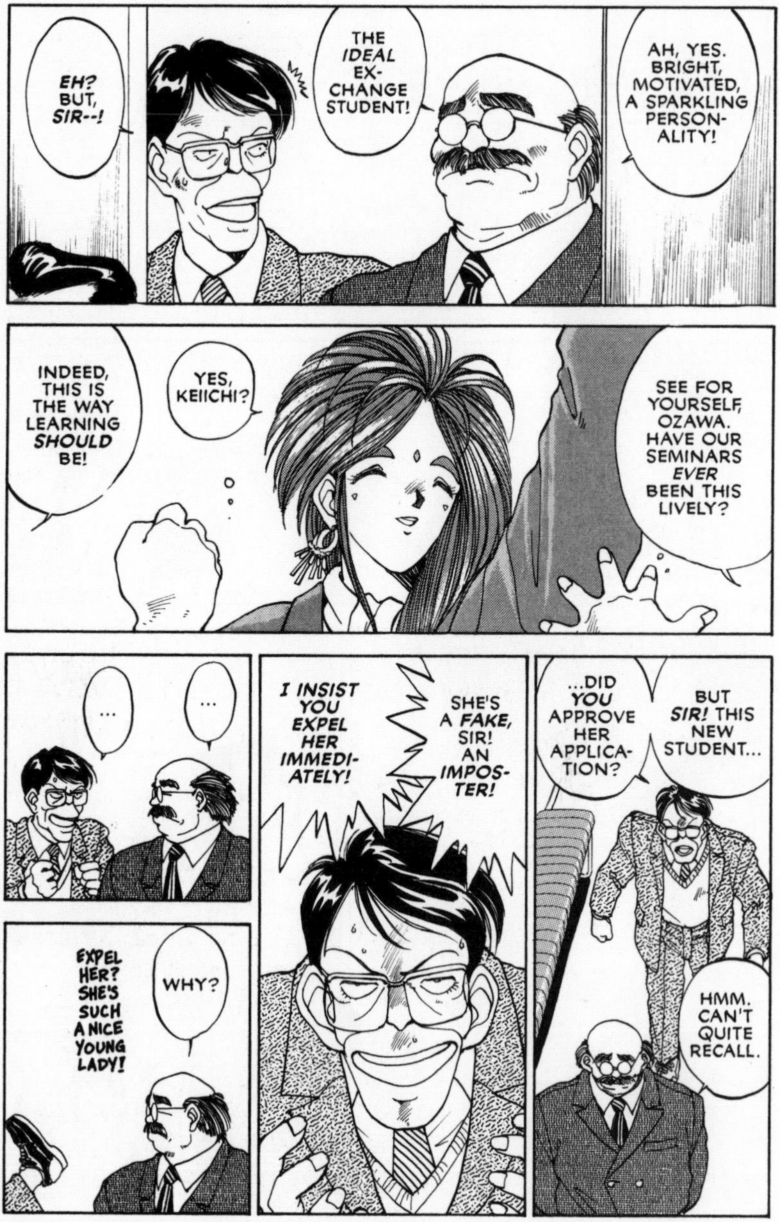
AH, YES. BRIGHT, MOTIVATED, A SPARKLING PERSONALITY!
THE *IDEAL* EXCHANGE STUDENT!
EH? BUT, SIR--!
SEE FOR YOURSELF, OZAWA. HAVE OUR SEMINARS *EVER* BEEN THIS LIVELY?
YES, KEIICHI?
INDEED, THIS IS THE WAY LEARNING ***SHOULD*** BE!
BUT *SIR!* THIS NEW STUDENT...
...DID *YOU* APPROVE HER APPLICATION?
HMM. CAN'T QUITE RECALL.
SHE'S A *FAKE,* SIR! AN *IMPOSTER!*
I INSIST YOU EXPEL HER IMMEDIATELY!
...
...
WHY?
EXPEL HER? SHE'S SUCH A NICE YOUNG LADY!

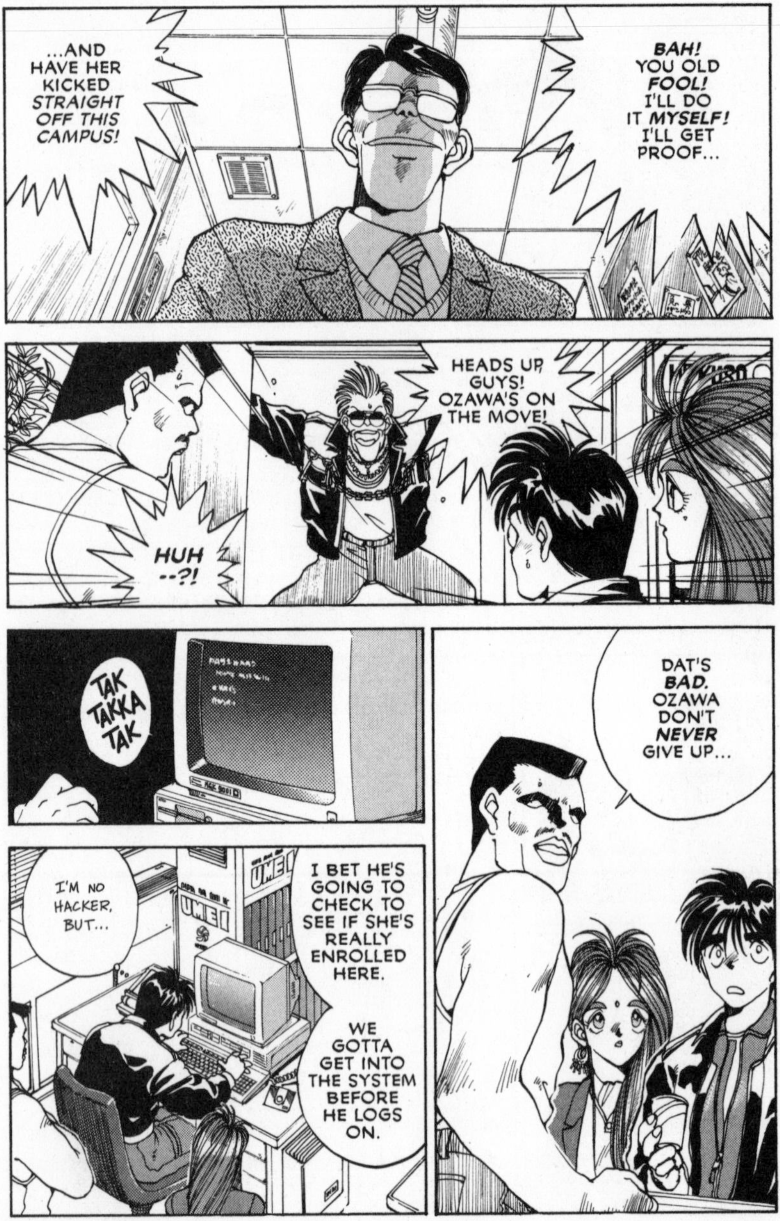
BAH! YOU OLD FOOL! I'LL DO IT MYSELF! I'LL GET PROOF...
...AND HAVE HER KICKED STRAIGHT OFF THIS CAMPUS!
HEADS UP, GUYS! OZAWA'S ON THE MOVE!
HUH --?!
DAT'S BAD. OZAWA DON'T NEVER GIVE UP...
TAK TAKKA TAK
I BET HE'S GOING TO CHECK TO SEE IF SHE'S REALLY ENROLLED HERE.
I'M NO HACKER, BUT...
WE GOTTA GET INTO THE SYSTEM BEFORE HE LOGS ON.

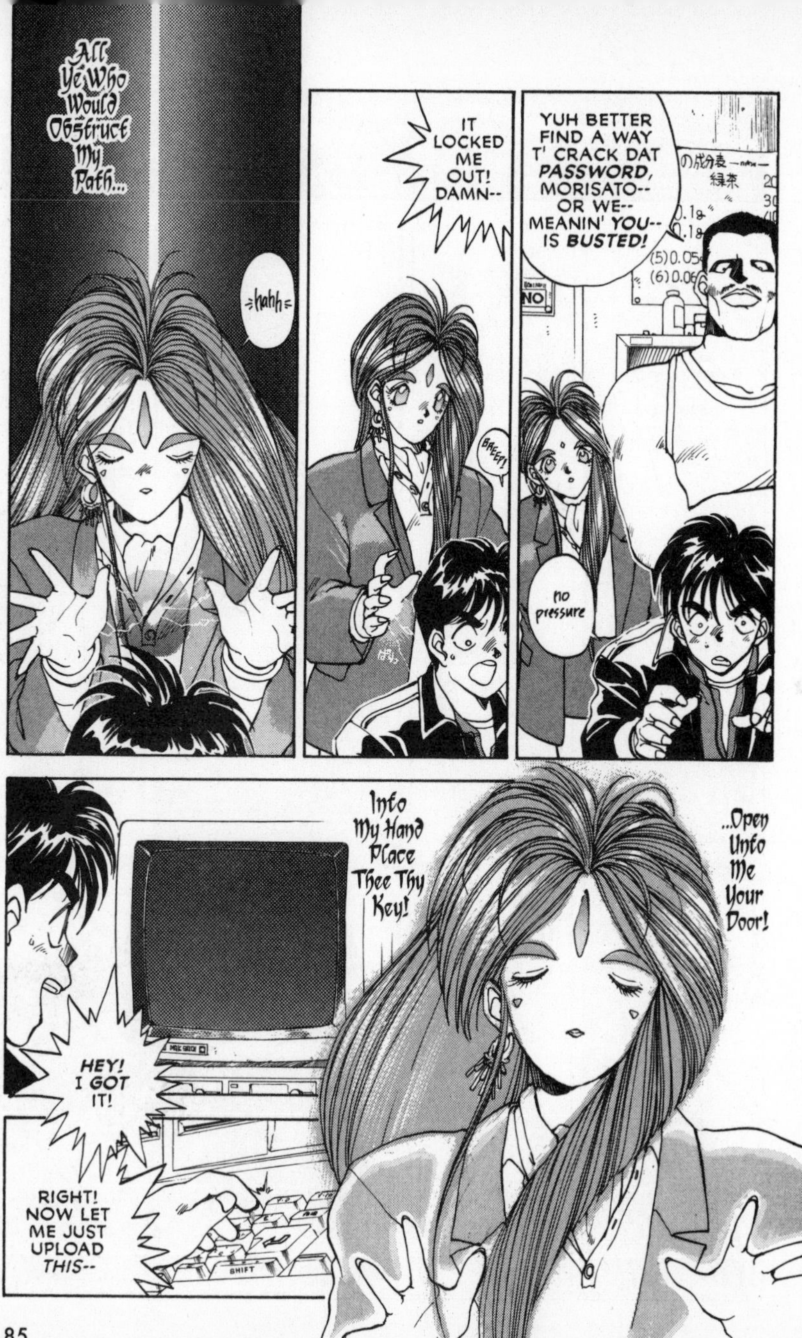
YUH BETTER FIND A WAY T' CRACK DAT PASSWORD, MORISATO-- OR WE-- MEANIN' YOU-- IS BUSTED!
no pressure
IT LOCKED ME OUT! DAMN--
BREEP!
All Ye Who Would Obstruct My Path...
hahh
Into My Hand Place Thee Thy Key!
...Open Unto Me Your Door!
HEY! I GOT IT!
RIGHT! NOW LET ME JUST UPLOAD THIS--

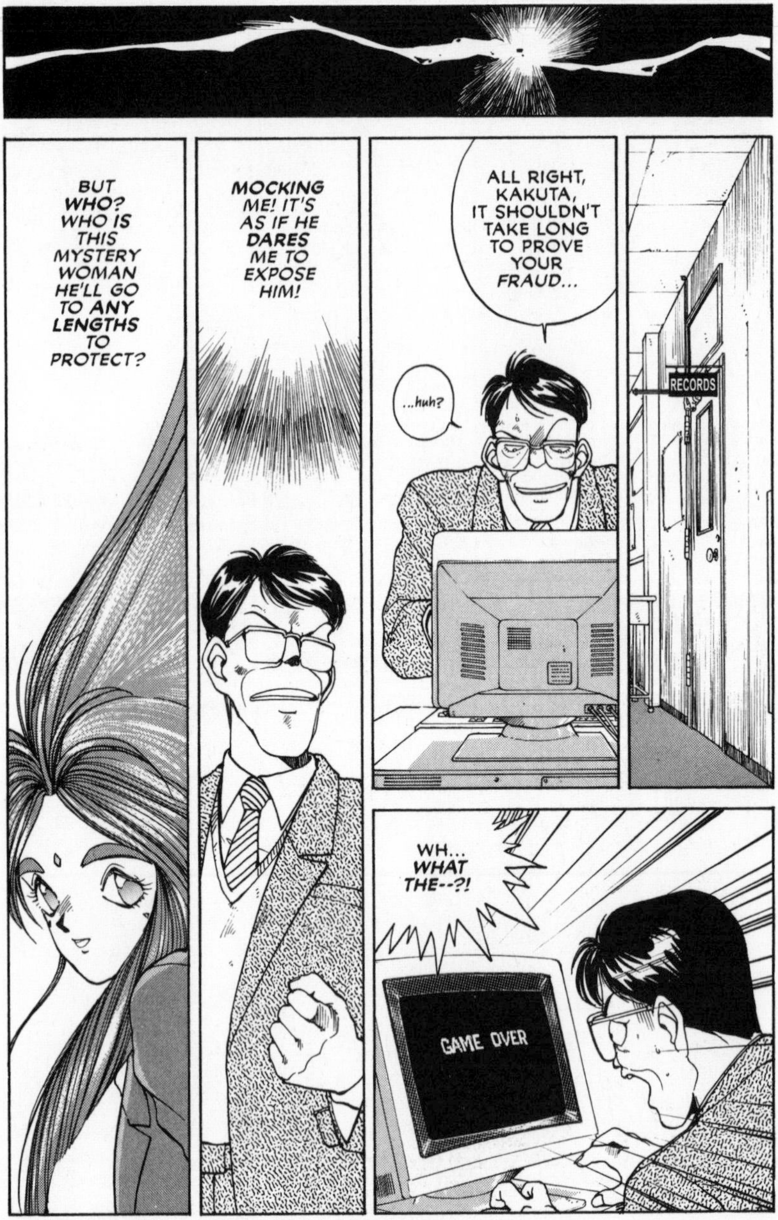
RECORDS
ALL RIGHT, KAKUTA, IT SHOULDN'T TAKE LONG TO PROVE YOUR FRAUD...
...huh?
WH... WHAT THE--?!
GAME OVER
MOCKING ME! IT'S AS IF HE DARES ME TO EXPOSE HIM!
BUT WHO? WHO IS THIS MYSTERY WOMAN HE'LL GO TO ANY LENGTHS TO PROTECT?

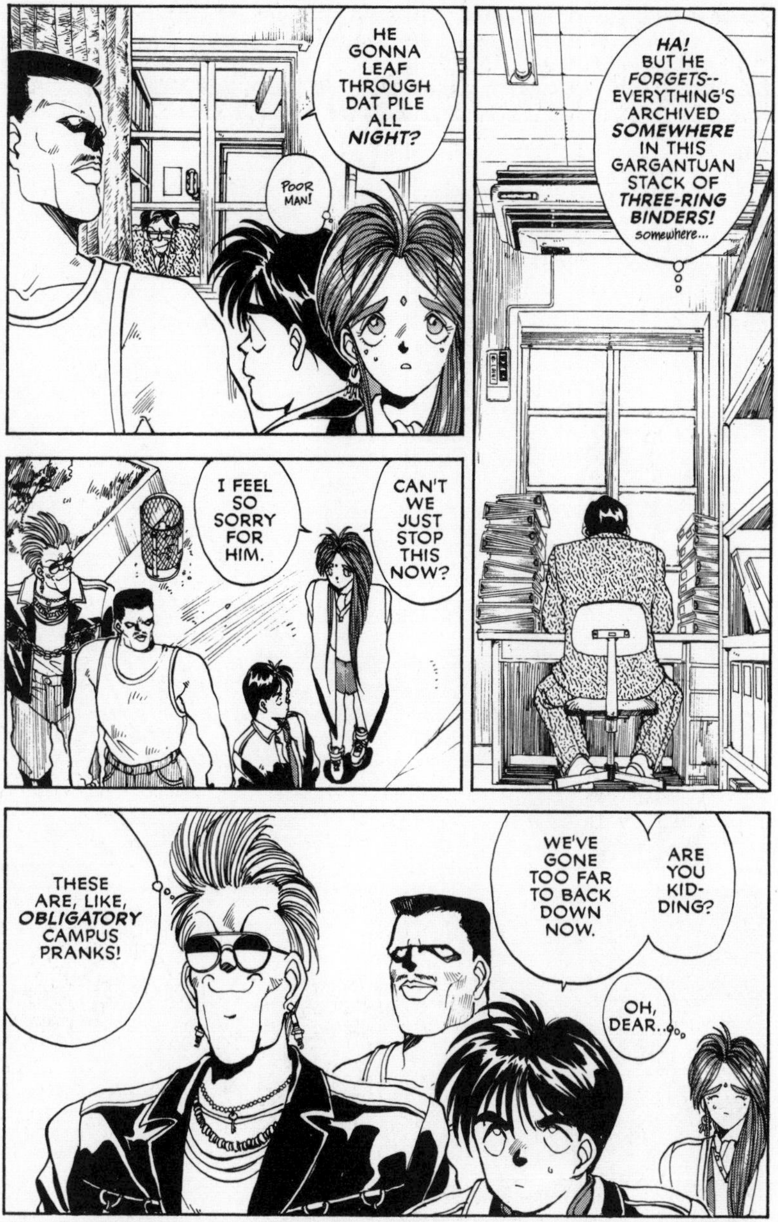
HA! BUT HE FORGETS-- EVERYTHING'S ARCHIVED SOMEWHERE IN THIS GARGANTUAN STACK OF THREE-RING BINDERS! somewhere...
HE GONNA LEAF THROUGH DAT PILE ALL NIGHT?
POOR MAN!
CAN'T WE JUST STOP THIS NOW?
I FEEL SO SORRY FOR HIM.
ARE YOU KID-DING?
WE'VE GONE TOO FAR TO BACK DOWN NOW.
THESE ARE, LIKE, OBLIGATORY CAMPUS PRANKS!
OH, DEAR...

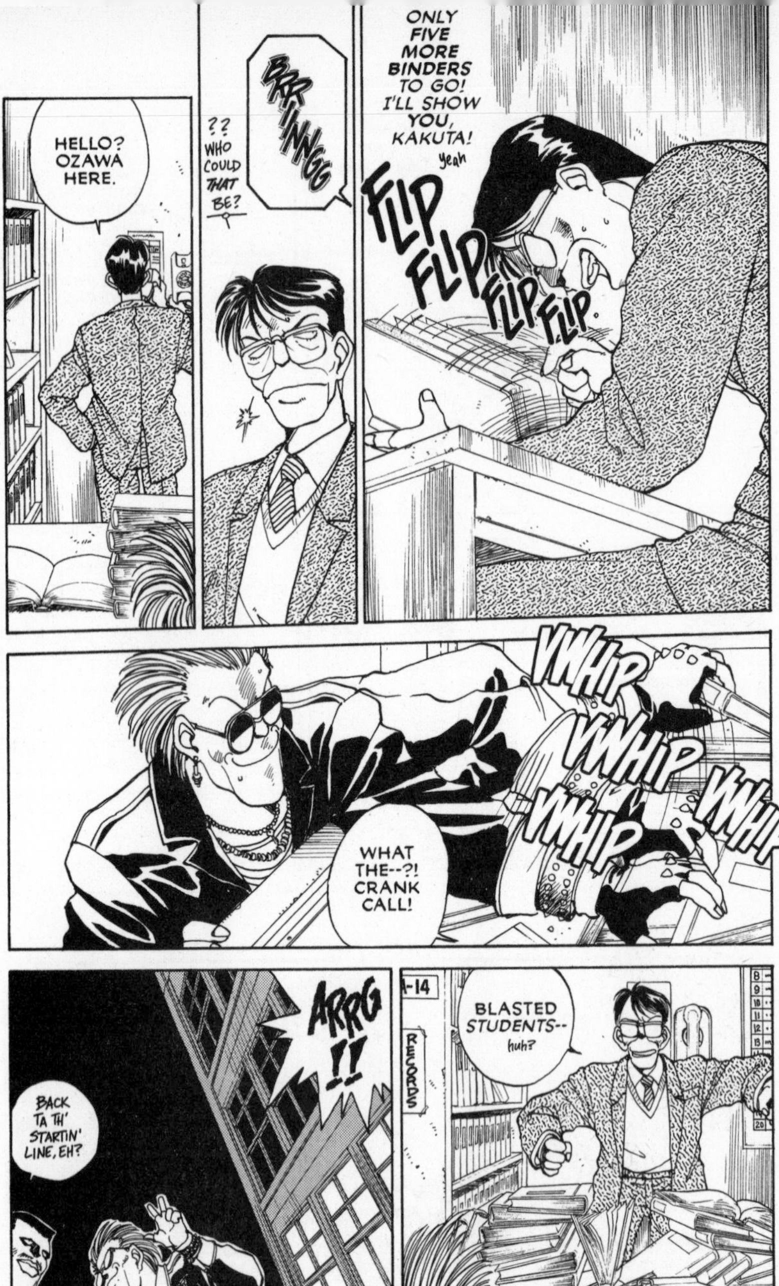
ONLY FIVE MORE BINDERS TO GO! I'LL SHOW YOU, KAKUTA!
yeah
FLIP FLIP FLIP FLIP
BRRINNGG
?? WHO COULD THAT BE?
HELLO? OZAWA HERE.
VWHIP VWHIP VWHIP VWHIP
WHAT THE--?! CRANK CALL!
A-14
RECORDS
BLASTED STUDENTS--
huh?
ARRG!!
BACK TA TH' STARTIN' LINE, EH?

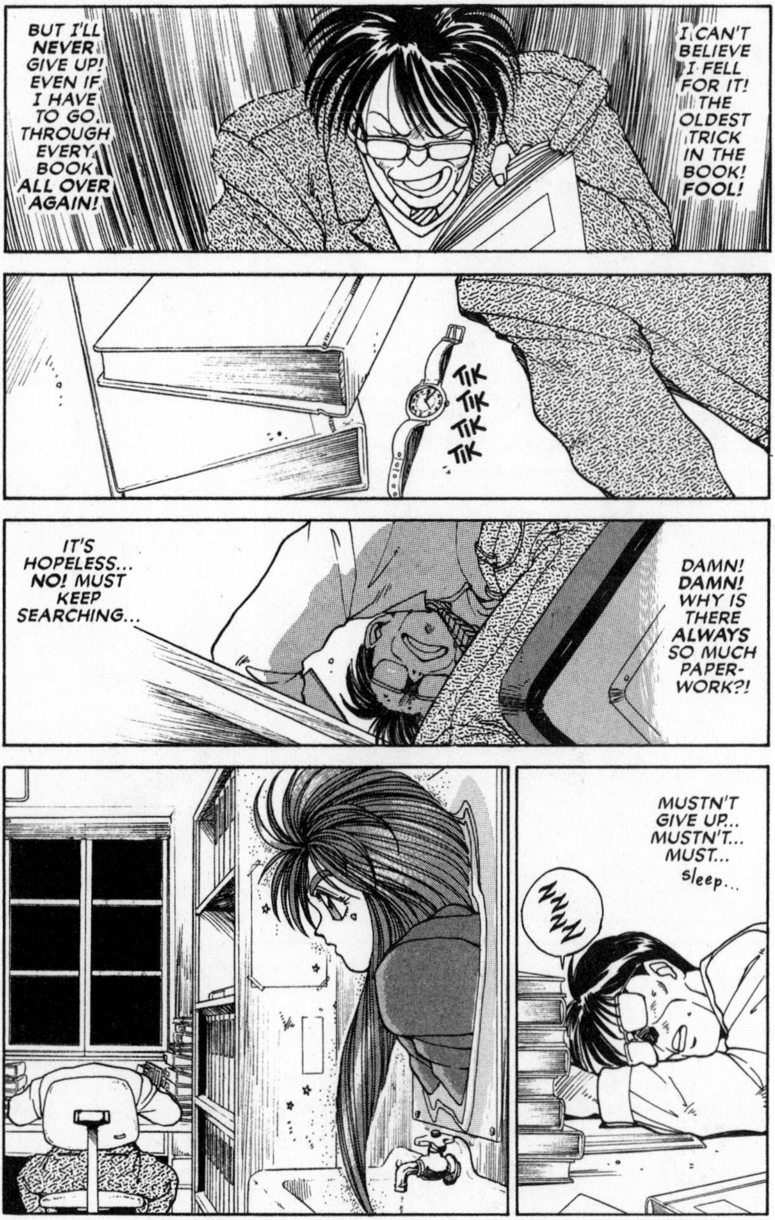
I CAN'T BELIEVE I FELL FOR IT! THE OLDEST TRICK IN THE BOOK! FOOL!
BUT I'LL NEVER GIVE UP! EVEN IF I HAVE TO GO THROUGH EVERY BOOK ALL OVER AGAIN!
TIK TIK TIK TIK
DAMN! DAMN! WHY IS THERE ALWAYS SO MUCH PAPER-WORK?!
IT'S HOPELESS... NO! MUST KEEP SEARCHING...
MUSTN'T GIVE UP... MUSTN'T... MUST... sleep...

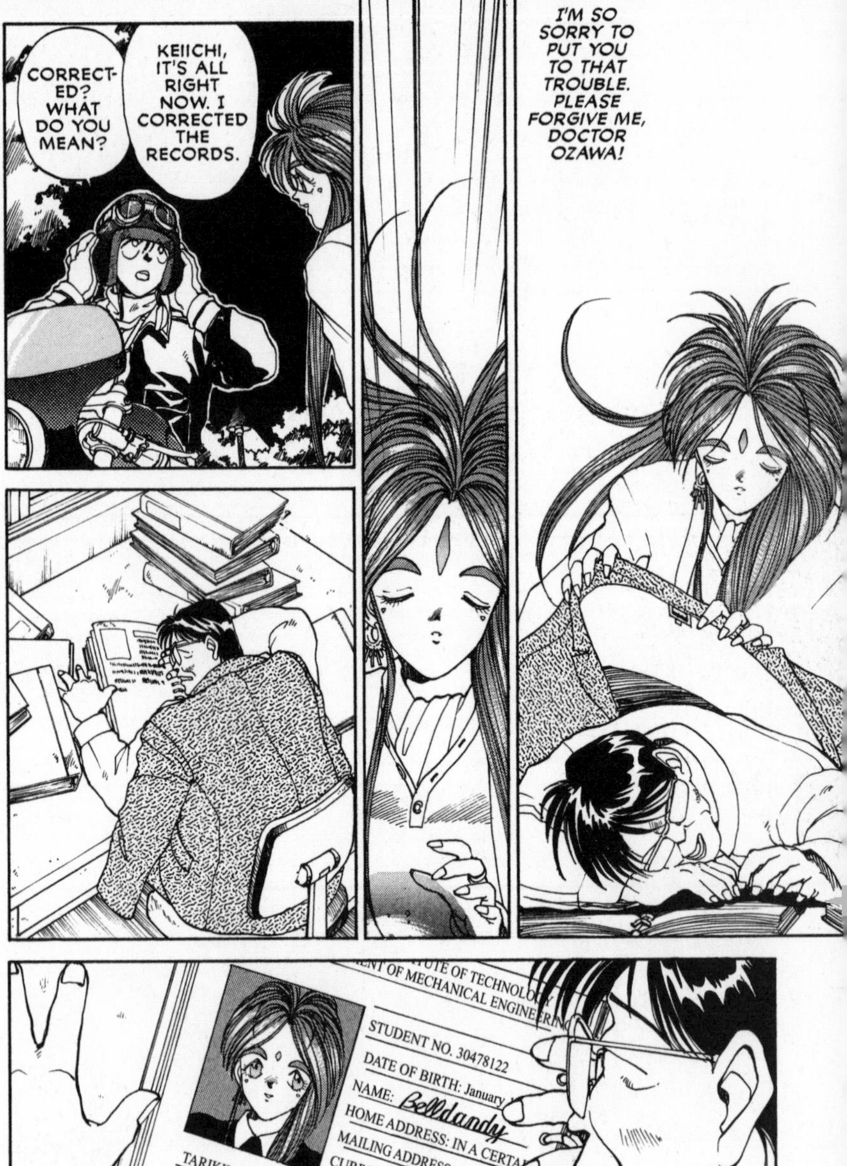

I'M SO SORRY TO PUT YOU TO THAT TROUBLE. PLEASE FORGIVE ME, DOCTOR OZAWA!
KEIICHI, IT'S ALL RIGHT NOW. I CORRECTED THE RECORDS.
CORRECTED? WHAT DO YOU MEAN?
TUTE OF TECHNOLOGY
ENT OF MECHANICAL ENGINEERIN
STUDENT NO. 30478122
DATE OF BIRTH: January
NAME: Belldandy
HOME ADDRESS: IN A CERTA
MAILING ADDRESS: SEE BELOW
CURRENT ADDRESS:
TARIKIHONGAN TEMPLE, 3-4-106 NEKO
this special case
excepti

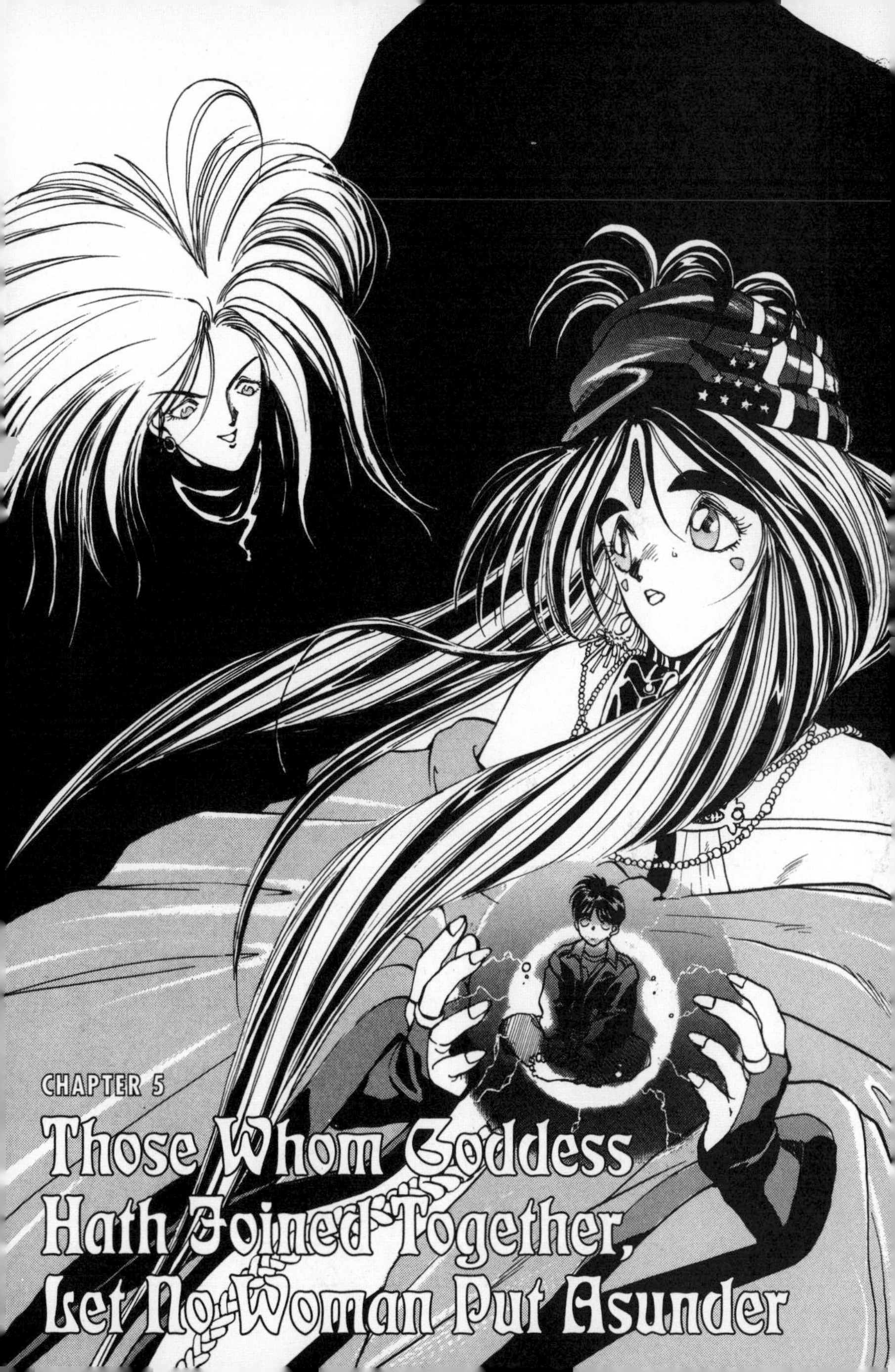
CHAPTER 5
Those Whom Goddess
Hath Joined Together,
Let No Woman Put Asunder

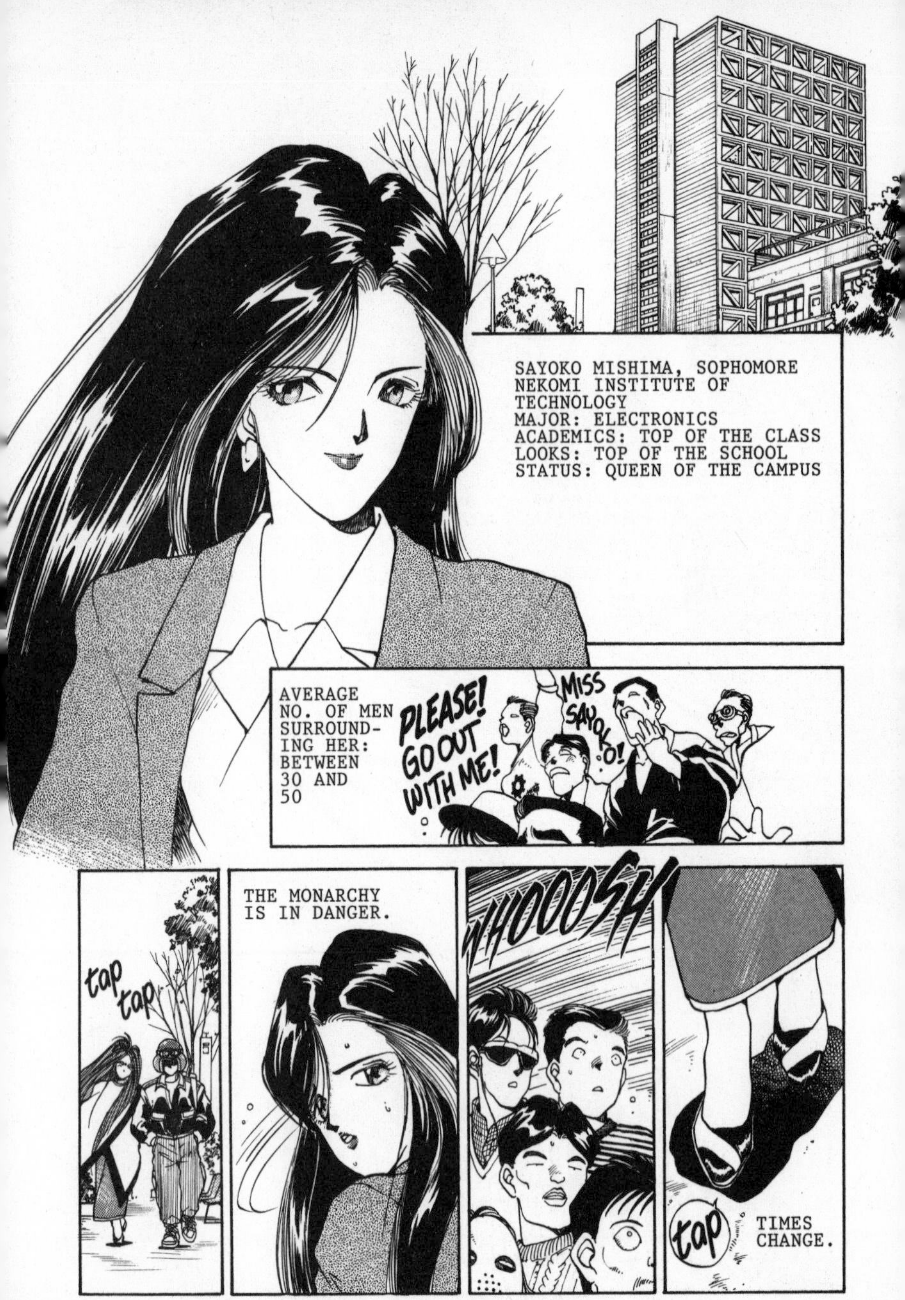
SAYOKO MISHIMA, SOPHOMORE
NEKOMI INSTITUTE OF TECHNOLOGY
MAJOR: ELECTRONICS
ACADEMICS: TOP OF THE CLASS
LOOKS: TOP OF THE SCHOOL
STATUS: QUEEN OF THE CAMPUS
MISS SAYOKO!
PLEASE! GO OUT WITH ME!
AVERAGE NO. OF MEN SURROUNDING HER: BETWEEN 30 AND 50
TIMES CHANGE.
tap
WHOOOOSH
THE MONARCHY IS IN DANGER.
tap tap

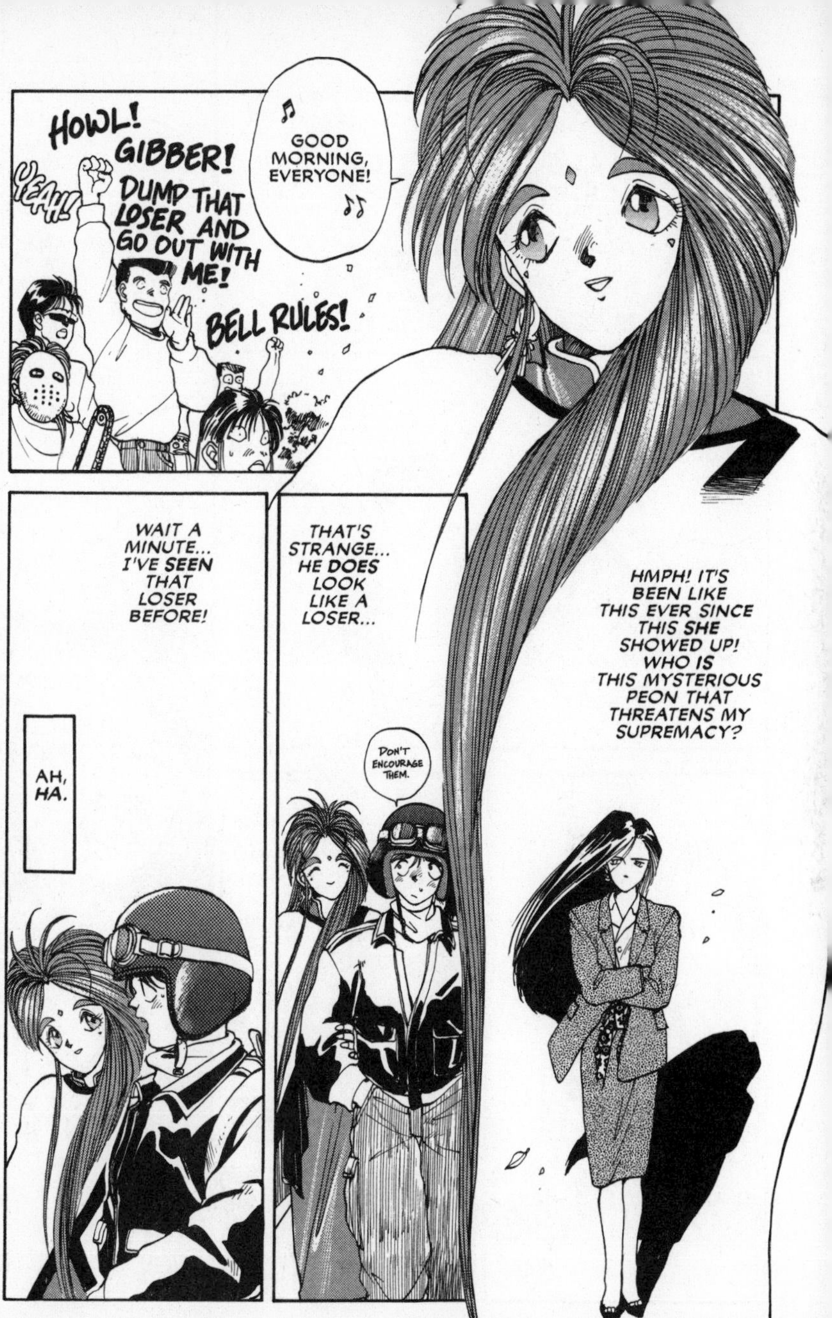
GOOD MORNING, EVERYONE!
HOWL!
GIBBER!
YEAH!!
DUMP THAT LOSER AND GO OUT WITH ME!
BELL RULES!
THAT'S STRANGE... HE DOES LOOK LIKE A LOSER...
DON'T ENCOURAGE THEM.
WAIT A MINUTE... I'VE SEEN THAT LOSER BEFORE!
AH, HA.
HMPH! IT'S BEEN LIKE THIS EVER SINCE THIS SHE SHOWED UP! WHO IS THIS MYSTERIOUS PEON THAT THREATENS MY SUPREMACY?

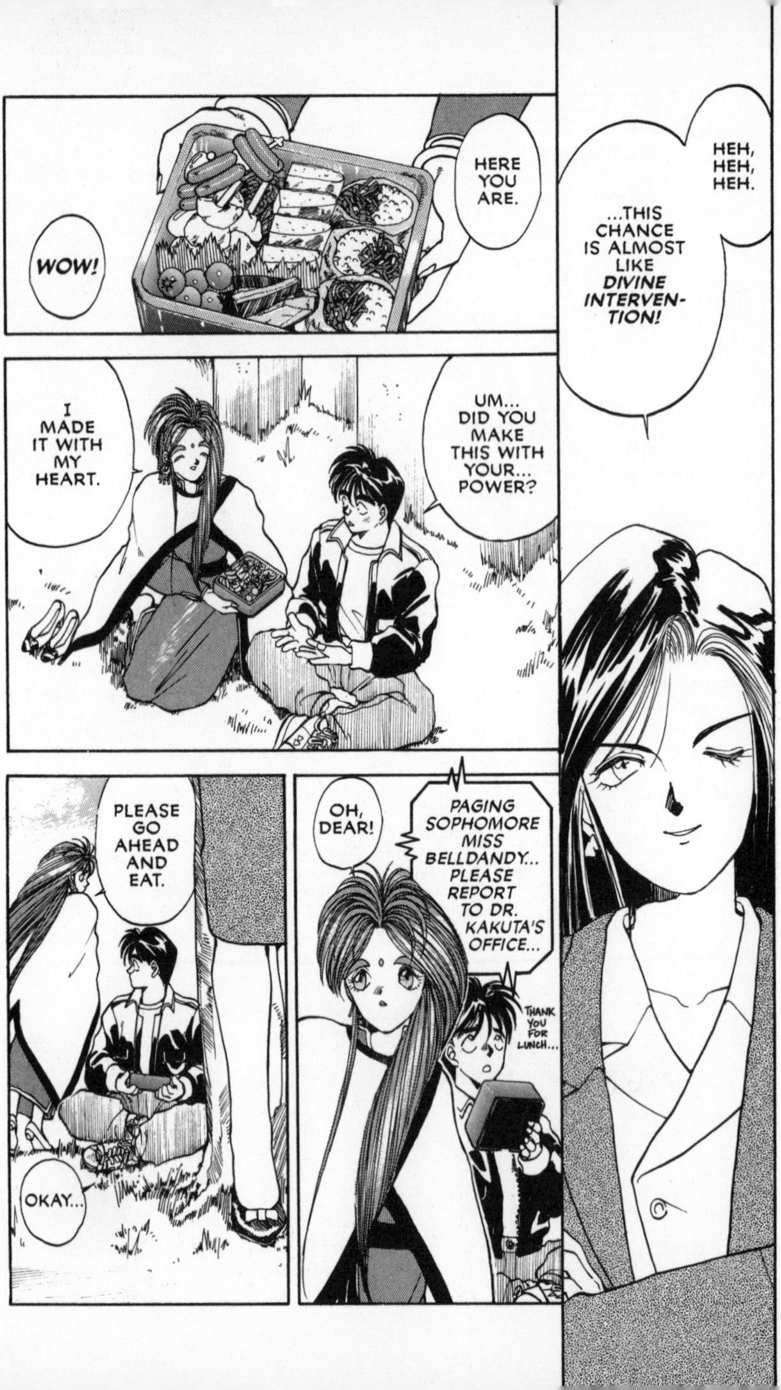
HEH, HEH, HEH.
...THIS CHANCE IS ALMOST LIKE *DIVINE INTERVENTION!*
HERE YOU ARE.
WOW!
UM... DID YOU MAKE THIS WITH YOUR... POWER?
I MADE IT WITH MY HEART.
PAGING SOPHOMORE MISS BELLDANDY... PLEASE REPORT TO DR. KAKUTA'S OFFICE...
OH, DEAR!
THANK YOU FOR LUNCH...
PLEASE GO AHEAD AND EAT.
OKAY...

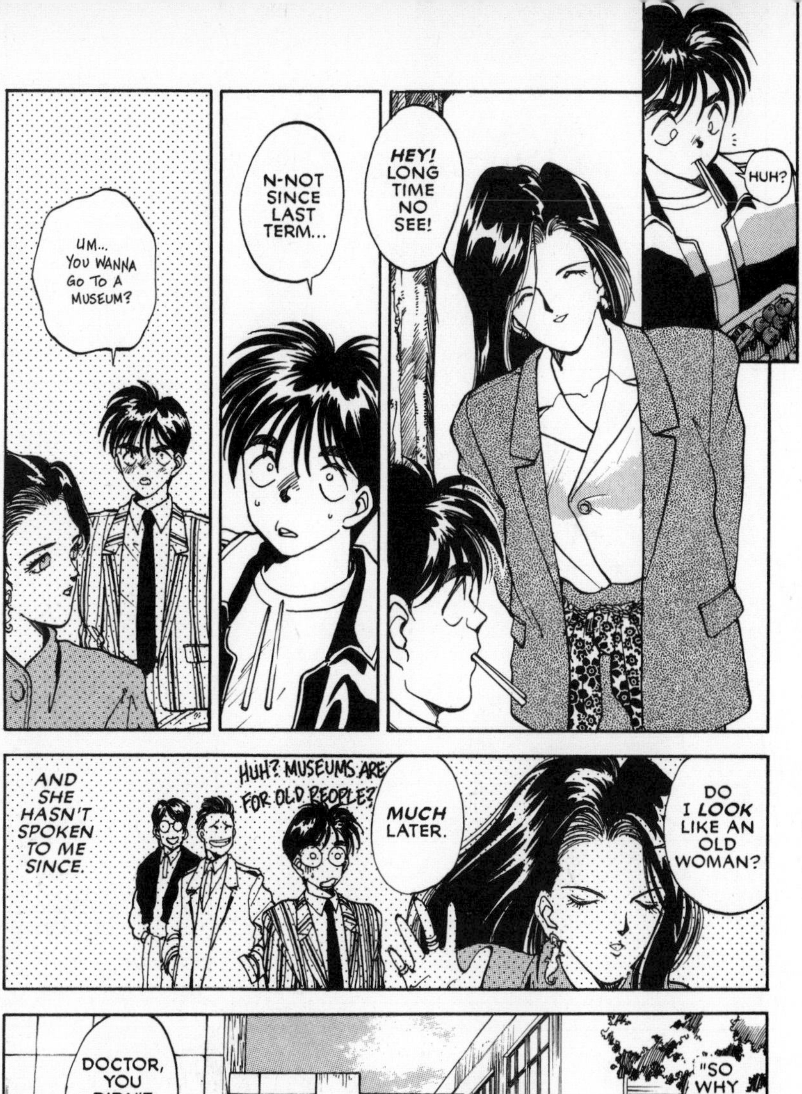
HUH?
HEY! LONG TIME NO SEE!
N-NOT SINCE LAST TERM...
UM... YOU WANNA GO TO A MUSEUM?
DO I LOOK LIKE AN OLD WOMAN?
MUCH LATER.
HUH? MUSEUMS ARE FOR OLD PEOPLE?
AND SHE HASN'T SPOKEN TO ME SINCE.
"SO WHY NOW...?"
DOCTOR, YOU DIDN'T HAVE ME PAGED?

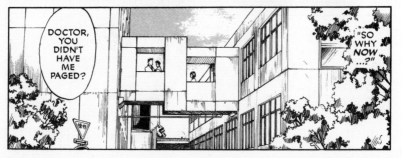

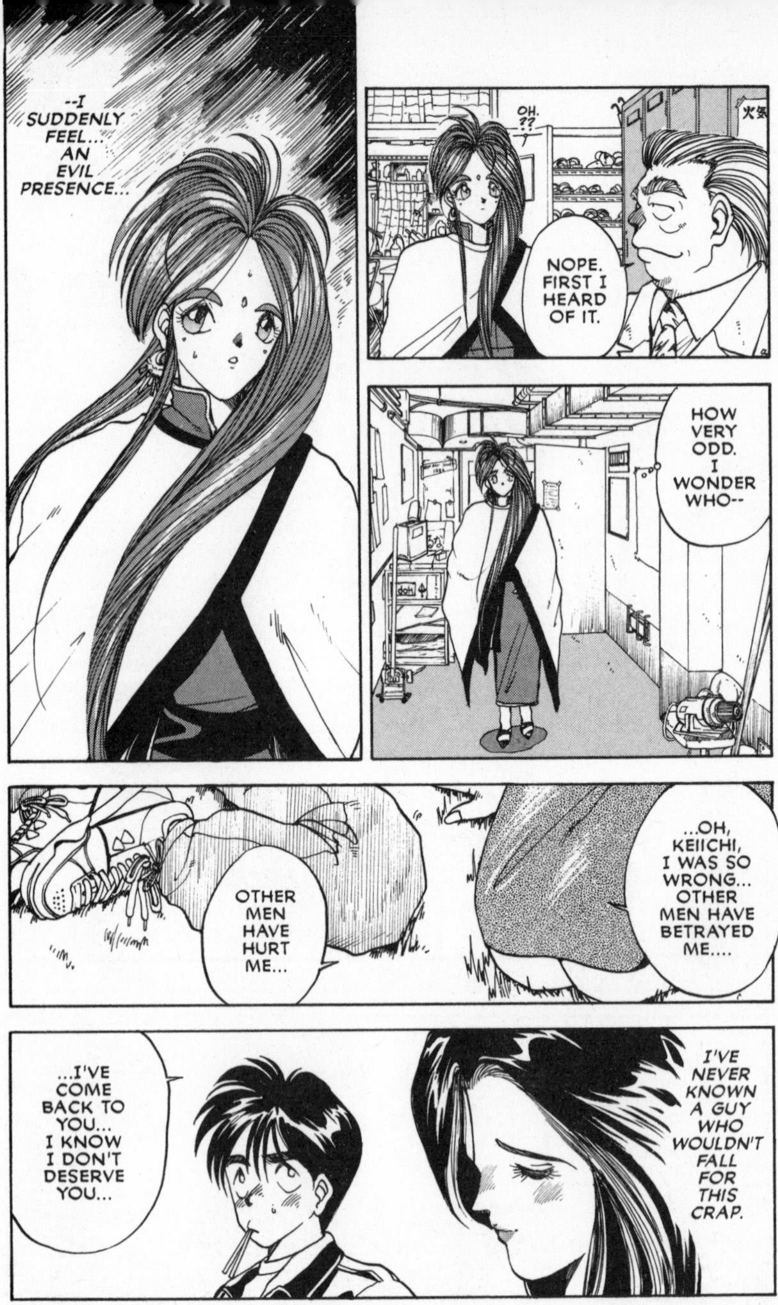
OH. ??
NOPE. FIRST I HEARD OF IT.
HOW VERY ODD. I WONDER WHO--
--I SUDDENLY FEEL... AN EVIL PRESENCE...
...OH, KEIICHI, I WAS SO WRONG... OTHER MEN HAVE BETRAYED ME....
OTHER MEN HAVE HURT ME...
I'VE NEVER KNOWN A GUY WHO WOULDN'T FALL FOR THIS CRAP.
...I'VE COME BACK TO YOU... I KNOW I DON'T DESERVE YOU...

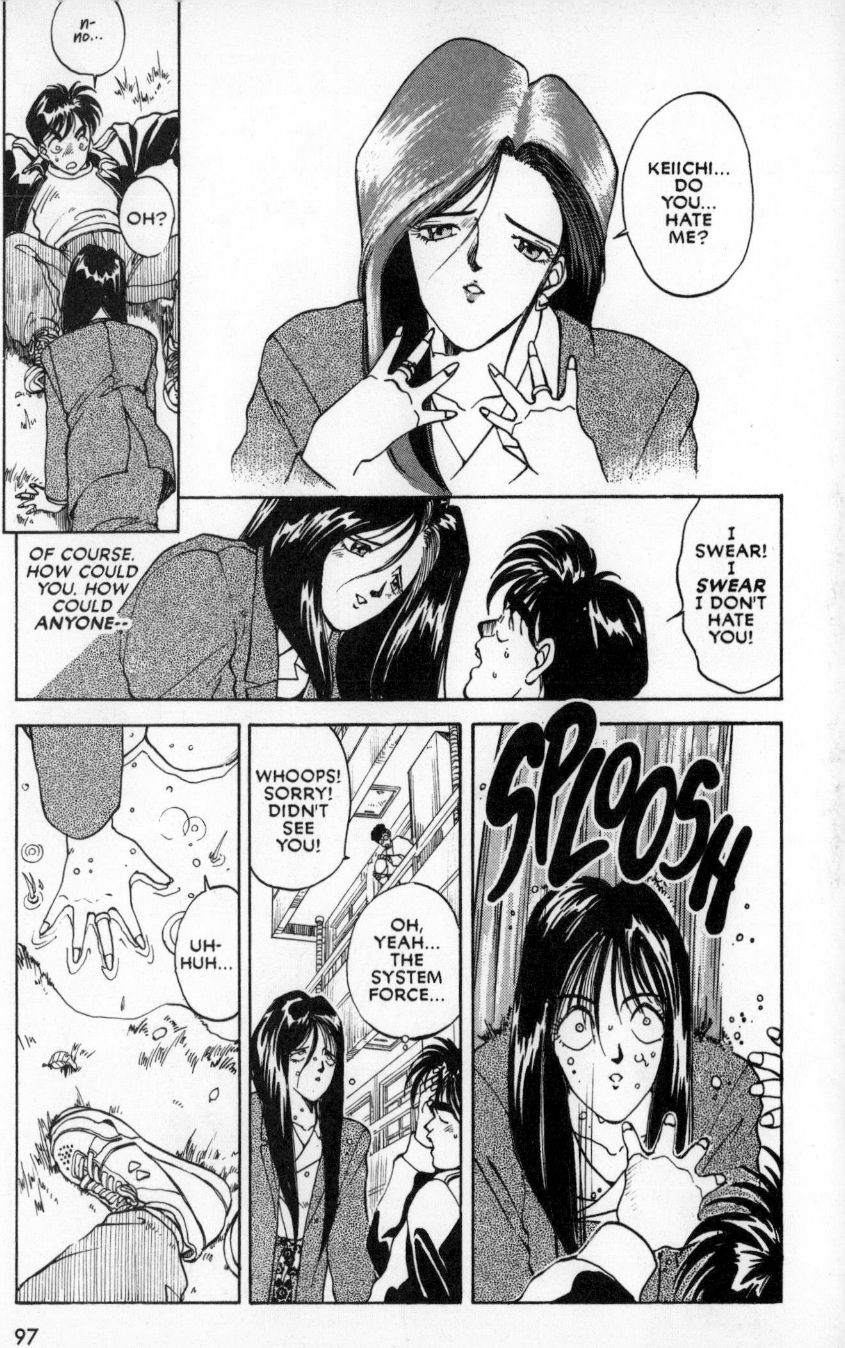

KEIICHI... DO YOU... HATE ME?
n-no...
OH?
I SWEAR! I SWEAR I DON'T HATE YOU!
OF COURSE. HOW COULD YOU. HOW COULD ANYONE--
SPLOOSH
WHOOPS! SORRY! DIDN'T SEE YOU!
OH, YEAH... THE SYSTEM FORCE...
UH-HUH...

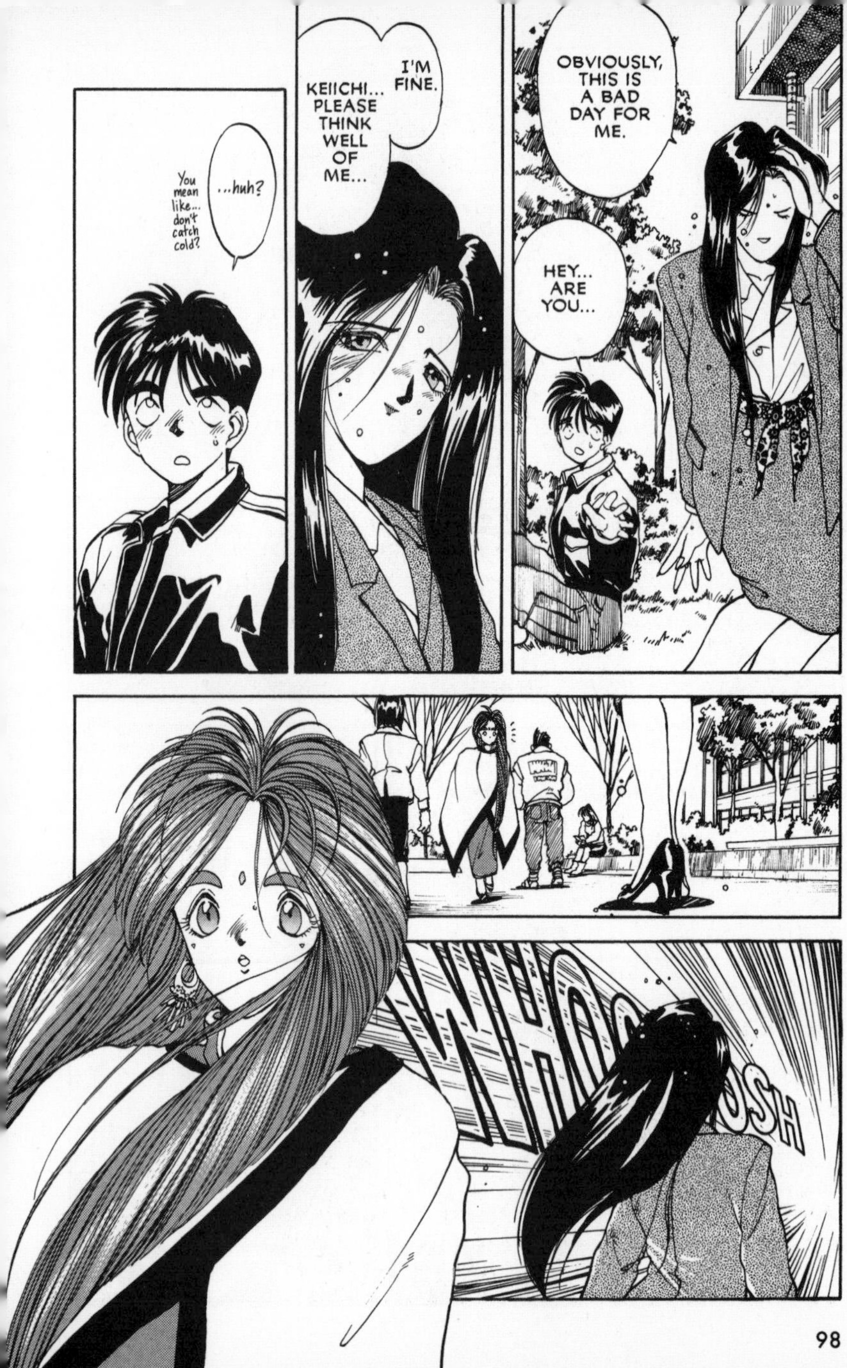
OBVIOUSLY, THIS IS A BAD DAY FOR ME.
HEY... ARE YOU...
I'M FINE.
KEIICHI... PLEASE THINK WELL OF ME...
...huh?
You mean like... don't catch cold?
WHOOSH

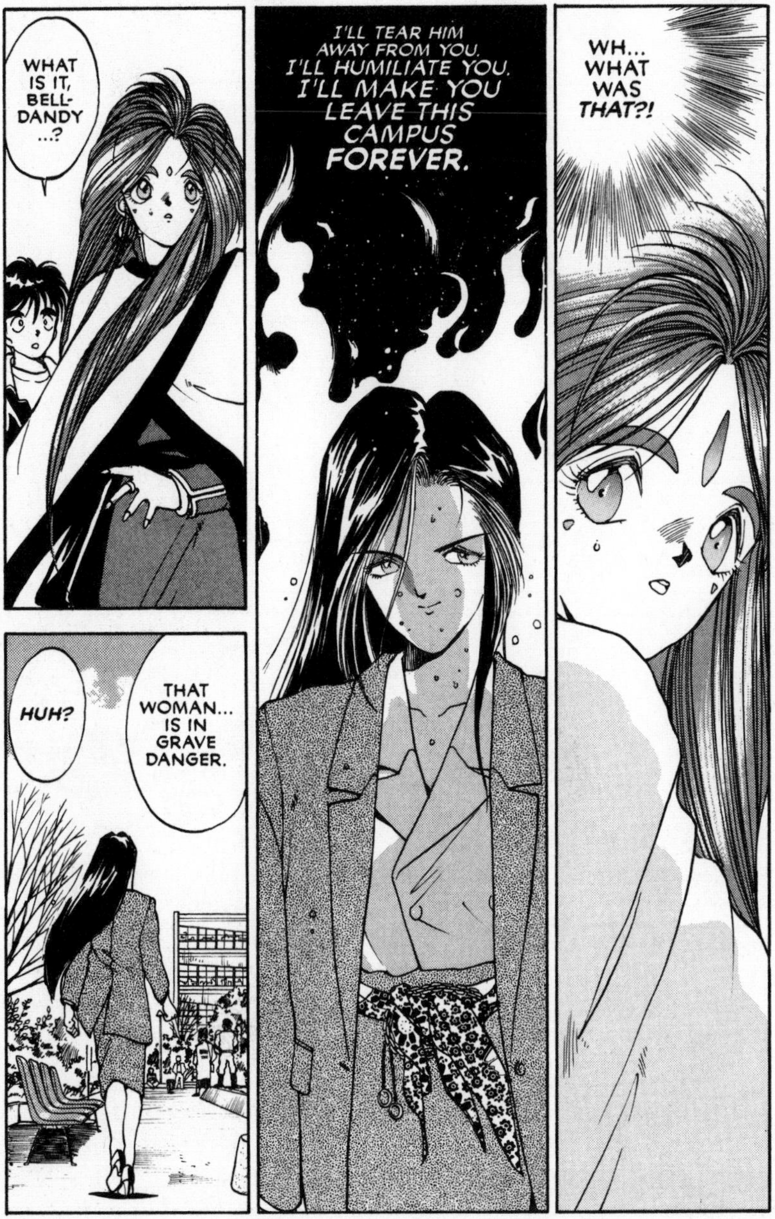
WH... WHAT WAS *THAT?!*
I'LL TEAR HIM AWAY FROM YOU. I'LL HUMILIATE YOU. I'LL MAKE YOU LEAVE THIS CAMPUS **FOREVER.**
WHAT IS IT, BELL-DANDY ...?
THAT WOMAN... IS IN GRAVE DANGER.
HUH?

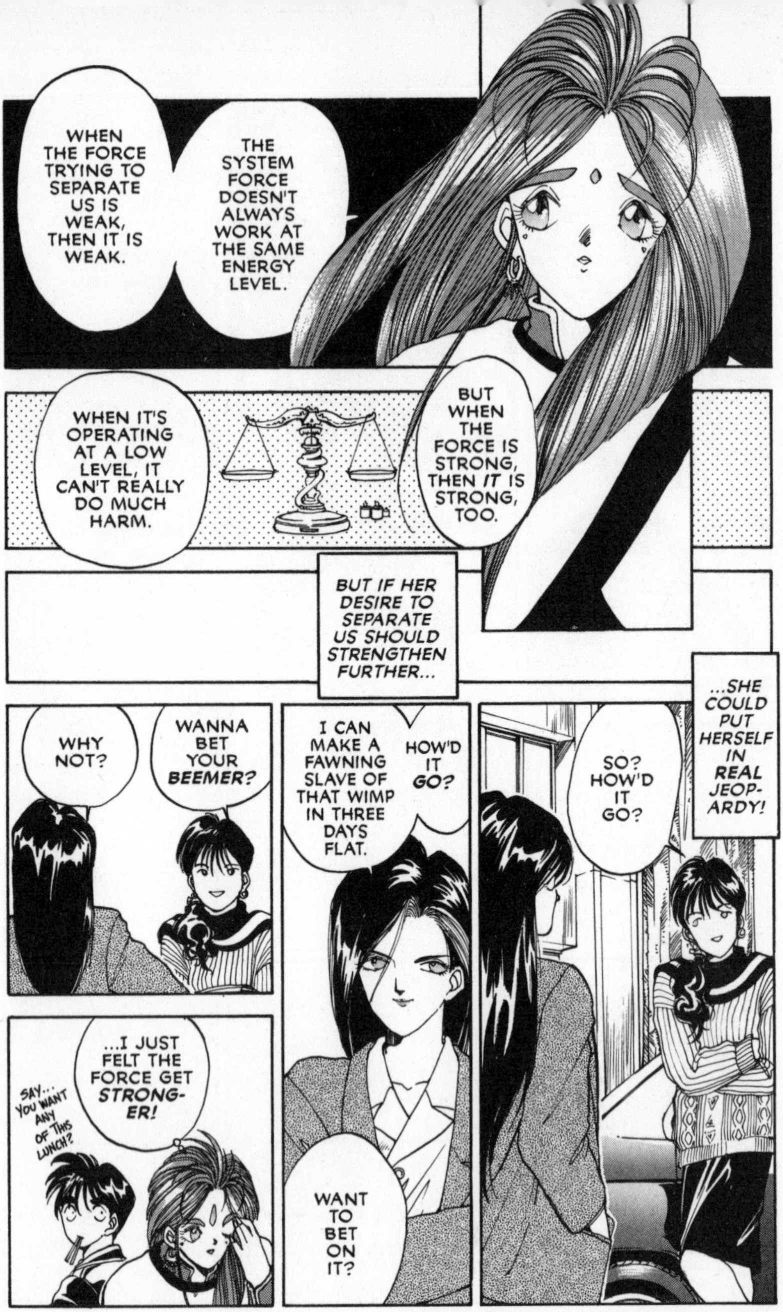

THE SYSTEM FORCE DOESN'T ALWAYS WORK AT THE SAME ENERGY LEVEL.
WHEN THE FORCE TRYING TO SEPARATE US IS WEAK, THEN IT IS WEAK.
WHEN IT'S OPERATING AT A LOW LEVEL, IT CAN'T REALLY DO MUCH HARM.
BUT WHEN THE FORCE IS STRONG, THEN *IT* IS STRONG, TOO.
BUT IF HER DESIRE TO SEPARATE US SHOULD STRENGTHEN FURTHER...
...SHE COULD PUT HERSELF IN REAL JEOPARDY!
SO? HOW'D IT GO?
HOW'D IT *GO?*
I CAN MAKE A FAWNING SLAVE OF THAT WIMP IN THREE DAYS FLAT.
WANT TO BET ON IT?
WANNA BET YOUR *BEEMER?*
WHY NOT?
...I JUST FELT THE FORCE GET *STRONGER!*
SAY... YOU WANT ANY OF THIS LUNCH?

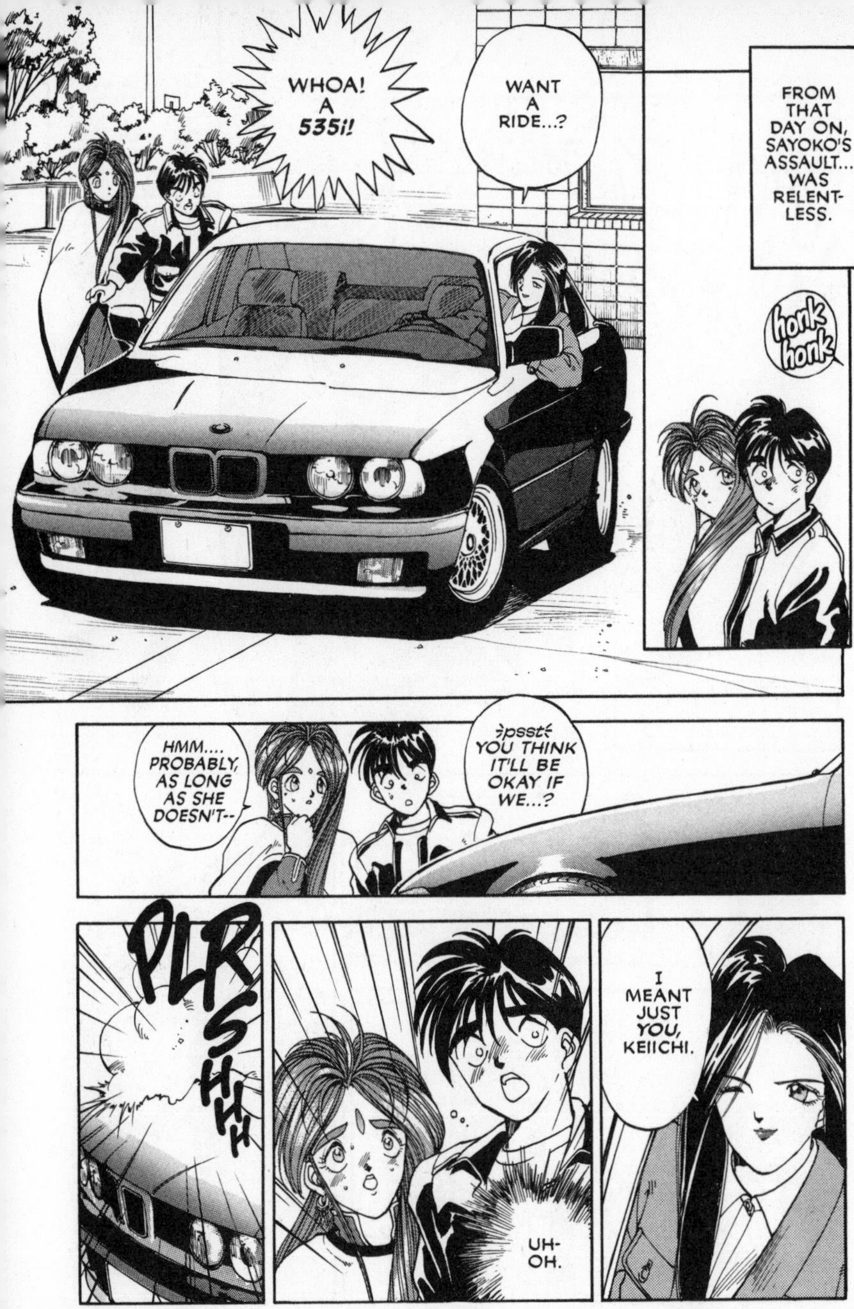

FROM THAT DAY ON, SAYOKO'S ASSAULT... WAS RELENTLESS.
honk honk
WANT A RIDE...?
WHOA! A 535i!
psst YOU THINK IT'LL BE OKAY IF WE...?
HMM.... PROBABLY, AS LONG AS SHE DOESN'T--
I MEANT JUST YOU, KEIICHI.
UH-OH.
PLR SHHH

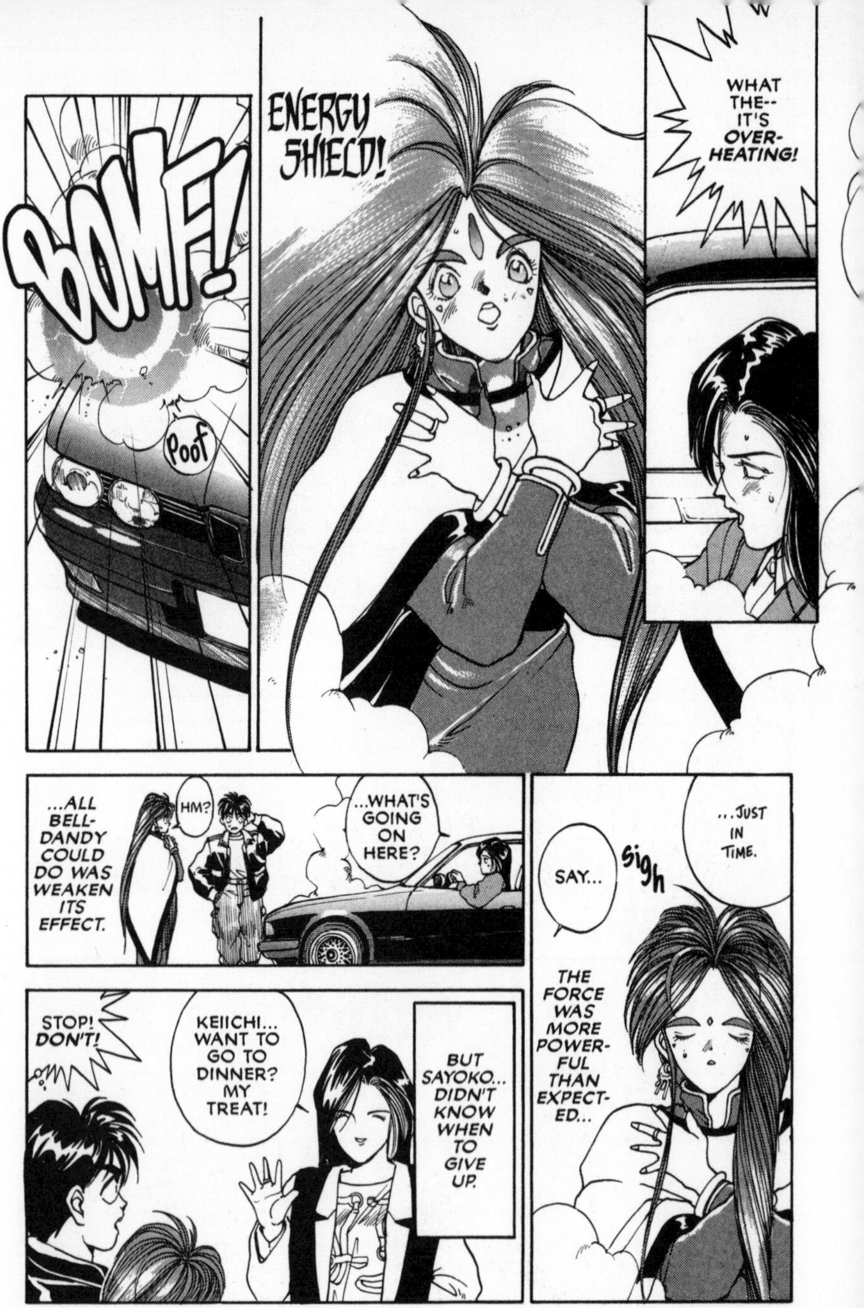
WHAT THE-- IT'S OVER-HEATING!
ENERGY SHIELD!
BOMF!
Poof
...JUST IN TIME.
Sigh
SAY...
THE FORCE WAS MORE POWER-FUL THAN EXPECT-ED...
...WHAT'S GOING ON HERE?
HM?
...ALL BELL-DANDY COULD DO WAS WEAKEN ITS EFFECT.
BUT SAYOKO... DIDN'T KNOW WHEN TO GIVE UP.
KEIICHI... WANT TO GO TO DINNER? MY TREAT!
STOP! DON'T!

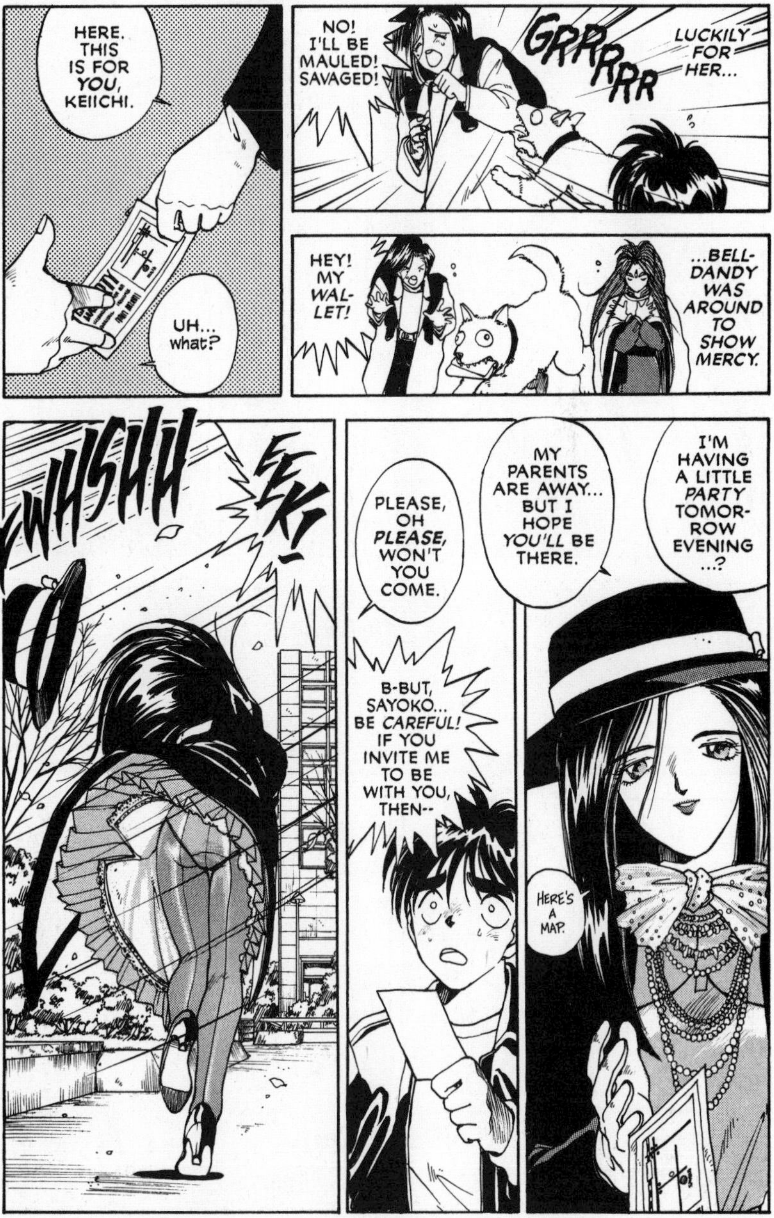
LUCKILY FOR HER...
GRRRRRR
NO! I'LL BE MAULED! SAVAGED!
...BELL-DANDY WAS AROUND TO SHOW MERCY.
HEY! MY WAL-LET!
HERE. THIS IS FOR YOU, KEIICHI.
UH... what?
I'M HAVING A LITTLE PARTY TOMOR-ROW EVENING ...?
MY PARENTS ARE AWAY... BUT I HOPE YOU'LL BE THERE.
HERE'S A MAP.
PLEASE, OH PLEASE, WON'T YOU COME.
B-BUT, SAYOKO... BE CAREFUL! IF YOU INVITE ME TO BE WITH YOU, THEN--
EEK!
FWHSHH

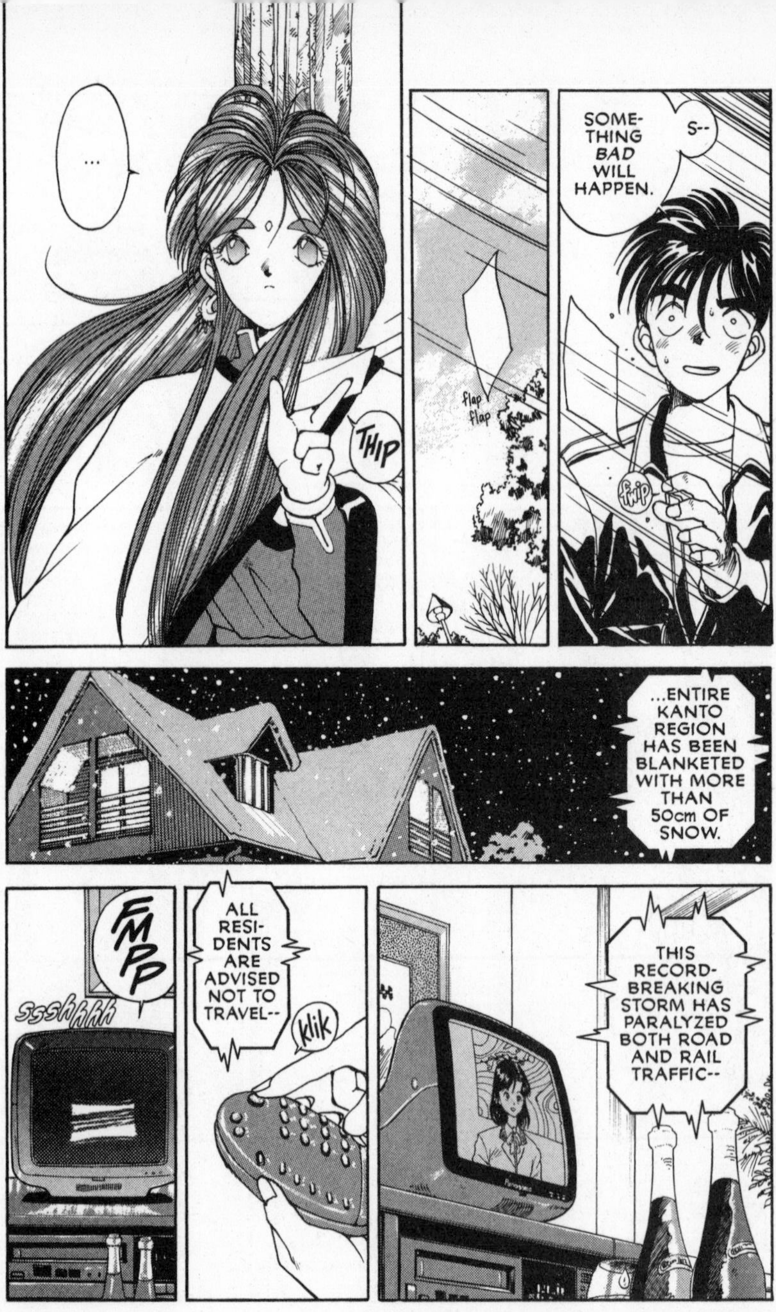
S--
SOME-THING BAD WILL HAPPEN.
fwip
flap flap
...
THIP
...ENTIRE KANTO REGION HAS BEEN BLANKETED WITH MORE THAN 50cm OF SNOW.
THIS RECORD-BREAKING STORM HAS PARALYZED BOTH ROAD AND RAIL TRAFFIC--
ALL RESI-DENTS ARE ADVISED NOT TO TRAVEL--
klik
FMPP
ssshhhh

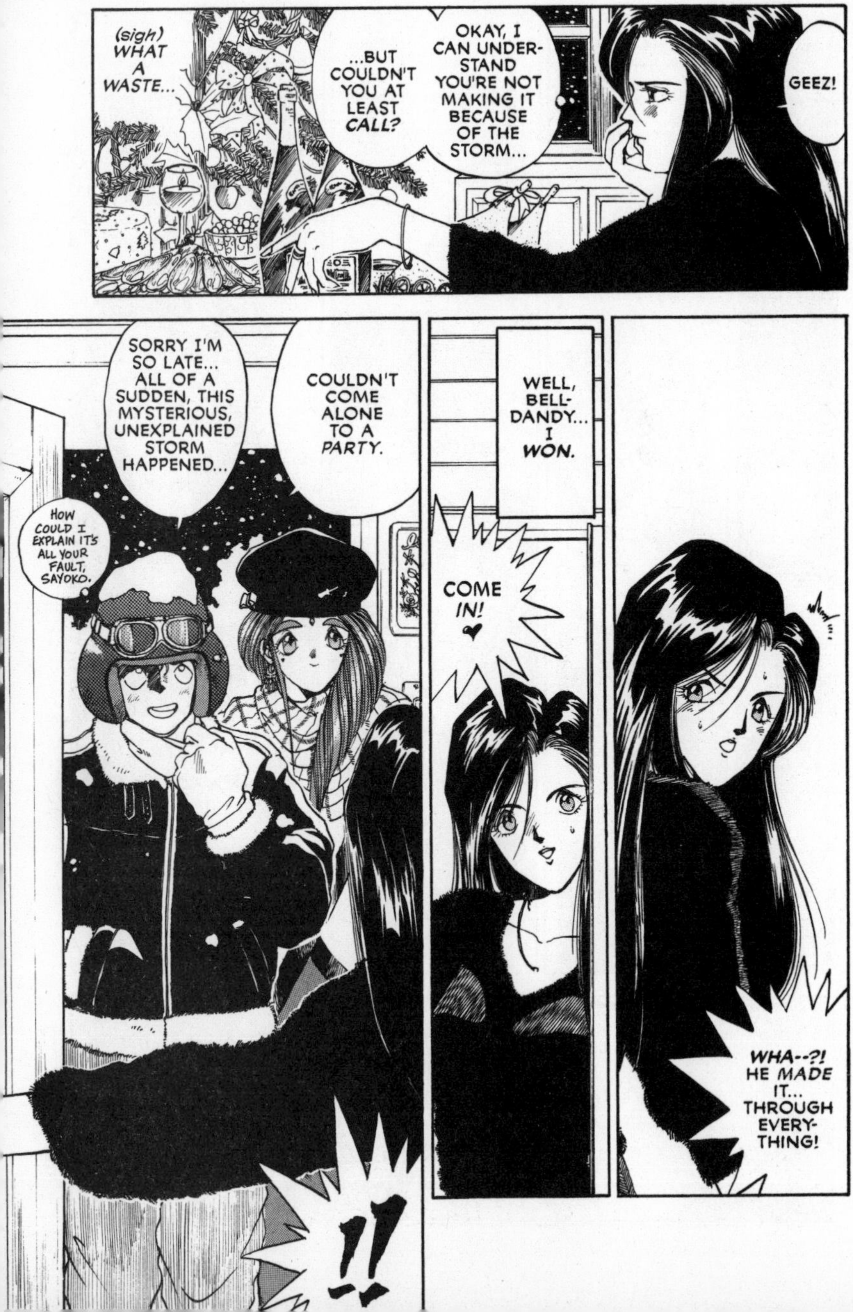

GEEZ!
OKAY, I CAN UNDER-STAND YOU'RE NOT MAKING IT BECAUSE OF THE STORM...
...BUT COULDN'T YOU AT LEAST *CALL?*
(sigh) WHAT A *WASTE*...
WHA--?! HE *MADE* IT... THROUGH EVERY-THING!
WELL, BELL-DANDY... I *WON.*
COME *IN!* ♥
COULDN'T COME ALONE TO A *PARTY.*
SORRY I'M SO LATE... ALL OF A SUDDEN, THIS MYSTERIOUS, UNEXPLAINED STORM HAPPENED...
HOW COULD I EXPLAIN IT'S ALL YOUR FAULT, SAYOKO.
!!

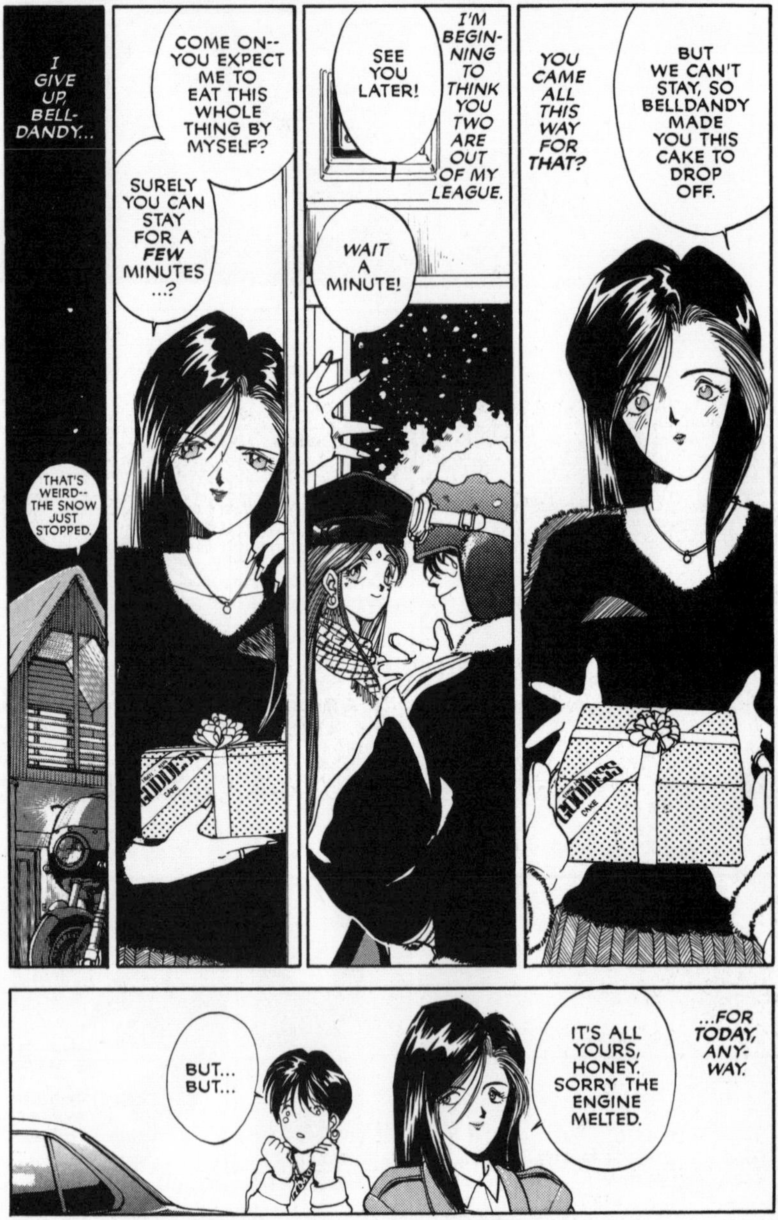

BUT WE CAN'T STAY, SO BELLDANDY MADE YOU THIS CAKE TO DROP OFF.
YOU CAME ALL THIS WAY FOR THAT?
I'M BEGIN-NING TO THINK YOU TWO ARE OUT OF MY LEAGUE.
SEE YOU LATER!
WAIT A MINUTE!
COME ON-- YOU EXPECT ME TO EAT THIS WHOLE THING BY MYSELF?
SURELY YOU CAN STAY FOR A FEW MINUTES ...?
I GIVE UP, BELL-DANDY...
THAT'S WEIRD-- THE SNOW JUST STOPPED.
...FOR TODAY, ANY-WAY.
IT'S ALL YOURS, HONEY. SORRY THE ENGINE MELTED.
BUT... BUT...

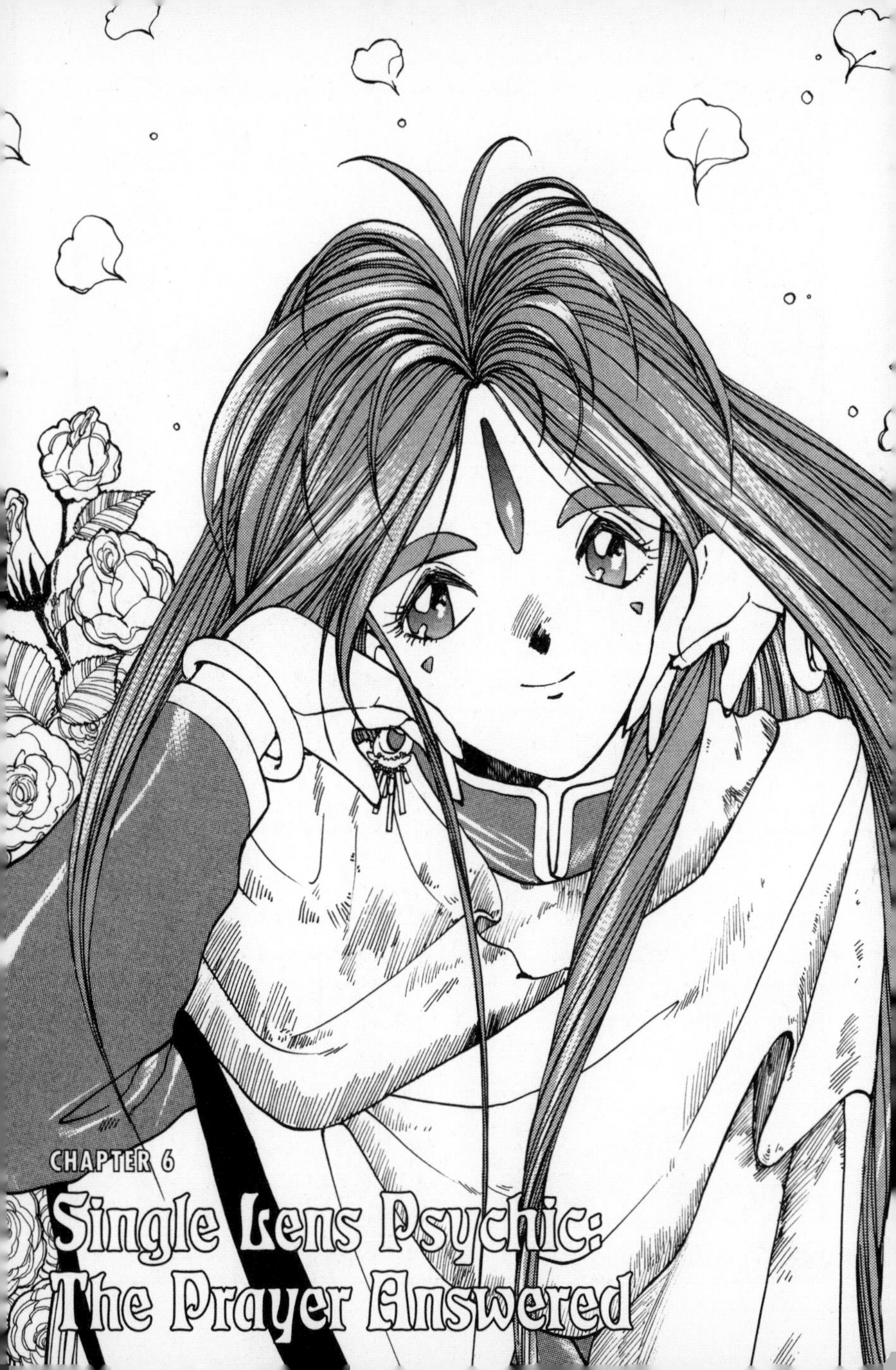

CHAPTER 6
Single Lens Psychic: The Prayer Answered

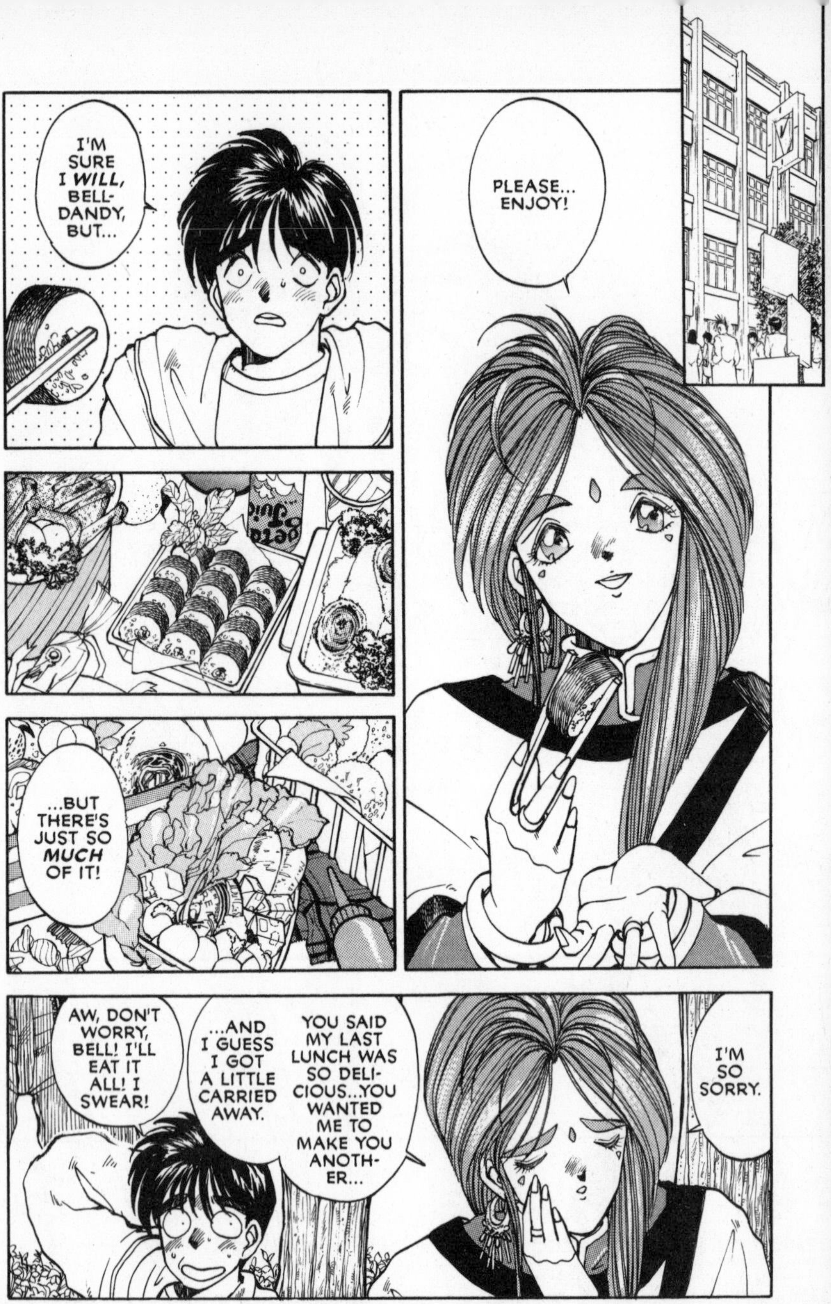
PLEASE... ENJOY!
I'M SURE I *WILL*, BELL-DANDY, BUT...
...BUT THERE'S JUST SO *MUCH* OF IT!
I'M SO SORRY.
YOU SAID MY LAST LUNCH WAS SO DELI-CIOUS...YOU WANTED ME TO MAKE YOU ANOTH-ER...
...AND I GUESS I GOT A LITTLE CARRIED AWAY.
AW, DON'T WORRY, BELL! I'LL EAT IT ALL! I SWEAR!

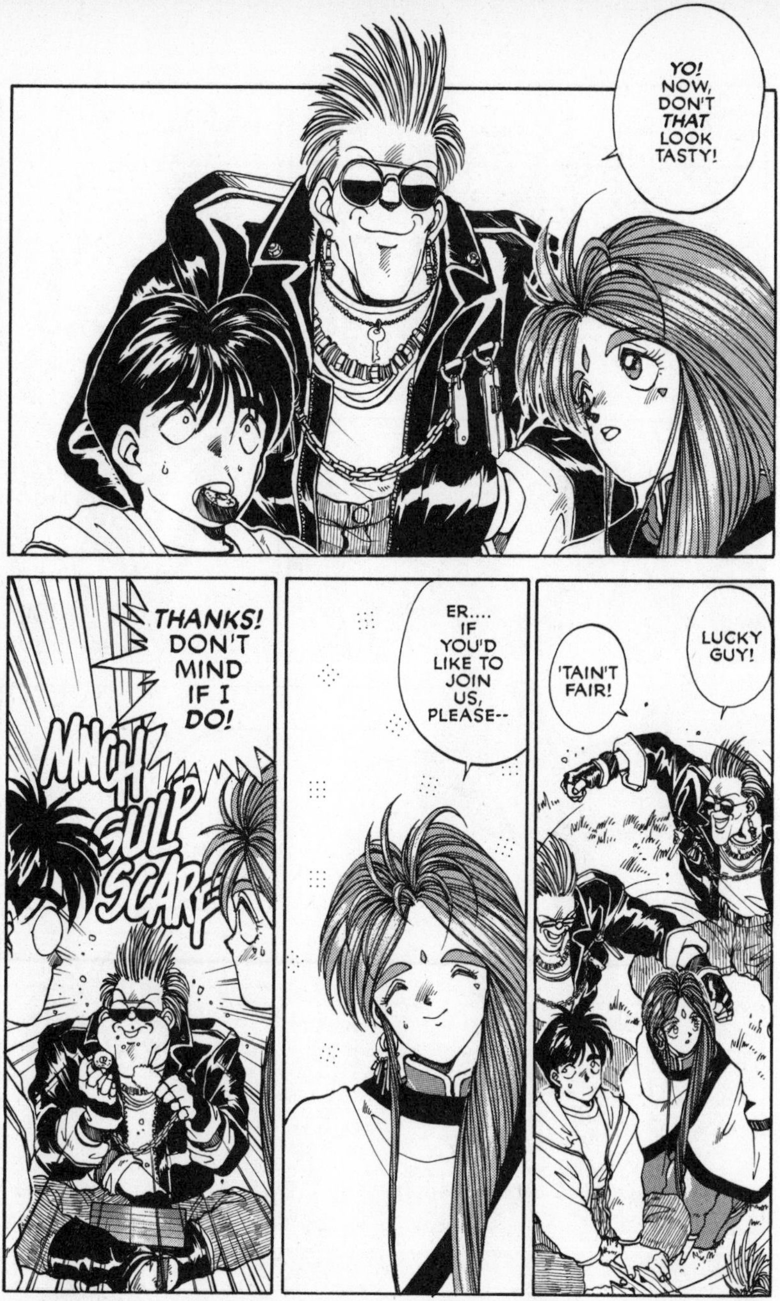
YO! NOW, DON'T THAT LOOK TASTY!
ER.... IF YOU'D LIKE TO JOIN US, PLEASE--
THANKS! DON'T MIND IF I DO!
MNCH
GULP
SCARF
'TAIN'T FAIR!
LUCKY GUY!

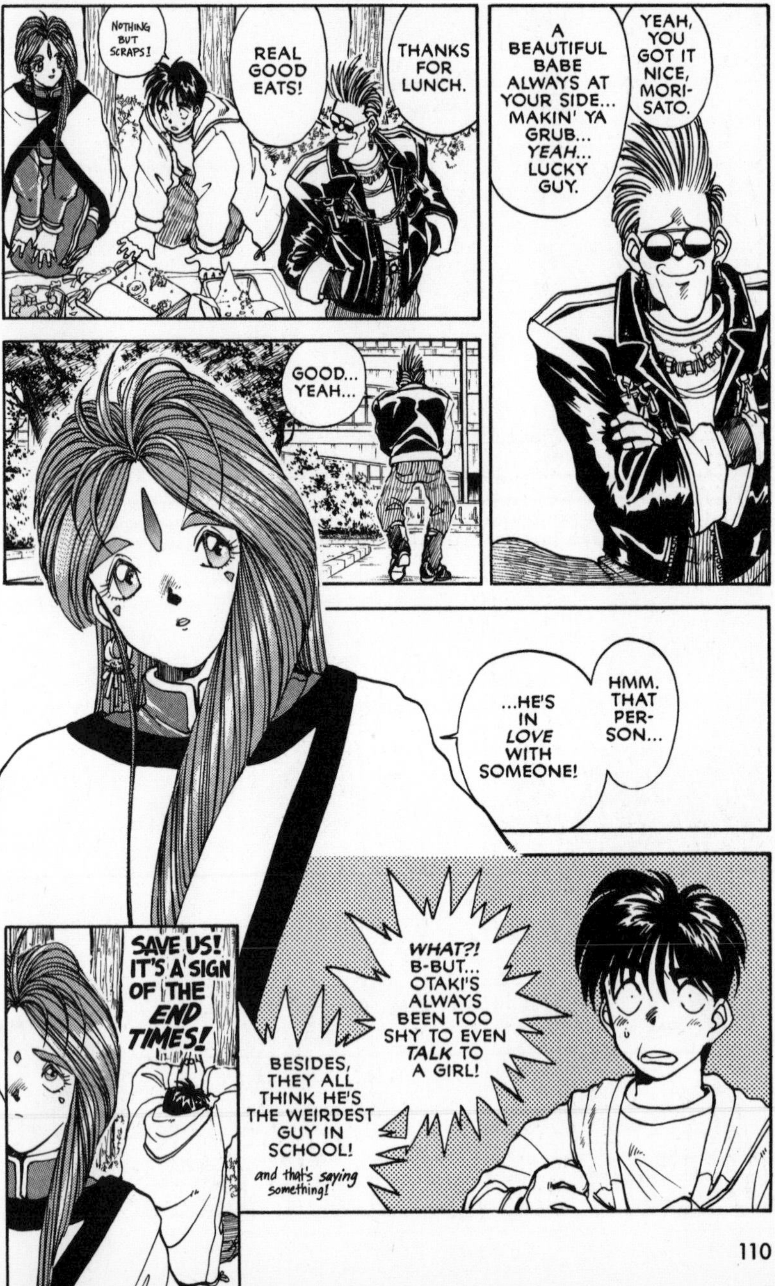
YEAH, YOU GOT IT NICE, MORI-SATO.
A BEAUTIFUL BABE ALWAYS AT YOUR SIDE... MAKIN' YA GRUB... YEAH... LUCKY GUY.
THANKS FOR LUNCH.
REAL GOOD EATS!
NOTHING BUT SCRAPS!
GOOD... YEAH...
HMM. THAT PER-SON...
...HE'S IN LOVE WITH SOMEONE!
WHAT?! B-BUT... OTAKI'S ALWAYS BEEN TOO SHY TO EVEN TALK TO A GIRL!
BESIDES, THEY ALL THINK HE'S THE WEIRDEST GUY IN SCHOOL!
and that's saying something!
SAVE US! IT'S A SIGN OF THE END TIMES!

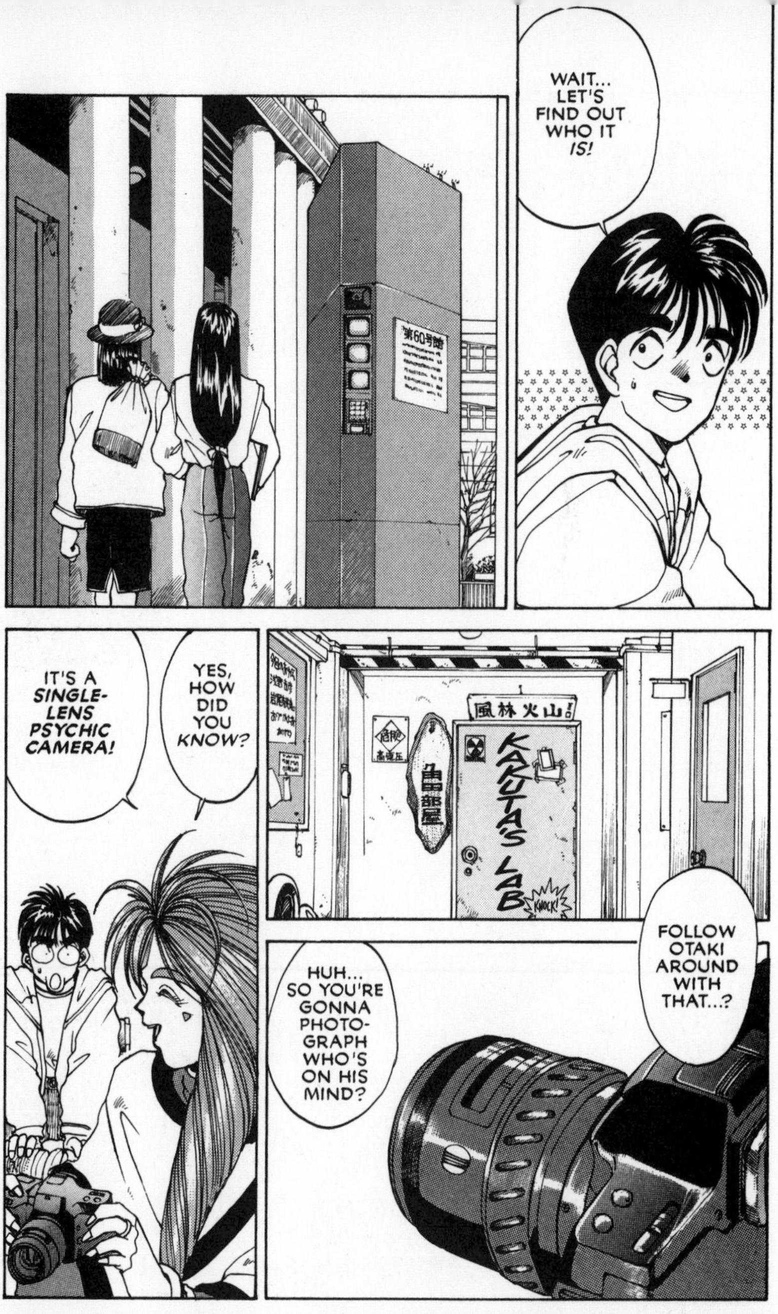
WAIT... LET'S FIND OUT WHO IT *IS!*
風林火山
角田部屋
KAKUTA'S LAB
KNOCK!
FOLLOW OTAKI AROUND WITH THAT...?
HUH... SO YOU'RE GONNA PHOTOGRAPH WHO'S ON HIS MIND?
YES, HOW DID YOU KNOW?
IT'S A *SINGLE-LENS PSYCHIC* CAMERA!

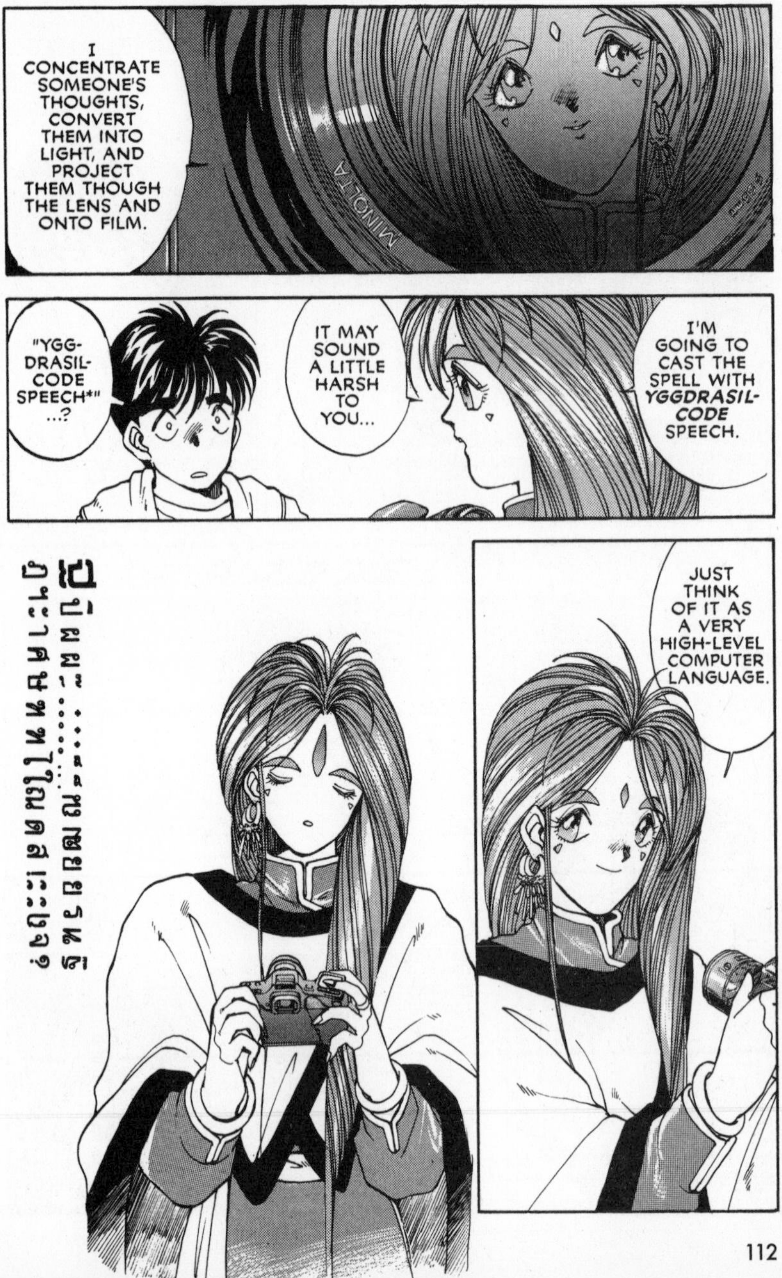
I CONCENTRATE SOMEONE'S THOUGHTS, CONVERT THEM INTO LIGHT, AND PROJECT THEM THOUGH THE LENS AND ONTO FILM.
MINOLTA
I'M GOING TO CAST THE SPELL WITH *YGGDRASIL-CODE* SPEECH.
IT MAY SOUND A LITTLE HARSH TO YOU...
"YGG-DRASIL-CODE SPEECH*" ...?
JUST THINK OF IT AS A VERY HIGH-LEVEL COMPUTER LANGUAGE.

*EACH PULSE-CODE MODULATION EQUALS 5,000 WORDS!

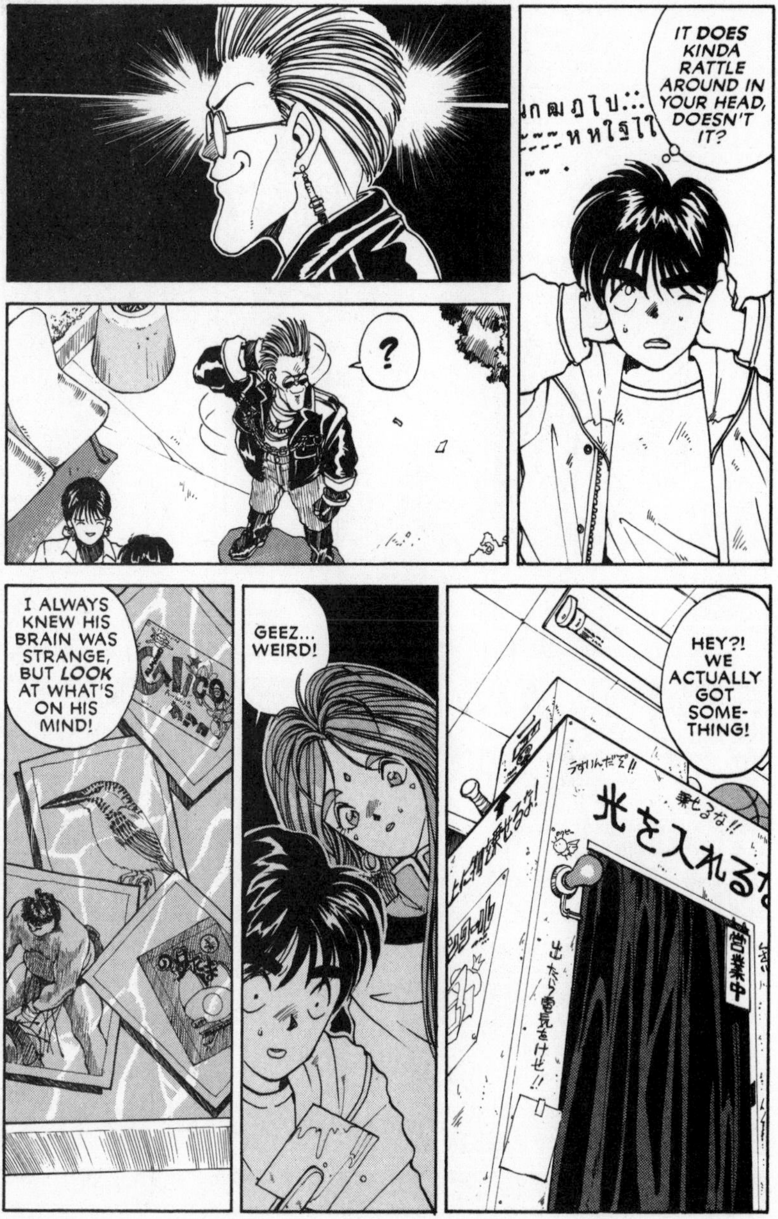
IT DOES KINDA RATTLE AROUND IN YOUR HEAD, DOESN'T IT?
?
HEY?! WE ACTUALLY GOT SOME-THING!
光を入れるな
営業中
GEEZ... WEIRD!
I ALWAYS KNEW HIS BRAIN WAS STRANGE, BUT LOOK AT WHAT'S ON HIS MIND!

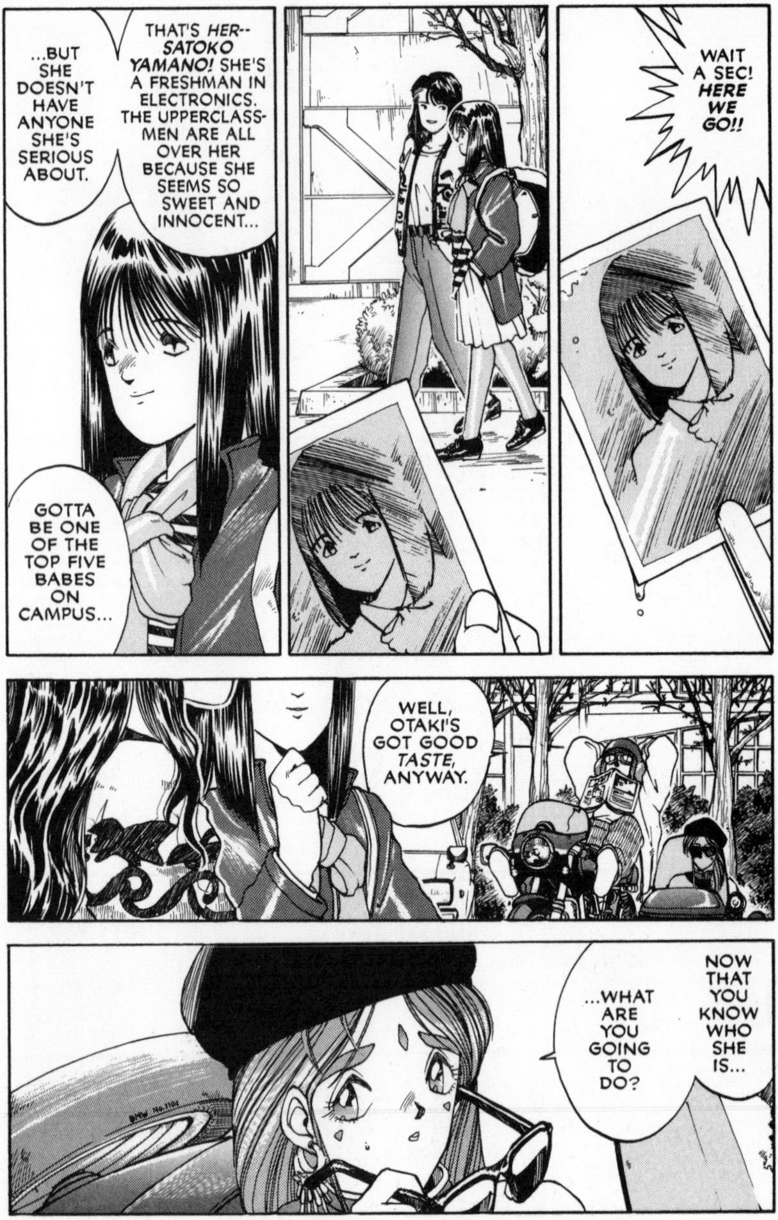
WAIT A SEC! HERE WE GO!!
THAT'S HER-- SATOKO YAMANO! SHE'S A FRESHMAN IN ELECTRONICS. THE UPPERCLASSMEN ARE ALL OVER HER BECAUSE SHE SEEMS SO SWEET AND INNOCENT...
...BUT SHE DOESN'T HAVE ANYONE SHE'S SERIOUS ABOUT.
GOTTA BE ONE OF THE TOP FIVE BABES ON CAMPUS...
WELL, OTAKI'S GOT GOOD TASTE, ANYWAY.
NOW THAT YOU KNOW WHO SHE IS...
...WHAT ARE YOU GOING TO DO?

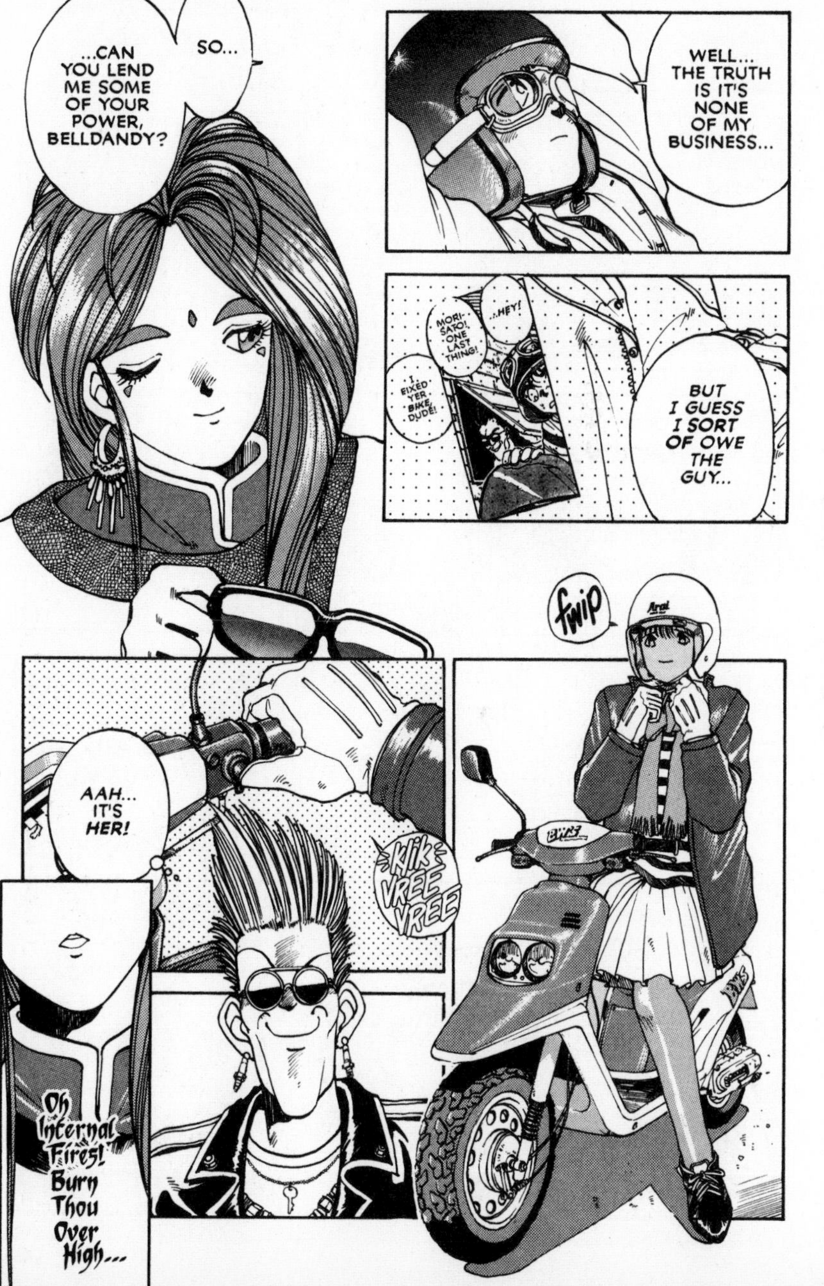
WELL... THE TRUTH IS IT'S NONE OF MY BUSINESS...
...HEY!
MORI-SATO!, ONE LAST THING!
I FIXED YER BIKE, DUDE!
BUT I GUESS I SORT OF OWE THE GUY...
SO...
...CAN YOU LEND ME SOME OF YOUR POWER, BELLDANDY?
fwip
AAH... IT'S HER!
klik VREE VREE
Oh Internal Fires! Burn Thou Over High...

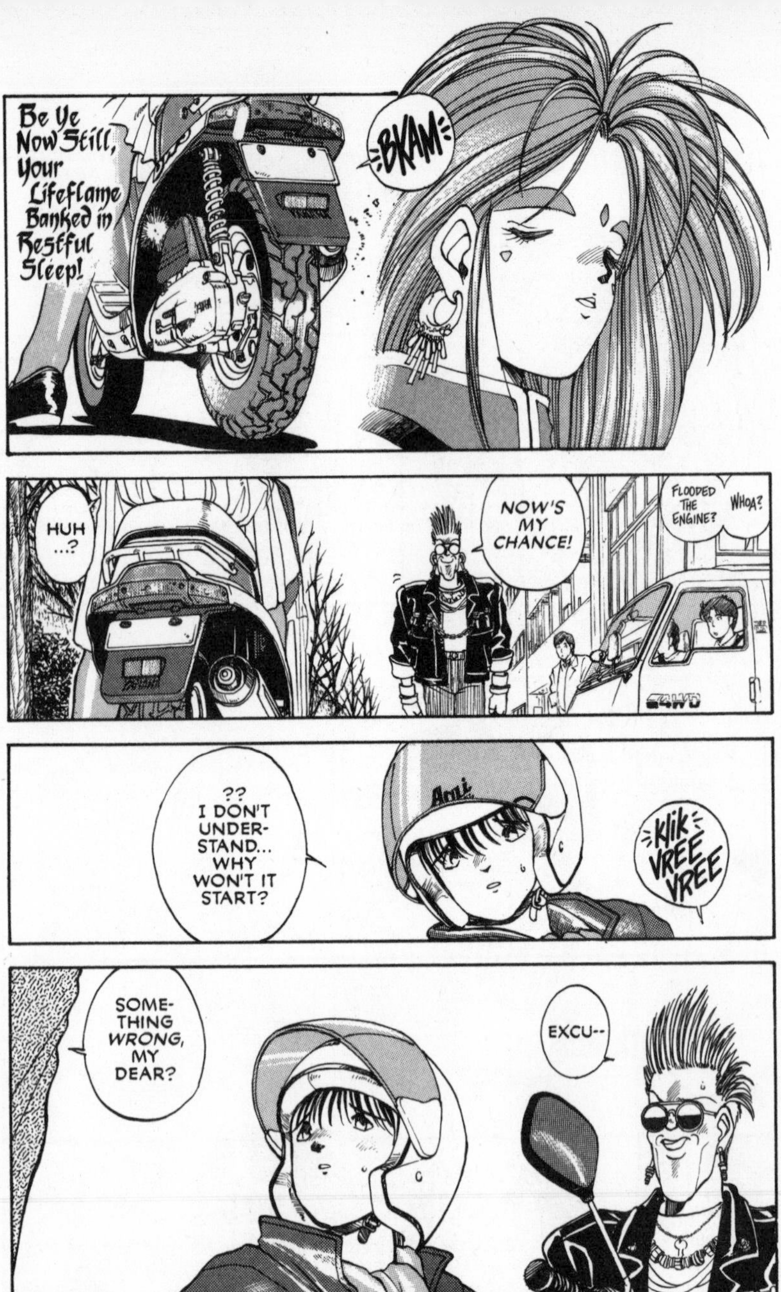

Be Ye Now Still, Your Lifeflame Banked in Restful Sleep!
BKAM
HUH ...?
NOW'S MY CHANCE!
FLOODED THE ENGINE?
WHOA?
?? I DON'T UNDER-STAND... WHY WON'T IT START?
KLIK VREE VREE
SOME-THING WRONG, MY DEAR?
EXCU--

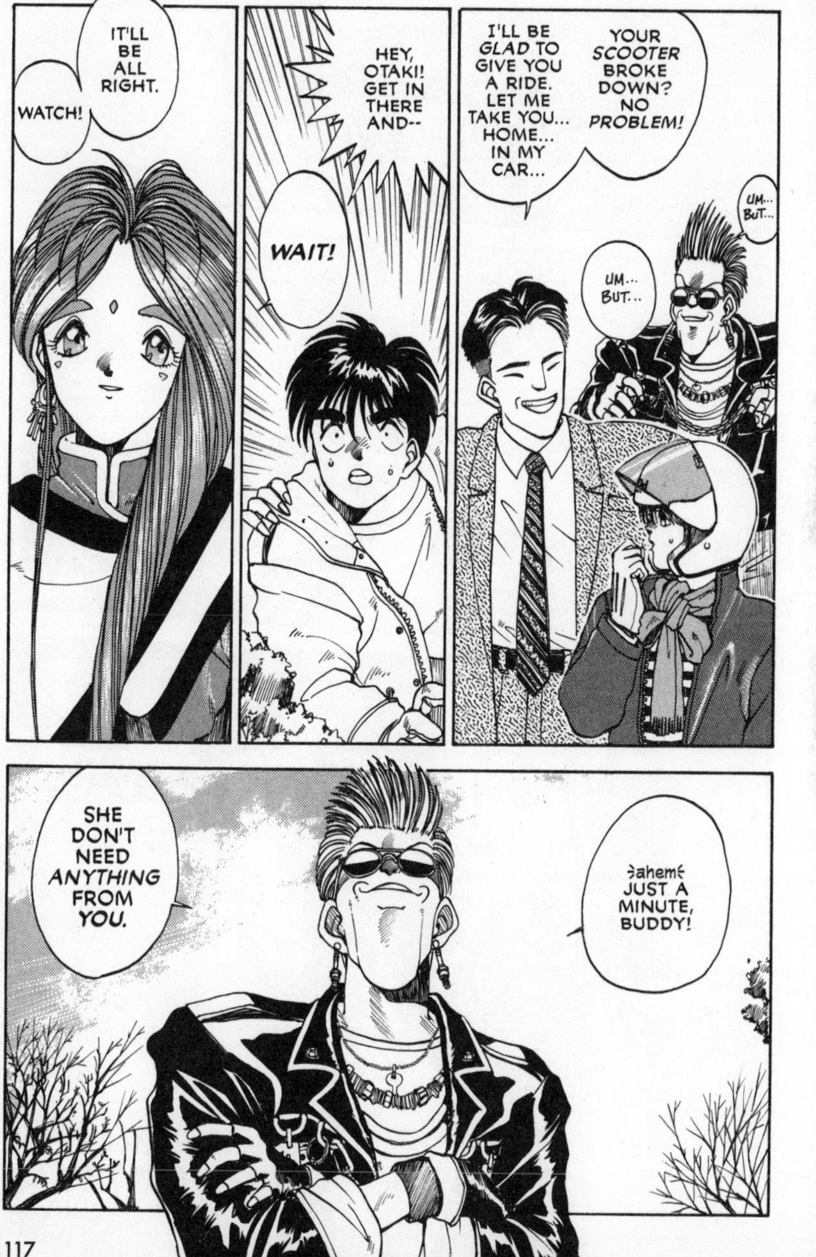
YOUR SCOOTER BROKE DOWN? NO PROBLEM!
I'LL BE GLAD TO GIVE YOU A RIDE. LET ME TAKE YOU... HOME... IN MY CAR...
UM... BUT...
UM... BUT...
HEY, OTAKI! GET IN THERE AND--
WAIT!
IT'LL BE ALL RIGHT.
WATCH!
ahem JUST A MINUTE, BUDDY!
SHE DON'T NEED ANYTHING FROM YOU.

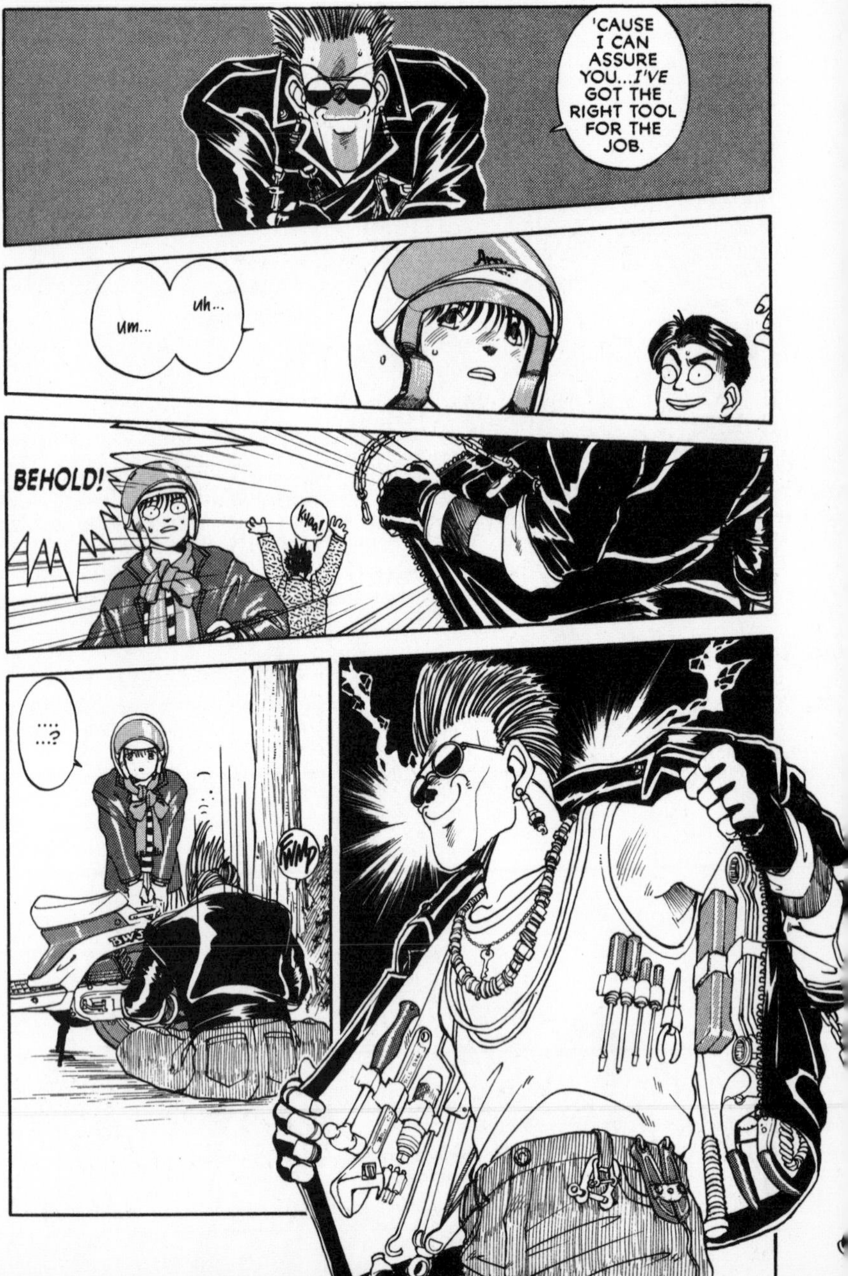
'CAUSE I CAN ASSURE YOU...I'VE GOT THE RIGHT TOOL FOR THE JOB.
uh...
um...
Kyaa!
BEHOLD!
FWMP
....
...?

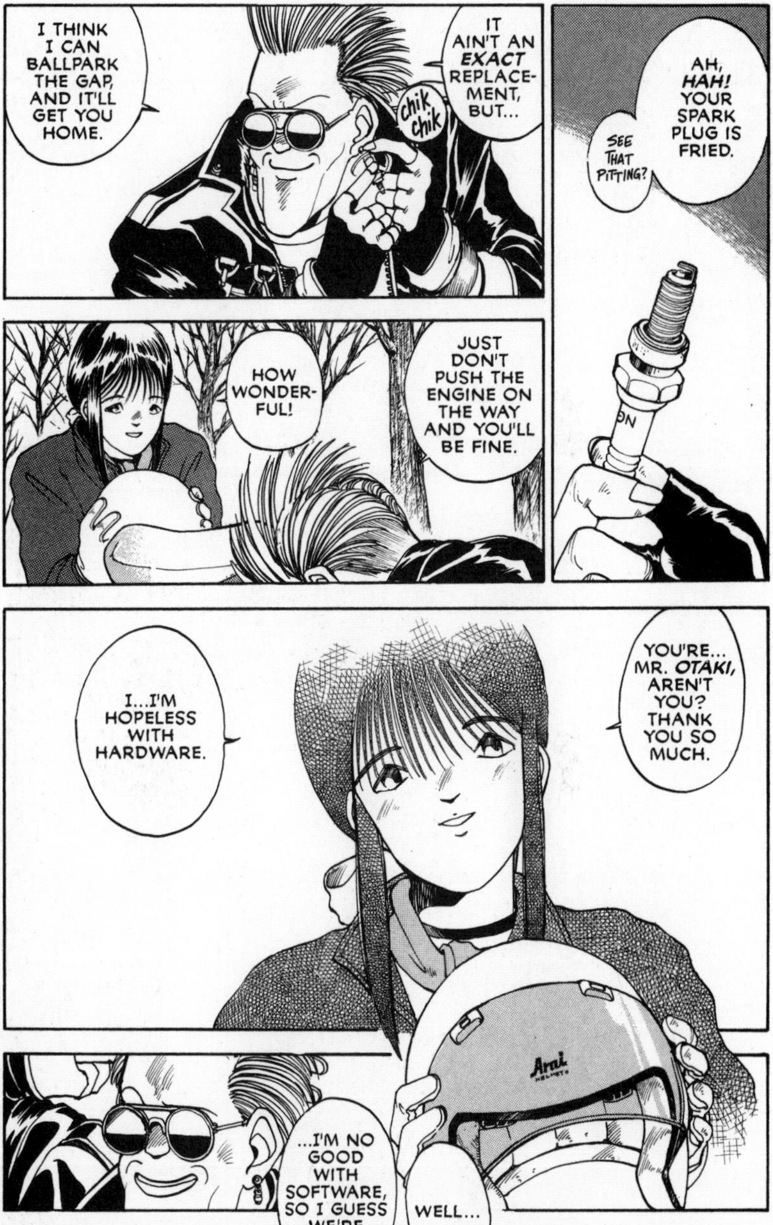
AH, HAH! YOUR SPARK PLUG IS FRIED.
SEE THAT PITTING?
IT AIN'T AN EXACT REPLACEMENT, BUT...
chik chik
I THINK I CAN BALLPARK THE GAP, AND IT'LL GET YOU HOME.
JUST DON'T PUSH THE ENGINE ON THE WAY AND YOU'LL BE FINE.
HOW WONDERFUL!
YOU'RE... MR. OTAKI, AREN'T YOU? THANK YOU SO MUCH.
I...I'M HOPELESS WITH HARDWARE.
Arai
WELL...
...I'M NO GOOD WITH SOFTWARE, SO I GUESS WE'RE EVEN.

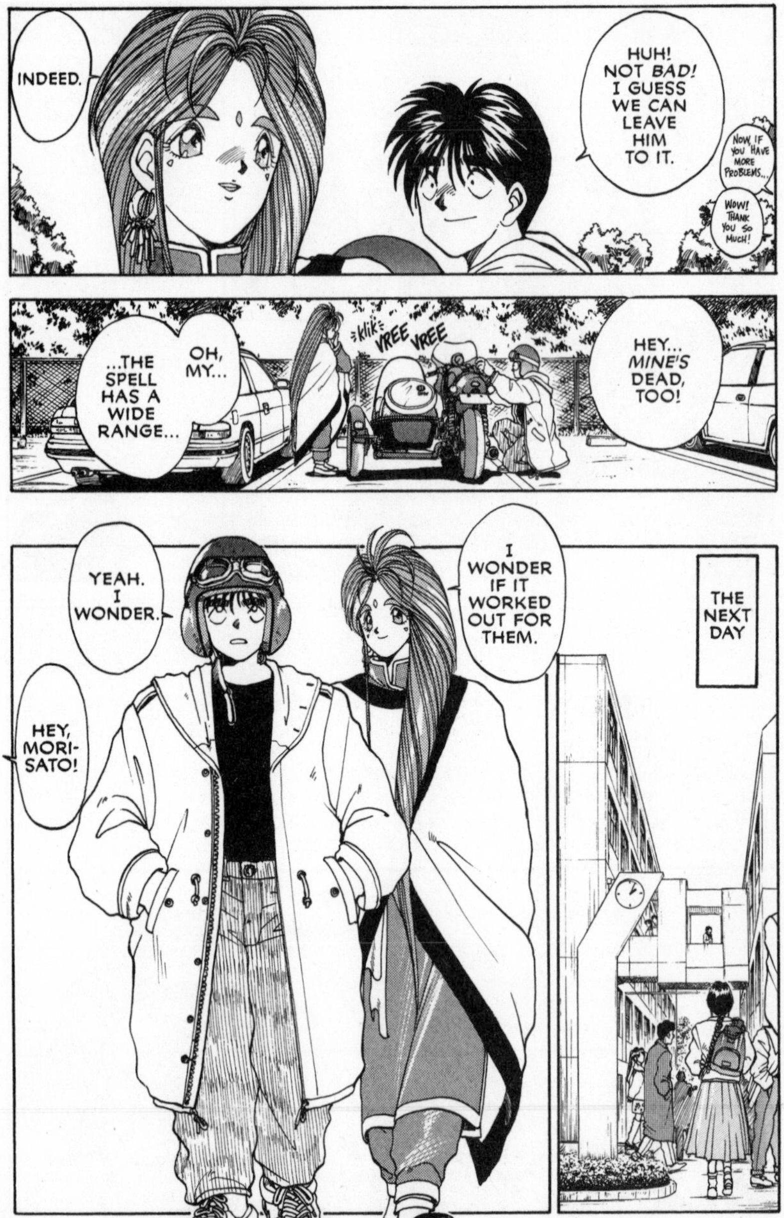
HUH! NOT *BAD!* I GUESS WE CAN LEAVE HIM TO IT.
NOW, IF YOU HAVE MORE PROBLEMS...
WOW! THANK YOU SO MUCH!
INDEED.
HEY... *MINE'S* DEAD, TOO!
klik
VREE VREE
OH, MY...
...THE SPELL HAS A WIDE RANGE...
THE NEXT DAY
I WONDER IF IT WORKED OUT FOR THEM.
YEAH. I WONDER.
HEY, MORI-SATO!

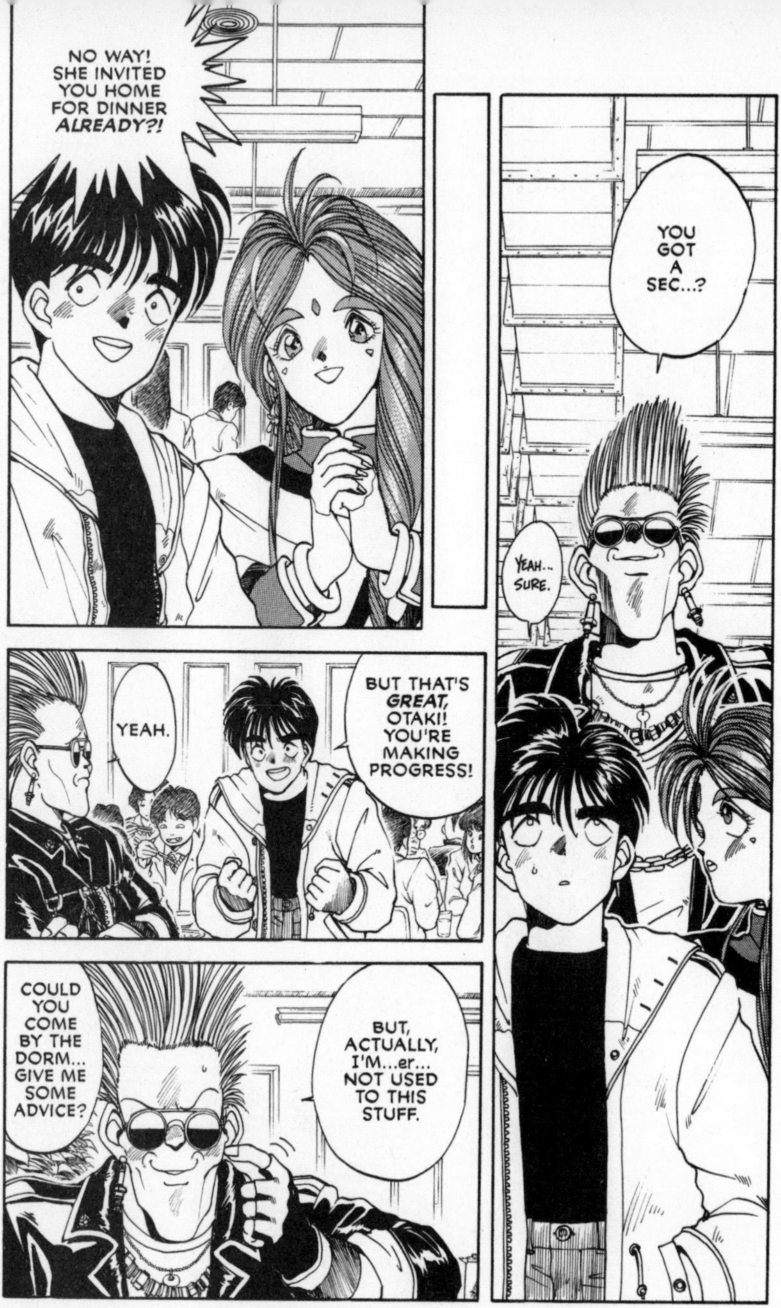
NO WAY! SHE INVITED YOU HOME FOR DINNER *ALREADY?!*
YEAH.
BUT THAT'S *GREAT,* OTAKI! YOU'RE MAKING PROGRESS!
COULD YOU COME BY THE DORM... GIVE ME SOME ADVICE?
BUT, ACTUALLY, I'M...er... NOT USED TO THIS STUFF.
YOU GOT A SEC...?
YEAH... SURE.

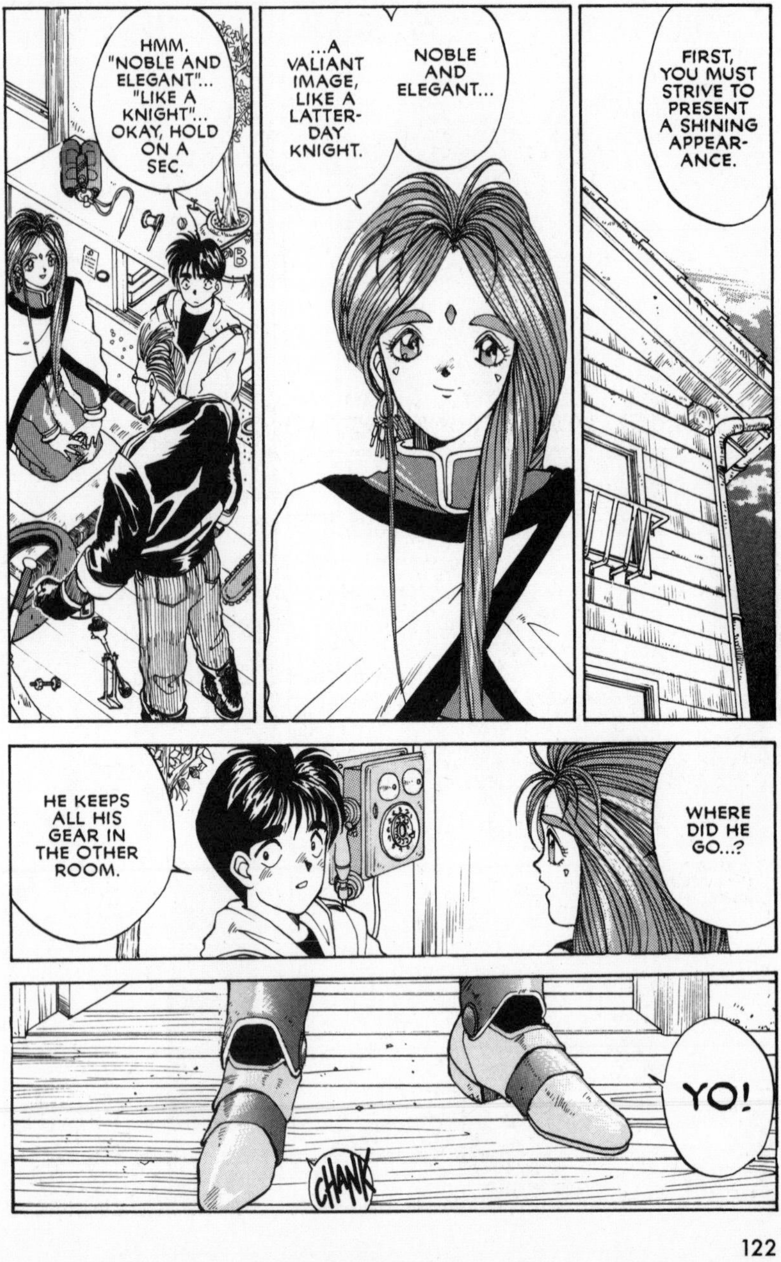
FIRST, YOU MUST STRIVE TO PRESENT A SHINING APPEARANCE.
NOBLE AND ELEGANT...
...A VALIANT IMAGE, LIKE A LATTER-DAY KNIGHT.
HMM. "NOBLE AND ELEGANT"... "LIKE A KNIGHT"... OKAY, HOLD ON A SEC.
WHERE DID HE GO...?
HE KEEPS ALL HIS GEAR IN THE OTHER ROOM.
YO!
CHANK

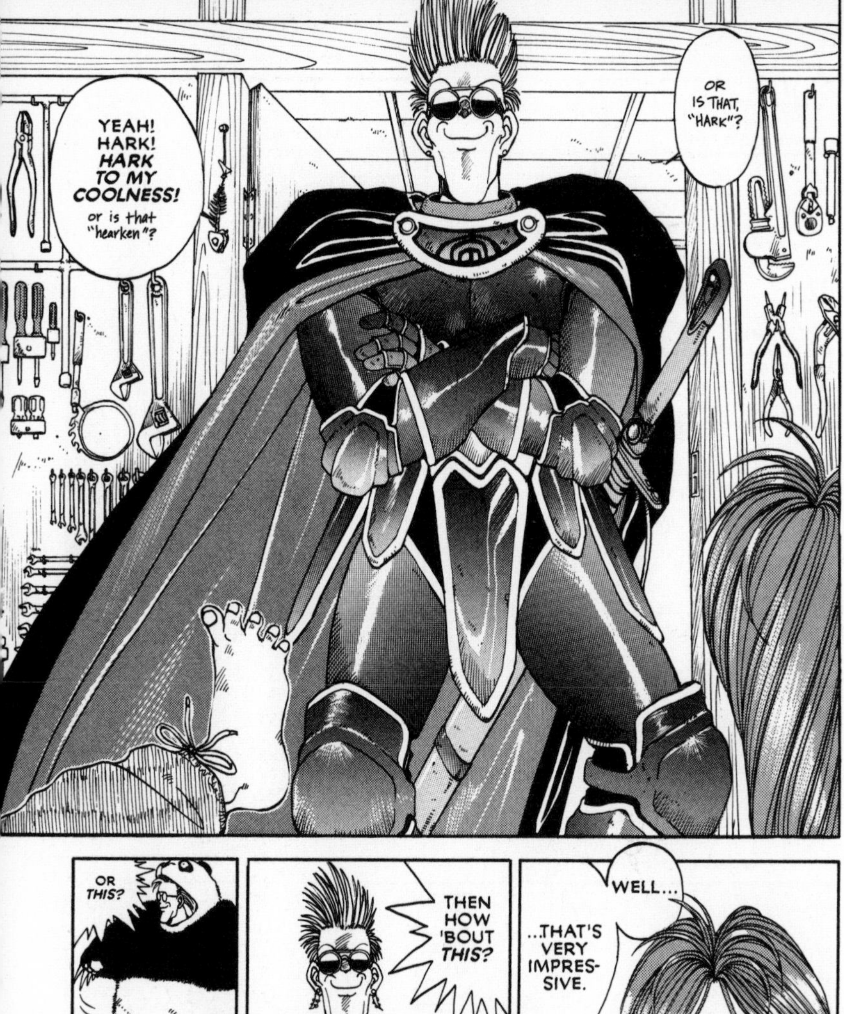
YEAH! HARK! HARK TO MY COOLNESS!
or is that "hearken"?
OR IS THAT, "HARK"?

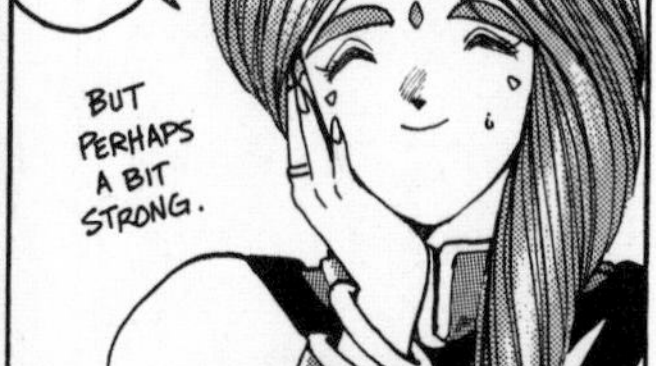
WELL...
...THAT'S VERY IMPRES-SIVE.
BUT PERHAPS A BIT STRONG.

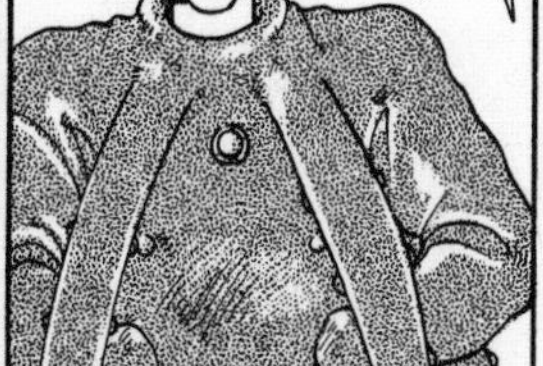
THEN HOW 'BOUT THIS?

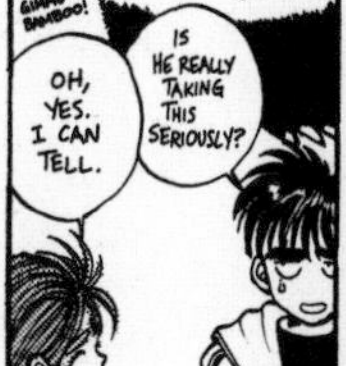
OR THIS?
ARGH! GIMME BAMBOO!
IS HE REALLY TAKING THIS SERIOUSLY?
OH, YES. I CAN TELL.

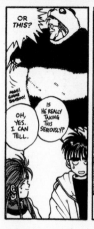

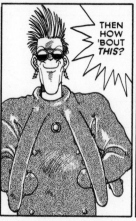

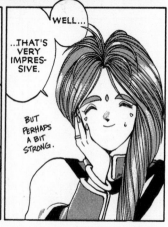

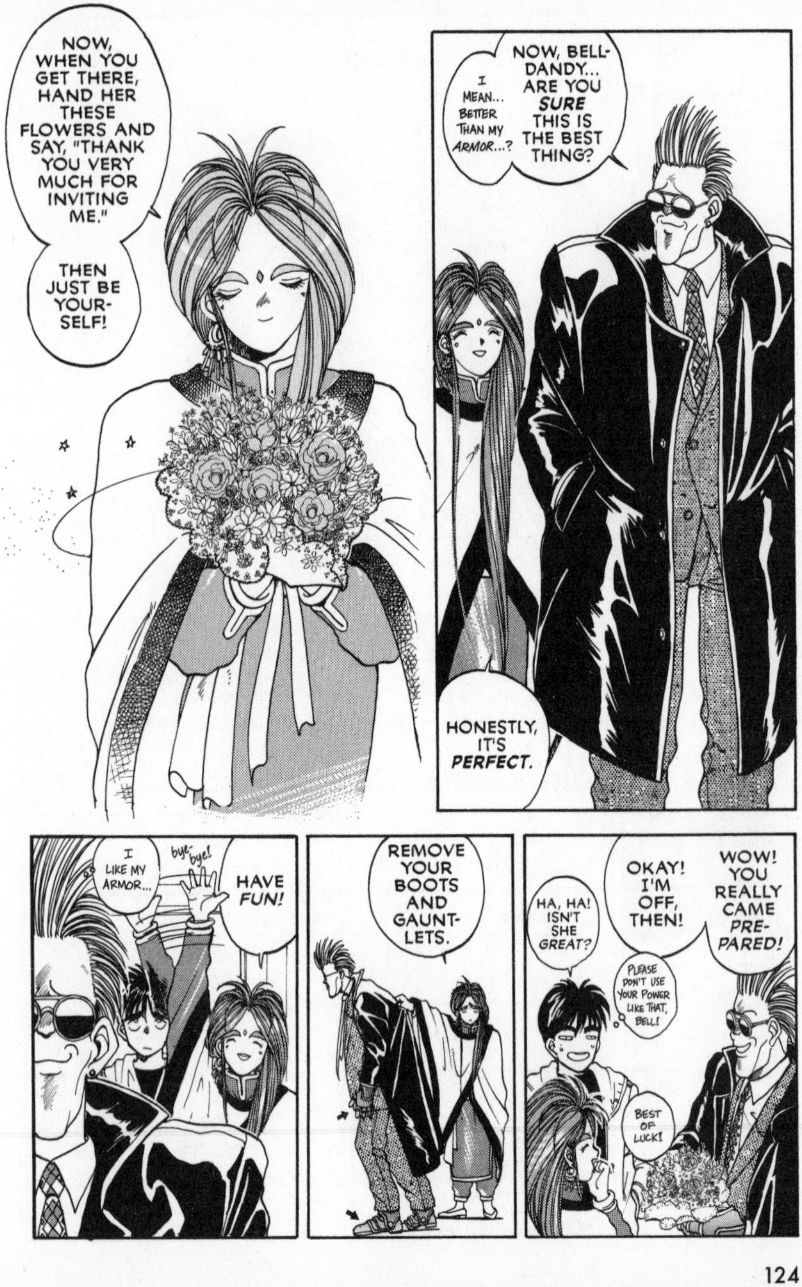
NOW, BELL-DANDY... ARE YOU *SURE* THIS IS THE BEST THING?
I MEAN... BETTER THAN MY *ARMOR*...?
HONESTLY, IT'S *PERFECT*.
NOW, WHEN YOU GET THERE, HAND HER THESE FLOWERS AND SAY, "THANK YOU VERY MUCH FOR INVITING ME."
THEN JUST BE YOUR-SELF!
WOW! YOU REALLY CAME *PRE-PARED!*
OKAY! I'M OFF, THEN!
HA, HA! ISN'T SHE *GREAT?*
PLEASE DON'T USE YOUR POWER LIKE THAT, BELL!
BEST OF LUCK!
REMOVE YOUR BOOTS AND GAUNT-LETS.
HAVE *FUN!*
bye-bye!
I LIKE MY ARMOR...

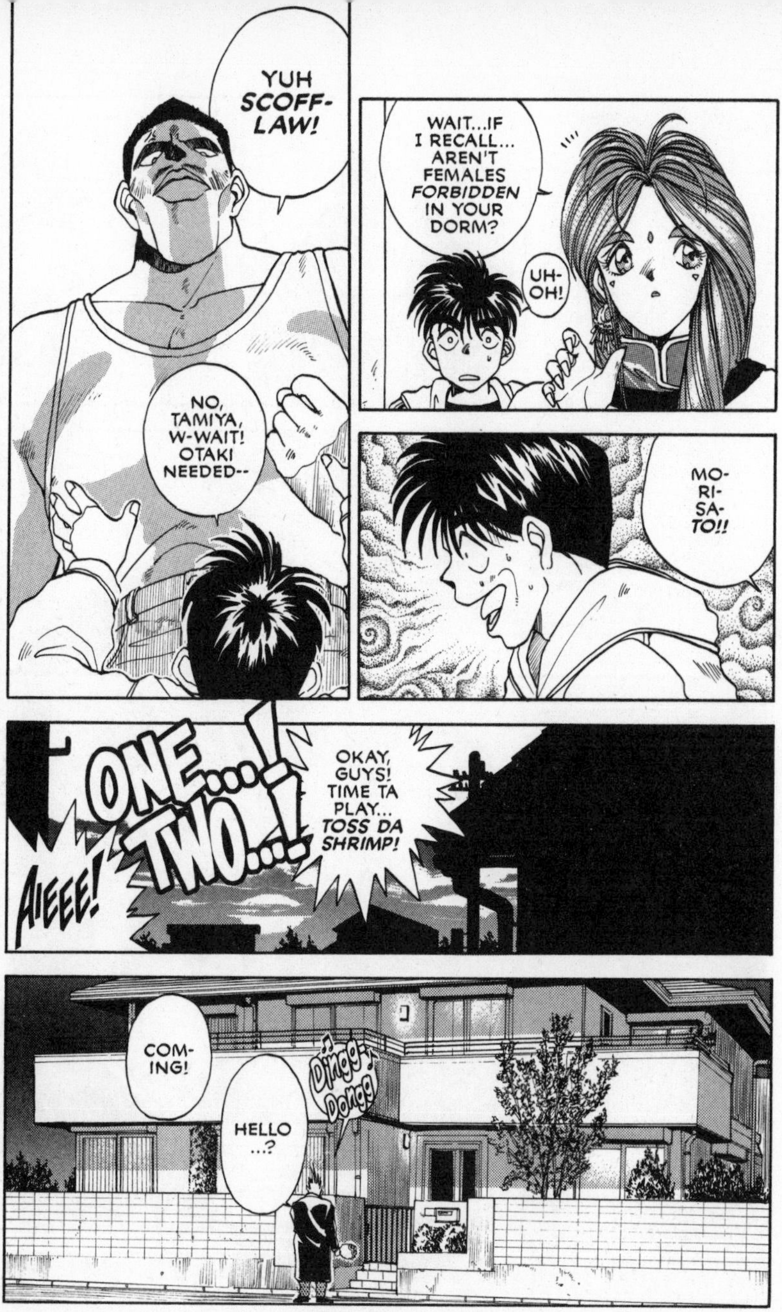
WAIT...IF I RECALL... AREN'T FEMALES *FORBIDDEN* IN YOUR DORM?
UH-OH!
MO-RI-SA-*TO!!*
YUH *SCOFF-LAW!*
NO, TAMIYA, W-WAIT! OTAKI NEEDED--
OKAY, GUYS! TIME TA PLAY... *TOSS DA SHRIMP!*
ONE...!
TWO...!
AIEEE!
Dingg Dongg
HELLO ...?
COM-ING!

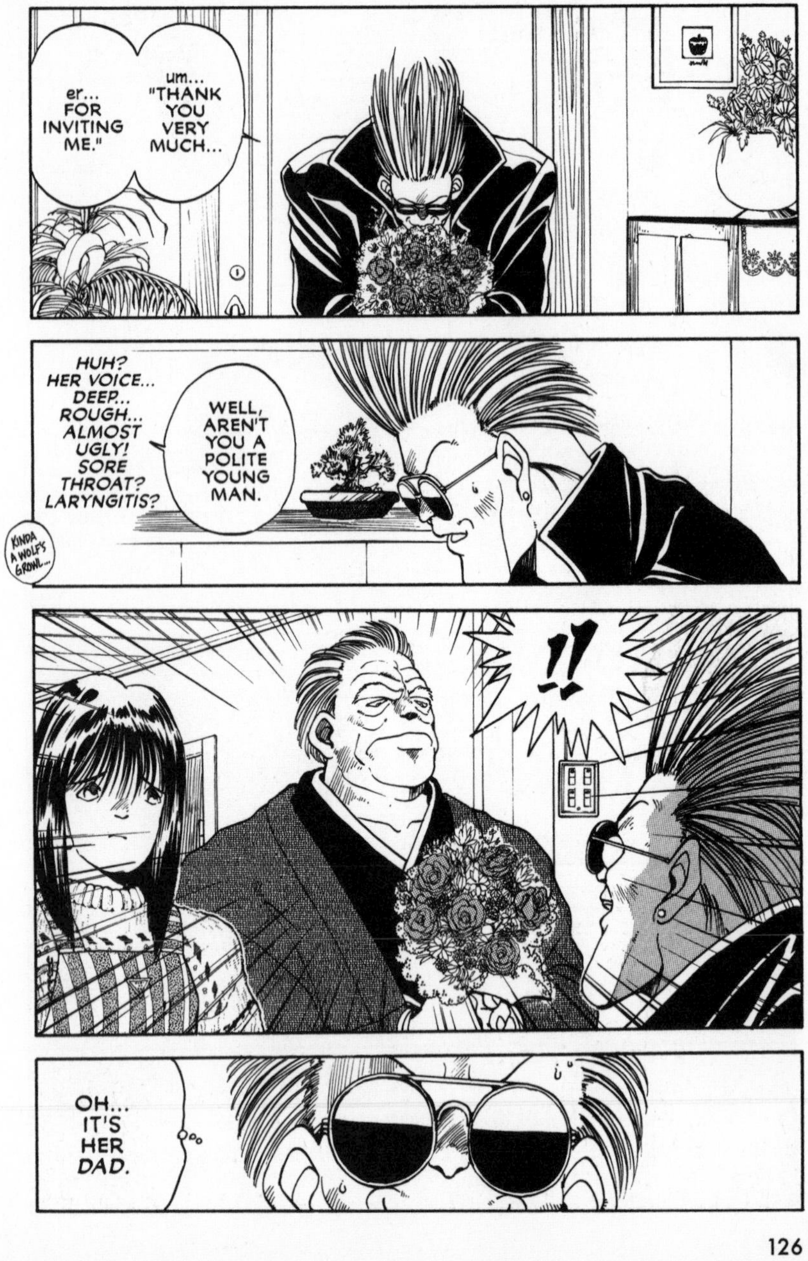
um... "THANK YOU VERY MUCH...
er... FOR INVITING ME."
WELL, AREN'T YOU A POLITE YOUNG MAN.
HUH? HER VOICE... DEEP... ROUGH... ALMOST UGLY! SORE THROAT? LARYNGITIS?
KINDA A WOLF'S GROWL...
!!
OH... IT'S HER DAD.

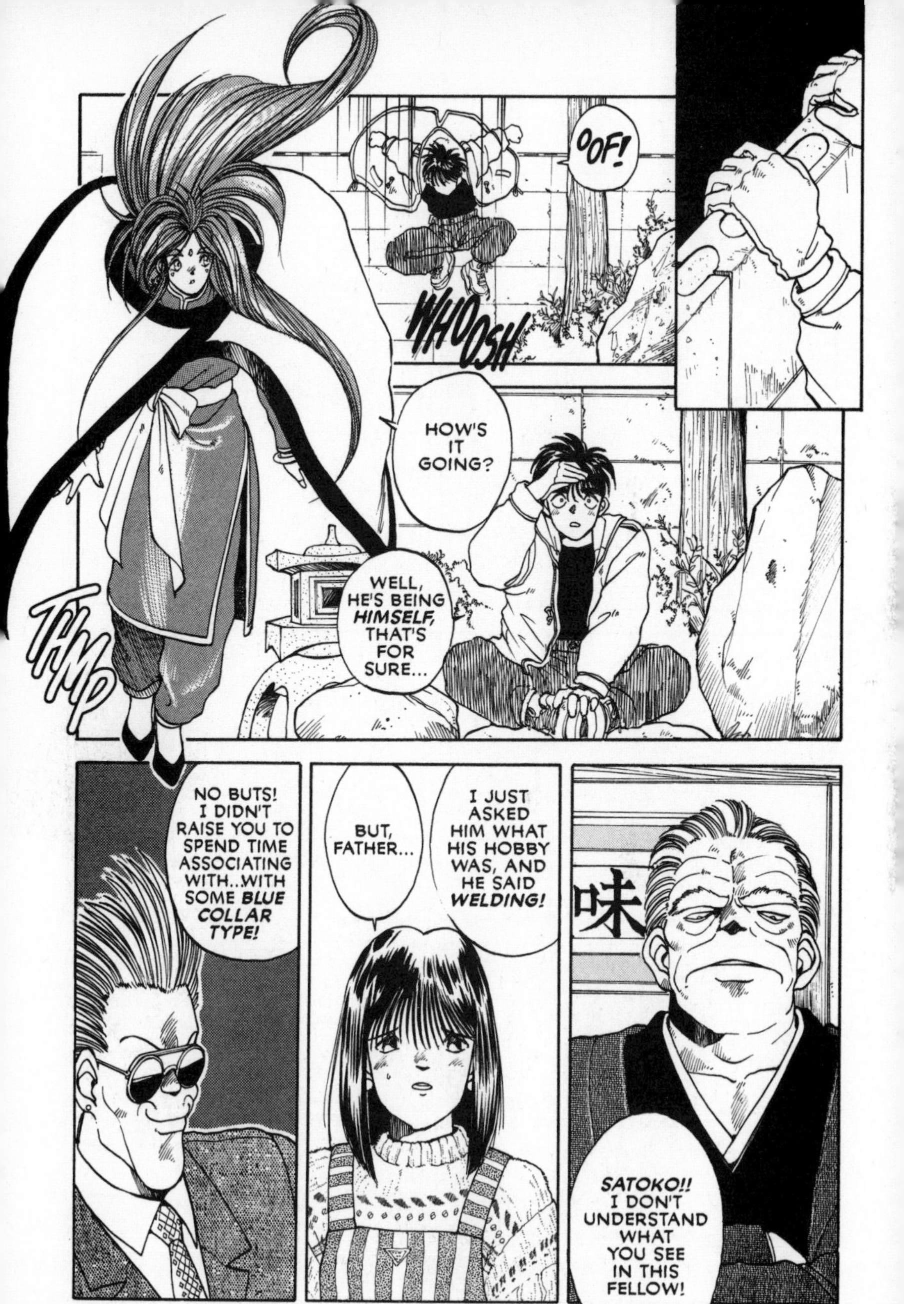

OOF!
WHOOSH
HOW'S IT GOING?
WELL, HE'S BEING *HIMSELF,* THAT'S FOR SURE...
THMP
SATOKO!! I DON'T UNDERSTAND WHAT YOU SEE IN THIS FELLOW!
I JUST ASKED HIM WHAT HIS HOBBY WAS, AND HE SAID *WELDING!*
BUT, FATHER...
NO BUTS! I DIDN'T RAISE YOU TO SPEND TIME ASSOCIATING WITH...WITH SOME *BLUE COLLAR TYPE!*

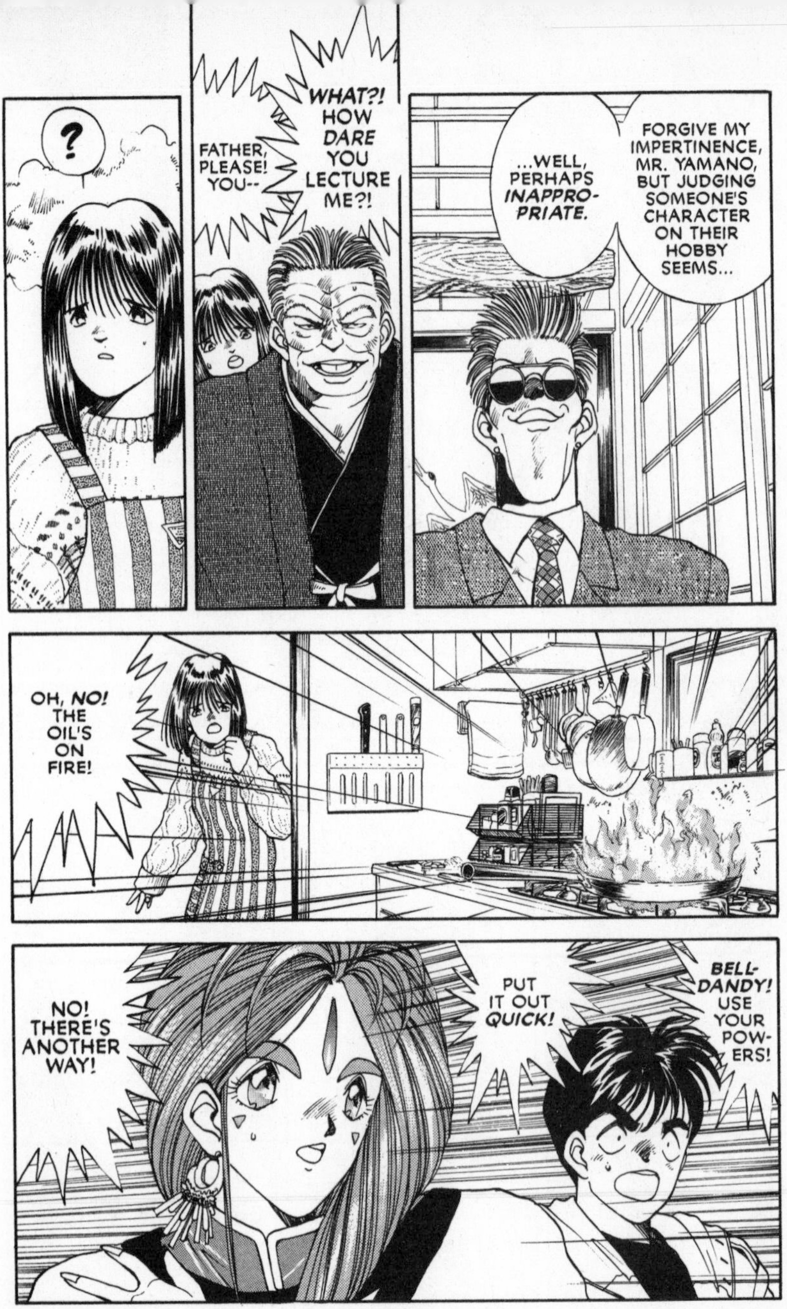

FORGIVE MY IMPERTINENCE, MR. YAMANO, BUT JUDGING SOMEONE'S CHARACTER ON THEIR HOBBY SEEMS...
...WELL, PERHAPS *INAPPROPRIATE.*
WHAT?! HOW *DARE* YOU LECTURE ME?!
FATHER, PLEASE! YOU--
?
OH, *NO!* THE OIL'S ON FIRE!
BELL-DANDY! USE YOUR POWERS!
PUT IT OUT *QUICK!*
NO! THERE'S ANOTHER WAY!

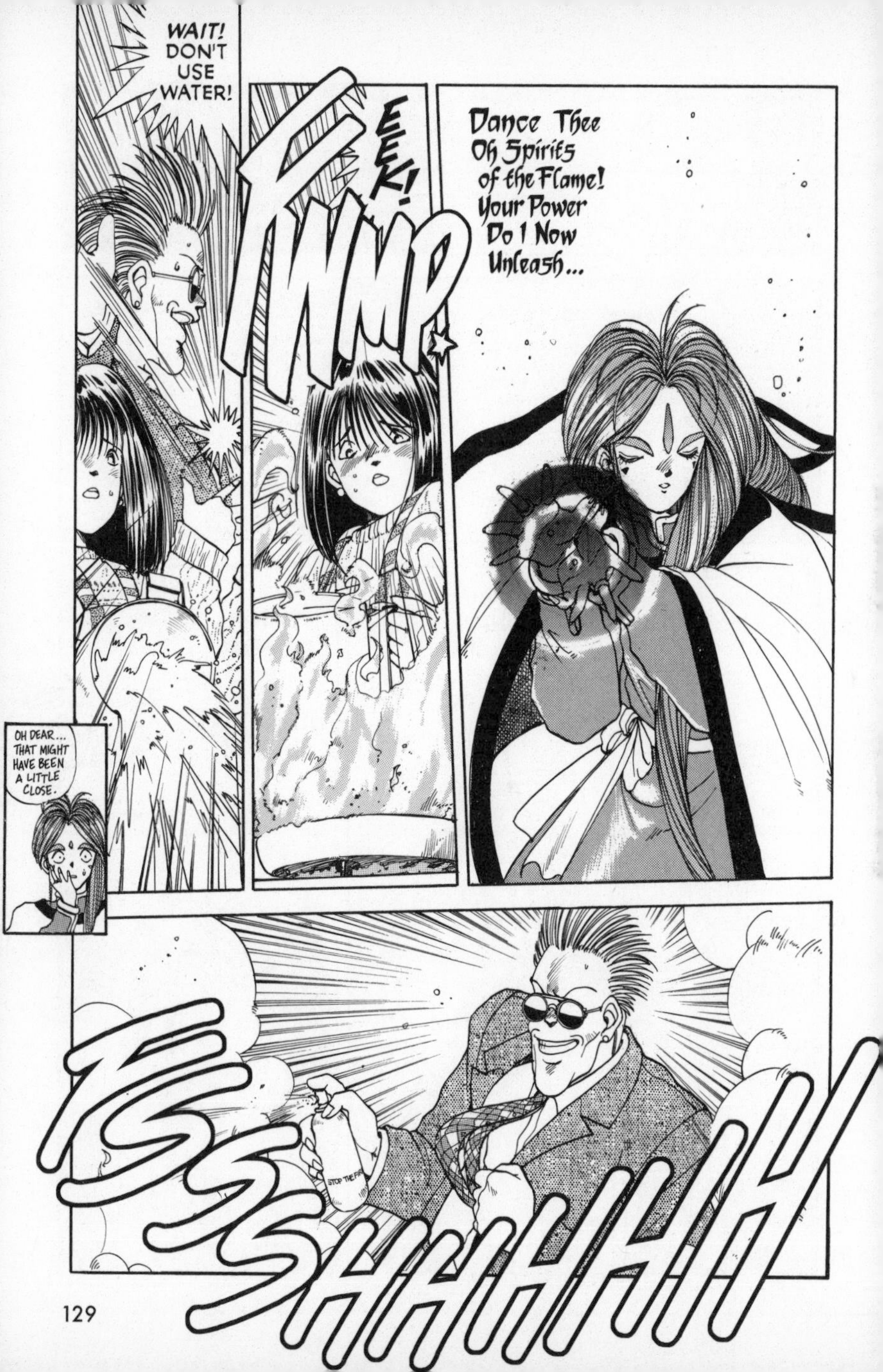
Dance Thee Oh Spirits of the Flame! Your Power Do I Now Unleash...
EEEK!
FWMP!
WAIT! DON'T USE WATER!
OH DEAR... THAT MIGHT HAVE BEEN A LITTLE CLOSE.
ISSSHHHHHH

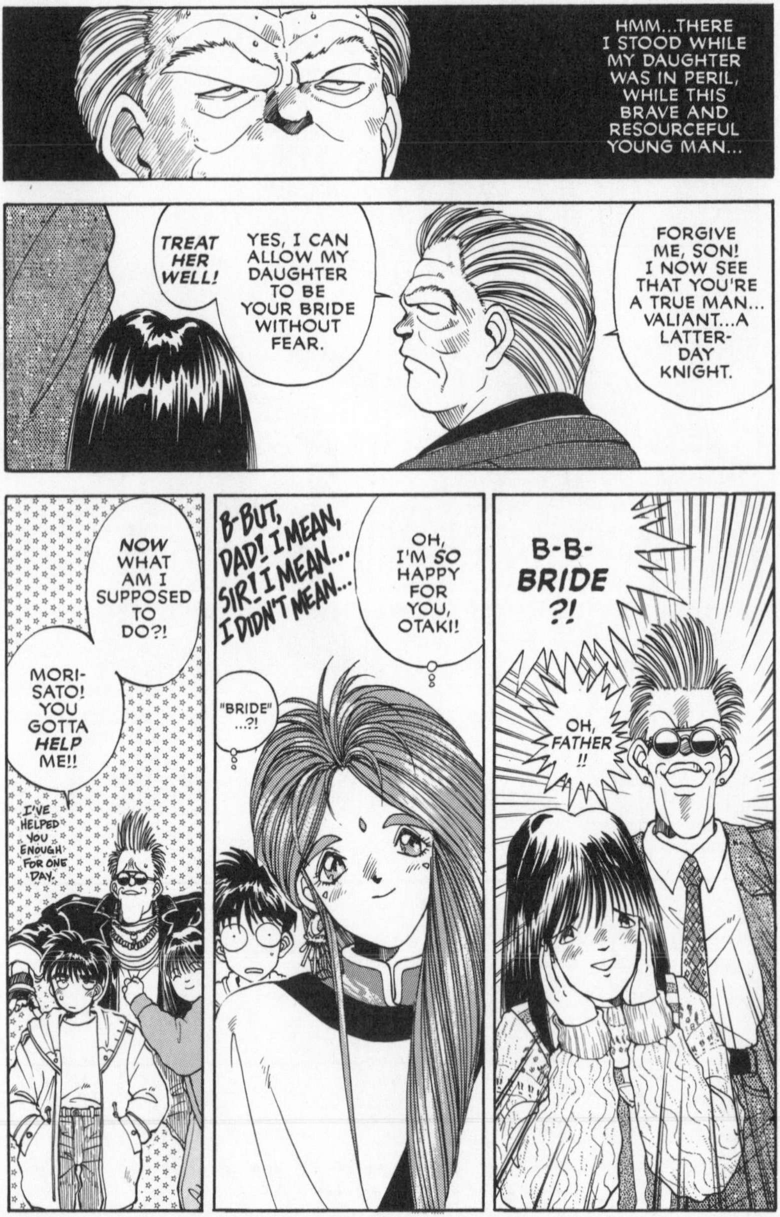
HMM...THERE I STOOD WHILE MY DAUGHTER WAS IN PERIL, WHILE THIS BRAVE AND RESOURCEFUL YOUNG MAN...
FORGIVE ME, SON! I NOW SEE THAT YOU'RE A TRUE MAN... VALIANT...A LATTER-DAY KNIGHT.
YES, I CAN ALLOW MY DAUGHTER TO BE YOUR BRIDE WITHOUT FEAR.
TREAT HER WELL!
B-B-BRIDE ?!
OH, FATHER !!
OH, I'M SO HAPPY FOR YOU, OTAKI!
B-BUT, DAD! I MEAN, SIR! I MEAN... I DIDN'T MEAN...
"BRIDE" ...?!
NOW WHAT AM I SUPPOSED TO DO?!
MORI-SATO! YOU GOTTA HELP ME!!
I'VE HELPED YOU ENOUGH FOR ONE DAY.

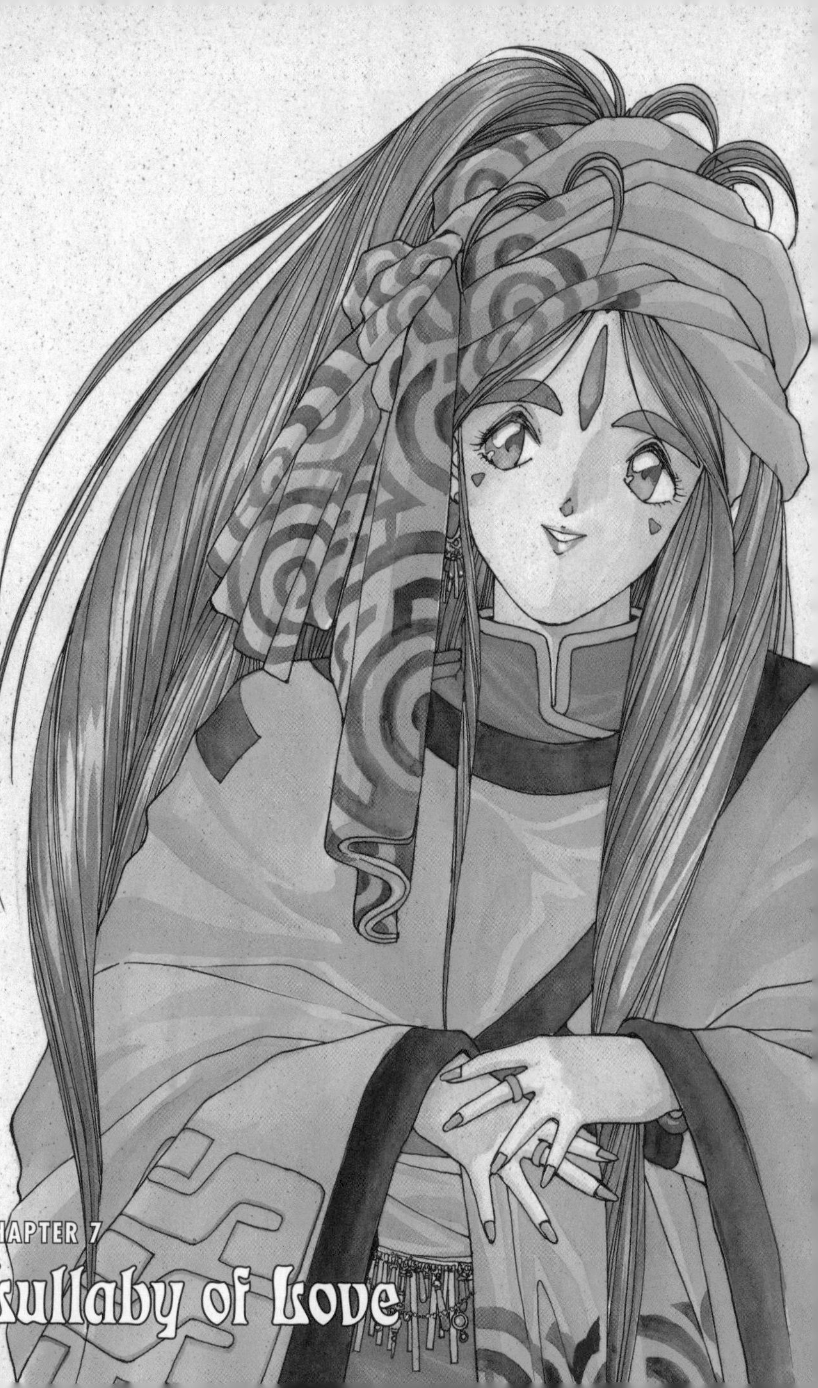

CHAPTER 7

Lullaby of Love

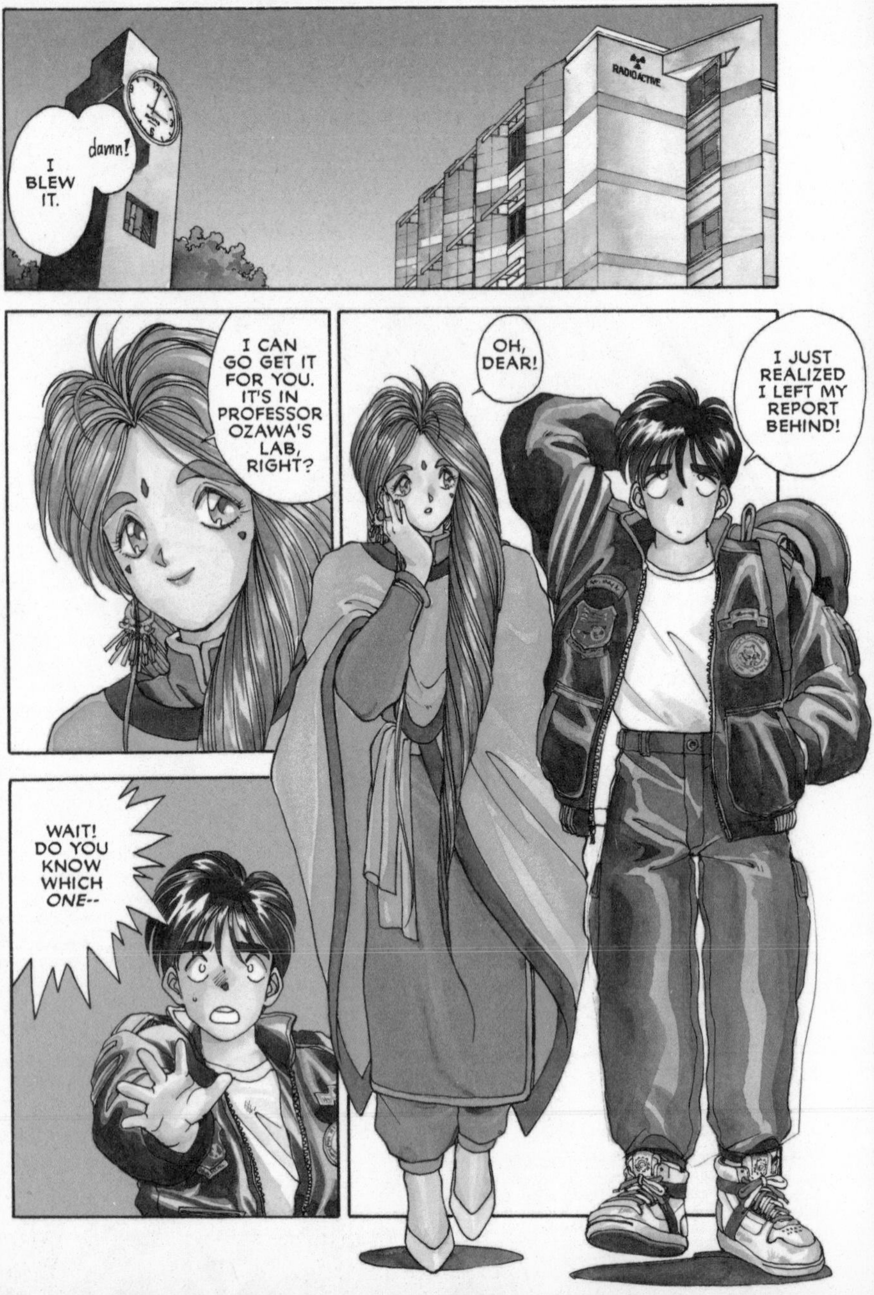
RADIO ACTIVE
damn!
I BLEW IT.
I JUST REALIZED I LEFT MY REPORT BEHIND!
OH, DEAR!
I CAN GO GET IT FOR YOU. IT'S IN PROFESSOR OZAWA'S LAB, RIGHT?
WAIT! DO YOU KNOW WHICH *ONE*--

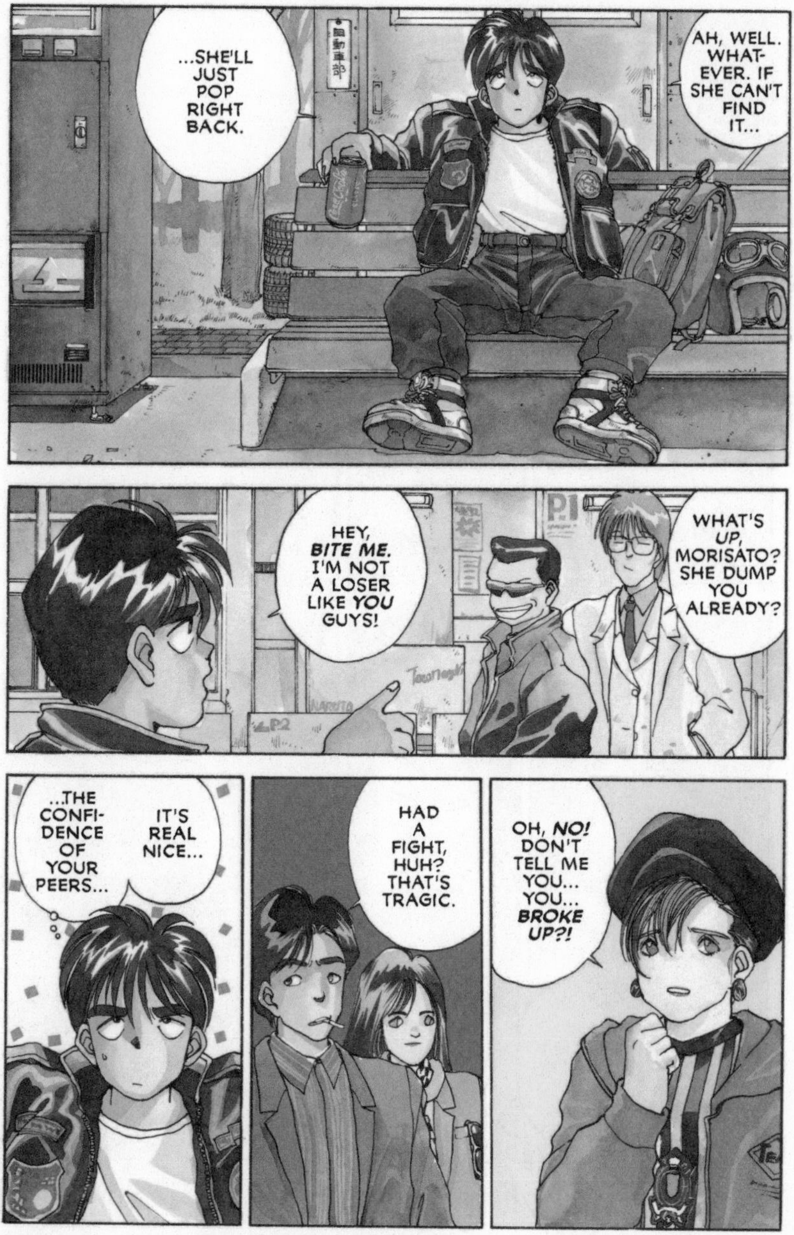

AH, WELL. WHATEVER. IF SHE CAN'T FIND IT...
自動車部
...SHE'LL JUST POP RIGHT BACK.
WHAT'S *UP*, MORISATO? SHE DUMP YOU ALREADY?
HEY, ***BITE ME.*** I'M NOT A LOSER LIKE ***YOU*** GUYS!
OH, ***NO!*** DON'T TELL ME YOU... YOU... ***BROKE UP?!***
HAD A FIGHT, HUH? THAT'S TRAGIC.
IT'S REAL NICE...
...THE CONFIDENCE OF YOUR PEERS...

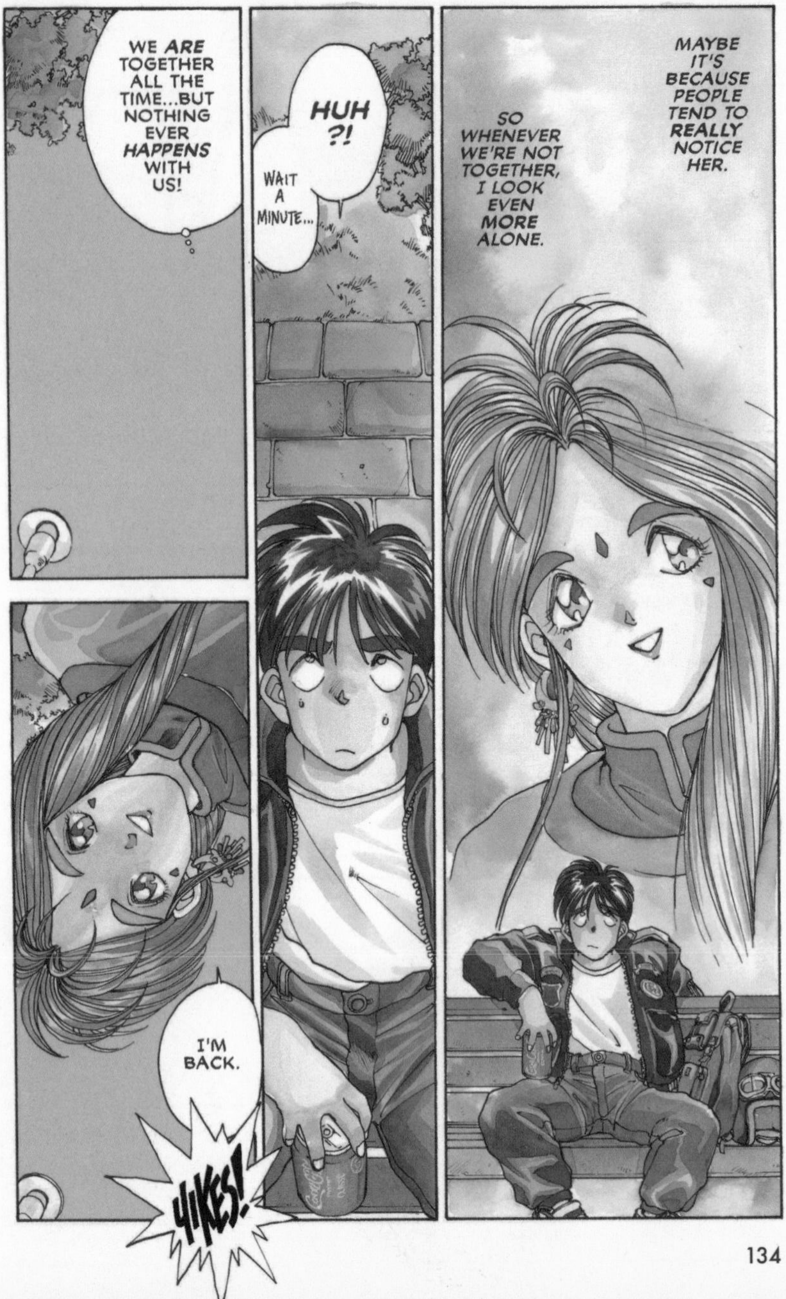
MAYBE IT'S BECAUSE PEOPLE TEND TO REALLY NOTICE HER.
SO WHENEVER WE'RE NOT TOGETHER, I LOOK EVEN MORE ALONE.
HUH ?!
WAIT A MINUTE...
WE ARE TOGETHER ALL THE TIME...BUT NOTHING EVER HAPPENS WITH US!
I'M BACK.
YIKES!

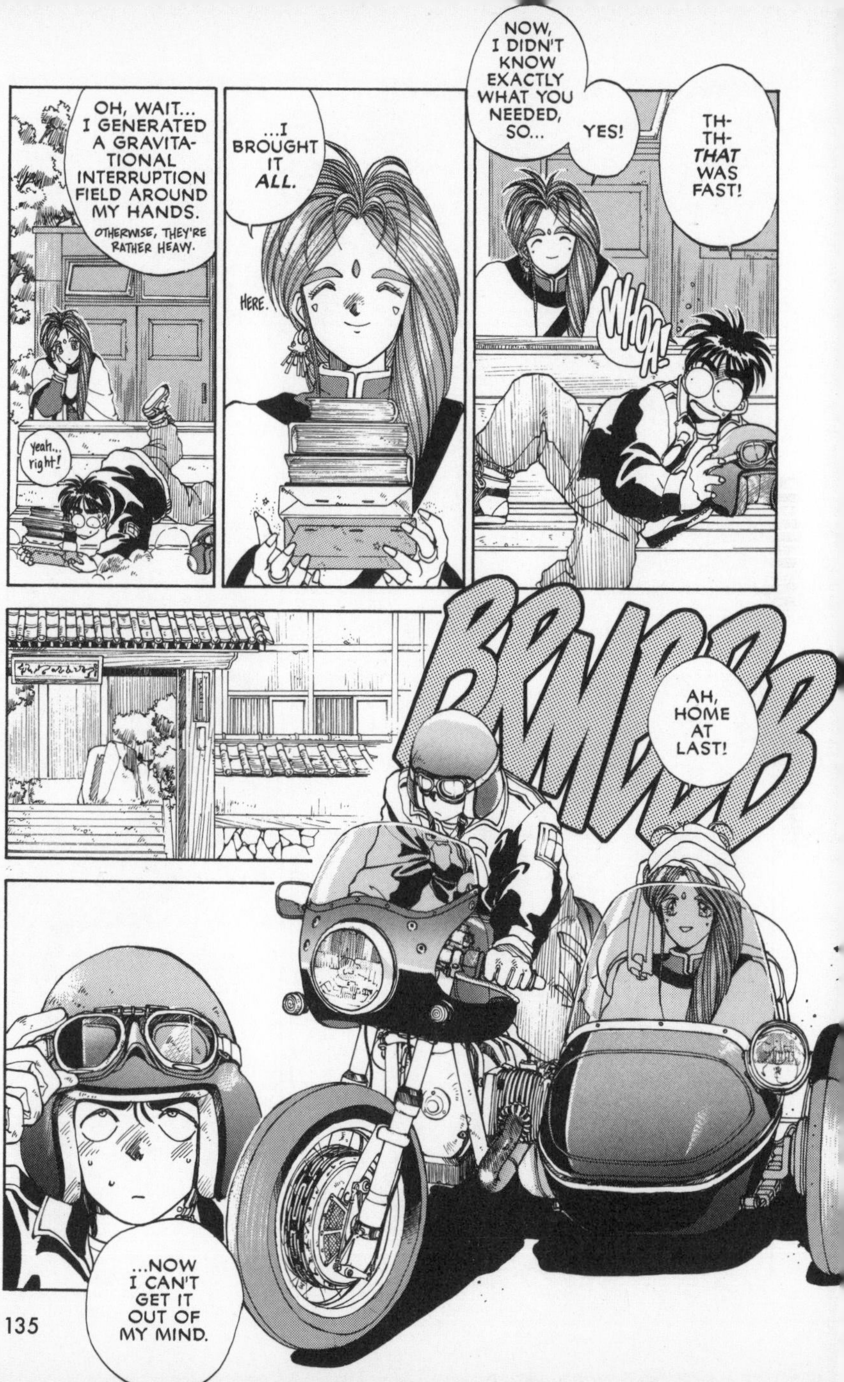
TH- TH- THAT WAS FAST!
YES!
NOW, I DIDN'T KNOW EXACTLY WHAT YOU NEEDED, SO...
WHOA!
...I BROUGHT IT ALL.
HERE.
OH, WAIT... I GENERATED A GRAVITA- TIONAL INTERRUPTION FIELD AROUND MY HANDS.
OTHERWISE, THEY'RE RATHER HEAVY.
yeah... right!
AH, HOME AT LAST!
...NOW I CAN'T GET IT OUT OF MY MIND.

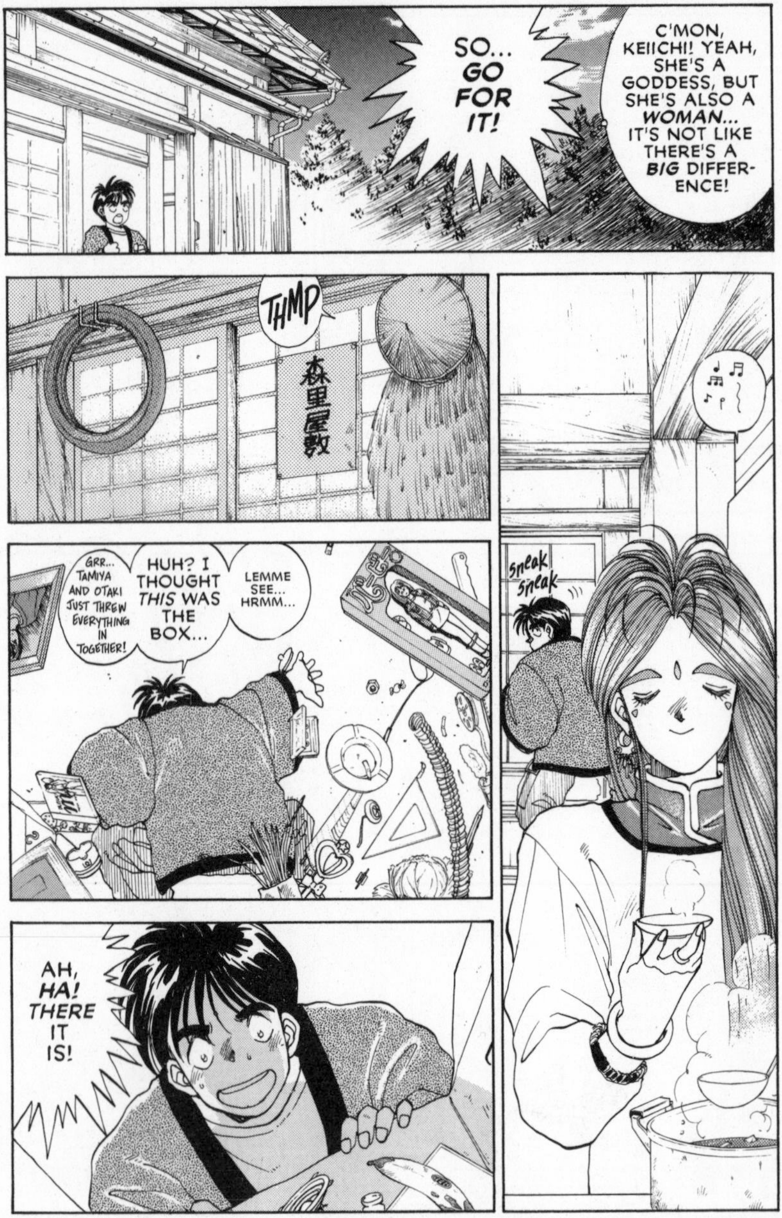
C'MON, KEIICHI! YEAH, SHE'S A GODDESS, BUT SHE'S ALSO A *WOMAN*... IT'S NOT LIKE THERE'S A *BIG* DIFFERENCE!
SO... *GO FOR IT!*
SNEAK SNEAK
THMP
森里屋敷
LEMME SEE... HRMM...
HUH? I THOUGHT *THIS* WAS THE BOX...
GRR... TAMIYA AND OTAKI JUST THREW EVERYTHING IN TOGETHER!
AH, *HA! THERE IT IS!*

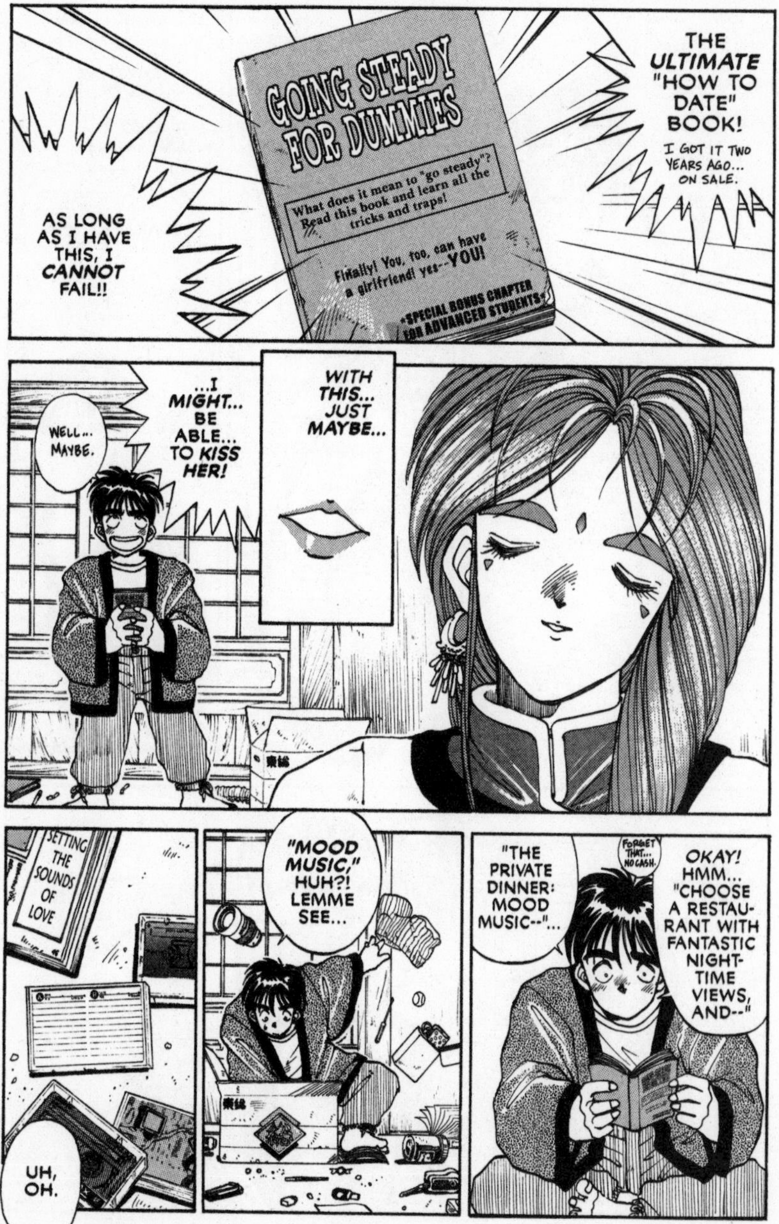
THE ULTIMATE "HOW TO DATE" BOOK!
I GOT IT TWO YEARS AGO... ON SALE.
GOING STEADY FOR DUMMIES
What does it mean to "go steady"? Read this book and learn all the tricks and traps!
Finally! You, too, can have a girlfriend! yes--YOU!
•SPECIAL BONUS CHAPTER FOR ADVANCED STUDENTS•
AS LONG AS I HAVE THIS, I CANNOT FAIL!!
WITH THIS... JUST MAYBE...
...I MIGHT... BE ABLE... TO KISS HER!
WELL... MAYBE.
OKAY! HMM... "CHOOSE A RESTAURANT WITH FANTASTIC NIGHT-TIME VIEWS, AND--"
FORGET THAT... NO CASH.
"THE PRIVATE DINNER: MOOD MUSIC--"...
"MOOD MUSIC," HUH?! LEMME SEE...
SETTING THE SOUNDS OF LOVE
UH, OH.

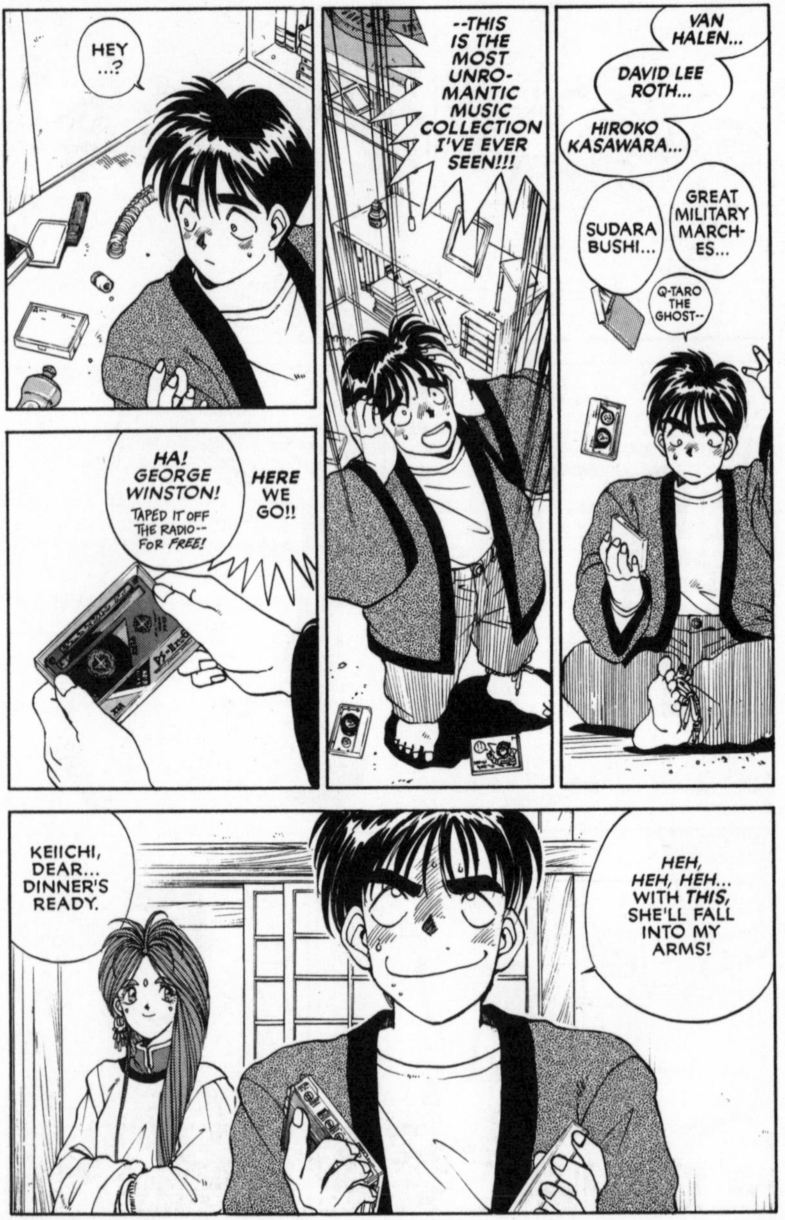
VAN HALEN...
DAVID LEE ROTH...
HIROKO KASAWARA...
GREAT MILITARY MARCH-ES...
SUDARA BUSHI...
Q-TARO THE GHOST--
--THIS IS THE MOST UNRO-MANTIC MUSIC COLLECTION I'VE EVER SEEN!!!
HEY ...?
HA! GEORGE WINSTON! TAPED IT OFF THE RADIO-- FOR FREE!
HERE WE GO!!
HEH, HEH, HEH... WITH THIS, SHE'LL FALL INTO MY ARMS!
KEIICHI, DEAR... DINNER'S READY.

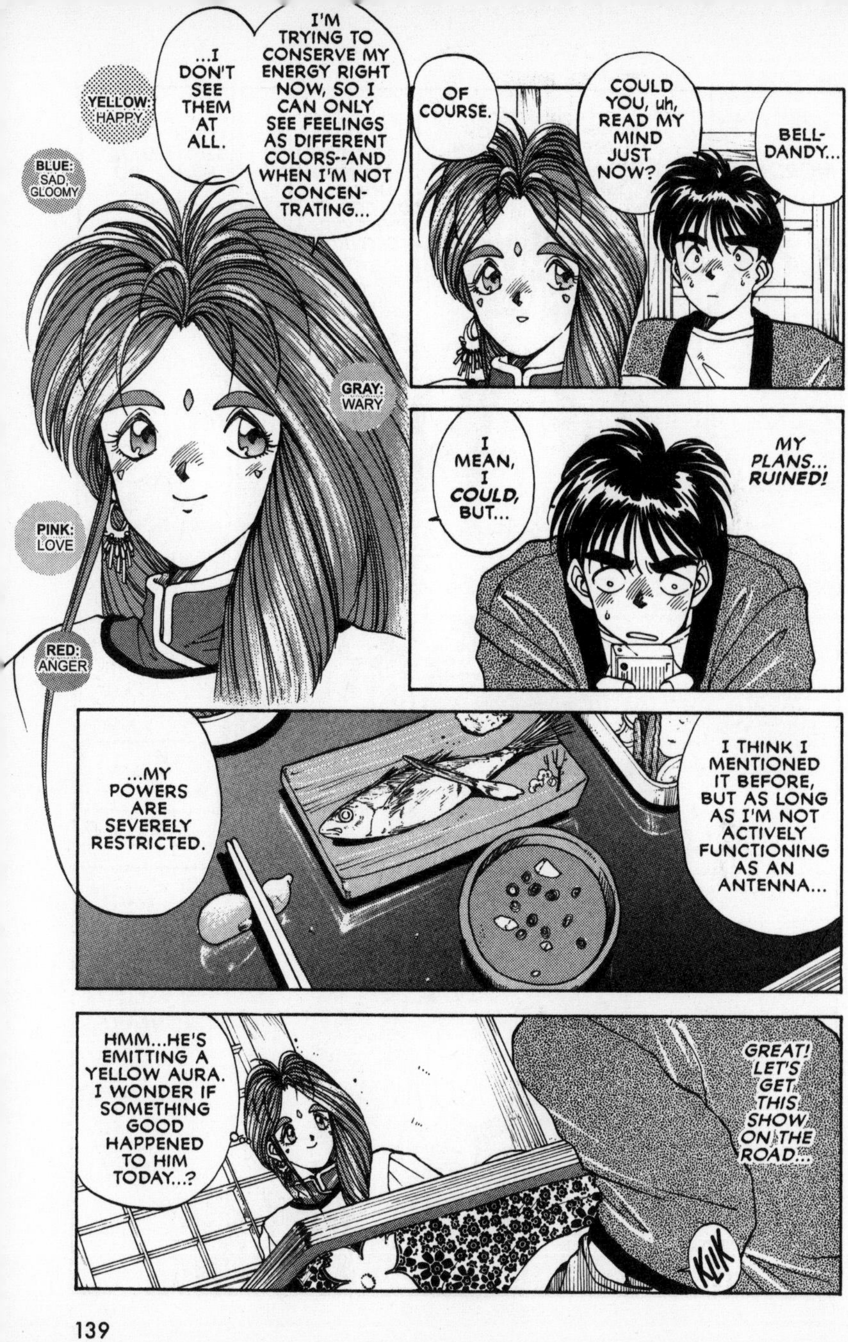
BELL-DANDY...
COULD YOU, uh, READ MY MIND JUST NOW?
OF COURSE.
MY PLANS... RUINED!
I MEAN, I COULD, BUT...
I'M TRYING TO CONSERVE MY ENERGY RIGHT NOW, SO I CAN ONLY SEE FEELINGS AS DIFFERENT COLORS--AND WHEN I'M NOT CONCEN-TRATING...
...I DON'T SEE THEM AT ALL.
YELLOW: HAPPY
BLUE: SAD, GLOOMY
GRAY: WARY
PINK: LOVE
RED: ANGER
I THINK I MENTIONED IT BEFORE, BUT AS LONG AS I'M NOT ACTIVELY FUNCTIONING AS AN ANTENNA...
...MY POWERS ARE SEVERELY RESTRICTED.
GREAT! LET'S GET THIS SHOW ON THE ROAD...
KLIK
HMM...HE'S EMITTING A YELLOW AURA. I WONDER IF SOMETHING GOOD HAPPENED TO HIM TODAY...?

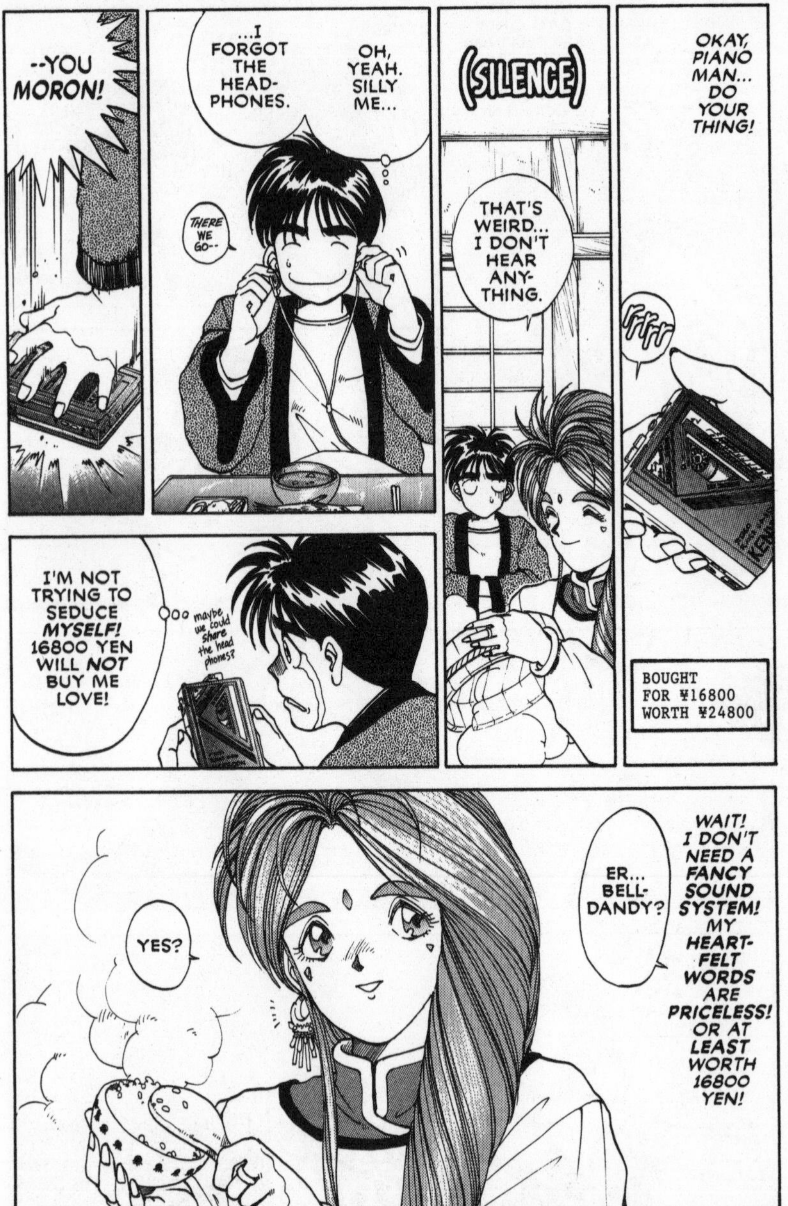
OKAY, PIANO MAN... DO YOUR THING!
BOUGHT FOR ¥16800 WORTH ¥24800
(SILENCE)
THAT'S WEIRD... I DON'T HEAR ANYTHING.
OH, YEAH. SILLY ME...
...I FORGOT THE HEAD-PHONES.
THERE WE GO--
--YOU MORON!
maybe we could share the head phones?
I'M NOT TRYING TO SEDUCE MYSELF! 16800 YEN WILL NOT BUY ME LOVE!
WAIT! I DON'T NEED A FANCY SOUND SYSTEM! MY HEART-FELT WORDS ARE PRICELESS! OR AT LEAST WORTH 16800 YEN!
ER... BELL-DANDY?
YES?

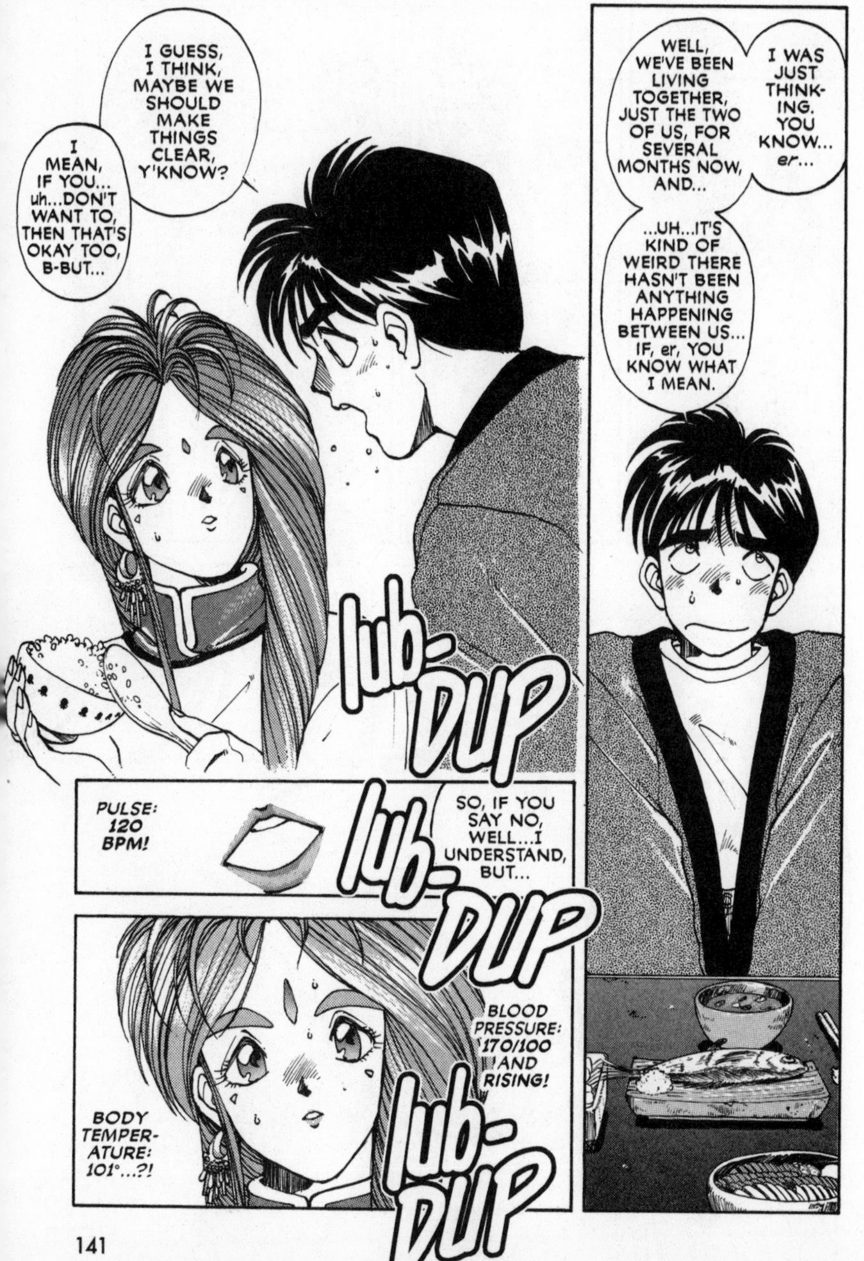
I WAS JUST THINKING. YOU KNOW... er...
WELL, WE'VE BEEN LIVING TOGETHER, JUST THE TWO OF US, FOR SEVERAL MONTHS NOW, AND...
...UH...IT'S KIND OF WEIRD THERE HASN'T BEEN ANYTHING HAPPENING BETWEEN US... IF, er, YOU KNOW WHAT I MEAN.
I GUESS, I THINK, MAYBE WE SHOULD MAKE THINGS CLEAR, Y'KNOW?
I MEAN, IF YOU... uh...DON'T WANT TO, THEN THAT'S OKAY TOO, B-BUT...
lub-DUP
SO, IF YOU SAY NO, WELL...I UNDERSTAND, BUT...
PULSE: 120 BPM!
lub-DUP
BLOOD PRESSURE: 170/100 AND RISING!
BODY TEMPERATURE: 101°...?!
lub-DUP

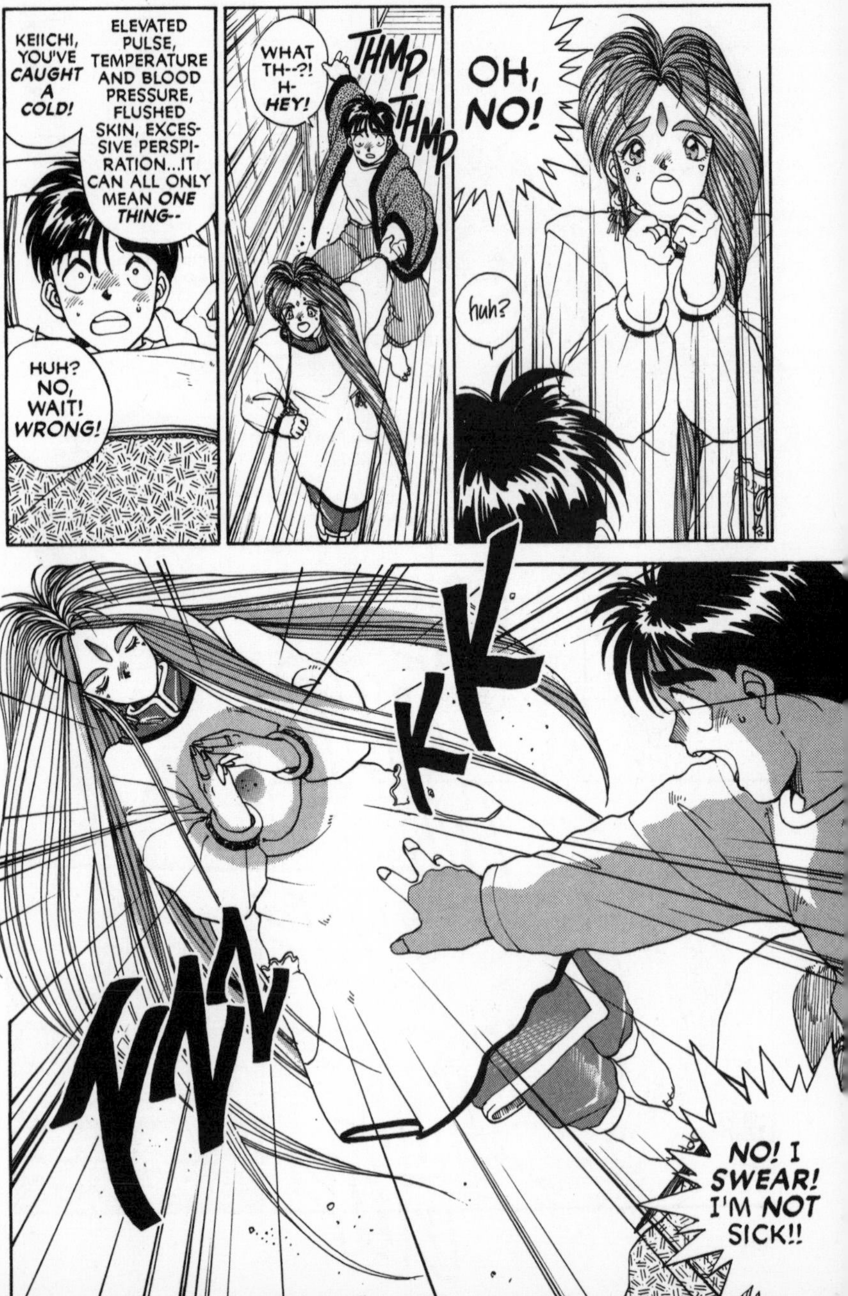
OH, NO!
huh?
WHAT TH--?! H-HEY!
THMP THMP
ELEVATED PULSE, TEMPERATURE AND BLOOD PRESSURE, FLUSHED SKIN, EXCESSIVE PERSPIRATION...IT CAN ALL ONLY MEAN ONE THING--
KEIICHI, YOU'VE CAUGHT A COLD!
HUH? NO, WAIT! WRONG!
NO! I SWEAR! I'M NOT SICK!!

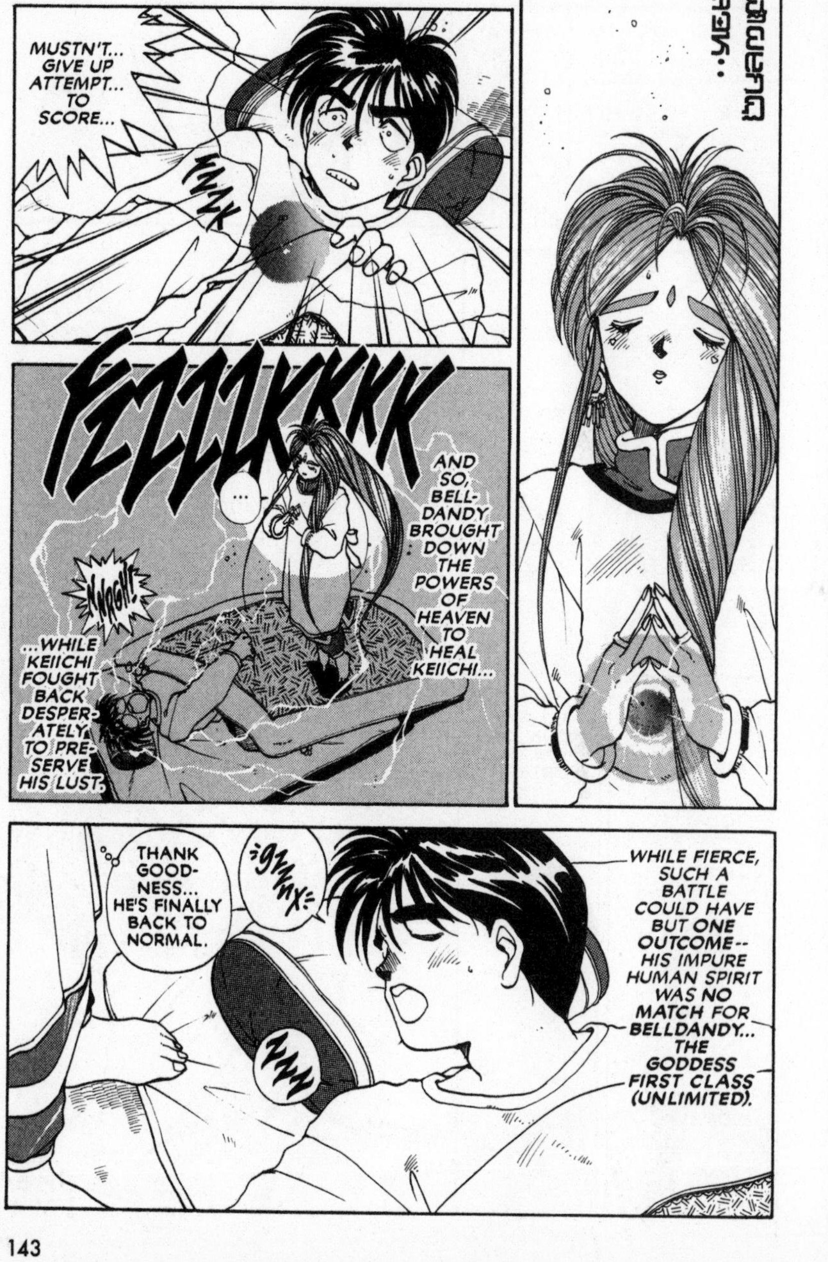
MUSTN'T... GIVE UP ATTEMPT... TO SCORE...
AND SO, BELLDANDY BROUGHT DOWN THE POWERS OF HEAVEN TO HEAL KEIICHI...
...
NNRGH!
...WHILE KEIICHI FOUGHT BACK DESPERATELY TO PRESERVE HIS LUST.
WHILE FIERCE, SUCH A BATTLE COULD HAVE BUT ONE OUTCOME-- HIS IMPURE HUMAN SPIRIT WAS NO MATCH FOR BELLDANDY... THE GODDESS FIRST CLASS (UNLIMITED).
THANK GOODNESS... HE'S FINALLY BACK TO NORMAL.

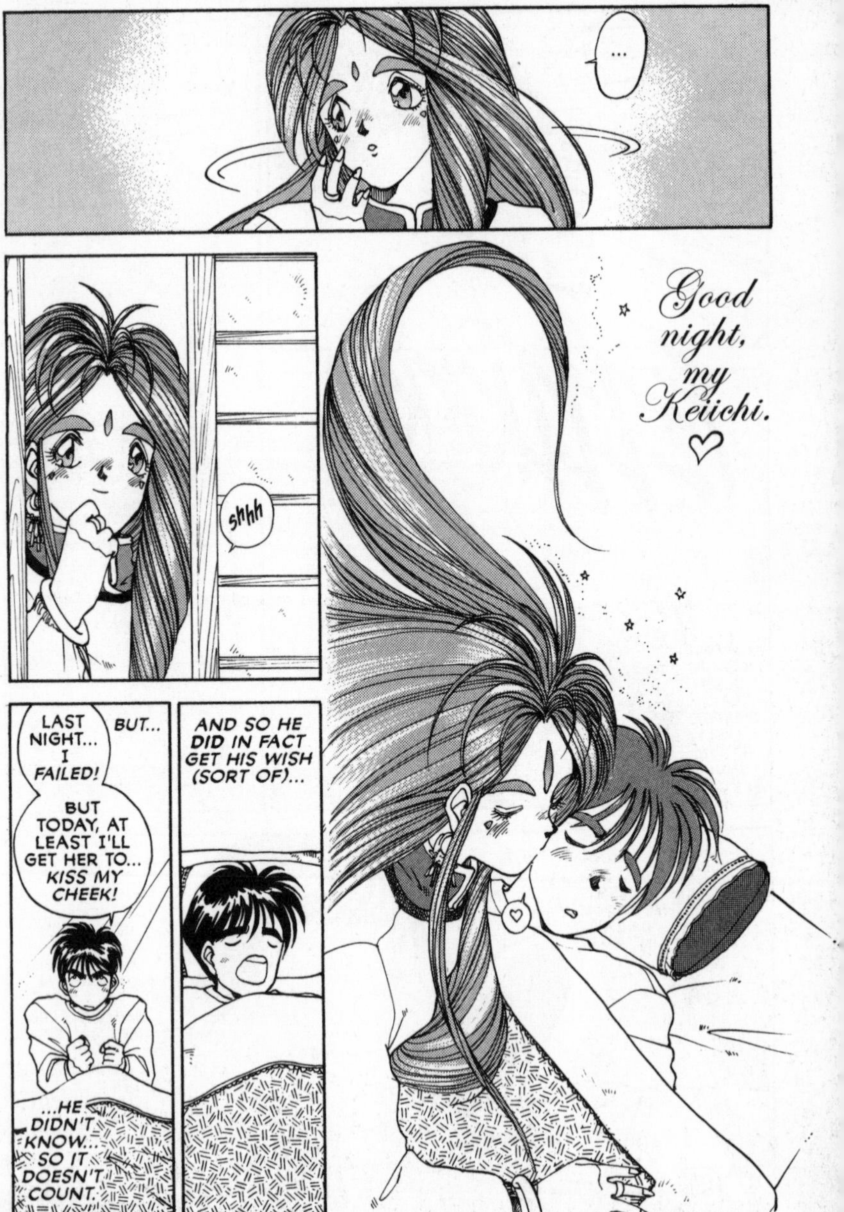
...
Good night, my Keiichi. ♡
shhh
AND SO HE DID IN FACT GET HIS WISH (SORT OF)...
BUT...
LAST NIGHT... I FAILED!
BUT TODAY, AT LEAST I'LL GET HER TO... KISS MY CHEEK!
...HE DIDN'T KNOW... SO IT DOESN'T COUNT.

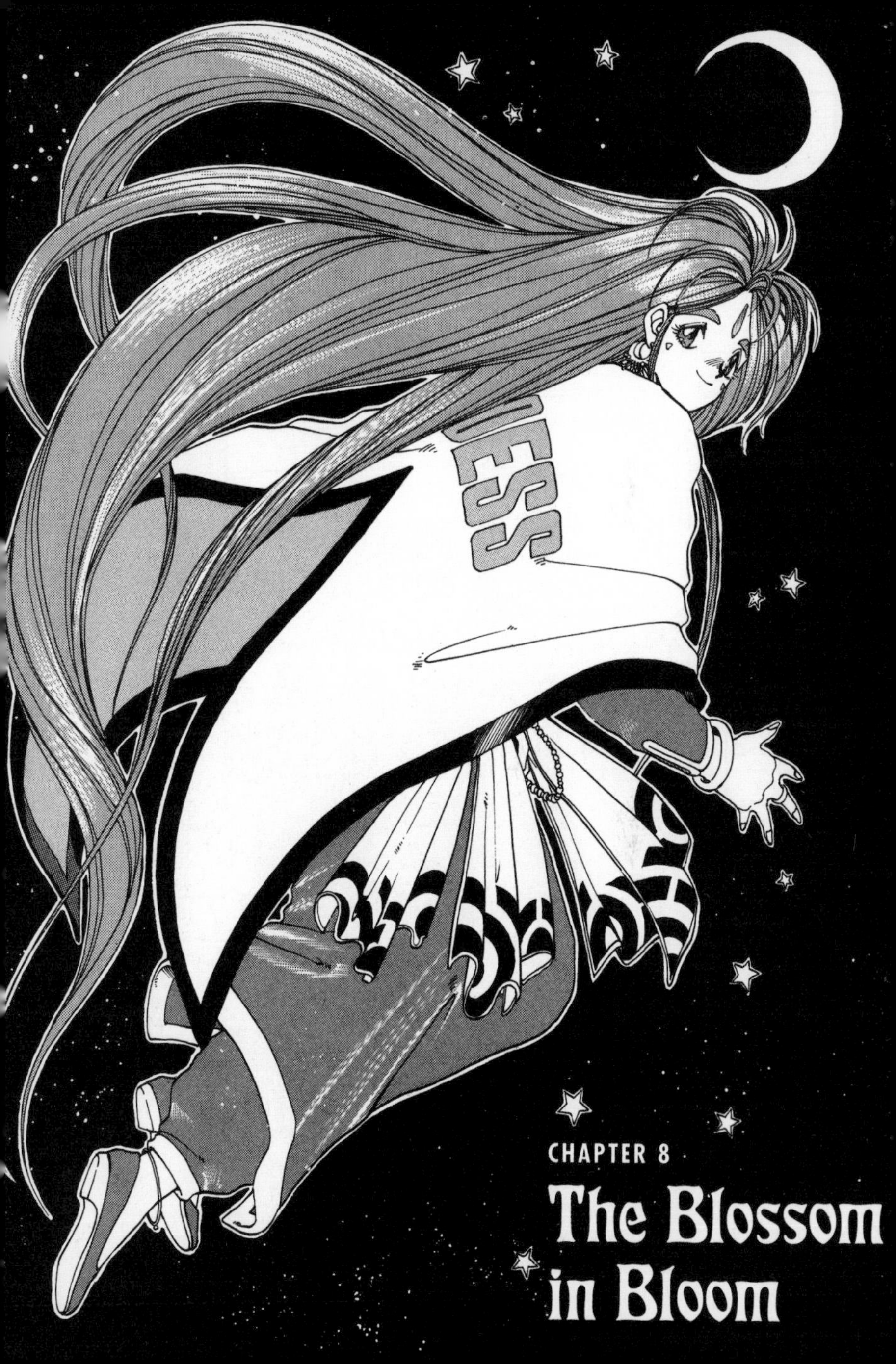

CHAPTER 8

The Blossom in Bloom

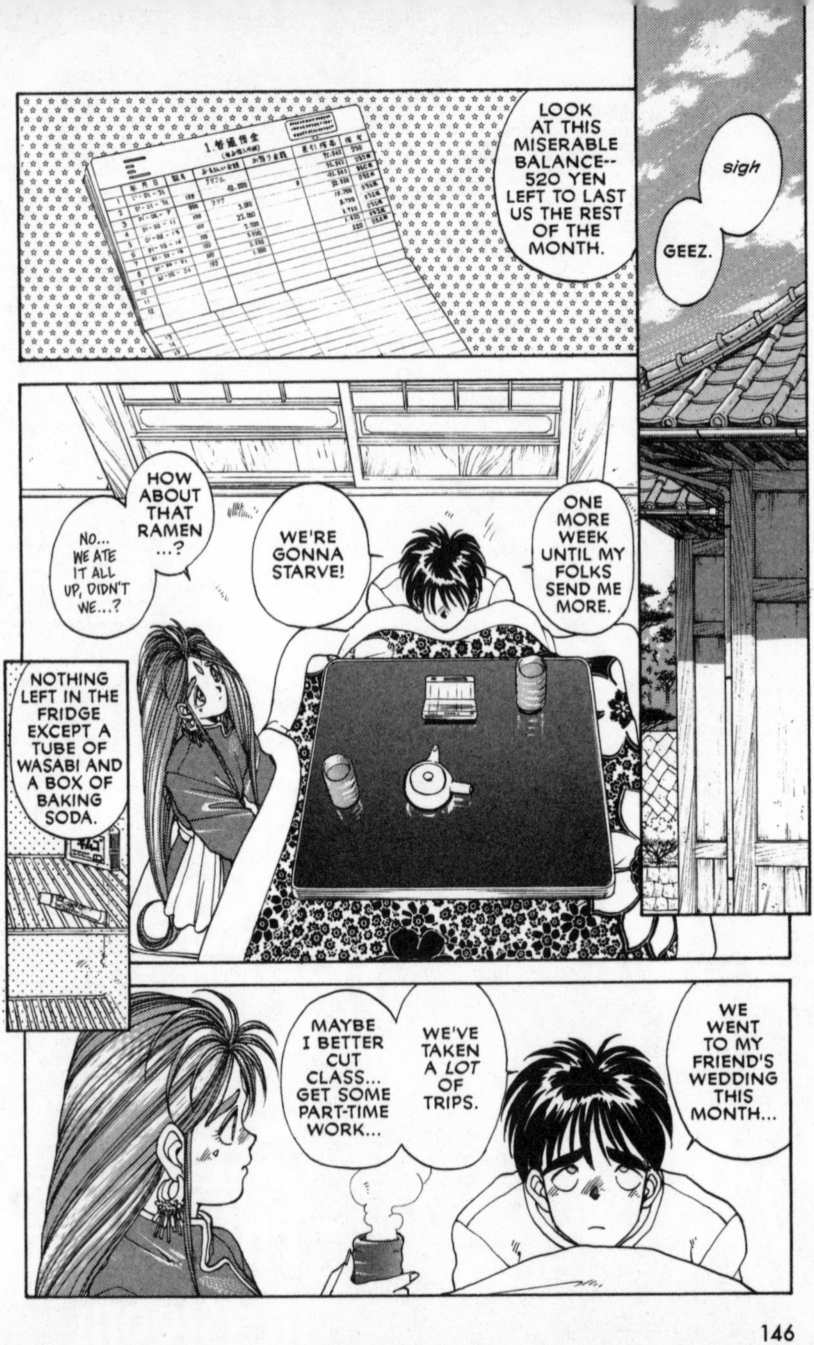
sigh
GEEZ.
LOOK AT THIS MISERABLE BALANCE-- 520 YEN LEFT TO LAST US THE REST OF THE MONTH.
ONE MORE WEEK UNTIL MY FOLKS SEND ME MORE.
WE'RE GONNA STARVE!
HOW ABOUT THAT RAMEN ...?
NO... WE ATE IT ALL UP, DIDN'T WE...?
NOTHING LEFT IN THE FRIDGE EXCEPT A TUBE OF WASABI AND A BOX OF BAKING SODA.
WE WENT TO MY FRIEND'S WEDDING THIS MONTH...
WE'VE TAKEN A *LOT* OF TRIPS.
MAYBE I BETTER CUT CLASS... GET SOME PART-TIME WORK...

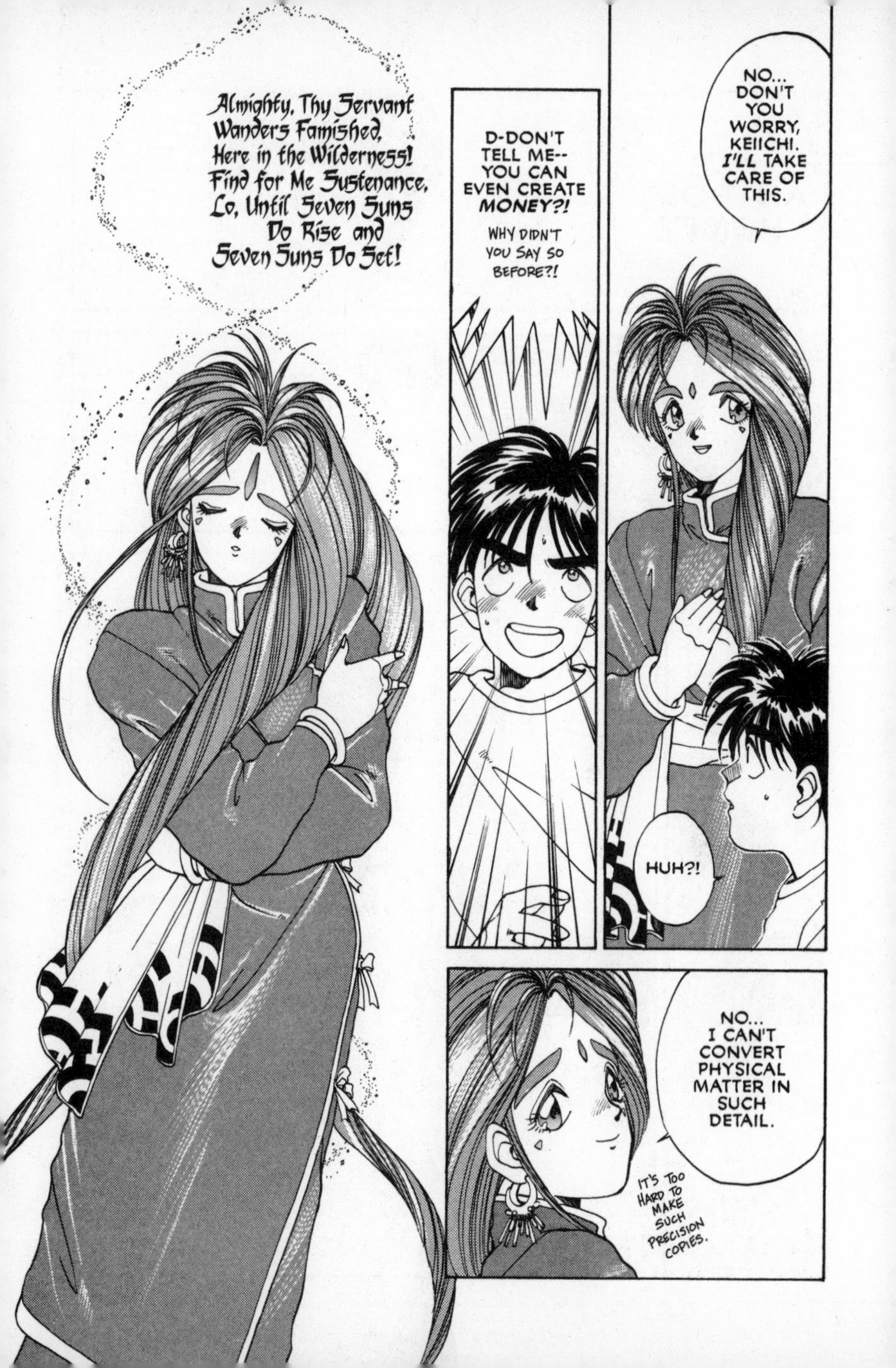
NO... DON'T YOU WORRY, KEIICHI. I'LL TAKE CARE OF THIS.
HUH?!
D-DON'T TELL ME-- YOU CAN EVEN CREATE MONEY?!
WHY DIDN'T YOU SAY SO BEFORE?!
NO... I CAN'T CONVERT PHYSICAL MATTER IN SUCH DETAIL.
IT'S TOO HARD TO MAKE SUCH PRECISION COPIES.
Almighty, Thy Servant Wanders Famished, Here in the Wilderness! Find for Me Sustenance, Lo, Until Seven Suns Do Rise and Seven Suns Do Set!

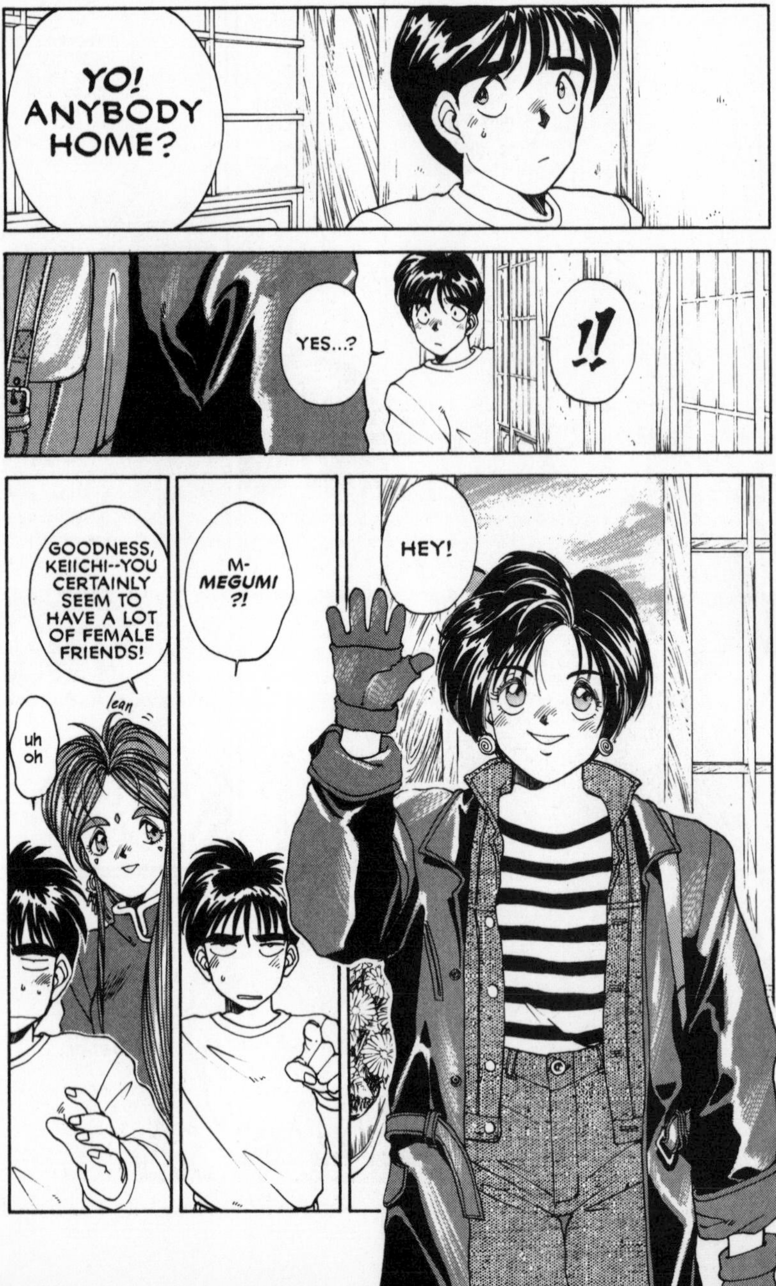
YO! ANYBODY HOME?
!!
YES...?
HEY!
M- MEGUMI ?!
GOODNESS, KEIICHI--YOU CERTAINLY SEEM TO HAVE A LOT OF FEMALE FRIENDS!
lean
uh oh

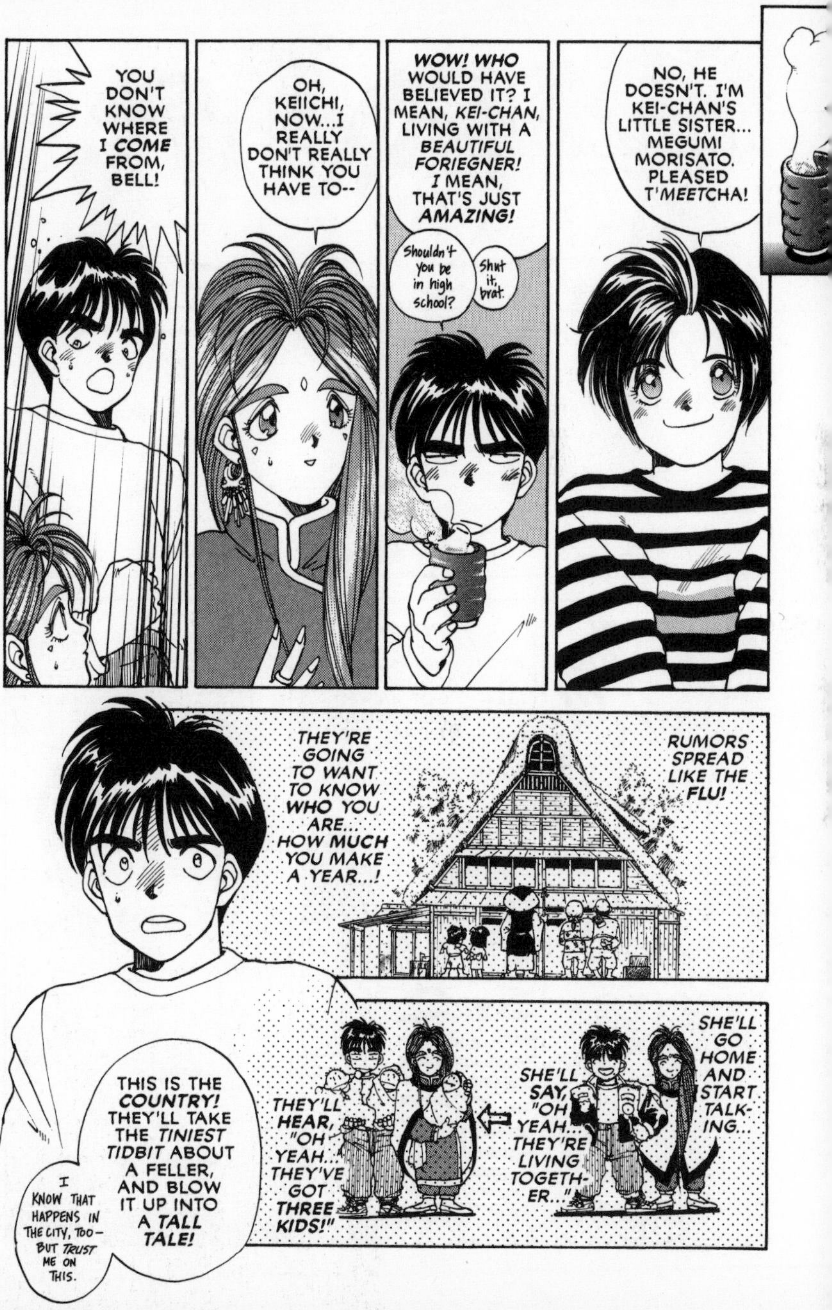
NO, HE DOESN'T. I'M KEI-CHAN'S LITTLE SISTER... MEGUMI MORISATO. PLEASED T'MEETCHA!
WOW! WHO WOULD HAVE BELIEVED IT? I MEAN, KEI-CHAN, LIVING WITH A BEAUTIFUL FORIEGNER! I MEAN, THAT'S JUST AMAZING!
Shut it, brat.
Shouldn't you be in high school?
OH, KEIICHI, NOW...I REALLY DON'T REALLY THINK YOU HAVE TO--
YOU DON'T KNOW WHERE I COME FROM, BELL!
RUMORS SPREAD LIKE THE FLU!
THEY'RE GOING TO WANT TO KNOW WHO YOU ARE... HOW MUCH YOU MAKE A YEAR...!
SHE'LL GO HOME AND START TALKING...
SHE'LL SAY, "OH YEAH... THEY'RE LIVING TOGETHER..."
THEY'LL HEAR, "OH YEAH... THEY'VE GOT THREE KIDS!"
THIS IS THE COUNTRY! THEY'LL TAKE THE TINIEST TIDBIT ABOUT A FELLER, AND BLOW IT UP INTO A TALL TALE!
I KNOW THAT HAPPENS IN THE CITY, TOO-- BUT TRUST ME ON THIS.

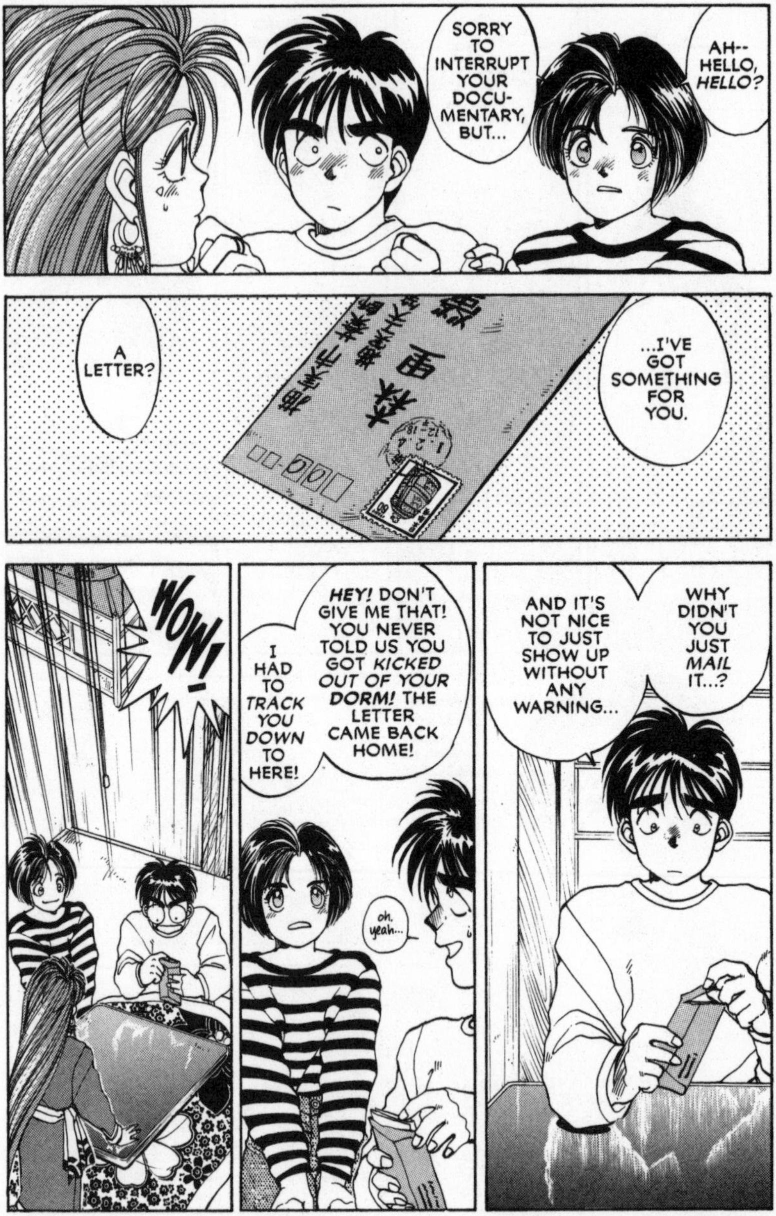
AH-- HELLO, *HELLO?*
SORRY TO INTERRUPT YOUR DOCU-MENTARY, BUT...
...I'VE GOT SOMETHING FOR YOU.
A LETTER?
WHY DIDN'T YOU JUST *MAIL* IT...?
AND IT'S NOT NICE TO JUST SHOW UP WITHOUT ANY WARNING...
HEY! DON'T GIVE ME THAT! YOU NEVER TOLD US YOU GOT *KICKED OUT OF YOUR DORM!* THE LETTER CAME BACK HOME!
I HAD TO *TRACK* YOU DOWN TO HERE!
oh. yeah...
WOW!-

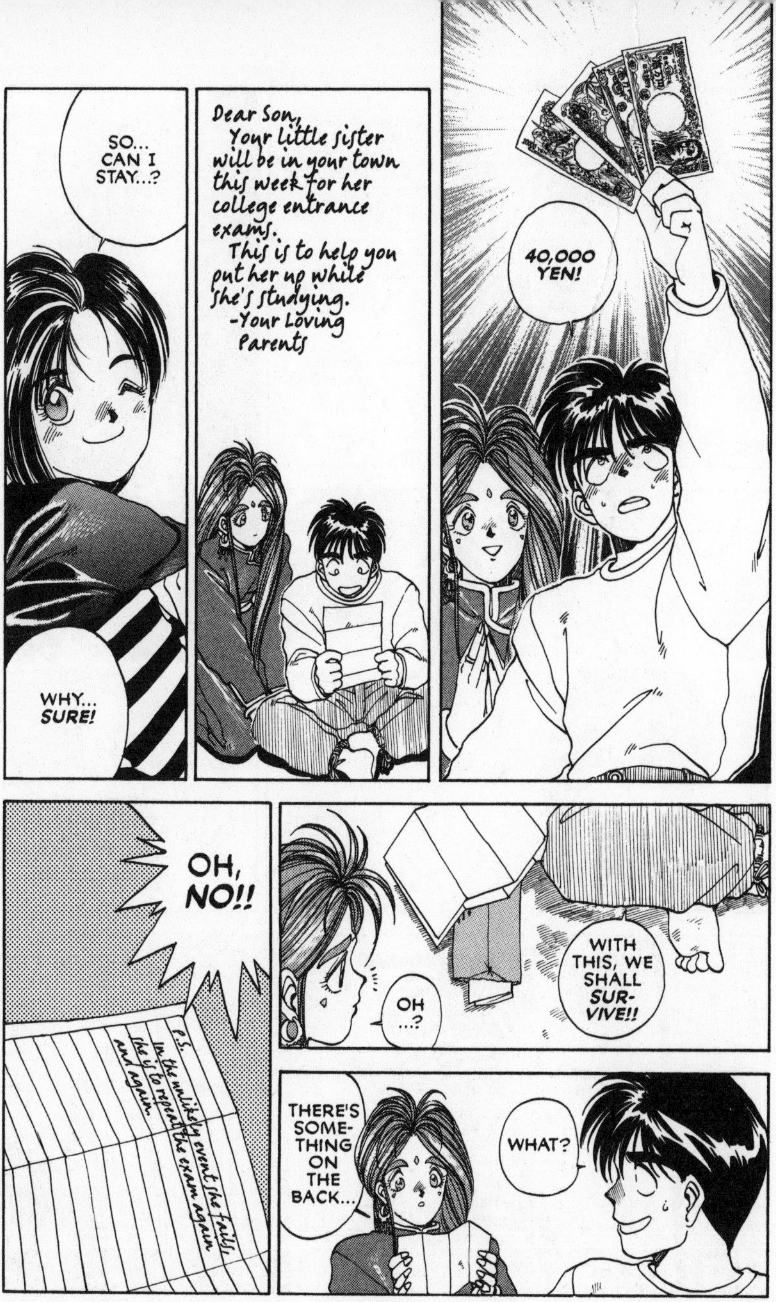
40,000 YEN!
Dear Son,
Your little sister will be in your town this week for her college entrance exams.
This is to help you put her up while she's studying.
-Your Loving Parents
SO... CAN I STAY...?
WHY... SURE!
WITH THIS, WE SHALL SUR-VIVE!!
OH ...?
THERE'S SOME-THING ON THE BACK...
WHAT?
OH, NO!!
P.S.
In the unlikely event she fails, she is to repeat the exam again and again.

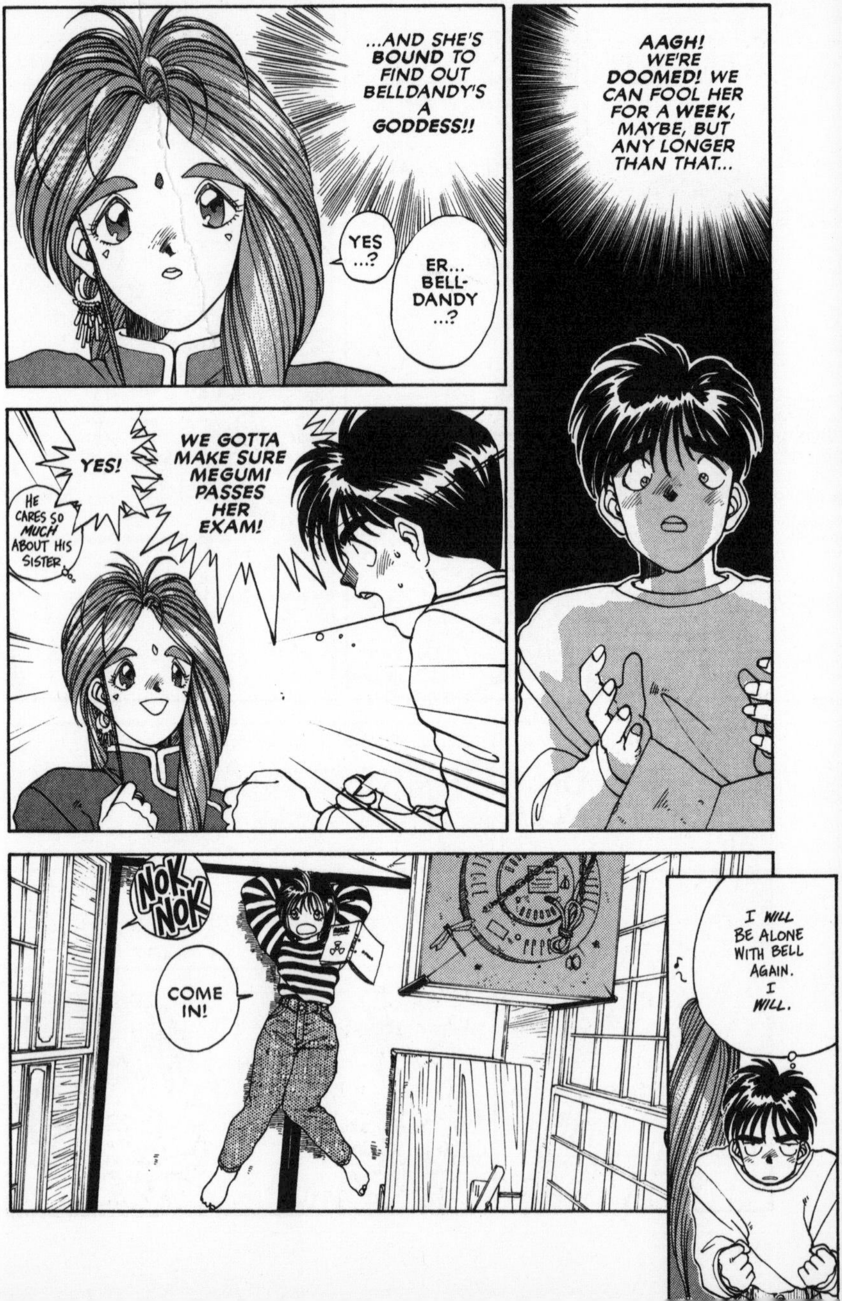
AAGH! WE'RE DOOMED! WE CAN FOOL HER FOR A WEEK, MAYBE, BUT ANY LONGER THAN THAT...
...AND SHE'S BOUND TO FIND OUT BELLDANDY'S A GODDESS!!
ER... BELL-DANDY ...?
YES ...?
WE GOTTA MAKE SURE MEGUMI PASSES HER EXAM!
YES!
HE CARES SO MUCH ABOUT HIS SISTER
I WILL BE ALONE WITH BELL AGAIN. I WILL.
NOK NOK
COME IN!

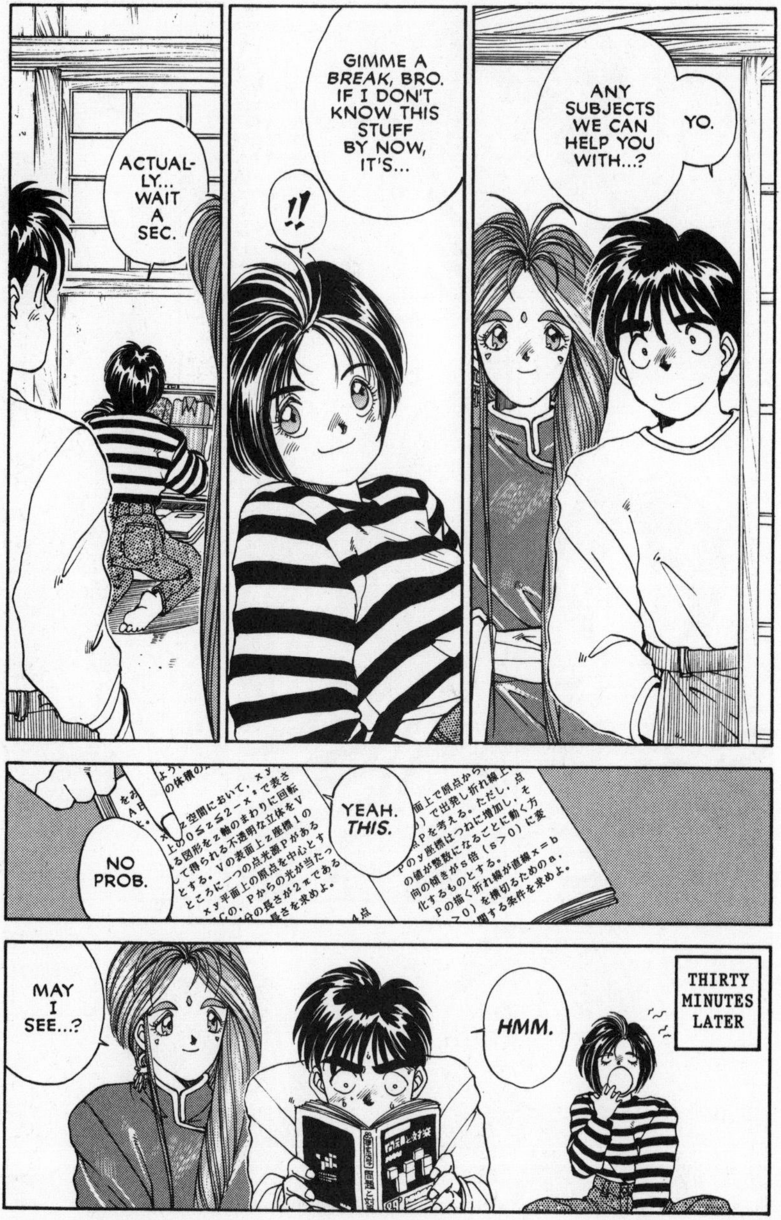
YO.
ANY SUBJECTS WE CAN HELP YOU WITH...?
GIMME A *BREAK*, BRO. IF I DON'T KNOW THIS STUFF BY NOW, IT'S...
!!
ACTUAL-LY... WAIT A SEC.
YEAH. *THIS.*
NO PROB.
THIRTY MINUTES LATER
HMM.
MAY I SEE...?

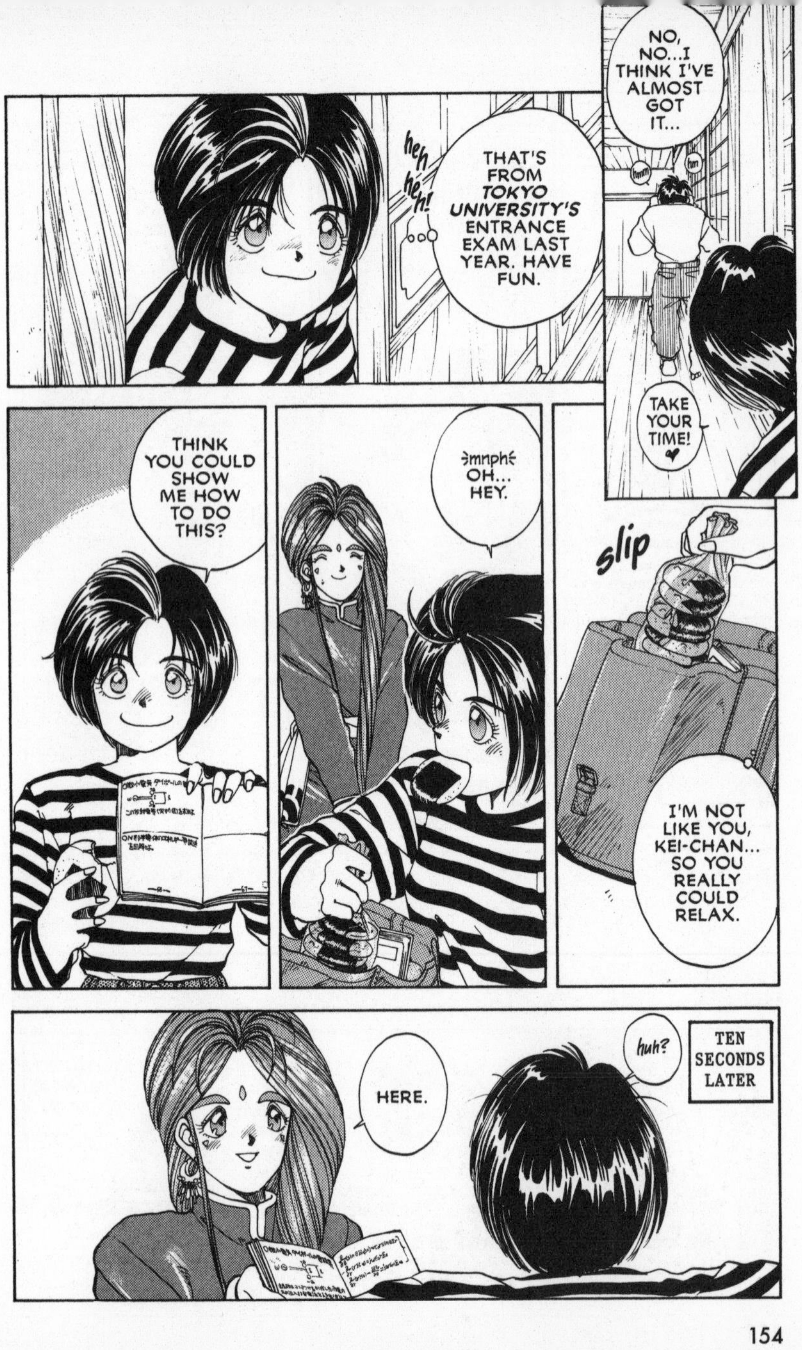
NO, NO...I THINK I'VE ALMOST GOT IT...
hmm
hm
TAKE YOUR TIME! ♥
heh heh!
THAT'S FROM *TOKYO UNIVERSITY'S* ENTRANCE EXAM LAST YEAR. HAVE FUN.
slip
I'M NOT LIKE YOU, KEI-CHAN... SO YOU REALLY COULD RELAX.
mnph OH... HEY.
THINK YOU COULD SHOW ME HOW TO DO THIS?
TEN SECONDS LATER
huh?
HERE.

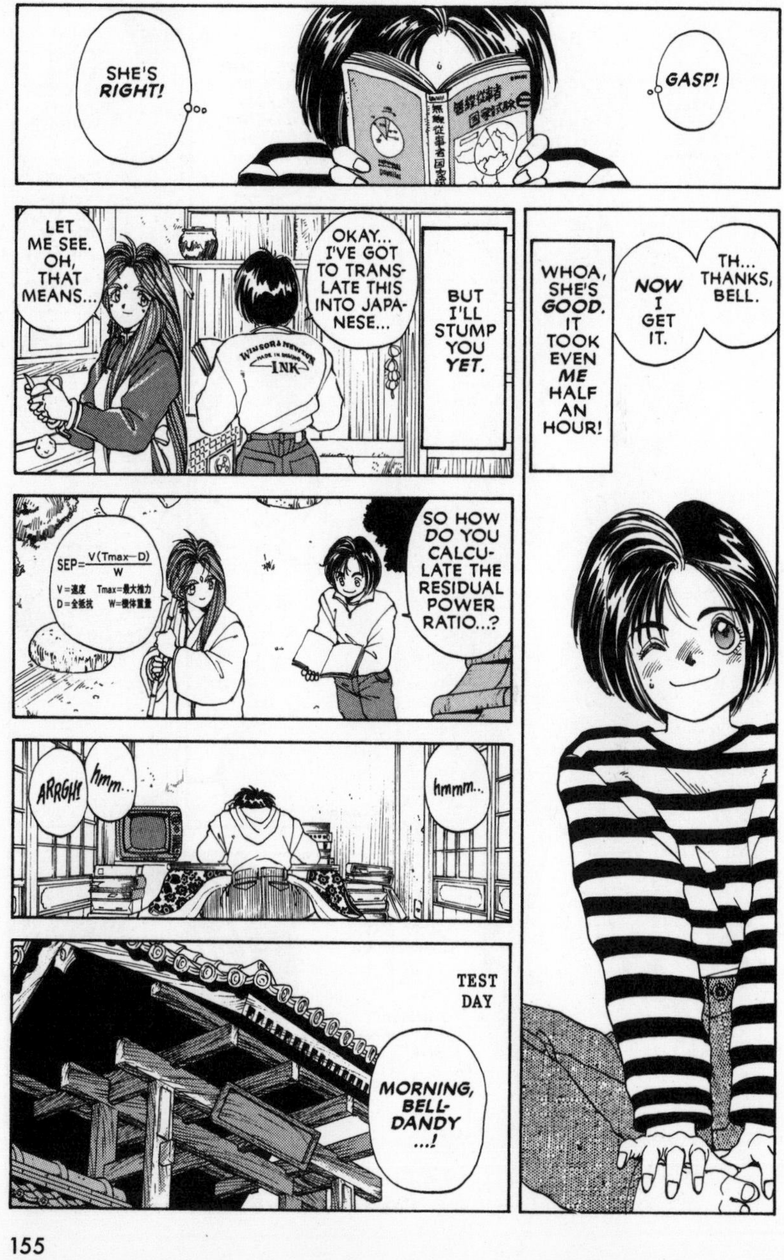
GASP!
SHE'S RIGHT!
TH... THANKS, BELL.
NOW I GET IT.
WHOA, SHE'S GOOD. IT TOOK EVEN ME HALF AN HOUR!
BUT I'LL STUMP YOU YET.
OKAY... I'VE GOT TO TRANSLATE THIS INTO JAPANESE...
LET ME SEE. OH, THAT MEANS...
WINSOR & NEWTON MADE IN ENGLAND INK
SO HOW DO YOU CALCULATE THE RESIDUAL POWER RATIO...?
SEP=V(Tmax−D)/W
V=速度 Tmax=最大推力
D=全抵抗 W=機体重量
hmmm...
hmm...
ARRGH!
TEST DAY
MORNING, BELL-DANDY ...!

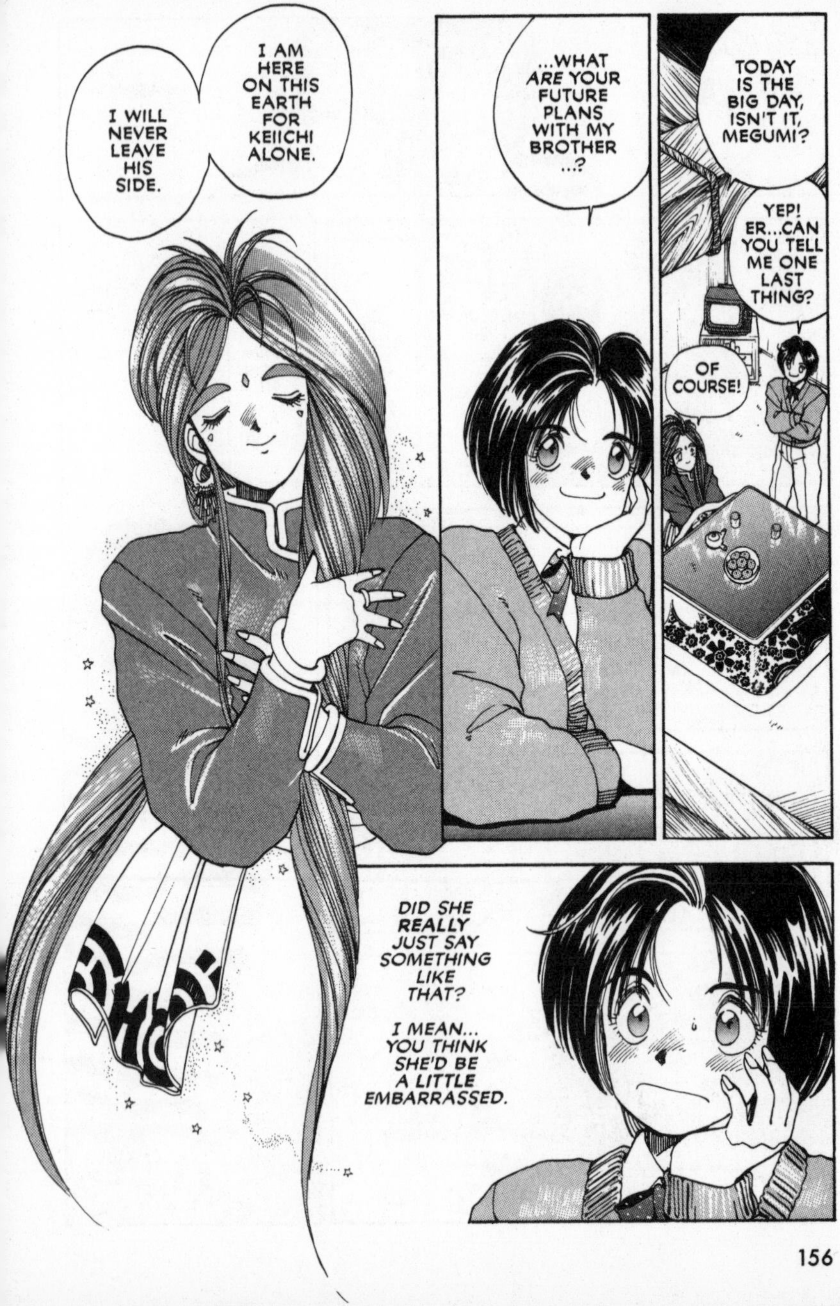
TODAY IS THE BIG DAY, ISN'T IT, MEGUMI?
YEP! ER...CAN YOU TELL ME ONE LAST THING?
OF COURSE!
...WHAT *ARE* YOUR FUTURE PLANS WITH MY BROTHER ...?
I AM HERE ON THIS EARTH FOR KEIICHI ALONE.
I WILL NEVER LEAVE HIS SIDE.
DID SHE **REALLY** JUST SAY SOMETHING LIKE THAT?
I MEAN... YOU THINK SHE'D BE A LITTLE EMBARRASSED.

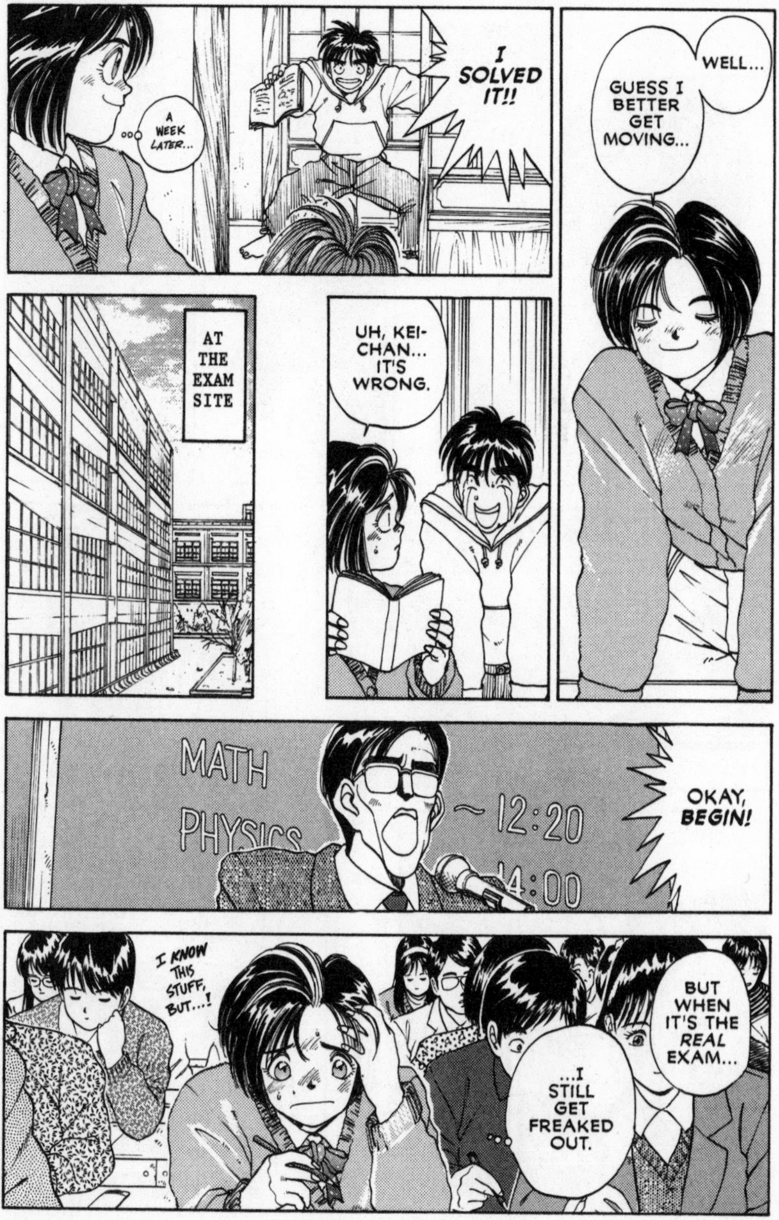

WELL...
GUESS I BETTER GET MOVING...
I SOLVED IT!!
A WEEK LATER...
UH, KEI-CHAN... IT'S WRONG.
AT THE EXAM SITE
OKAY, BEGIN!
MATH
PHYSICS
~12:20
14:00
BUT WHEN IT'S THE REAL EXAM...
...I STILL GET FREAKED OUT.
I KNOW THIS STUFF, BUT...!

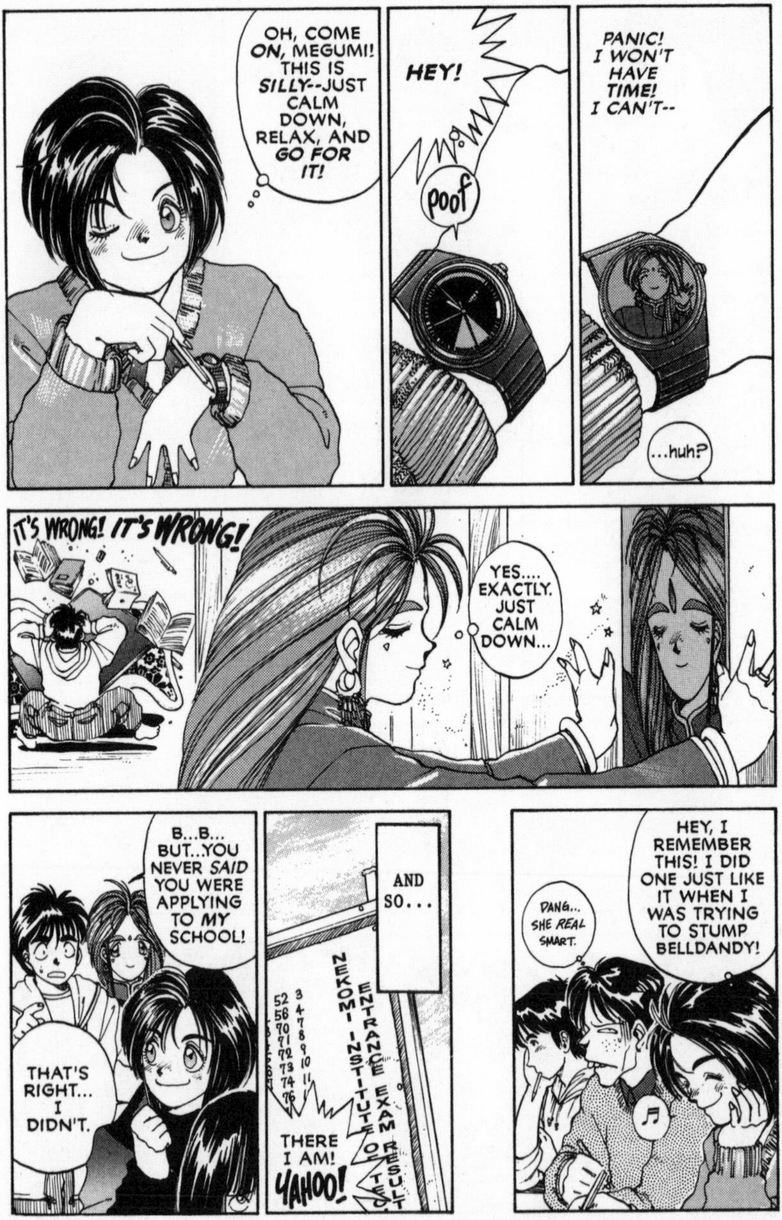
PANIC! I WON'T HAVE TIME! I CAN'T--
...huh?
HEY!
poof
OH, COME ON, MEGUMI! THIS IS SILLY--JUST CALM DOWN, RELAX, AND GO FOR IT!
YES.... EXACTLY. JUST CALM DOWN...
IT'S WRONG! IT'S WRONG!
HEY, I REMEMBER THIS! I DID ONE JUST LIKE IT WHEN I WAS TRYING TO STUMP BELLDANDY!
DANG... SHE REAL SMART.
AND SO...
NEKOMI INSTITUTE OF TEC
ENTRANCE EXAM RESULT
THERE I AM!
YAHOO!
B...B... BUT...YOU NEVER SAID YOU WERE APPLYING TO MY SCHOOL!
THAT'S RIGHT... I DIDN'T.

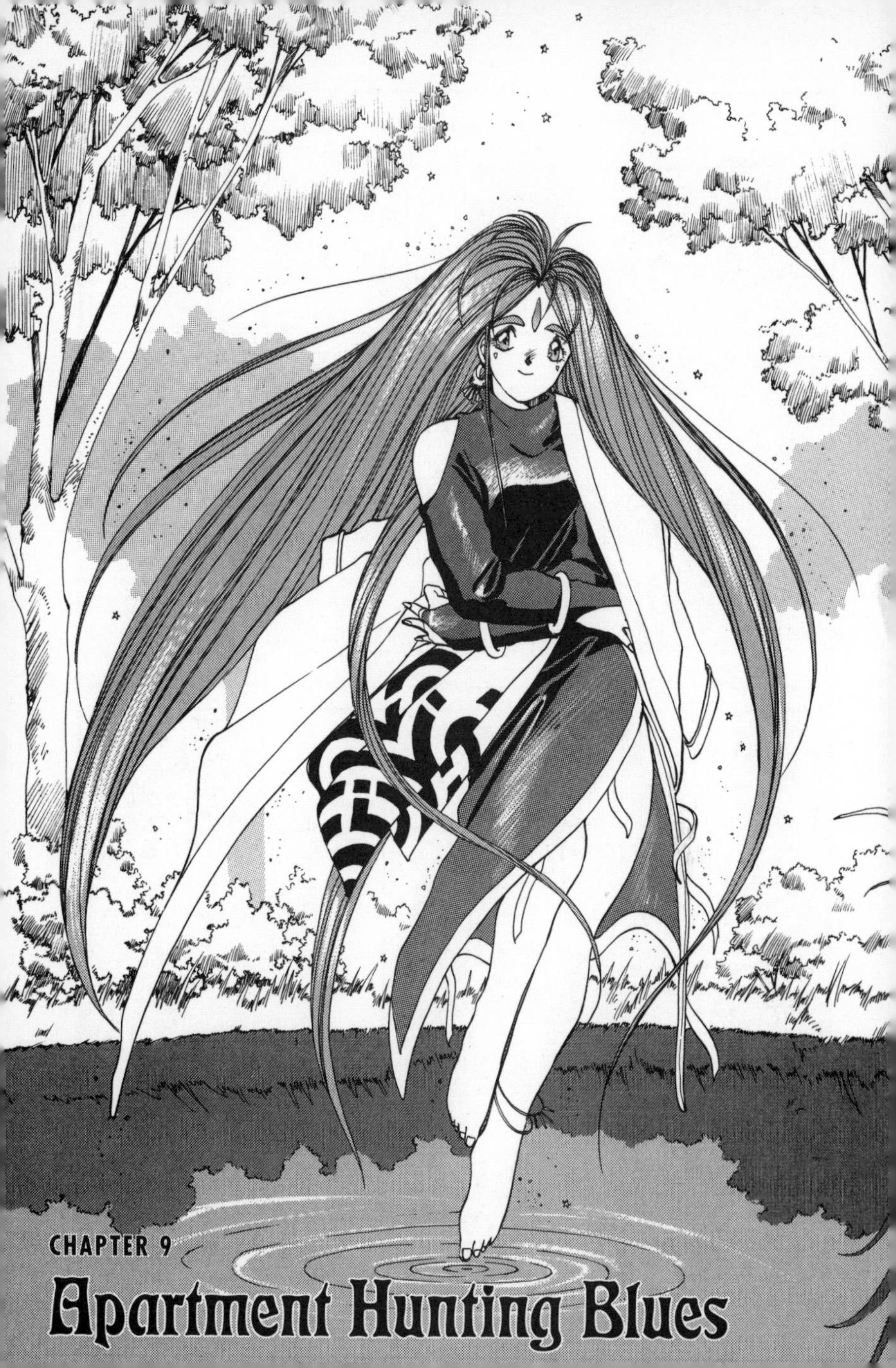

CHAPTER 9

Apartment Hunting Blues

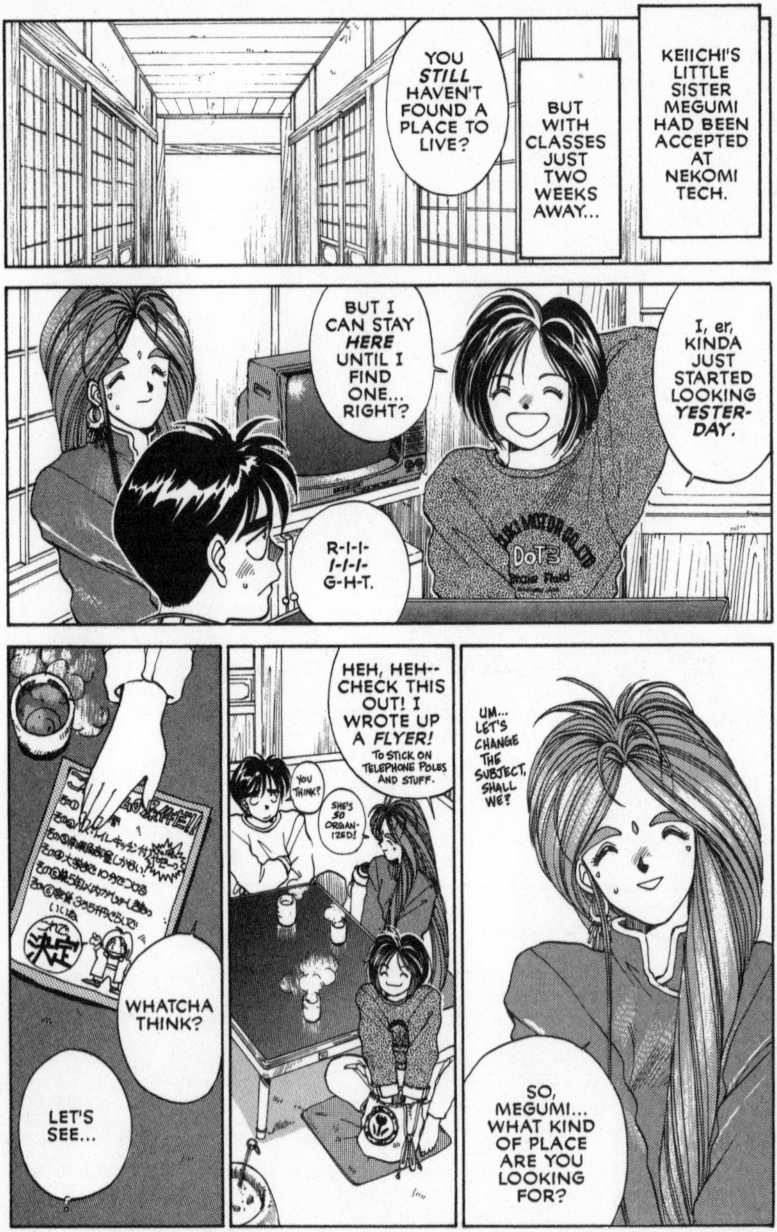
KEIICHI'S LITTLE SISTER MEGUMI HAD BEEN ACCEPTED AT NEKOMI TECH.
BUT WITH CLASSES JUST TWO WEEKS AWAY...
YOU *STILL* HAVEN'T FOUND A PLACE TO LIVE?
I, er, KINDA JUST STARTED LOOKING *YESTER-DAY.*
BUT I CAN STAY *HERE* UNTIL I FIND ONE... RIGHT?
R-I-I-*I-I-I-*G-H-T.
UM... LET'S CHANGE THE SUBJECT, SHALL WE?
SO, MEGUMI... WHAT KIND OF PLACE ARE YOU LOOKING FOR?
HEH, HEH-- CHECK THIS OUT! I WROTE UP A *FLYER!* TO STICK ON TELEPHONE POLES AND STUFF.
YOU THINK?
SHE'S *SO* ORGAN-IZED!
WHATCHA THINK?
LET'S SEE...

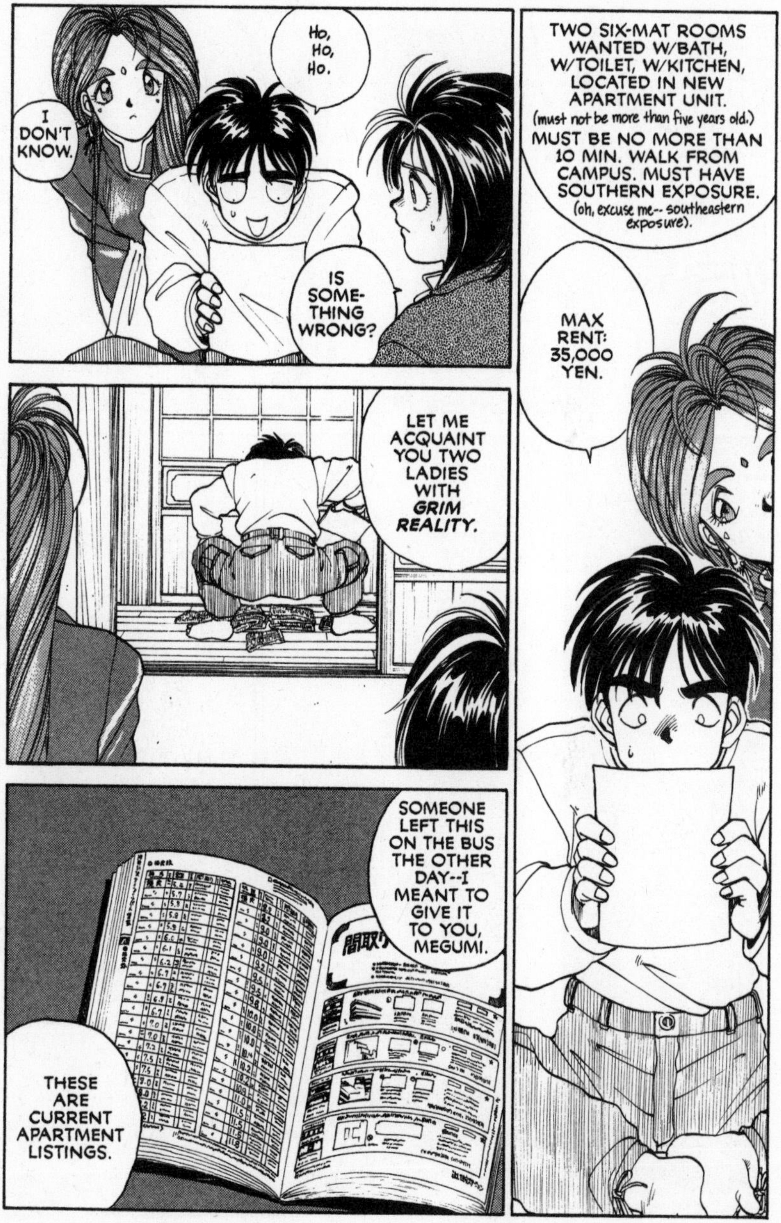

TWO SIX-MAT ROOMS WANTED W/BATH, W/TOILET, W/KITCHEN, LOCATED IN NEW APARTMENT UNIT. (must not be more than five years old.) MUST BE NO MORE THAN 10 MIN. WALK FROM CAMPUS. MUST HAVE SOUTHERN EXPOSURE. (oh, excuse me-- southeastern exposure).
MAX RENT: 35,000 YEN.
Ho, Ho, Ho.
IS SOMETHING WRONG?
I DON'T KNOW.
LET ME ACQUAINT YOU TWO LADIES WITH *GRIM REALITY*.
SOMEONE LEFT THIS ON THE BUS THE OTHER DAY--I MEANT TO GIVE IT TO YOU, MEGUMI.
THESE ARE CURRENT APARTMENT LISTINGS.

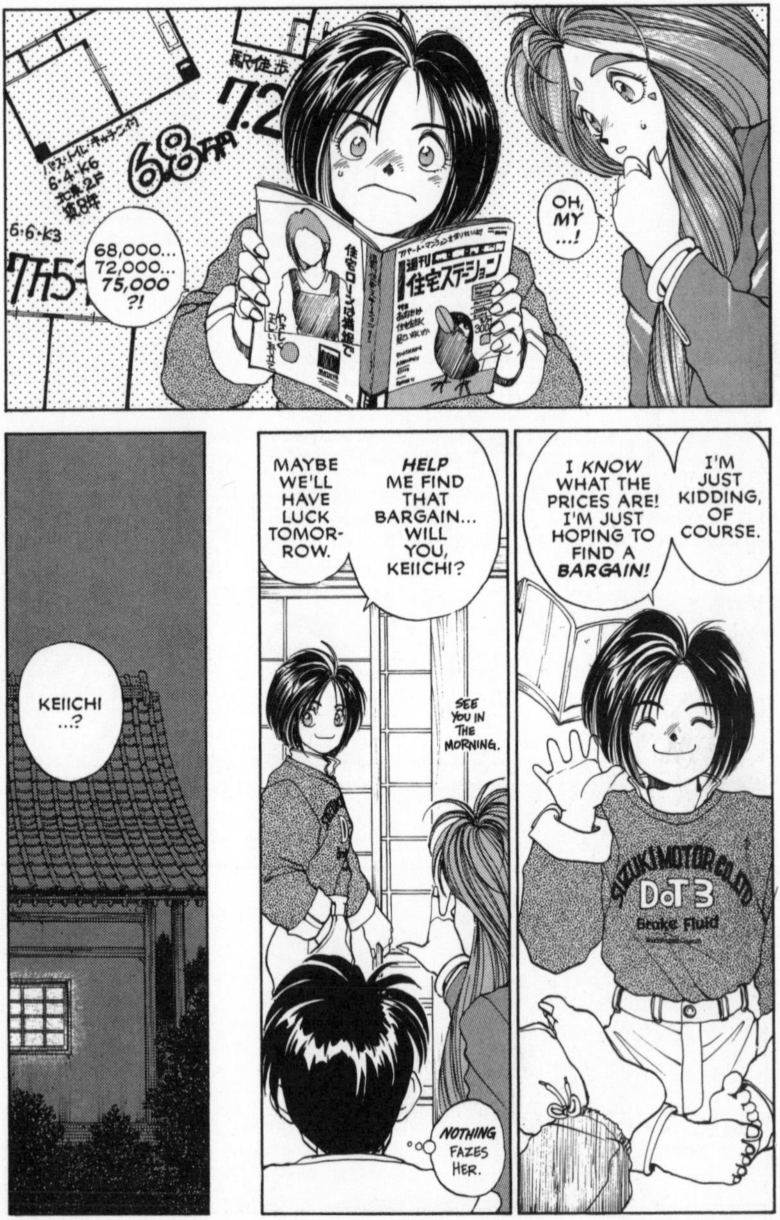

OH, MY ...!
68,000... 72,000... 75,000?!
I'M JUST KIDDING, OF COURSE.
I KNOW WHAT THE PRICES ARE! I'M JUST HOPING TO FIND A BARGAIN!
HELP ME FIND THAT BARGAIN... WILL YOU, KEIICHI?
MAYBE WE'LL HAVE LUCK TOMOR-ROW.
SEE YOU IN THE MORNING.
NOTHING FAZES HER.
KEIICHI ...?

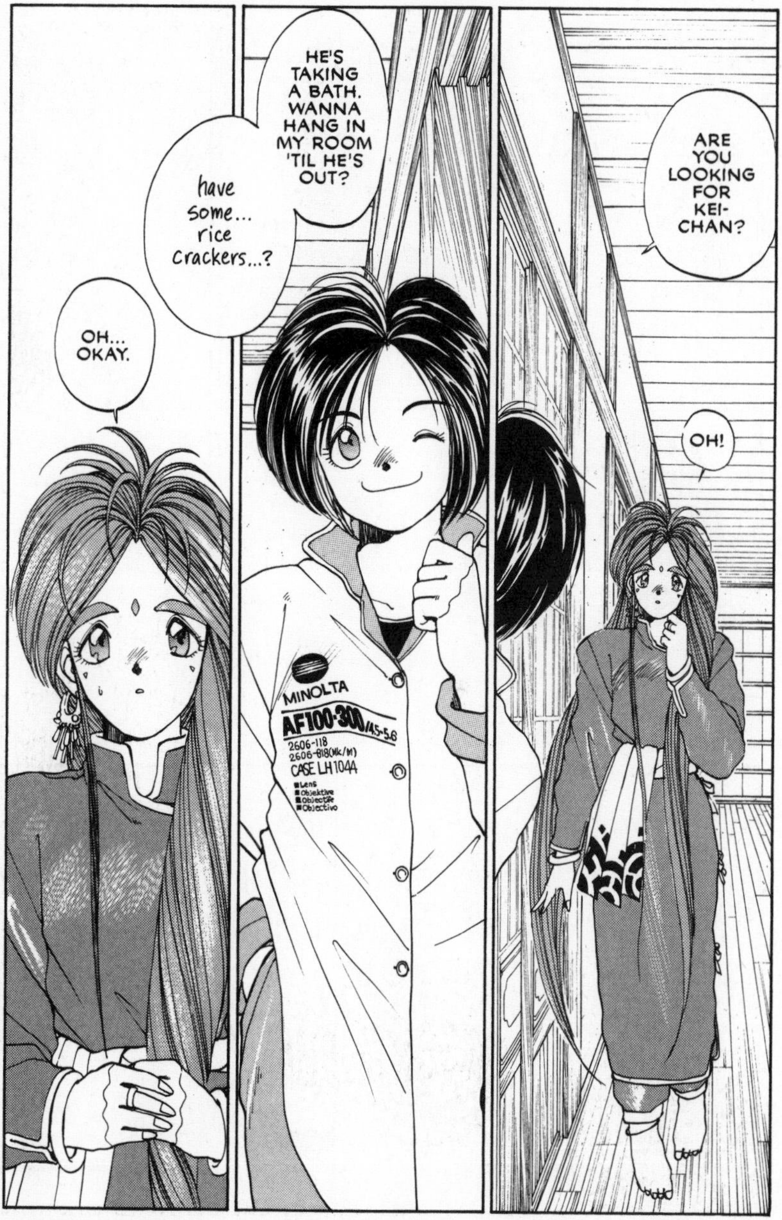
ARE YOU LOOKING FOR KEI-CHAN?
OH!
HE'S TAKING A BATH. WANNA HANG IN MY ROOM 'TIL HE'S OUT?
have some... rice crackers...?
MINOLTA
AF100·300/4.5-5.6
2606-118
2606-818(Mk/M)
CASE LH1044
Lens
Objektive
Objectivo
OH... OKAY.

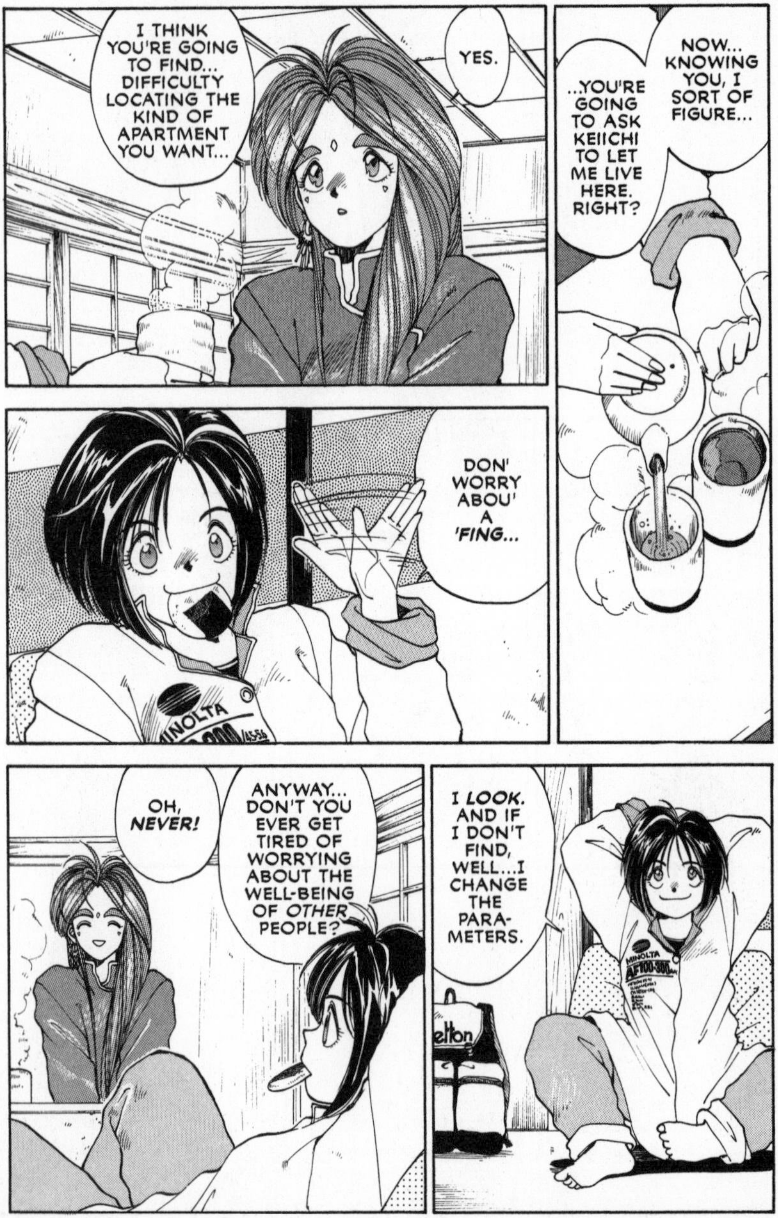
NOW... KNOWING YOU, I SORT OF FIGURE...
...YOU'RE GOING TO ASK KEIICHI TO LET ME LIVE HERE. RIGHT?
YES.
I THINK YOU'RE GOING TO FIND... DIFFICULTY LOCATING THE KIND OF APARTMENT YOU WANT...
DON' WORRY ABOU' A *'FING...*
I *LOOK.* AND IF I DON'T FIND, WELL...I CHANGE THE PARA-METERS.
ANYWAY... DON'T YOU EVER GET TIRED OF WORRYING ABOUT THE WELL-BEING OF *OTHER* PEOPLE?
OH, *NEVER!*

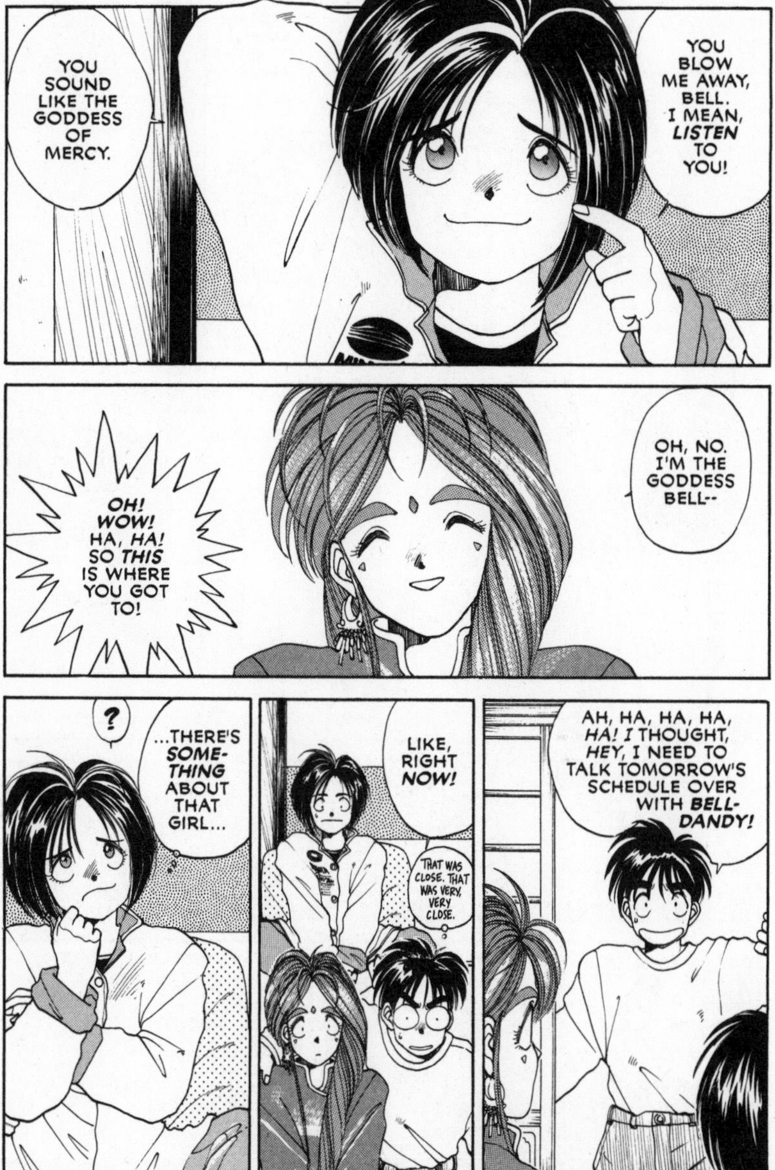
YOU BLOW ME AWAY, BELL. I MEAN, *LISTEN* TO YOU!
YOU SOUND LIKE THE GODDESS OF MERCY.
OH, NO. I'M THE GODDESS BELL--
OH! WOW! HA, *HA!* SO *THIS* IS WHERE YOU GOT TO!
AH, HA, HA, HA, *HA! I* THOUGHT, *HEY,* I NEED TO TALK TOMORROW'S SCHEDULE OVER WITH *BELL-DANDY!*
LIKE, RIGHT *NOW!*
THAT WAS CLOSE. THAT WAS VERY, VERY CLOSE.
?
...THERE'S *SOME-THING* ABOUT THAT GIRL...

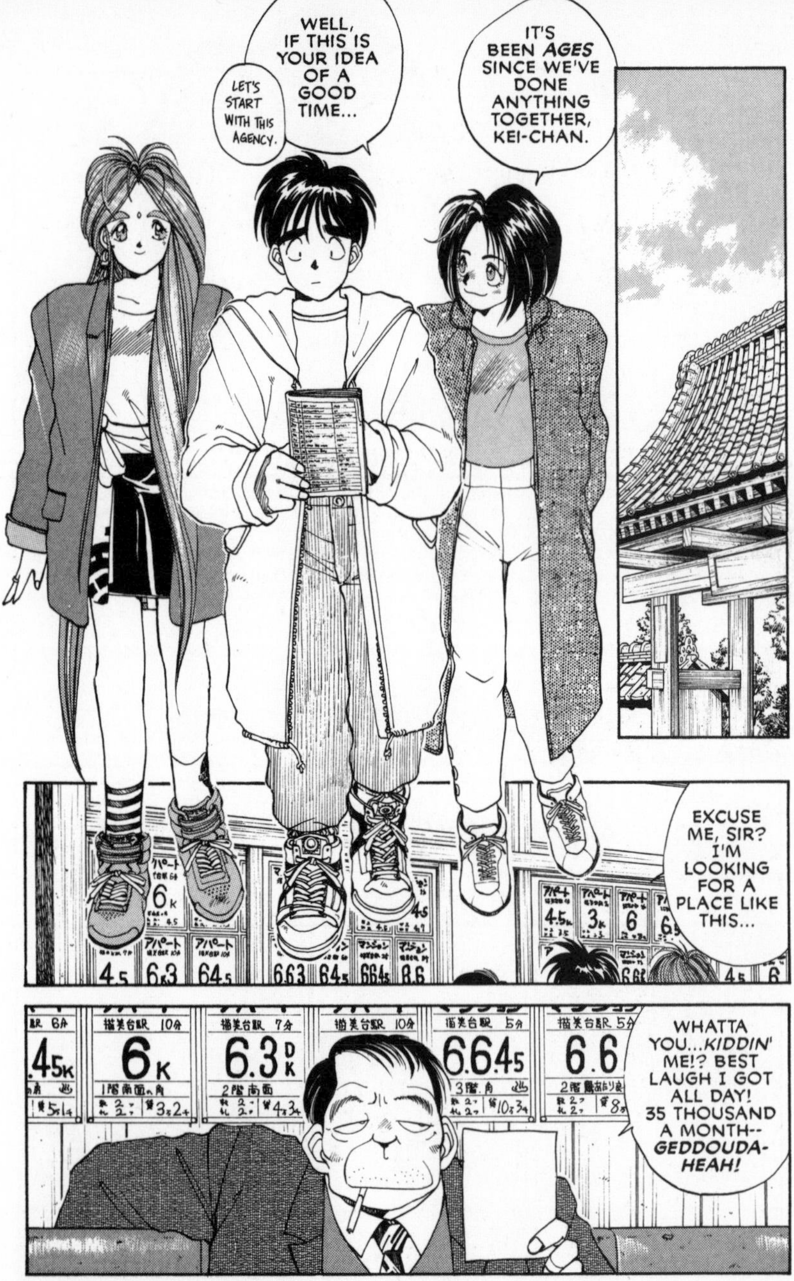
IT'S BEEN *AGES* SINCE WE'VE DONE ANYTHING TOGETHER, KEI-CHAN.
WELL, IF THIS IS YOUR IDEA OF A GOOD TIME...
LET'S START WITH THIS AGENCY.
EXCUSE ME, SIR? I'M LOOKING FOR A PLACE LIKE THIS...
WHATTA YOU...*KIDDIN'* ME!? BEST LAUGH I GOT ALL DAY! 35 THOUSAND A MONTH-- ***GEDDOUDA-HEAH!***

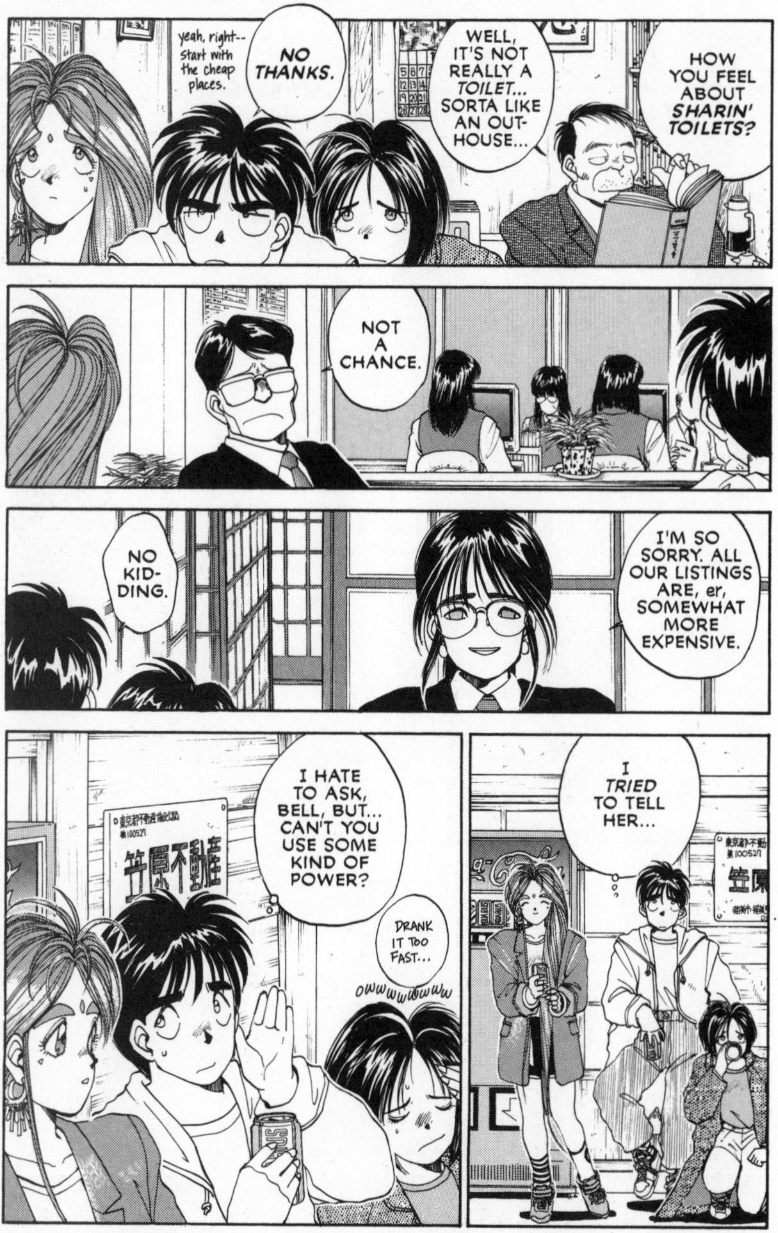
HOW YOU FEEL ABOUT *SHARIN' TOILETS?*
WELL, IT'S NOT REALLY A *TOILET...* SORTA LIKE AN OUT-HOUSE...
NO THANKS.
yeah, right-- start with the cheap places.
NOT A CHANCE.
I'M SO SORRY. ALL OUR LISTINGS ARE, er, SOMEWHAT MORE EXPENSIVE.
NO KID-DING.
I *TRIED* TO TELL HER...
I HATE TO ASK, BELL, BUT... CAN'T YOU USE SOME KIND OF POWER?
笠原不動産
DRANK IT TOO FAST...
OWWWWWWWW

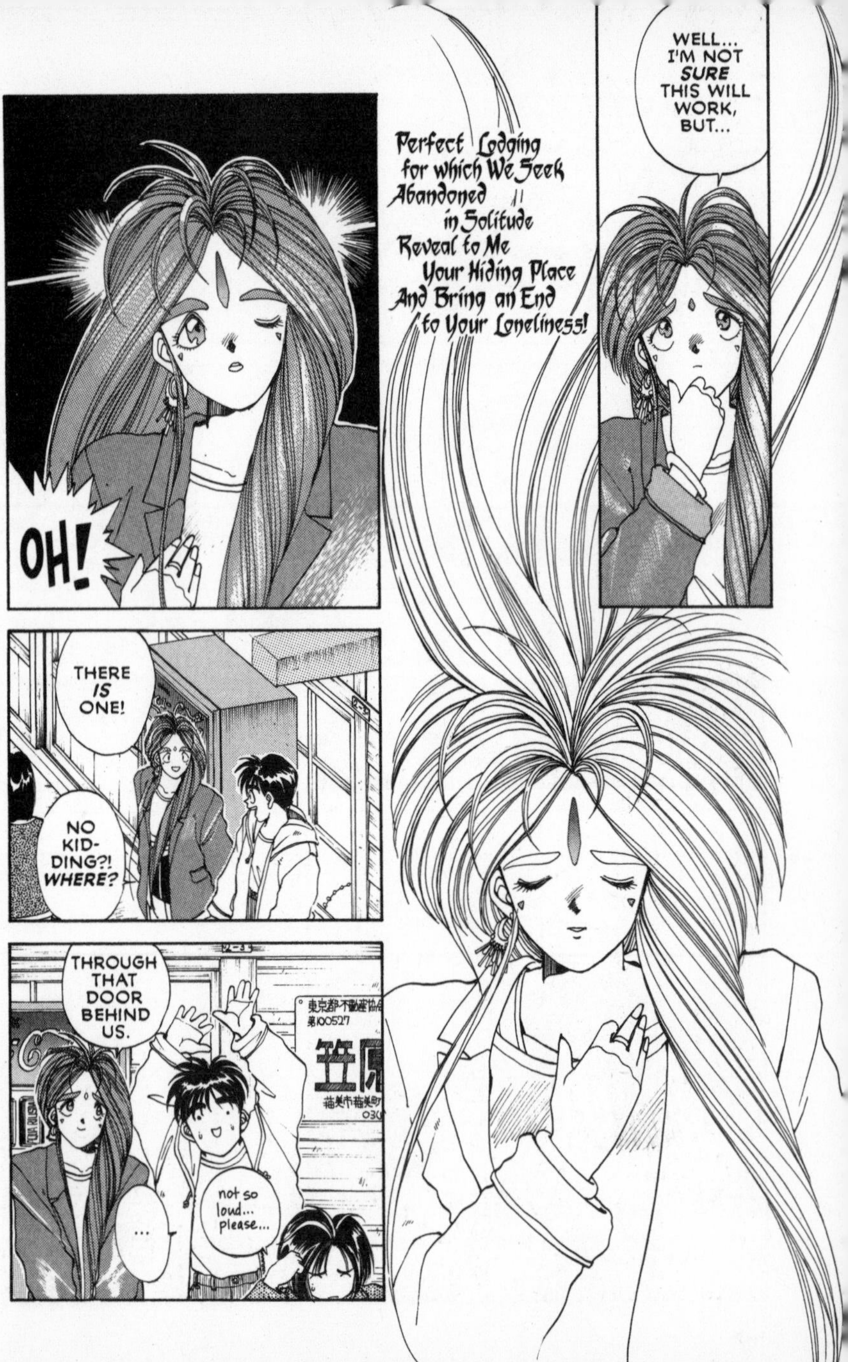
WELL... I'M NOT *SURE* THIS WILL WORK, BUT...
Perfect Lodging for which We Seek Abandoned in Solitude Reveal to Me Your Hiding Place And Bring an End to Your Loneliness!
OH!
THERE *IS* ONE!
NO KID-DING?! *WHERE?*
THROUGH THAT DOOR BEHIND US.
not so loud... please...
...

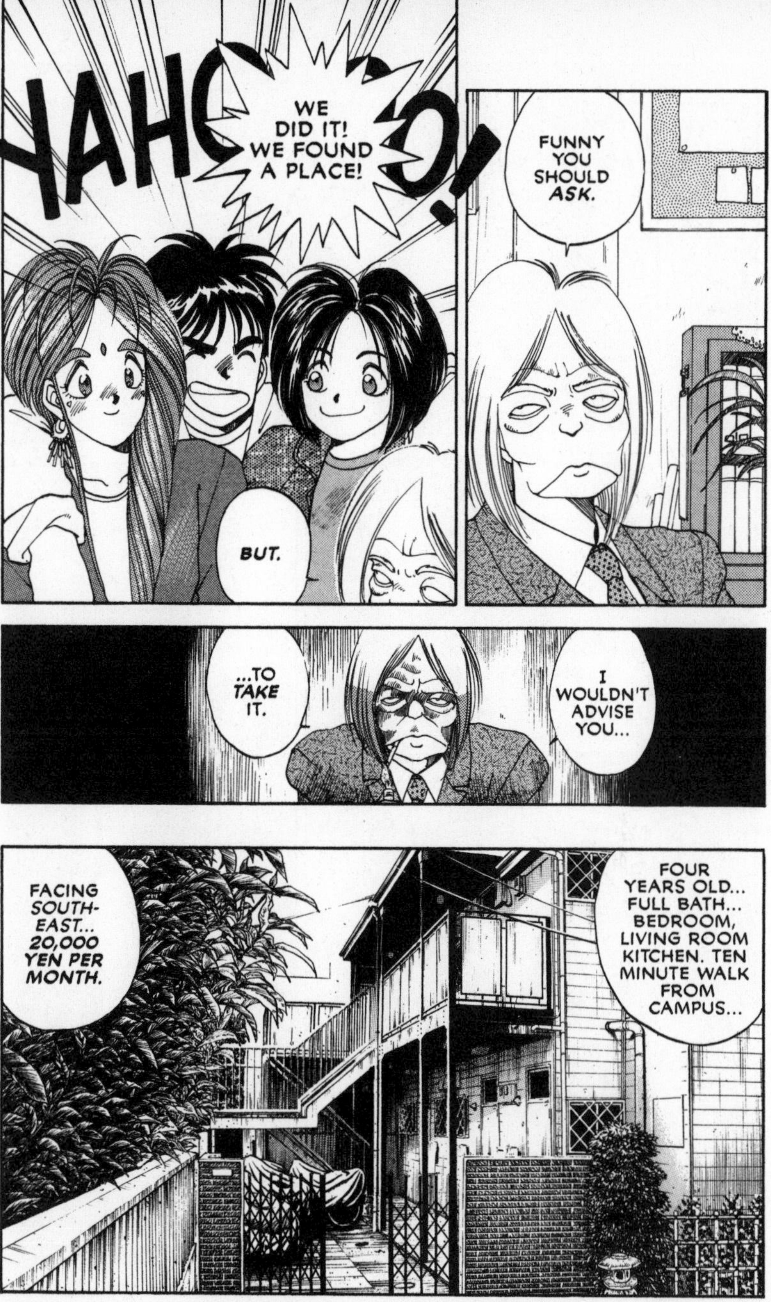
FUNNY YOU SHOULD ASK.
YAHOOO!
WE DID IT! WE FOUND A PLACE!
BUT.
I WOULDN'T ADVISE YOU...
...TO TAKE IT.
FOUR YEARS OLD... FULL BATH... BEDROOM, LIVING ROOM KITCHEN. TEN MINUTE WALK FROM CAMPUS...
FACING SOUTH-EAST... 20,000 YEN PER MONTH.

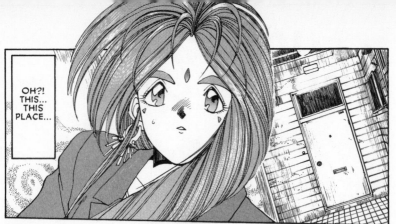

OH?! THIS... THIS PLACE...
WELL, OKAY-- I'LL TAKE IT!
...
HUH? WHERE'D THE MYSTERIOUS OLD MAN GO?
WHO KNOWS.
I'M GONNA SCOPE OUT THE GARDEN. ❤
....

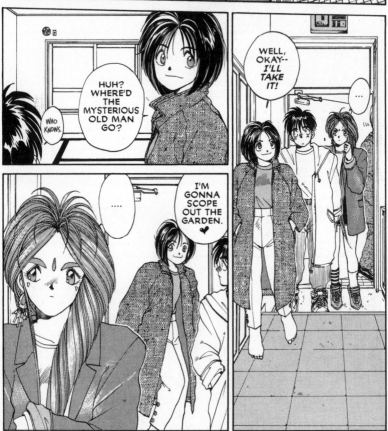

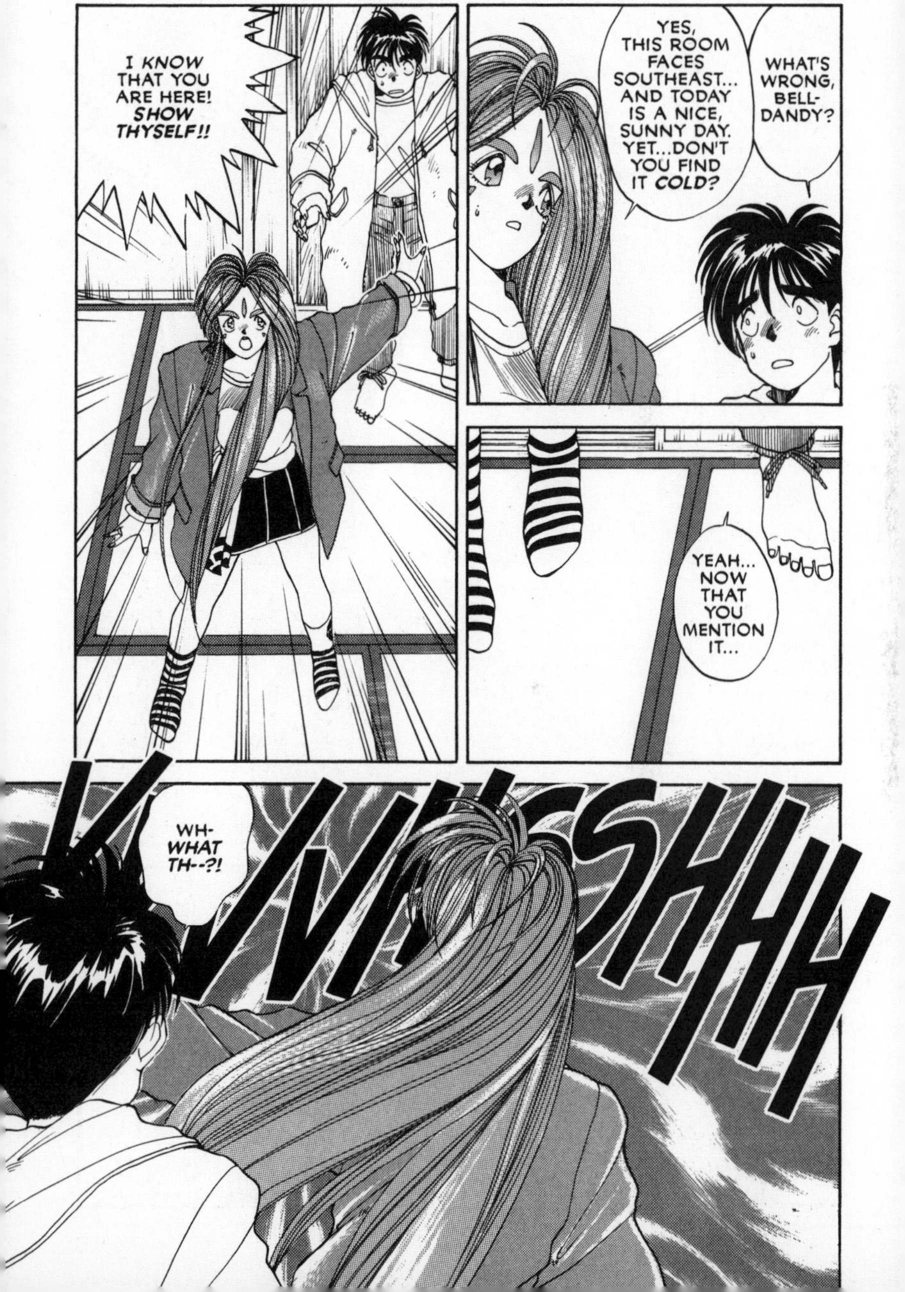
WHAT'S WRONG, BELL-DANDY?
YES, THIS ROOM FACES SOUTHEAST... AND TODAY IS A NICE, SUNNY DAY. YET...DON'T YOU FIND IT *COLD?*
YEAH... NOW THAT YOU MENTION IT...
I *KNOW* THAT YOU ARE HERE! ***SHOW THYSELF!!***
WH-WHAT TH--?!

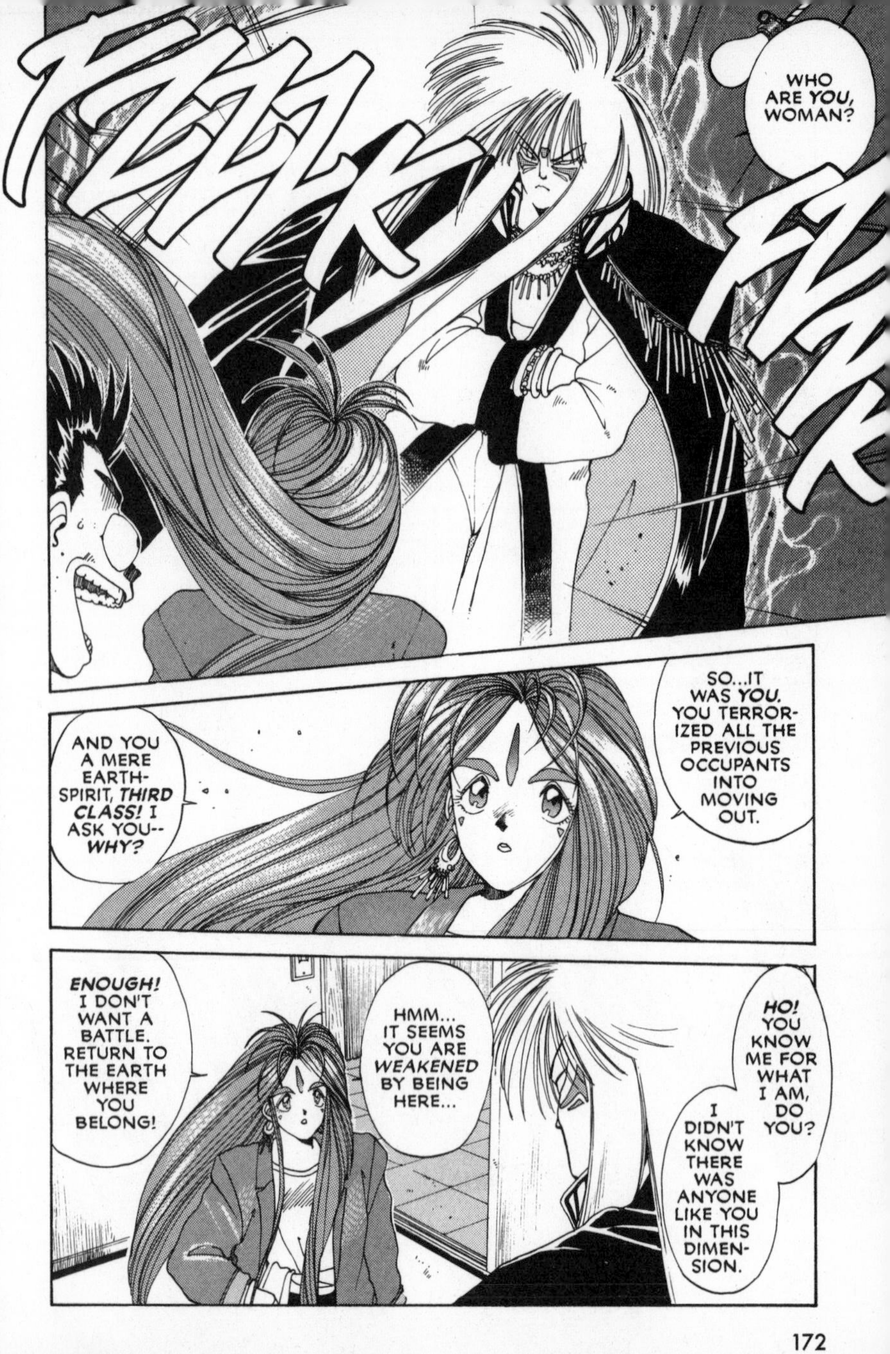
WHO ARE *YOU*, WOMAN?
SO...IT WAS *YOU.* YOU TERRORIZED ALL THE PREVIOUS OCCUPANTS INTO MOVING OUT.
AND YOU A MERE EARTH-SPIRIT, *THIRD CLASS!* I ASK YOU-- *WHY?*
HO! YOU KNOW ME FOR WHAT I AM, DO YOU?
I DIDN'T KNOW THERE WAS ANYONE LIKE YOU IN THIS DIMENSION.
HMM... IT SEEMS YOU ARE *WEAKENED* BY BEING HERE...
ENOUGH! I DON'T WANT A BATTLE. RETURN TO THE EARTH WHERE YOU BELONG!

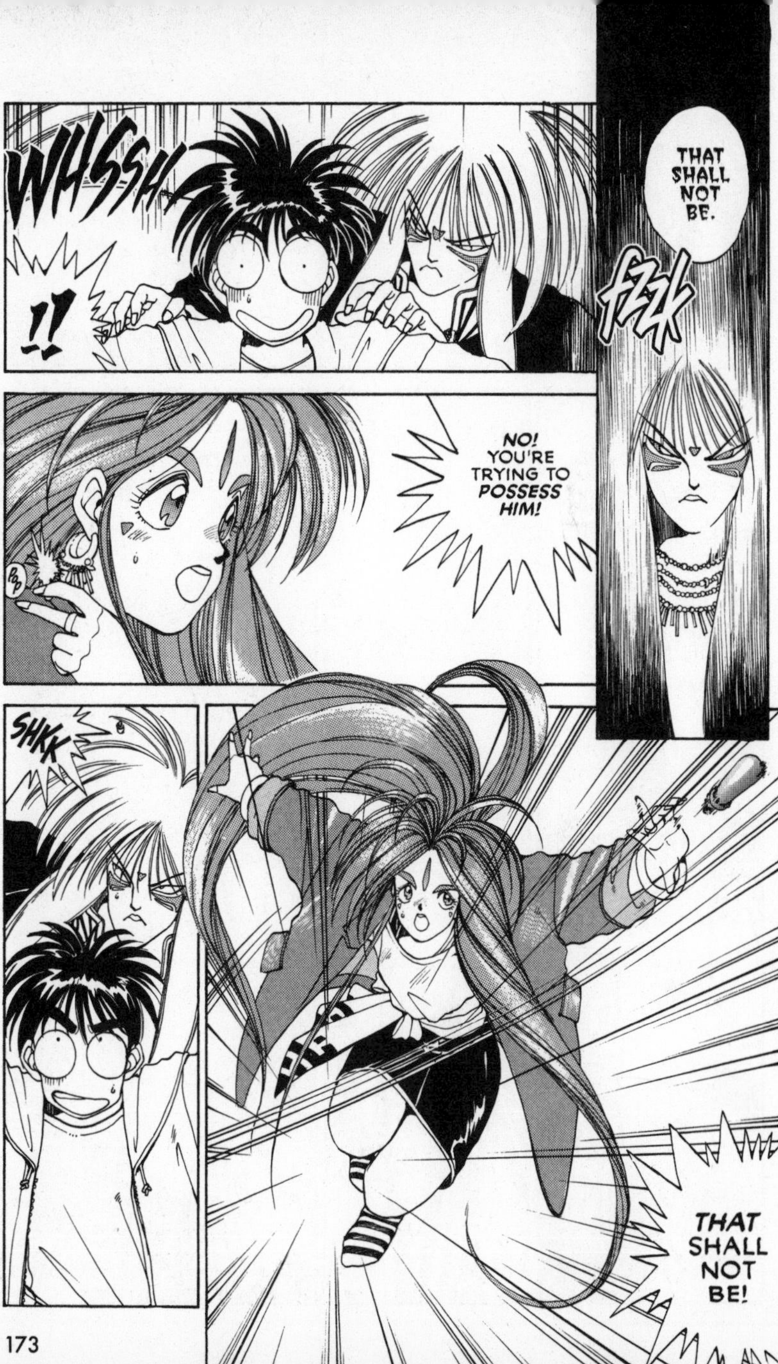
THAT SHALL NOT BE.
FZZK
WHSSH
!!
NO! YOU'RE TRYING TO *POSSESS* HIM!
POP
THAT SHALL NOT BE!
SHKK

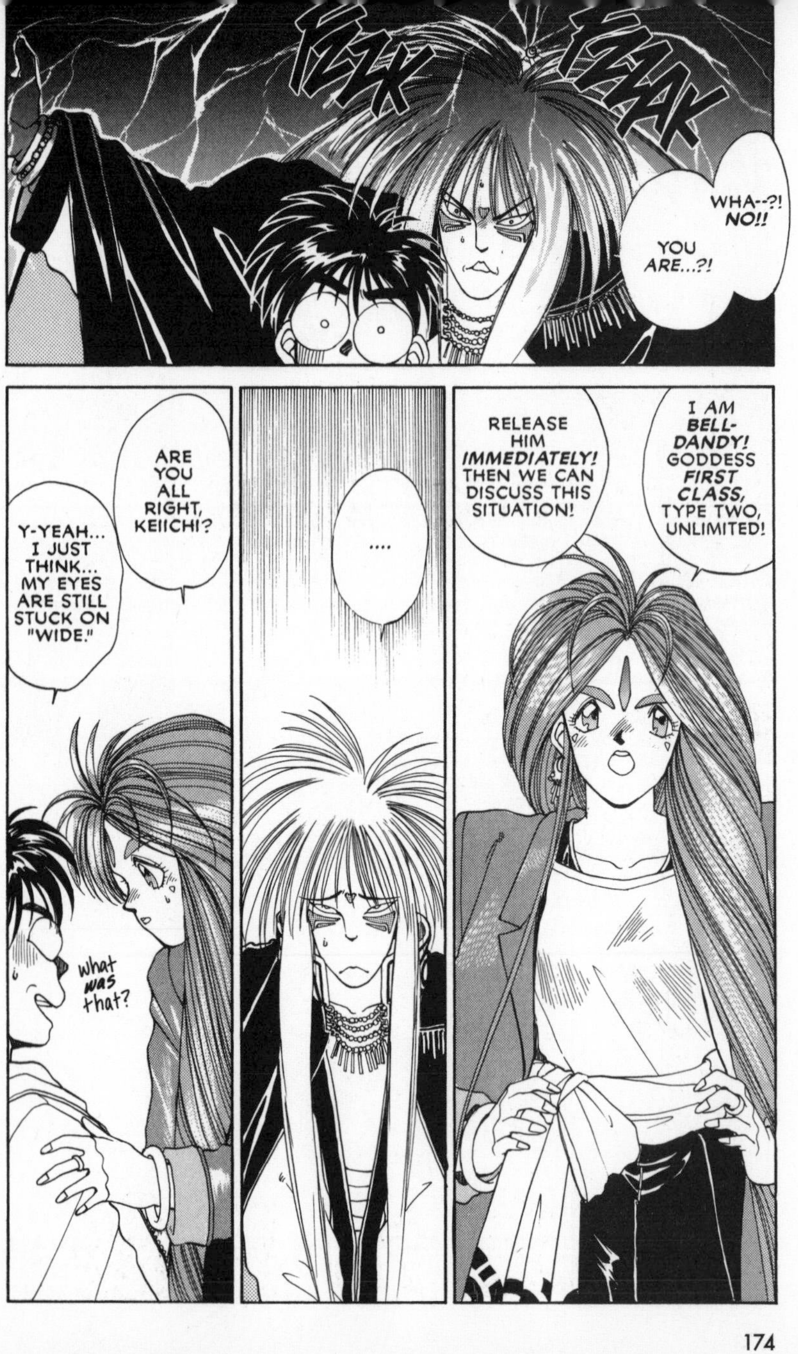
FZZAK
FZZK
WHA--?! NO!!
YOU ARE...?!
I AM BELL-DANDY! GODDESS FIRST CLASS, TYPE TWO, UNLIMITED!
RELEASE HIM IMMEDIATELY! THEN WE CAN DISCUSS THIS SITUATION!
....
ARE YOU ALL RIGHT, KEIICHI?
Y-YEAH... I JUST THINK... MY EYES ARE STILL STUCK ON "WIDE."
what was that?

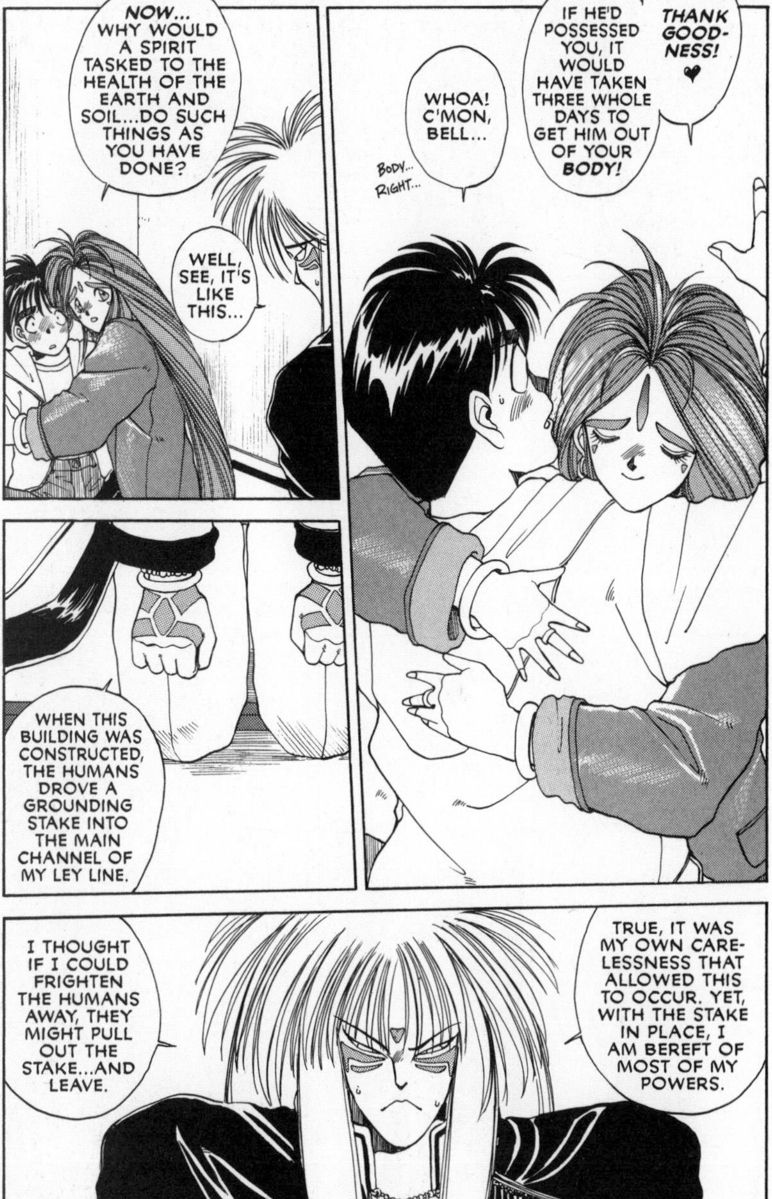
THANK GOODNESS!
IF HE'D POSSESSED YOU, IT WOULD HAVE TAKEN THREE WHOLE DAYS TO GET HIM OUT OF YOUR BODY!
WHOA! C'MON, BELL...
BODY... RIGHT...
NOW... WHY WOULD A SPIRIT TASKED TO THE HEALTH OF THE EARTH AND SOIL...DO SUCH THINGS AS YOU HAVE DONE?
WELL, SEE, IT'S LIKE THIS...
WHEN THIS BUILDING WAS CONSTRUCTED, THE HUMANS DROVE A GROUNDING STAKE INTO THE MAIN CHANNEL OF MY LEY LINE.
TRUE, IT WAS MY OWN CARELESSNESS THAT ALLOWED THIS TO OCCUR. YET, WITH THE STAKE IN PLACE, I AM BEREFT OF MOST OF MY POWERS.
I THOUGHT IF I COULD FRIGHTEN THE HUMANS AWAY, THEY MIGHT PULL OUT THE STAKE...AND LEAVE.

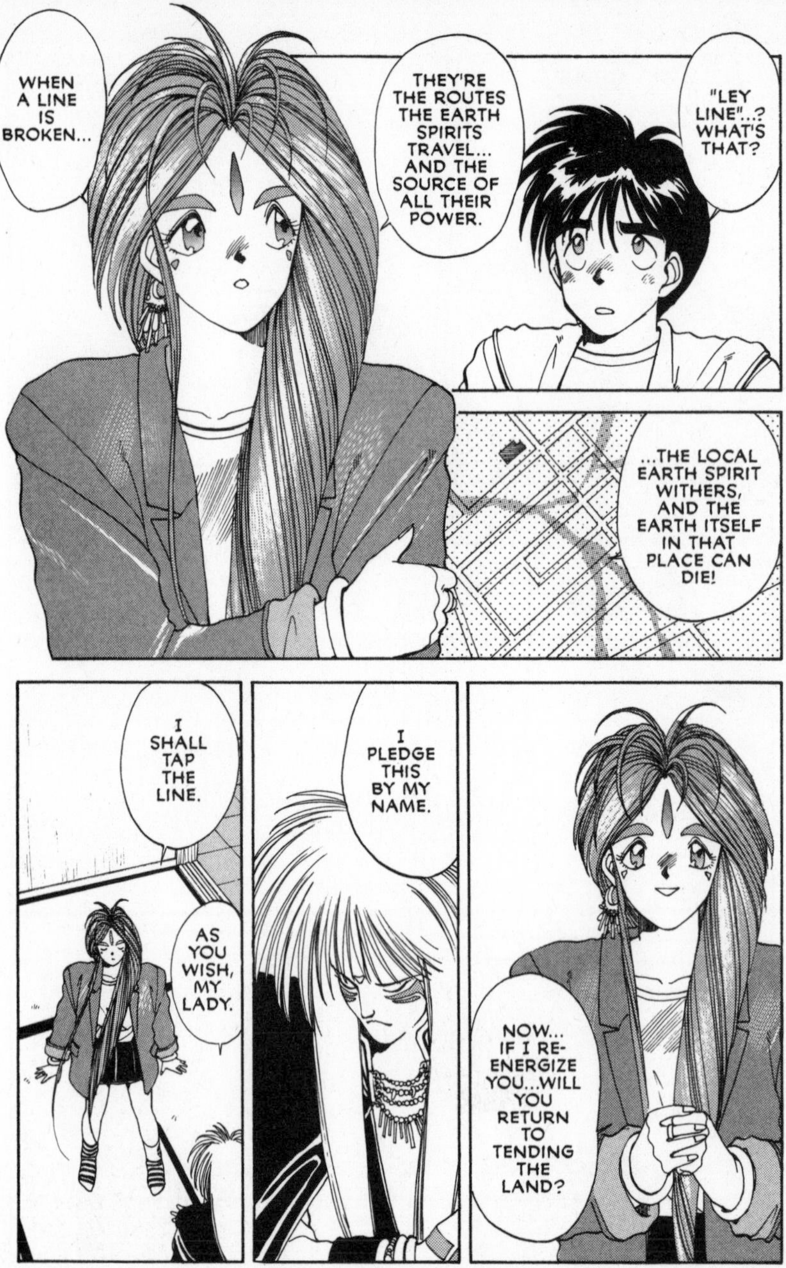
"LEY LINE"..? WHAT'S THAT?
THEY'RE THE ROUTES THE EARTH SPIRITS TRAVEL... AND THE SOURCE OF ALL THEIR POWER.
WHEN A LINE IS BROKEN...
...THE LOCAL EARTH SPIRIT WITHERS, AND THE EARTH ITSELF IN THAT PLACE CAN DIE!
NOW... IF I RE-ENERGIZE YOU...WILL YOU RETURN TO TENDING THE LAND?
I PLEDGE THIS BY MY NAME.
I SHALL TAP THE LINE.
AS YOU WISH, MY LADY.

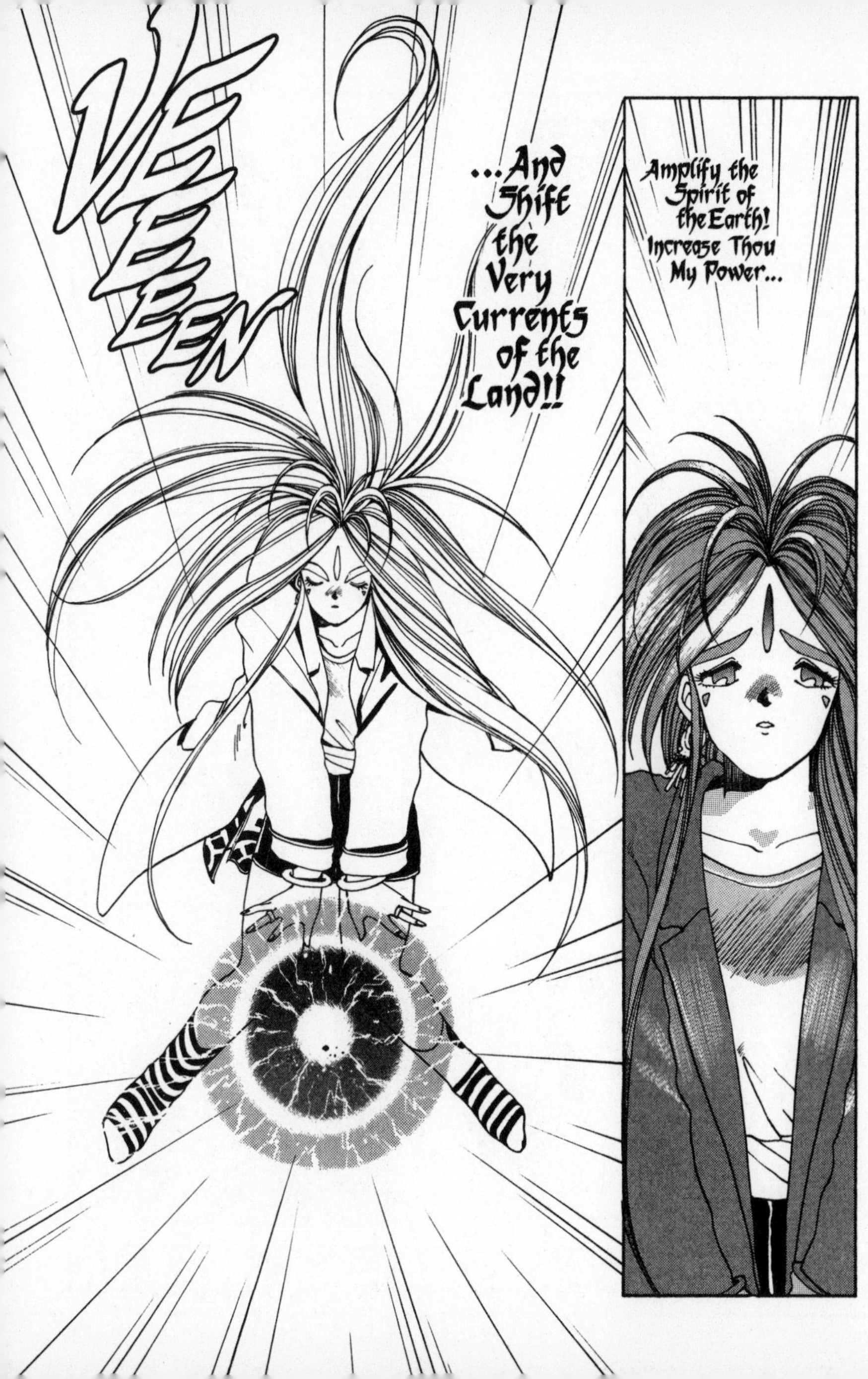
Amplify the Spirit of the Earth! Increase Thou My Power...
...And Shift the Very Currents of the Land!!
VEEEEEN

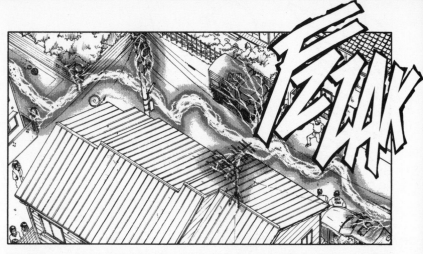

MY LADY...
I AM IN
YOUR DEBT.

OW!

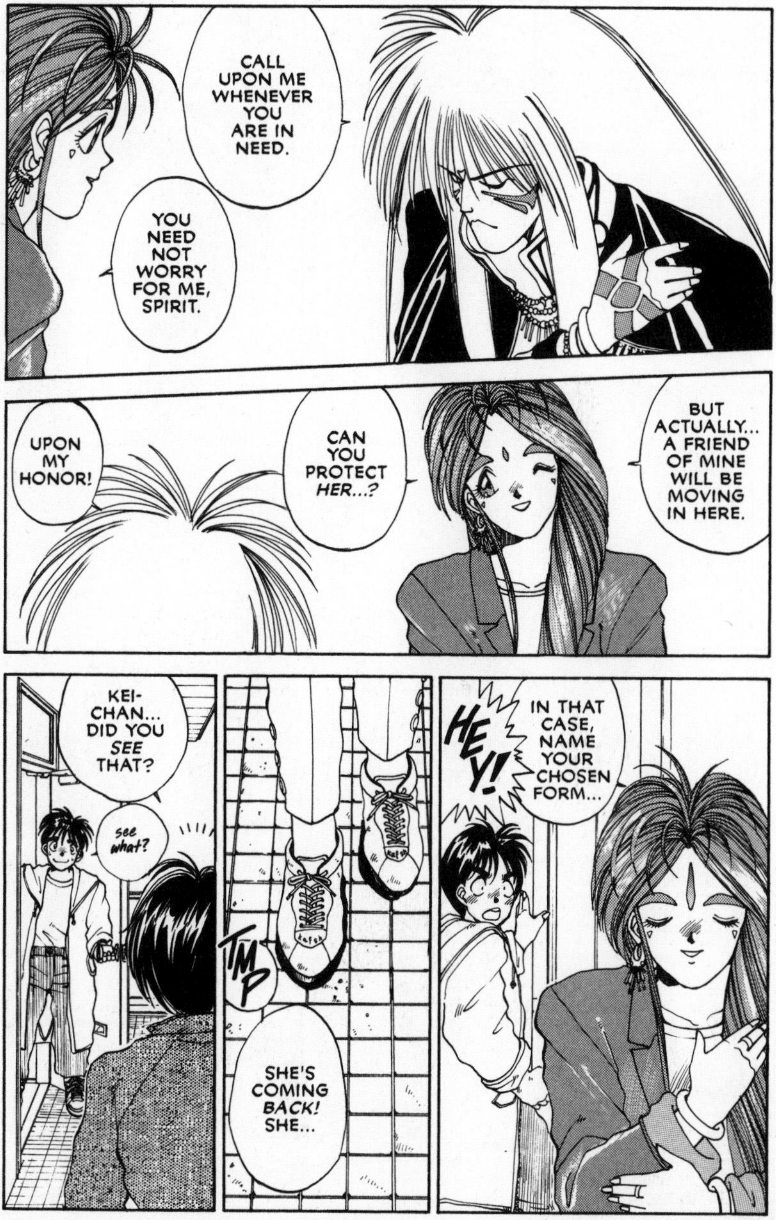
CALL UPON ME WHENEVER YOU ARE IN NEED.
YOU NEED NOT WORRY FOR ME, SPIRIT.
BUT ACTUALLY... A FRIEND OF MINE WILL BE MOVING IN HERE.
CAN YOU PROTECT *HER*...?
UPON MY HONOR!
IN THAT CASE, NAME YOUR CHOSEN FORM...
HEY!
TMP
SHE'S COMING *BACK!* SHE...
KEI-CHAN... DID YOU *SEE* THAT?
see what?

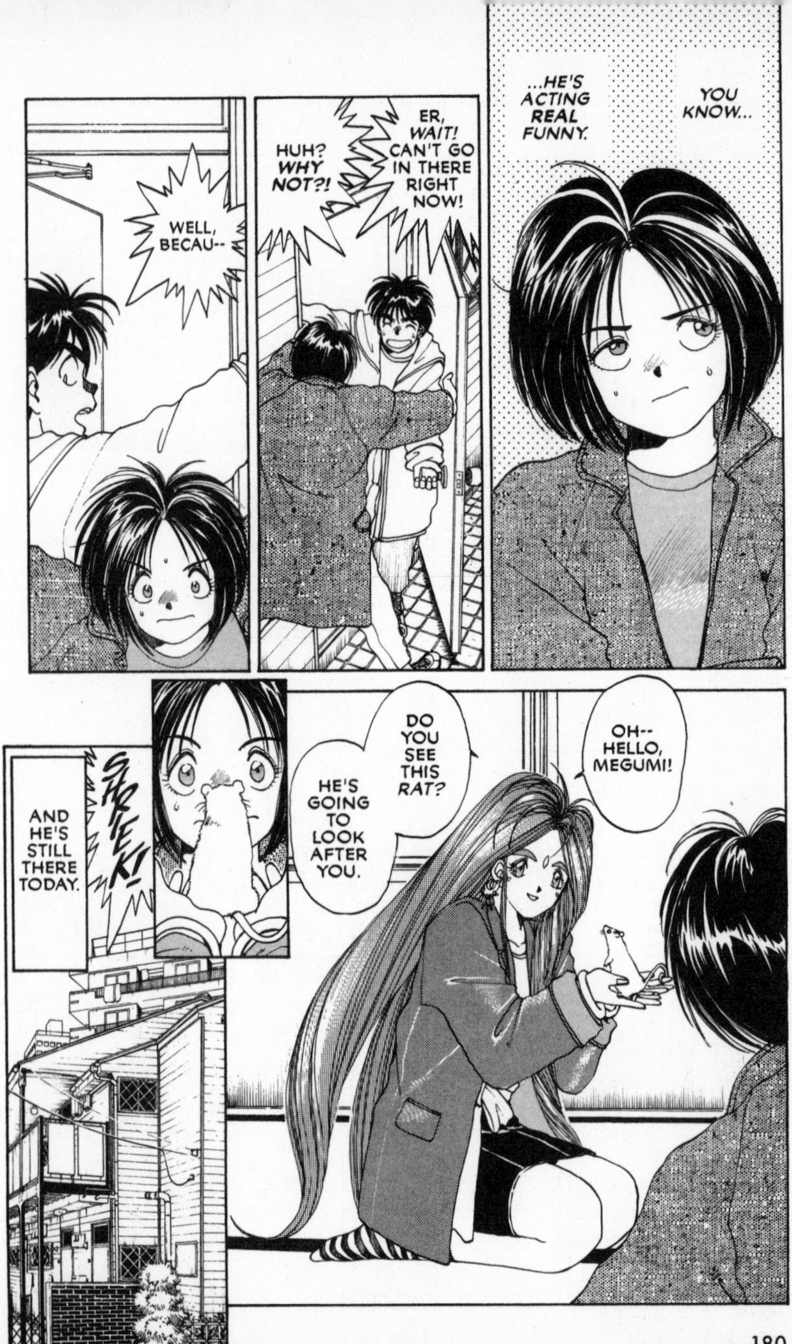
YOU KNOW...
...HE'S ACTING REAL FUNNY.
ER, WAIT! CAN'T GO IN THERE RIGHT NOW!
HUH? WHY NOT?!
WELL, BECAU--
OH-- HELLO, MEGUMI!
DO YOU SEE THIS RAT?
HE'S GOING TO LOOK AFTER YOU.
SHRIEK!
AND HE'S STILL THERE TODAY.

EDITOR
Carl Gustav Horn

DESIGNER
Debra Bailey

ART DIRECTOR
Lia Ribacchi

PUBLISHER
Mike Richardson

English-language version
produced by Dark Horse Comics

Published by Dark Horse Manga
A division of Dark Horse Comics, Inc.
10956 SE Main Street
Milwaukie, OR 97222
www.darkhorse.com

To find a comics shop in your area,
call the Comic Shop Locator Service
toll-free at 1-888-266-4226

First edition: October 2005
ISBN 978-1-59307-387-9

3 5 7 9 10 8 6 4

Printed at Lake Book Manufacturing, Inc.,
Melrose Park, IL, USA

letters to the
ENCHANTRESS

10956 SE Main Street, Milwaukie, Oregon 97222
omg@darkhorse.com • www.darkhorse.com

NOTE: Full addresses and e-mail addresses will not be printed, unless you ask! All fan artwork, letters, and e-mails submitted become the property of Dark Horse Comics.

First of all, thanks to all the readers for the positive reception of *Oh My Goddess!* Vol. 21 (see below). We received a number of responses to it, which will be printed in the "Letters to the Enchantress" section of Vol. 22. If you're starting the *OMG!* story right here with Vol. 1, though, we'd like *your* letters and fan art to print in Vol. 2! Read on . . .

Welcome to Vol. 1 of the new edition of *Oh My Goddess!* In July, Dark Horse released the first volume of *OMG!* in this new edition . . . which was actually Vol. 21. If you're brand new to this manga series, that last statement doesn't seem to make much sense, but please don't go. ^_^ Simply put, Dark Horse has already been releasing *Oh My Goddess!* in English for eleven years, but always in the "flopped," left-to-right reading (i.e., normal English direction) format, which was in fact the industry standard until just a few years ago.

After getting all the way up to Vol. 20 in left-to-right (and these volumes, by the way, are still available), Dark Horse decided to switch to right-to-left, the new industry standard. This switch means not only that all new volumes in the story are being re-released

right-to-left (hence, Vol. 21 in July), but Dark Horse is also going back and re-releasing all the *old* volumes, Vols. 1–20, in right-to-left format (hence, the book you're reading right now).

The idea is to serve both the fans who were already reading *Oh My Goddess!* in its old format, and the new fans we hope will discover this charming, and, shall we say, highly influential series. From now on, every two months, Dark Horse will switch off between "new" and "old" volumes. So, in January 2006 will come *OMG!* Vol. 22; in April 2006, *OMG!* Vol. 2; in June, *OMG!* Vol. 23, and so forth.

Oh My Goddess! is not only the second-longest continuously published manga series in the United States, it's been one of the more enduring manga series in Japan, too. The stories in this first volume ran originally in *OMG!*'s home magazine, the monthly *Afternoon* (also home of Dark Horse titles such as *Seraphic Feather*, *Blade of the Immortal*, *Gunsmith Cats*, and *Cannon God Exaxxion*), between November of 1988 and May of 1989. *Afternoon* magazine's very first issue had come out just the year before *Oh My Goddess!* started, so this manga has been very much a part of its history, and as of the October 2005 issue of *Afternoon*, the story is now up to Chapter 204.

It's a little startling to realize when *OMG!* began, Ronald Reagan was still president, and Osamu Tezuka was still alive. It was an interesting time both for Japan, and for manga. In 1988 Japan was known mainly to the West as a challenger for geopolitical prominence—the same way people talk about China today, but more so. The '80s had that very cyberpunk, *Blade Runner*-type vision of a future that would belong no longer to American, but to Japanese corporate imperialism. That didn't seem like such a bad thing to me when I was eighteen, if simply because Japanese corporate imperial products were much cooler.

Like Keiichi, I was a sophomore in college in the fall of 1988, and writing term papers about future economic conflict with Japan—or even future war. Never about anime or manga, though. Oddly enough, what was missing back then was mainstream American interest in Japanese *pop culture*. The big Japan-related stories that year were about the trade deficit, or how Japanese companies were buying American corporations and famous buildings, or whether American companies should use Japanese methods of organization—in other words, business and political issues. But anime and manga, as such, still barely existed on the radar of the American mass media, or indeed, in academia—these days it seems *most* of the university writing about Japan is about anime and manga.

Of course, there were otaku back then, too—I was already one—but you would sometimes get this weird vibe of a type you wouldn't really get today, where people would ask, shouldn't you be studying *serious* Japanese stuff so you can learn how to help America compete with Mitsubishi? As for professors hanging out at anime shows on campus, forget it; they wanted you to get a grounding in Japanese history and literature. I don't think that's such a bad idea for an anime fan either, as anime, like everything else, emerges out of a historical reality (although many have loved anime without knowing anything about Japan, or indeed, without even knowing it was Japanese).

It occurs to me now in writing this, that it's probably a good thing for Japanese studies departments that Americans are now so into anime and manga—because it eventually picked up the interest in Japan that had dipped after the Japanese economic bubble burst in the early '90s. You never know how these things are going to turn out; a friend of mine from high school completed his degree in Soviet Studies in 1991, the year the Soviet Union collapsed. To date there has been no compensating boom in Russian animation and comics.

EDITOR'S COMMENTARY ON VOL. 1:

3.6: The little dab of watercolor that goes over the top panel border between the word balloons was in the original. We are now so authentic it *hurts*.

7.2: The drawing tacked to the wall to the upper right of Bell-chan's head reads *shochuu*, meaning the middle of summer. Who drew it? A younger relative of one of the guys in the dorm?

14.1 The little octopus seen below Keiichi's left hand is a reference to *Kure Kure Takora* ("Gimme Gimme Octopus"), a wild Japanese live-action kid's show from 1973 about a greedy young, well, octopus, whose catchphrase is "Gimme! Gimme!" and whose eight arms come in handy for the task. Takora is said to also make a cameo near the beginning of the famous "Mr. Sparkle" ad in *The Simpsons*. Two Japanese sites about the show can be found at: http://www.kagurazaka. co.jp/kachimo/takora/takora.html (this one will play the theme song for you) and http:// www001.upp.so-net.ne.jp/kindan-hm/takora. html (more images up front).

19.2: Belldandy's parable of the TV antenna already seems a bit dated, as most Americans today get their TV through cable or digital satellite. However, Japan, which usually has a well-deserved reputation for being ahead of America on technical developments, didn't really start to introduce cable television until well into the 1980s.

27.1: When this story was first published in English in 2000, and later when it was collected in *OMG!* Vol. 1, it was called "Into The Lair of the Anime Otaku." Sada *is* recognizable as a stereotypical otaku (he even bears some physical resemblance to Tanaka, the "Otaking" of Gainax's must-see 1991 *Otaku no Video*, available in the U.S. through animeigo.com—also home to the original *Oh My Goddess!* anime series). But in fact the word "otaku" never appears in the original Japanese story; instead, the chapter title (and Keiichi) refer to Sada not as an "anime otaku," but as an "anime mania"—literally, using the English word "mania," which in Japanese becomes pronounced as "mah-nee-ah" instead of "may-nee-ah."

This is no more than speculation, but it is also possible that Fujishima *did* use "otaku" when this story first appeared in the December 1988 issue of *Afternoon*, but that it was changed for the graphic novel. The first printing of *Oh My Goddess!* Vol. 1 in Japan is dated August 23, 1989, exactly one month after the arrest of Tsutomu Miyazaki. An otaku who committed depraved serial killings, Miyazaki made the term notorious for a period of several years in the Japanese media (today it has been somewhat co-opted, if not always respected, as a marketable subculture, like gangster rap). In such an atmosphere of hysteria, it might have been deemed imprudent to refer to Sada as an otaku, even if he clearly is one—hence a change to the term "mania."

Again, however, that is no more than speculation, and the loan-word "mania"—the Japanese use "mania" where we would say "maniac"—to describe an obsessed fan is older in Japan than this meaning for "otaku," which didn't acquire that association until the early 1980s ("otaku" is just a form of the pronoun "you"—Jack Seward's 1969 book *Japanese in Action* recommended "otaku" as more masculine than the polite *anata* ordinarily taught in class!). But I found its use here intriguing, and it brought to mind a recollection that in the mid-'90s, scholar Kenji Sato (whose controversial essay on anime, "More Animated Than Life" was quoted in Donald Richie's 2002 book *A Hundred Years of Japanese Film*) was then trying to promote the term "mania" as a more positive substitute for "otaku"—an interesting reversal.

In any event, I don't believe Fujishima meant any special disrespect in his timeless portrayal of Sada; *Oh My Goddess!* found early affection among otaku audiences (it has been observed that the many imitations of *OMG!* over the years have progressively exploited its "harem" premise with overkill on fan service, without achieving Fujishima's sensitivity and elegance). Kosuke Fujishima himself trained as an assistant under the genuinely maniacal Tatsuya Egawa (best known in America for the anime based on his manga *Golden Boy*), who was even then a friend of Gainax's Hideaki Anno, and in fact used to draw covers for Gainax's *doujinshi*. It's fair to guess that Fujishima knew his way around otaku long before the general public had even heard the word.

It isn't the intention, by the way, of the new edition of *Oh My Goddess!* to make changes to the original English version merely for the sake of having it be "closer to the Japanese," if the so-called "closer" version actually makes things less clear. Changing "otaku" to "mania," as this edition does, in fact risks just that. But I thought the background behind the word was of sufficient interest to make the change; fortunately "anime mania" is readily understandable in English as an anime obsession, even if the reader doesn't realize at first that "mania" is being used here not to refer to the obsession, but to the obsessed person.

28.4: In this era, I'm surprised passersby didn't mistake her for Axl Rose.

32.6: Note Bell-chan clutching one of her shoes; Keiichi didn't even give her time to put them both back on (after taking them off to enter a Japanese house).

34.6: Probably a play on *Magical Emi* (1985) and/or *Creamy Mami* (1983), two "magical girl" shows that were early projects of industry titan Studio Pierrot, who more recently made the anime versions of *Great Teacher Onizuka, Naruto,* and *Bleach.*

37.4: Belldandy is holding a laserdisc. Before the Great Fire War destroyed human civilization, the Ancient Ones inscribed wondrous sounds and pictures on these shining plates, which resembled a DVD—yet so large that a warrior's hand's-breadth would not span its surface! Or so the elders of the tribe tell us.

37.5: To be a bit more specific, the 12-inch laserdisc, or LD, format, came onto the market in the late 1970s and, until the DVD supplanted it in the late 1990s, was basically the high-end alternative to watching movies on videotape. The LD format had a few advantages compared to DVD; you never had to worry about "artifacting" as you sometimes do with DVDs, as the visuals on an LD were stored in an uncompressed analog format. From a collector's standpoint, many movies (like the original cuts of the *Star Wars* films) had versions on LD different on their VHS or DVD releases; also, the large size of the LD envelope allowed the potential for beautiful layout and extras such as posters. Big disadvantages were the fact that, unlike DVDs, LDs weren't available as blank media, and could only store one hour of a movie (or half an hour, in the higher-quality "CAV" format—but never mind) before you had to flip them over and play the other side.

LDs were always bigger in Japan than in America, where they were generally confined to cinephiles and the tech-oriented; and of course, among those categories, quite a few otaku. Pioneer LDCA (now known as Geneon) was well-regarded for the high quality of their anime LDs in the mid-'90s; as well they might be, as Pioneer was the world's leading manufacturer of laserdiscs. Superelite status, however, was exuded by fans such as the editor, who bought import Japanese LDs (laserdiscs also had none of that DVD nonsense about region encoding) *despite having no LD player.* They sat on the shelf in their wrapper and were merely contemplated. It was a higher, spiritual way of enjoying the show.

38.2: Look at the little flying creature at top right; this is a close-up of the upper left corner of page 38, and probably takes the prize for the most obscure in-joke in Vol. 1 of *OMG!*—for the only way you would ever know it existed is if you had access to images of Mr. Fujishima's original manga art before it's laid out for printing. You can't actually *see* it on the page in either the Dark Horse or the original Japanese edition, because the doodle is above the top "bleed" line for page 38—a bleed is where an artist draws a panel deliberately so that the art will go off the edge of the page, as opposed to art drawn inside panel borders.

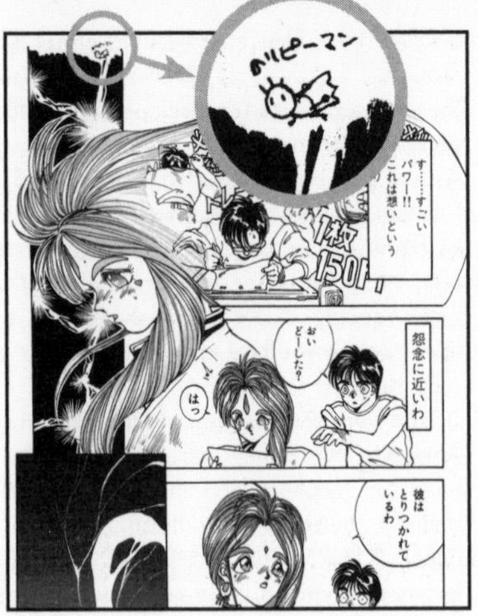
のりピーマン
す……すごい
パワー!!
これは想いという
怨念に近いわ
おい
どーした?
はっ
彼は
とりつかれて
いるわ

The doodle is apparently of "Noripii-Man," a character associated with Noriko Sakai, an idol singer and actress (official site http://www.sunmusic.org/noriko/index.html). Seventeen years old in December of 1988 when this story first appeared in *Afternoon,* she had just released her fourth album, *Lovely Times.* The same year, Noriko Sakai sang "Active Heart," the theme to Gainax's original *Gunbuster* anime series. "Noripii" (sometimes spelled "Nori-P") is her nickname, formed by shortening "Noriko" and adding the cute-sounding suffix "pii." Michael Gombos points out this usage is common among ko-gals; Ropponmatsu II also uses it in *Excel Saga.*

39.4: We honestly don't know what the tiny notes below the bottom panel border, "Garikin," and "Puupii," mean. They seem to be pointing to the spirits Belldandy senses to either side; they also sound a bit like manga sound FX. But as Morrissey said—although this isn't really his kind of manga—"there's always someone somewhere with a big nose who knows," so if you are that someone, please feel free to write in and inform *Letters to the Enchantress.* Big nose or not.

41.2: In the original Japanese, Sada said literally, "My world exists inside this 26-inch square;" which is not only a good line, but a surprising indication of TVs in Japan being marketed in inches—under most circumstances, of course, Japan is metric (see note for 166.3-4 below).

45.1: Satoshi Iwataki and Satoru Nakamura are the names of real people in the anime industry (for example, Satoshi Iwataki was a key animator on the recent *Tide-Line Blue* and Satoru Nakamura was an animation director on *Ghost in the Shell: Stand Alone Complex*). We're not absolutely sure if Fujishima-san was doing a shout-out to these same people, although it is certainly possible, as he knows a number of people in the anime industry (this will come up later) and Nakamura, at least, was working on the notorious *Angel Cop* at the time this story was first published (December of 1988). "Nozomi Omori" was a tribute to the Studio Proteus agent in Japan (Omori is also a SF critic and translator, having adapted Japanese versions of Rudy Rucker's *Freeware* and Joe Haldeman's *The Hemingway Hoax*). The original version didn't give the music composer's full name.

50.2: The video Sada gives Belldandy is called *Magical Masseuse Fashion Lele.* Did she ever watch it? By the way, it is in a so-called "clamshell" case, of the kind a video rental store would give you to take away the tape in (as opposed to the simple printed cardboard sleeve). In the late 1980s and early '90s, some American anime companies, most notably Pioneer, AnimEigo, and U.S. Renditions, sold tapes in a "clamshell" as a mark of prestige. I can't help but remember an incident at an anime convention—I think it was in 1999—where I was on a panel giving out free *Ranma 1/2* videos as prizes ... and the look on the audience's faces when they realized they were in VHS indicated that for otaku, at least, the DVD era was now firmly in place.

71.4: The monk seems to regard Belldandy's goddess mark as a *byakugo*, the third, "all-seeing" eye traditionally associated with portrayals of a *nyorai*, one who has achieved enlightenment in the Buddhist tradition (a category that includes the historical Buddha himself as well as those who achieved enlightenment after him).

73.1-2: In Zen Buddhism, *zazen* is the well-known sitting form of meditation. The relentless whacking of Keiichi with a bamboo stave is designed to help his concentration; an exaggeration of an actual Zen practice, but also an indication that many Japanese don't take religion perfectly seriously (for more on the Japanese relation to historical Buddhism, please see the notes in the back of the Dark Horse release *Katsuya Terada's The Monkey King*).

75.1: It's interesting that when Belldandy used her power to place shoes upon her bare goddess feet, she made them into New Balance, the same label as the editor's sneaks. Or "trainers," for our U.K. readership.

77.3: In the mid-'80s, Toyota was notably involved in research towards making auto engines out of advanced ceramics instead of metal. The theoretical advantages are great: not only would ceramic engines weigh less, increasing efficiency for the overall car (after all, the engine has to move its own weight as well as that of the car and its passengers), but ceramic engines can burn fuel at temperatures where a normal engine would overheat (not to mention melt into slag) which itself makes fuel use more efficient. However, while ceramic engines have been demonstrated in the lab, the industrial processes to mass-produce them safely (meaning, without cracks, because of the danger from their superheated fuel) has never been perfected. Some have voiced suspicion that ceramic engines are being kept off the market by conspiracy, but the Japanese have been the world leaders at marketing fuel-efficient technologies, so I am inclined to accept the simple engineering explanation.

84.5: Boy-oh-boy. Forget the LD, look at them 5 1/4" disc drives in the computer. They were just a little larger than a CD, except they were square, black, and had approximately 1/583 the storage capacity, limiting you to no more than a few "H".gifs at a time.

110.5: Otaki and Tamiya are probably named after the eponymous Japanese plastic model companies, but note that *otakki* is a variant on "otaku" sometimes used among otaku themselves. It's employed as both a noun and adjective—a slang use of a slang use, as if "otaku" were a Japanese adverb (which, of course, it isn't; see note for 27.1) ending in "ku" like *hayaku* ("quickly") that becomes an adjective when spelled with an "i" (so *hayai* means "fast").

It is sometimes reported that "otakki" was coined after the Tsutomu Miyazaki murders to distance the scene from the word otaku, but in fact the word is documented at least four years earlier than that, in Vol. 04, No. 014 of *Manga Puppeteer Tsushin* ("Manga Puppeteer Dispatch," a quarterly manga magazine published by General Products, the company called "Grand Prix" in *Otaku no Video*—see note for 27.1). Although no larger than an American comic book (ahem) at a stapled

38 pages, it featured short manga pieces by Hideaki Anno, *Cannon God Exaxxion's* Kenichi Sonoda, and, as aforementioned, covers by Kosuke Fujishima's mentor, Tatsuya Egawa.

The word appears on page 7 of this issue, within an astonishingly angry open letter to a "Mr. Komak"—who appears to be a magazine editor—written in equally astonishing English, verbatim: "You are the XXXX of mother XXXXing son of a Rich bich. Put your XXXX into your XXXXing XXX hole. You are just like a fore father of OTACKY people arnt you dummy?" The words represented here by Xs are considered unsuitable for a kind-hearted title like *Oh My Goddess!*.

The letter, incidentally is signed by a "Sakura Dai," (a.k.a. "Day Sakura,") whom, I believe, is the person listed in the credits of *Pop Chaser* as its director, and hence, would therefore be a pseudonym for Hiroyuki Kitakubo, later the internationally acclaimed director of *Blood the Last Vampire*, of which Andy Wachowski said, "it was as if the art of Francis Bacon had come to life."

Documentary evidence; from the embers of a flame war long-forgotten. It is good to be able to share this with you; this terrible burden of knowledge that an otacky carries inside.

111.3: The sign on the door above Kakuta Labs reads *Fu-Rin-Ka-Zan*, a maxim said to be from Sun Tzu's *The Art of War*, meaning "wind-forest-fire-mountain." In Japan it was made most famous as the banner of Takeda Shingen, one of the great lords of Japan's 16th century era of civil war. The idea behind the slogan is that a military strategy should incorporate the qualities of these natural features.

The kind of redwood burly-looking thing hanging to the left side of the door

reads *Kakuta-heya,* "(The) Kakuta Room" The sign tacked to the board on the right-hand side of the hall thanks "helpers Yoshihiko Asano, Namie Iwao, and Ozuka Kunio." Mr. Fujishima's assistants?

112.4: Belldandy appears to be expressing her spell here in the Thai alphabet, although the characters seem to be chosen at random.

113.4: The various graffiti written on the outside of the darkroom read, "Shut the lights when you leave!" "Stinks (in here)" "Please don't put anything on top," and more stridently, "Don't put anything up here!" (the request has been ignored, of course). Hanging down from the upper right corner of the darkroom curtain is an "Open for Business" sign that looks suspiciously swiped from some off-campus establishment.

113.6: Besides the bird and the Sumo wrestler, other objects on Otaki's mind are Almond Glico caramels, and a pack of Noritama-brand egg-flavored *furitake,* a flaky condiment that livens up any bowl of rice.

123.3: Otaki is wearing a Takora outfit, minus the head (see note for 14.1).

136.4: In Keiichi's frantic scattering of his chattels, we see he's got Yu's magic wand from *Creamy Mami* (see note for 34.6)—not to mention a Barbie doll, still in its collector's packaging. It kind of makes you wonder if his height isn't the only reason he's had poor luck with women.

138.1: Hiroko Kasahara is, as you might expect, a J-pop singer; she was nineteen years old when this story was first published in Japan, prompting the original Dark Horse English version to change her to "Tiffany," which by now would itself require its own lengthy note of explanation. Kasahara might be better-known today to most U.S. fans as an anime *seiyuu* (voice actor); she played Fuu in *Magic Knights Rayearth* and Misuki's mother, Hazuki, in *Full Moon wo Sagashite*.

"Sudara-bushi" is a famous, funny Japanese song from the early 1960s about various stupid things one is unable to stop doing, no matter how many times they go wrong. It was written by Tessho Hagiwara and first made famous by singer Hitoshi Ueki. In the original Dark Horse English version, "Weird Al" Yankovic was considered to be an equivalent.

Q-Taro the Ghost was a 1965 anime TV series, remade in 1971 and again in 1985, based on a manga by Fujiko Fujio, Hiroshi Fujimoto, and Motoo Abiko, the creators of *Doraemon.* It's also the subject of an extended joke in "Understanding *Oh My Goddess!* … In Eight Pages Or Less!" the fan manga by Yoshitoh Asari which opens Dark Horse's forthcoming book *Oh My Goddess! Colors.*

138.4: The original English version of Vol. 1 had Keiichi plotting to play Barry White, but interestingly, his own taste in romantic music runs to George Winston, a pianist who made the Windham Hill label famous for their "New Age" music with his 1982 album *December.*

149.5: The mental image Keiichi projects of the way people supposedly dress in his hometown would be like claiming American farmers today still look like the couple in Grant Wood's painting *American Gothic,* which you should really take the train to go see the next time you're attending Anime Central.

151.1: The guy on those four ¥10,000 notes is Yukichi Fukuzawa (1835-1901) both one of the last generation of samurai, and a founder of modern Japan. Fukuzawa played—as an educator, newspaper publisher, and advocate of self-reliance—roles comparable to those of Benjamin Franklin in the founding of America. In his own *Autobiography,* Fukuzawa talks about what it was like to try and study modern science in the twilight of the samurai era, when a single imported textbook (the only kind available) on electrical theory cost today's equivalent of US$20,000 in gold. Strangely, his own college days as he describes them—full of chemical experiments gone horribly wrong—sound not unlike a tale from Nekomi Tech, as do headings from that time in his *Autobiography* like, "We were capable of petty stealing," "Street fights for laughs," "Nudeness brings many adventures," and "Sanitation is all but disregarded."

Like Ben Franklin on the US $100 bill, today Yukichi is on Japan's 10,000-yen note, the highest-valued bill in circulation. And just as in America, where it's all about the Benjamins, in Japan, it's all about the Yukichis. Michael Gombos, Dark Horse's Japanese Licensing Manager, points out Rina Ayukawa ("A-Ayukawa!"), a Kobe girl on the recent TV Asahi show *London Hearts* (a comedy show produced by "London Boots," the troupe name of Atsushi and Ryo Tamura—official site, http://www.lonboo.com/, an English-language review at http://www.insitetokyo.com/column/hilo/index9.html) popularized the saying about men and their money or unfortunate lack thereof, *otoko wa yappari Yukichi da ne* (which means basically, "as far as guys go, you know it all comes down to the Yukichis"). It should be noted that Risa herself became known by the title *Shijo Saiaku Mashou Onna,* "The Most Witchiest Girl In History," which, appropriately enough, also sounds very much like an *Oh My Goddess!* story.

154.2: Tokyo University is, together with Keio University (which Yukichi Fukuzawa founded) often considered to be the top school in Japan. But, hell, you've read *Love Hina*; you know that.

155.4: Velocity times the product of maximum thrust force minus total resistance, the sum then divided by the weight of the fuselage. I think. At Pomona, I majored in history. N.I.T. was Harvey Mudd.

166.3-4: About the rentals listings that are up on the wall: the top line of each listing indicates how many minutes away the apartment is from Nekomi Tech, suggesting, of course, this place rents to a lot of students. The big number(s) in the center give the size of the apartment as measured in *jo*, which is the theoretical size of a Japanese tatami mat. I say *theoretical*, as exactly how big a "jo" is can vary by region in Japan, and also on the age of the building (it is said that a jo doesn't go as far as it used to), and whe-ther one is talking about an apartment, a condominium, or a house. This is one case where even the U.S.'s old-fashioned use of feet and inches is more specific. Having said that, a "typical" jo for an apartment is roughly 16 1/2 square feet.

Returning to the way these listings are written, a single big number (like the "6") means a one-room studio apartment; the "K" next to it confirms a kitchen. Two numbers (like the "6.3") mean a two-room apartment; here the "D" means a dining room. Three numbers (like the "6.6.45") means three rooms. The numbers themselves measure how many jo each room is; traditionally, you'll notice, in multiples of 1.5 (the "45" signifies 4.5). So a 3-jo room is about 49 1/2 sq. feet, a 4.5-jo room is about 74 sq. feet, and a 6-jo room is about 99 sq. feet. This is what happens, of course, when you have 127 million people living in a country the size of California.

The line below the big number(s) confirms the number of rooms. We know what you're getting for your money, but for how much money? The lower right numbers indicate the monthly rent for each unit; the first number shows how many tens of thousands, then how many thousands. So the "6" studio apartment (where you might have to share bathrooms, like in a dorm) costs 32,000 yen a month, whereas the "6.6.45" goes for a whopping 103,000. This particular chapter of *Oh My Goddess!* appeared in May of 1989; however, these rents are the same kind you might still find today around many universities—although in Tokyo you would probably pay at least a third more.

Finally, in the lower left corner of each listing are two numbers. The first is the number of months' rent that must be paid as *shikikin*, a security deposit refundable upon moving out. All of these units demand two months' rent for shikikin, but that's fair enough, like the standard American "first and last month's rent." But the second number is the disgusting practice of *reikin*, the so-called "remuneration" which is basically a bribe—or obligatory gift if you like—given to your landlord for the privilege of being allowed to pay rent to live there! As you can see, all these units also ask two months' rent for that, too—and needless to say, you don't get it back.

Nor is there any guarantee your landlord will look like Kyoko Otonashi. Sorry, but this volume *is* on the eighties tip.

—CGH

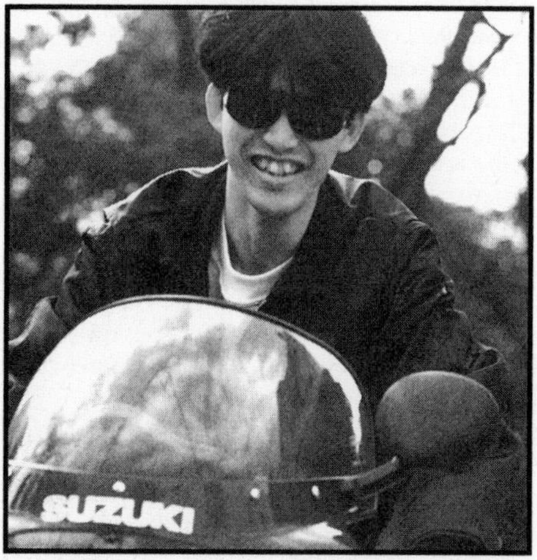
SUZUKI

Creator Kosuke Fujishima in 1989!

His message to fans in the original Japanese *Oh My Goddess!* Vol. 1:

"I've been so busy working on the manga that I haven't even had the chance to go outside; in fact, just now I found myself realizing that I literally hadn't so much as set foot out the door in the past three days. And it looks like I'm not going to get away anywhere this summer, either. So, remember the only leisure I'll get is from your fan mail."

STOP! This is the back of the book!

This manga collection is translated into English, but arranged in right-to-left reading format to maintain the artwork's visual orientation as originally drawn and published in Japan. If you've never read comics this way before, take a look at the diagram below to give yourself an idea of how to go about it. Basically, you'll be starting in the upper right-hand corner, and will read each word balloon and panel moving right-to-left. It may take a little getting used to, but you should get the hang of it very quickly. Have fun! If this is the millionth manga you've read this way, never mind.

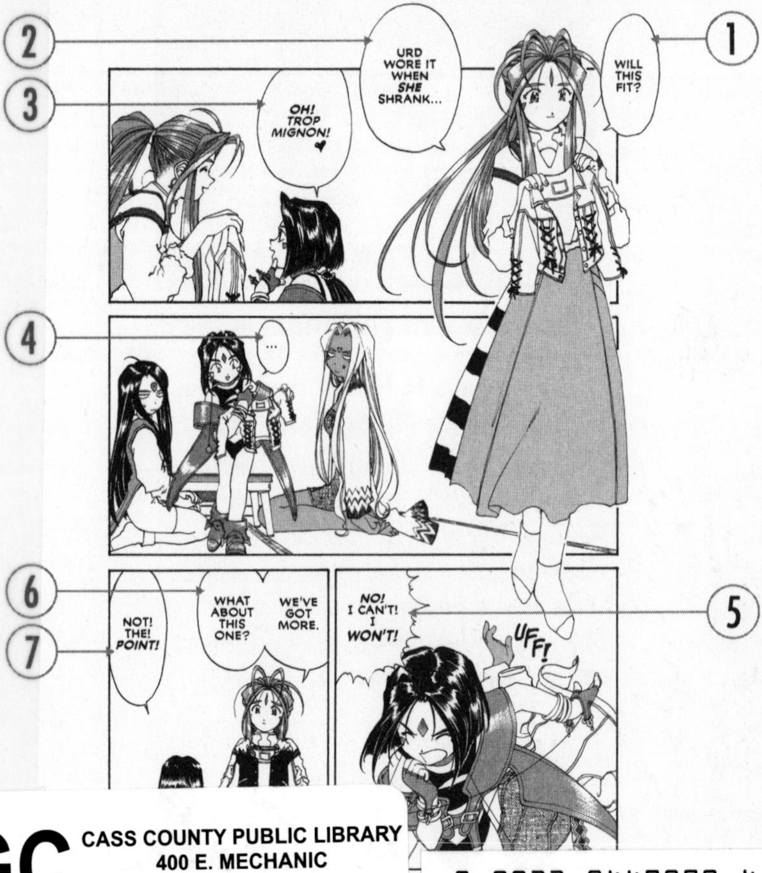
1
WILL THIS FIT?
2
URD WORE IT WHEN *SHE* SHRANK...
3
OH! TROP MIGNON!
4
...
5
NO! I CAN'T! I *WON'T!*
UFF!
WE'VE GOT MORE.
6
WHAT ABOUT THIS ONE?
7
NOT! THE! *POINT!*